# FAIRY TAIL

フェアリーテイル



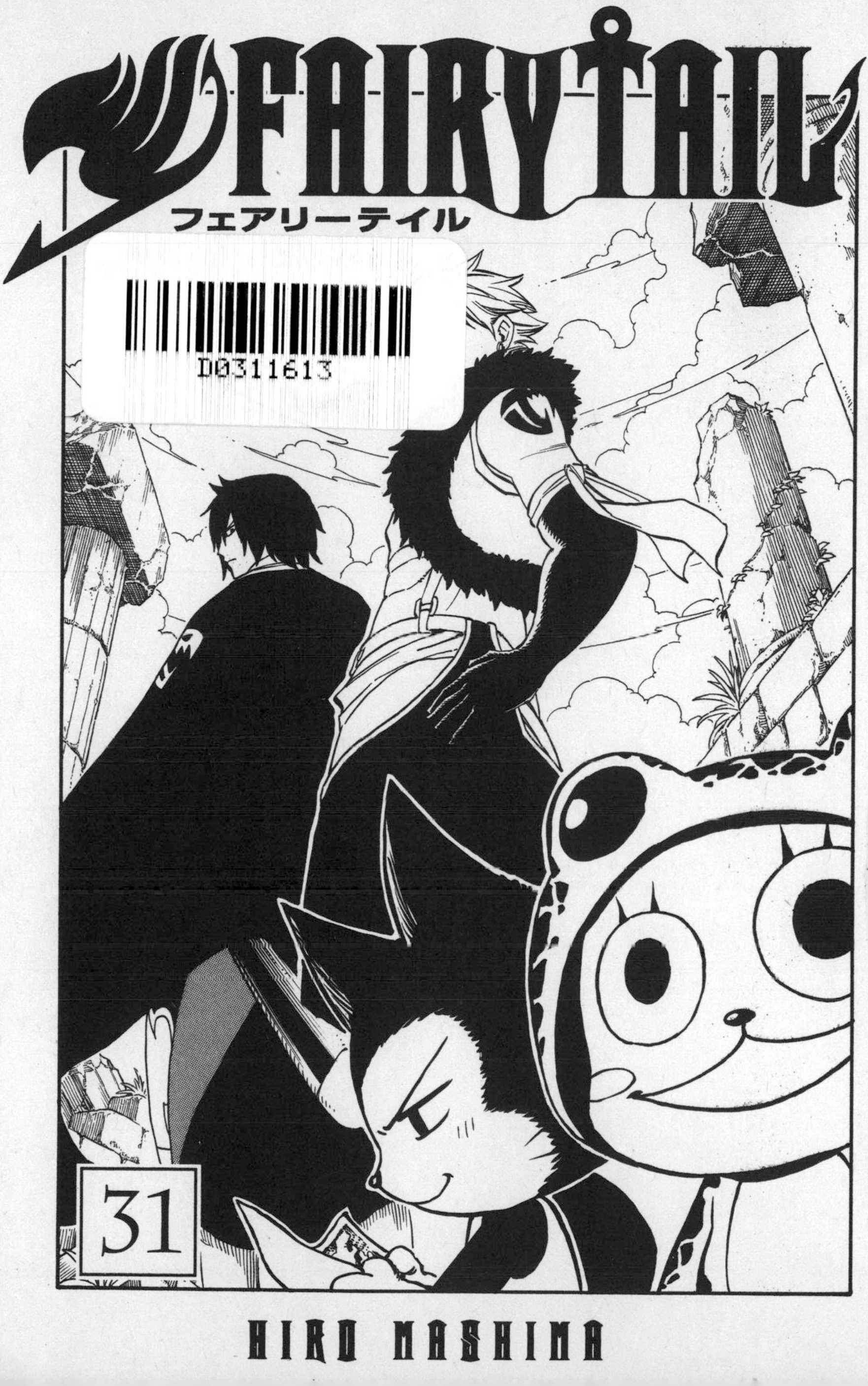

31

HIRO MASHIMA

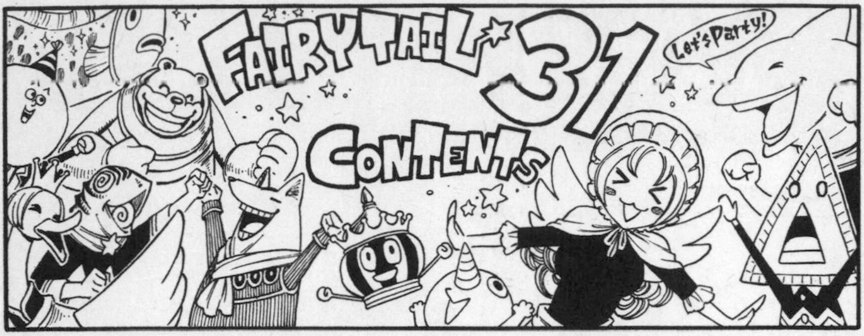
FAIRY TAIL 31
CONTENTS
Let's Party!

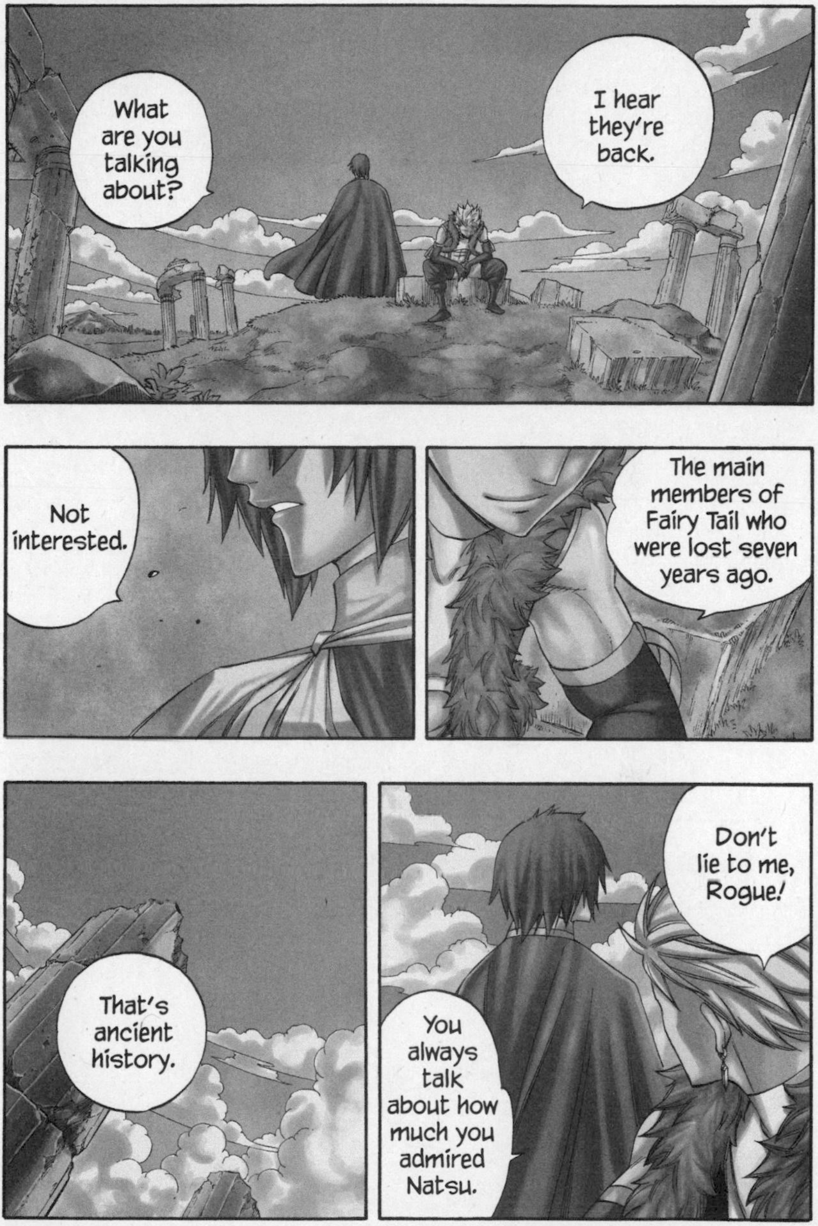
I hear they're back.
What are you talking about?
The main members of Fairy Tail who were lost seven years ago.
Not interested.
Don't lie to me, Rogue!
You always talk about how much you admired Natsu.
That's ancient history.

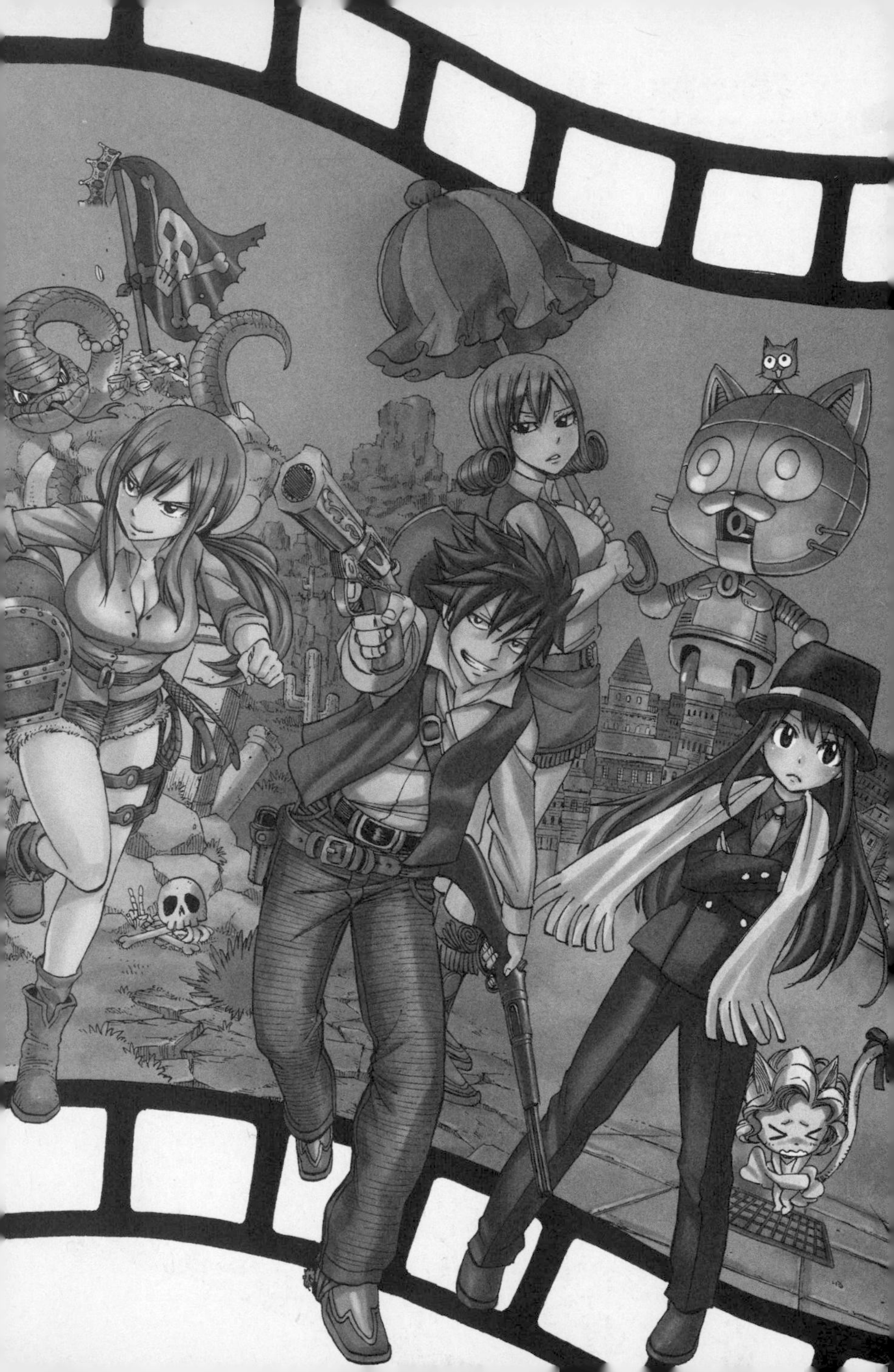

# Chapter 258: Saber Tooth

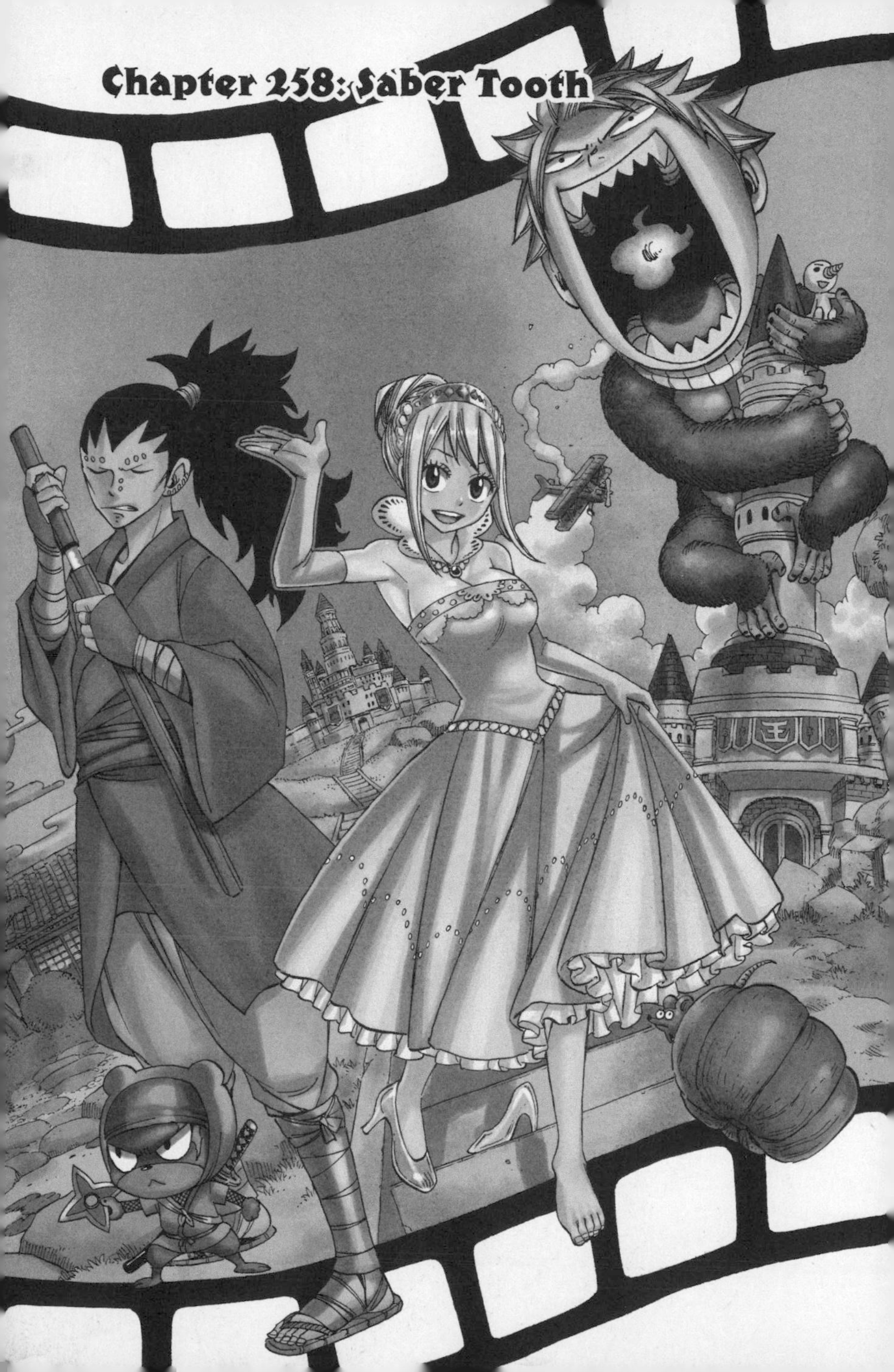

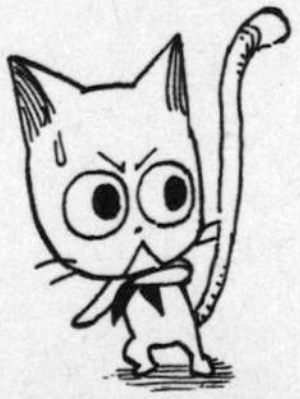

FAIRY TAIL

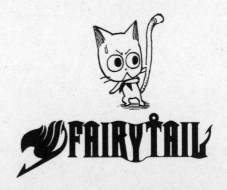

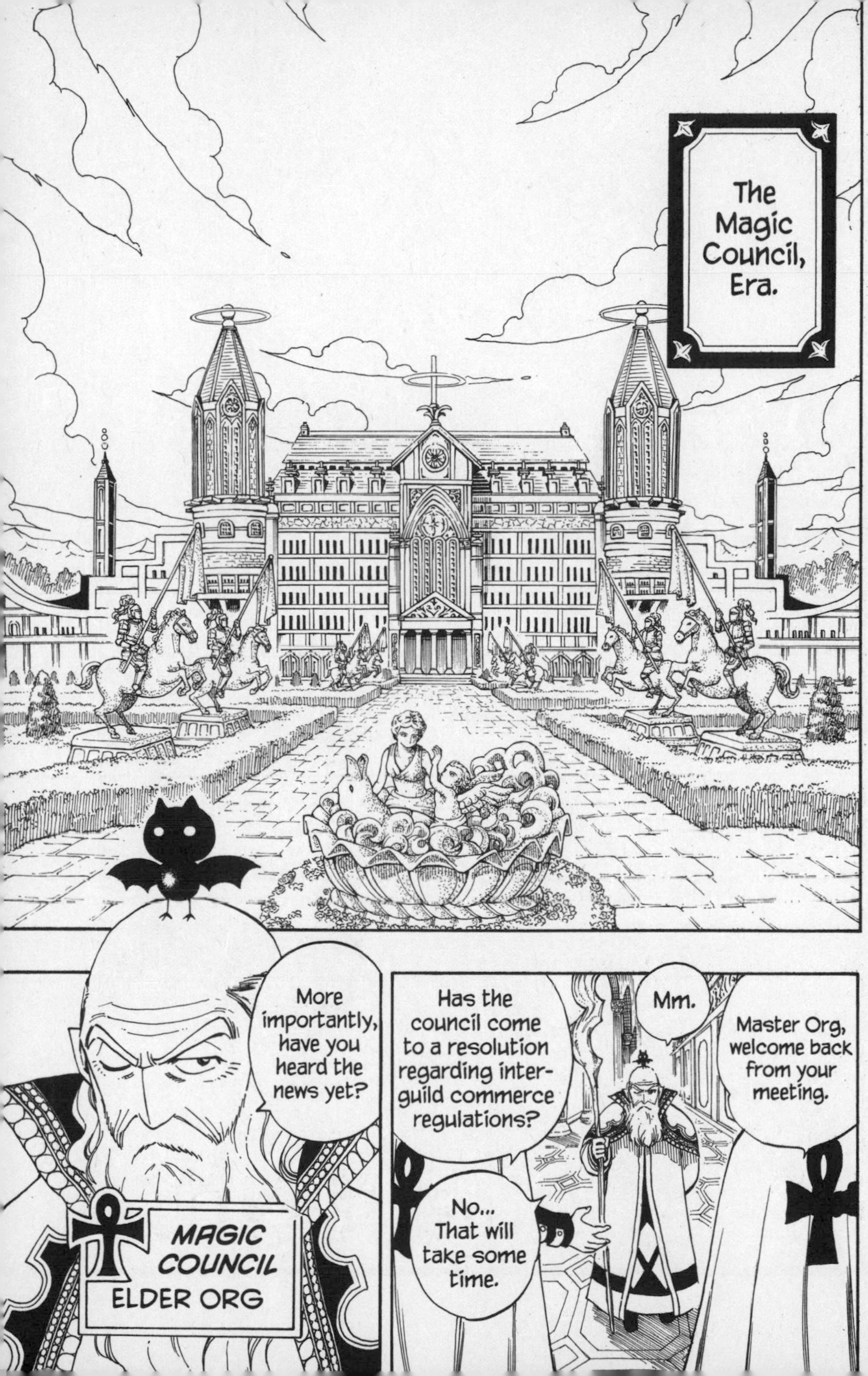
The Magic Council, Era.
Master Org, welcome back from your meeting.
Mm.
Has the council come to a resolution regarding inter-guild commerce regulations?
No... That will take some time.
More importantly, have you heard the news yet?
MAGIC COUNCIL
ELDER ORG

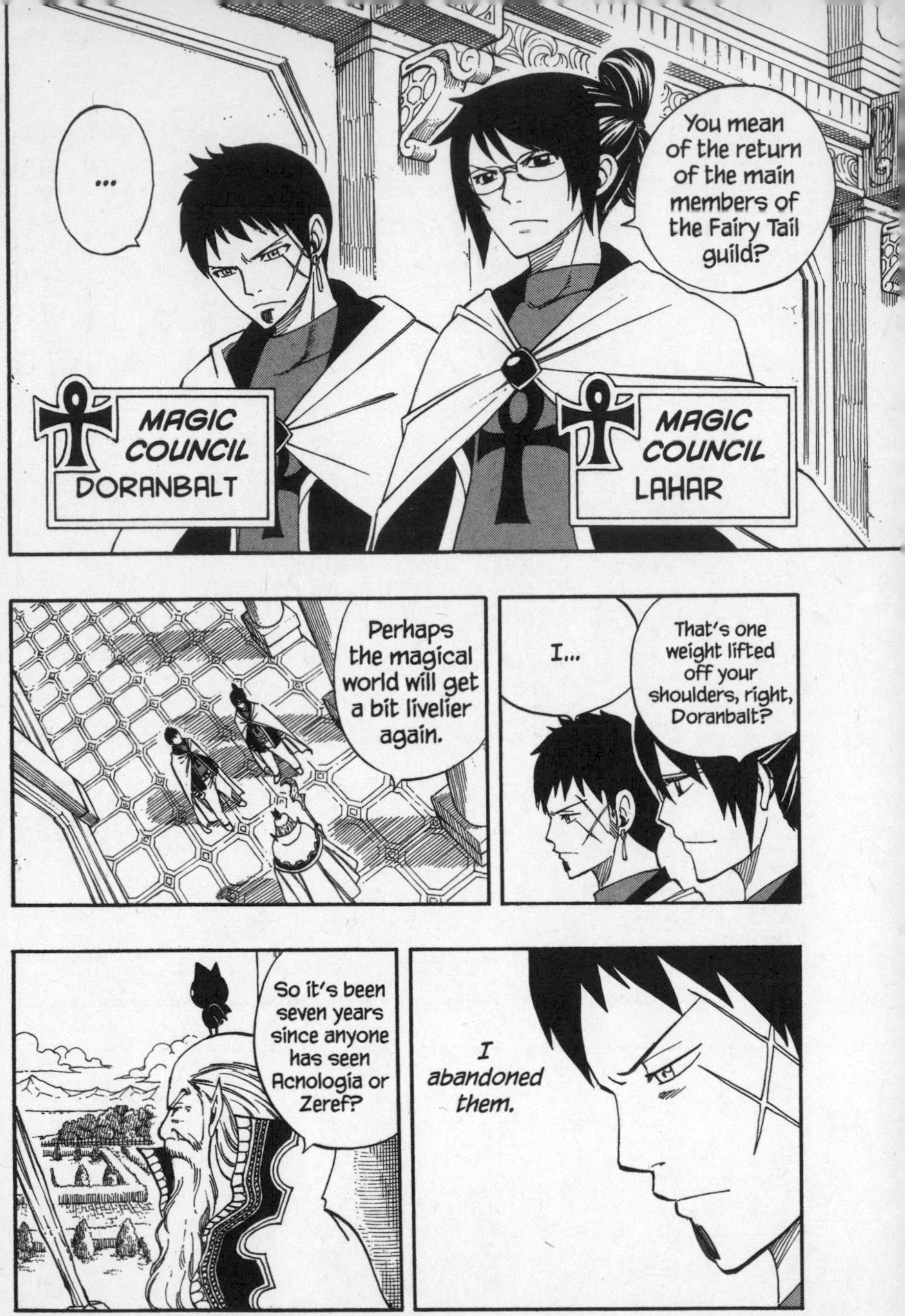
You mean of the return of the main members of the Fairy Tail guild?
...
MAGIC COUNCIL
LAHAR
MAGIC COUNCIL
DORANBALT
That's one weight lifted off your shoulders, right, Doranbalt?
I...
Perhaps the magical world will get a bit livelier again.
I abandoned them.
So it's been seven years since anyone has seen Acnologia or Zeref?

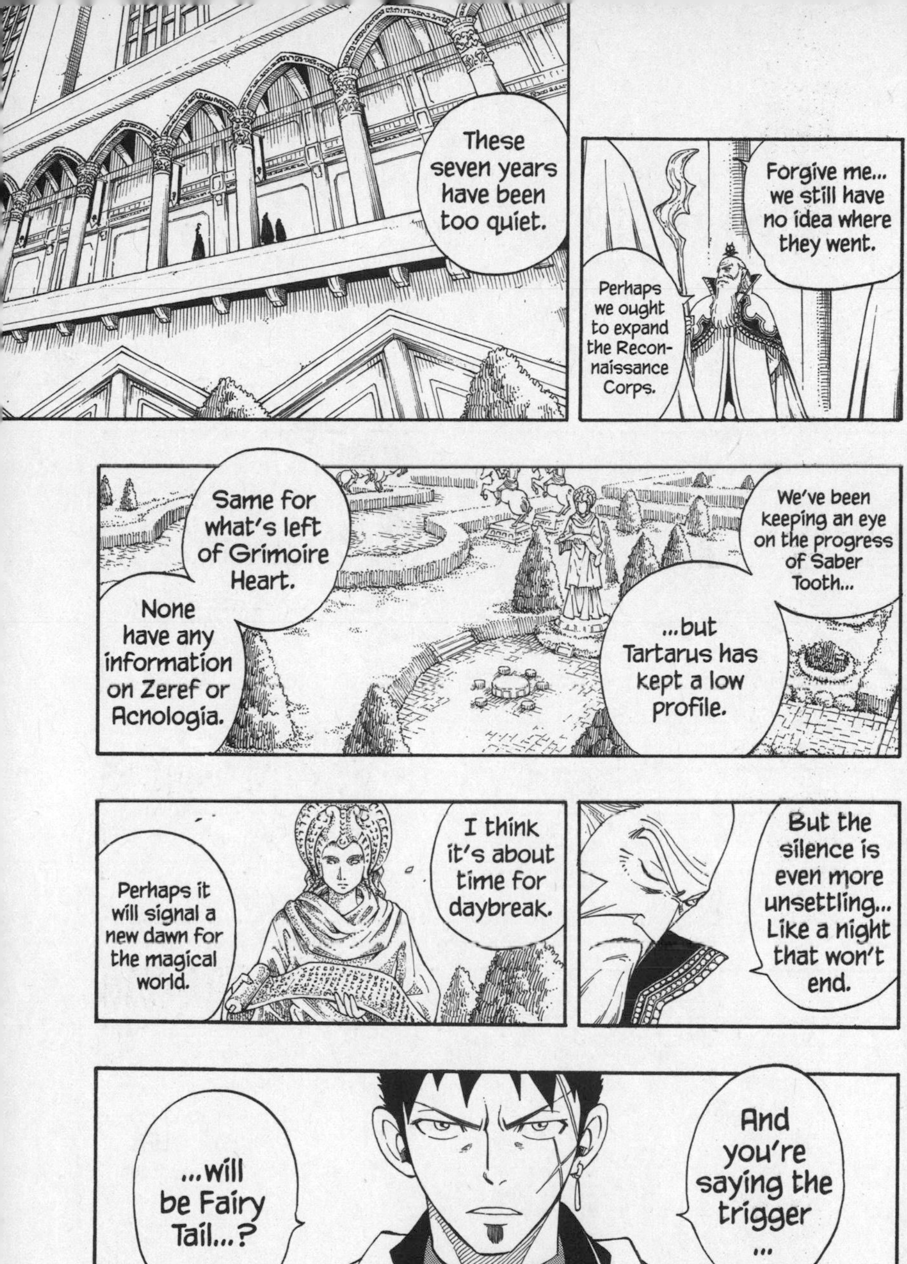
Forgive me... we still have no idea where they went.
Perhaps we ought to expand the Recon-naissance Corps.
These seven years have been too quiet.
We've been keeping an eye on the progress of Saber Tooth...
...but Tartarus has kept a low profile.
Same for what's left of Grimoire Heart.
None have any information on Zeref or Acnologia.
But the silence is even more unsettling... Like a night that won't end.
I think it's about time for daybreak.
Perhaps it will signal a new dawn for the magical world.
And you're saying the trigger ...
...will be Fairy Tail...?

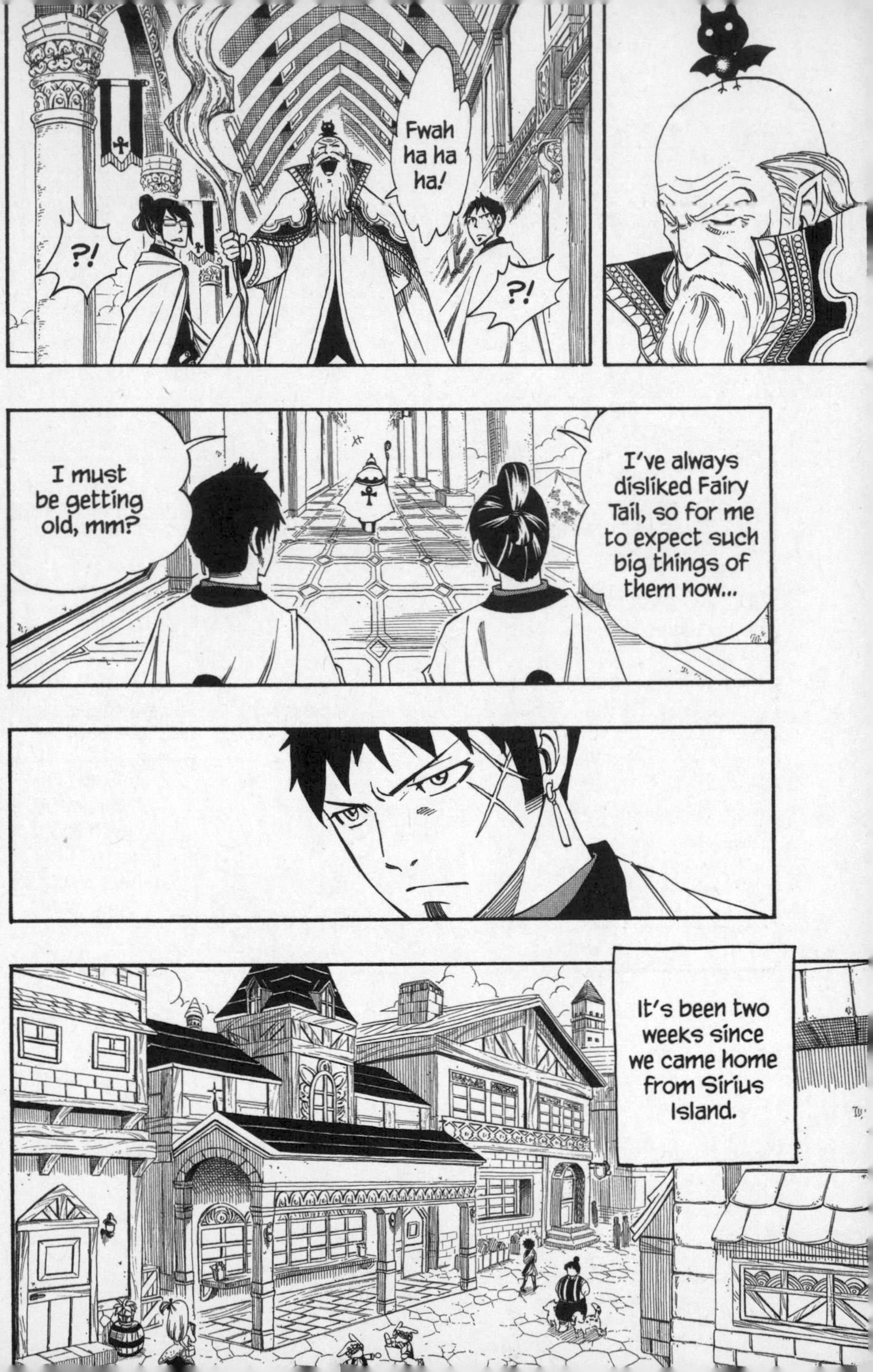
Fwah ha ha ha!
?!
?!
I've always disliked Fairy Tail, so for me to expect such big things of them now...
I must be getting old, mm?
It's been two weeks since we came home from Sirius Island.

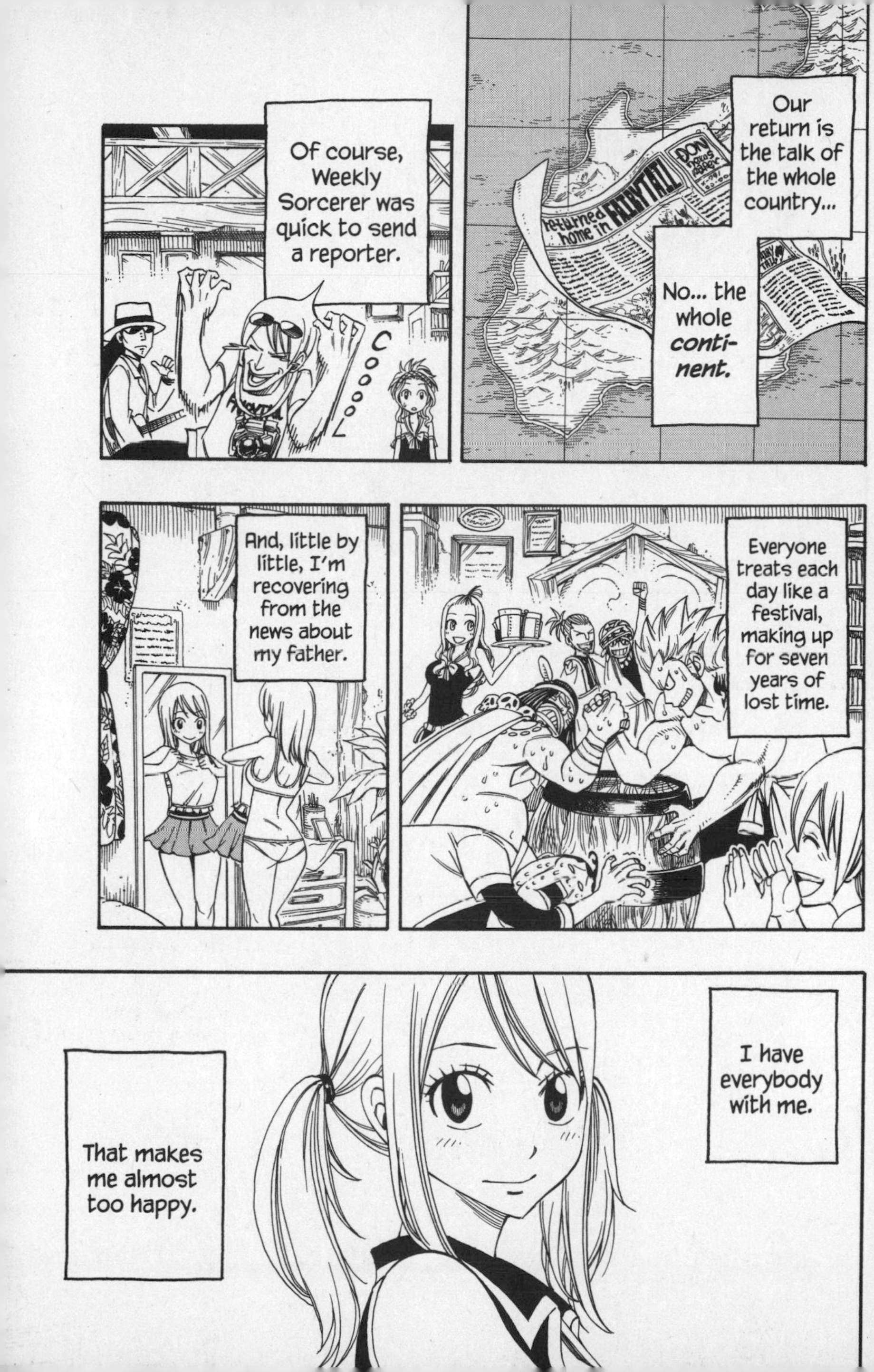
Our return is the talk of the whole country...
returned home in FAIRY TAIL
No... the whole *conti-nent.*
Of course, Weekly Sorcerer was quick to send a reporter.
Cooool
Everyone treats each day like a festival, making up for seven years of lost time.
And, little by little, I'm recovering from the news about my father.
I have everybody with me.
That makes me almost too happy.

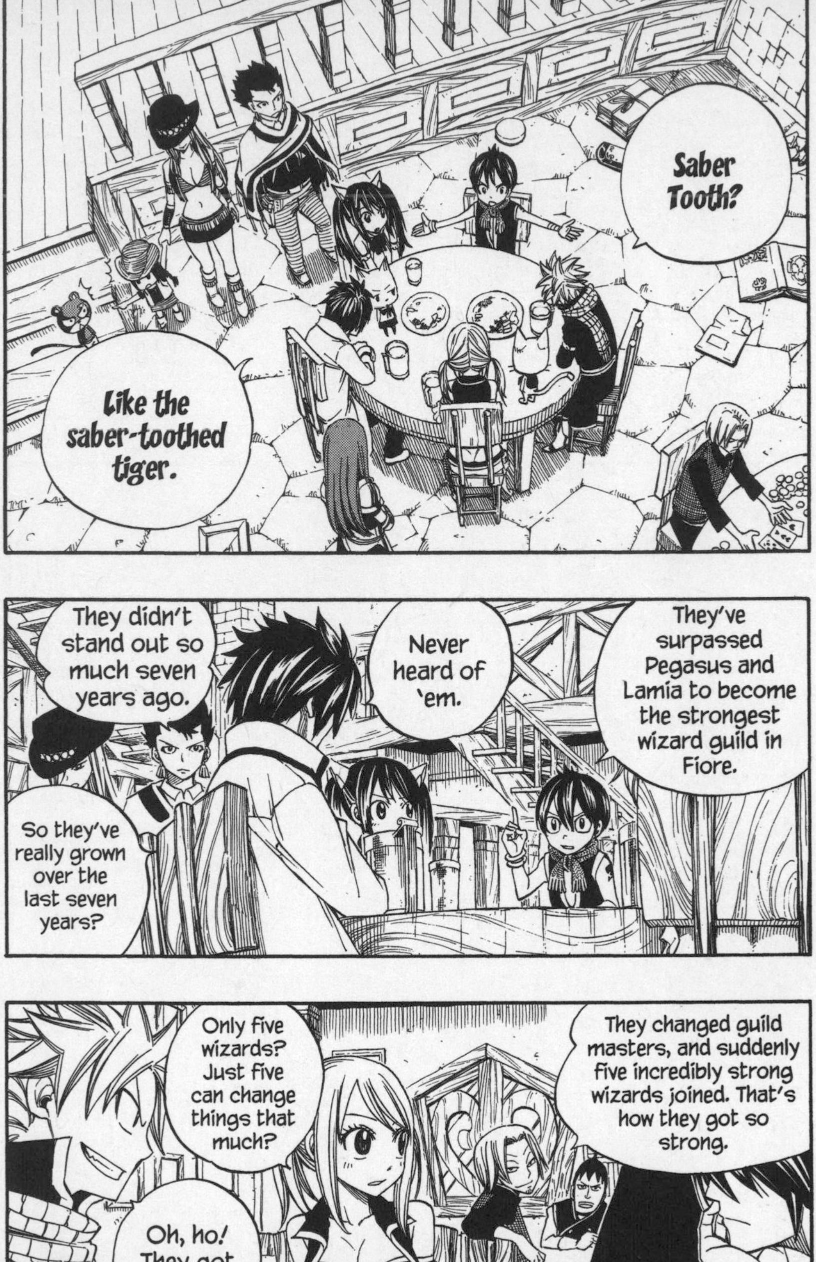
Saber Tooth?
Like the saber-toothed tiger.
They've surpassed Pegasus and Lamia to become the strongest wizard guild in Fiore.
Never heard of 'em.
They didn't stand out so much seven years ago.
So they've really grown over the last seven years?
They changed guild masters, and suddenly five incredibly strong wizards joined. That's how they got so strong.
Only five wizards? Just five can change things that much?
Oh, ho! They got guts!

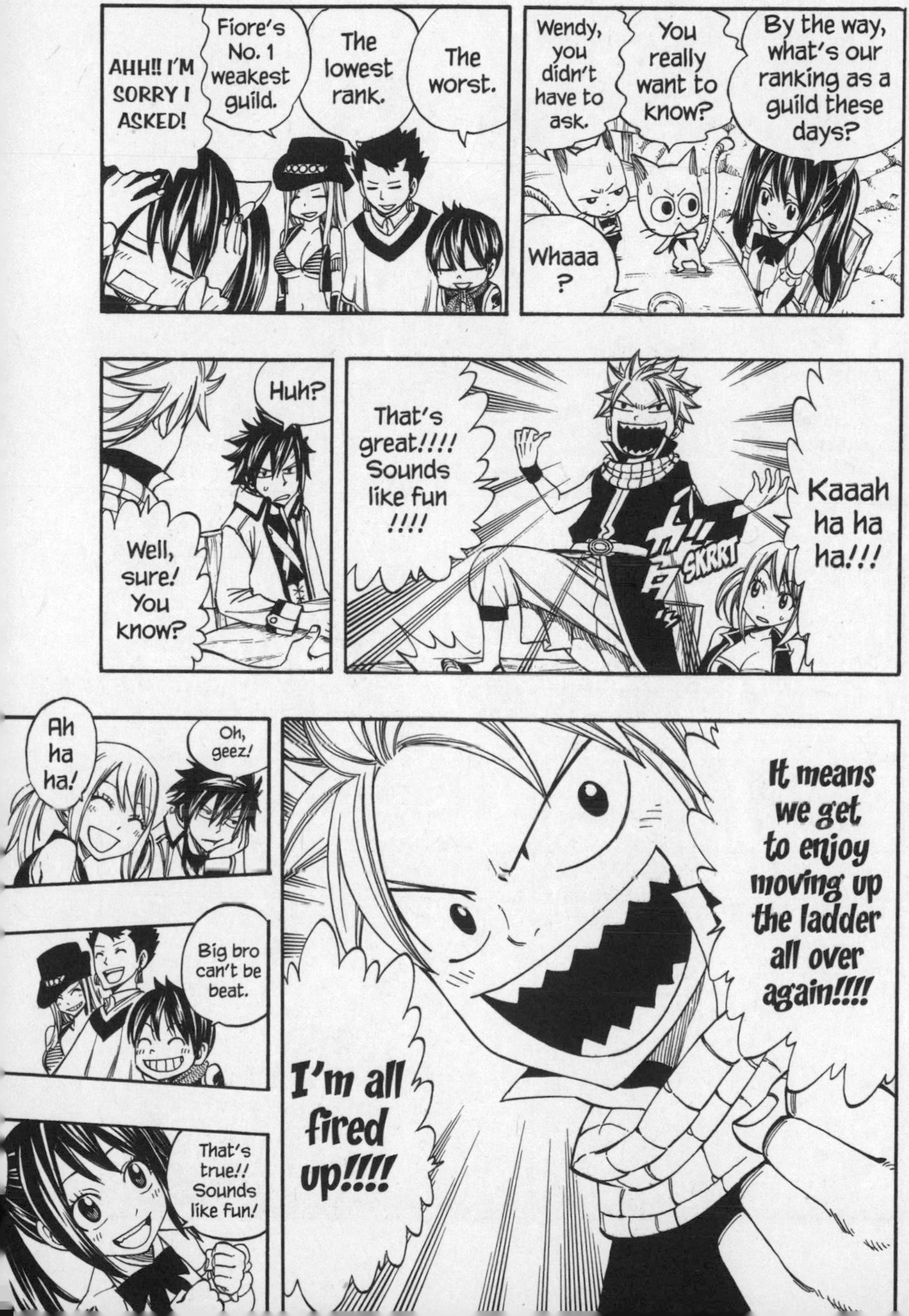
By the way, what's our ranking as a guild these days?
You really want to know?
Wendy, you didn't have to ask.
Whaaa?
The worst.
The lowest rank.
Fiore's No. 1 weakest guild.
AHH!! I'M SORRY I ASKED!
Kaaah ha ha ha!!!
SKRRT
That's great!!!! Sounds like fun !!!!
Huh?
Well, sure! You know?
It means we get to enjoy moving up the ladder all over again!!!!
I'm all fired up!!!!
Oh, geez!
Ah ha ha!
Big bro can't be beat.
That's true!! Sounds like fun!

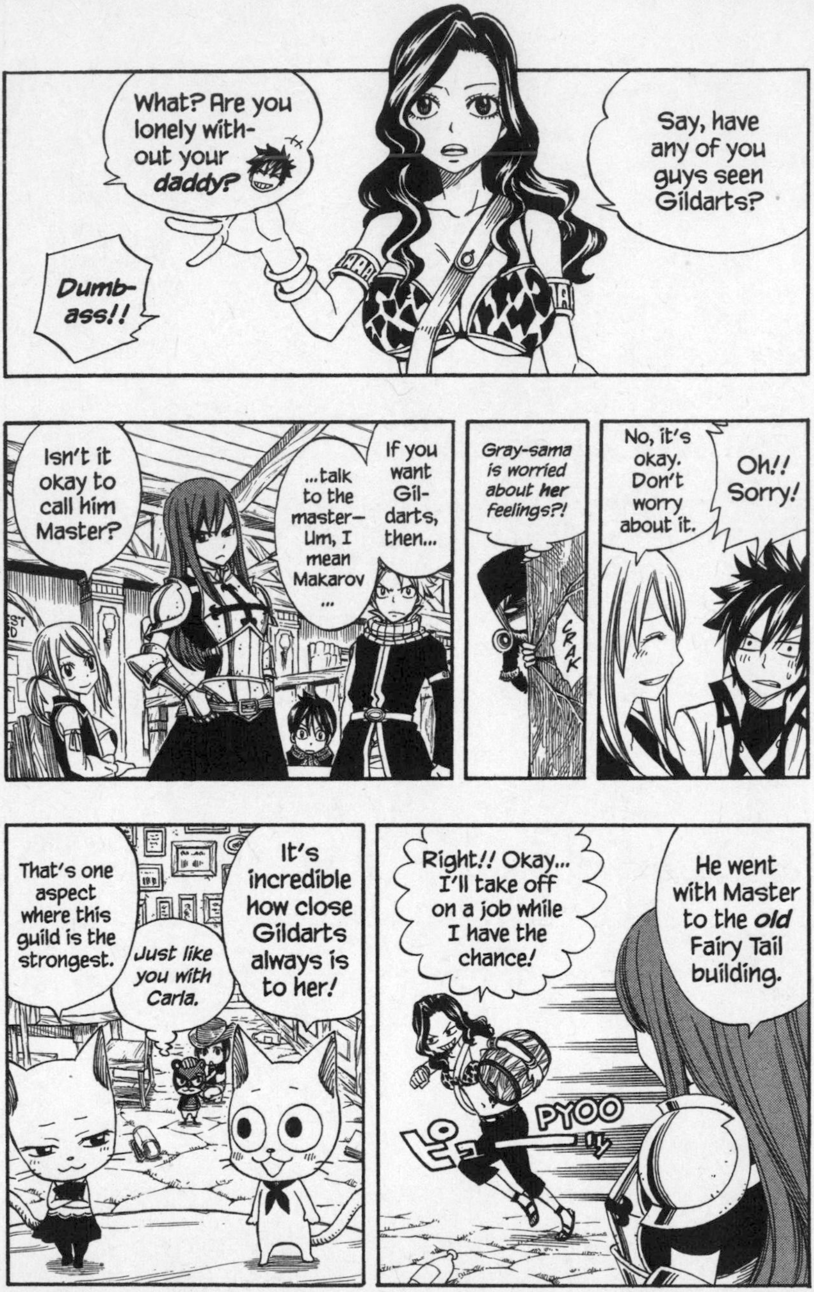
Say, have any of you guys seen Gildarts?
What? Are you lonely with-out your daddy?
Dumb-ass!!
Oh!! Sorry!
No, it's okay. Don't worry about it.
Gray-sama is worried about her feelings?!
CRAK
If you want Gil-darts, then...
...talk to the master— Um, I mean Makarov ...
Isn't it okay to call him Master?
He went with Master to the old Fairy Tail building.
Right!! Okay... I'll take off on a job while I have the chance!
PYOO
It's incredible how close Gildarts always is to her!
Just like you with Carla.
That's one aspect where this guild is the strongest.

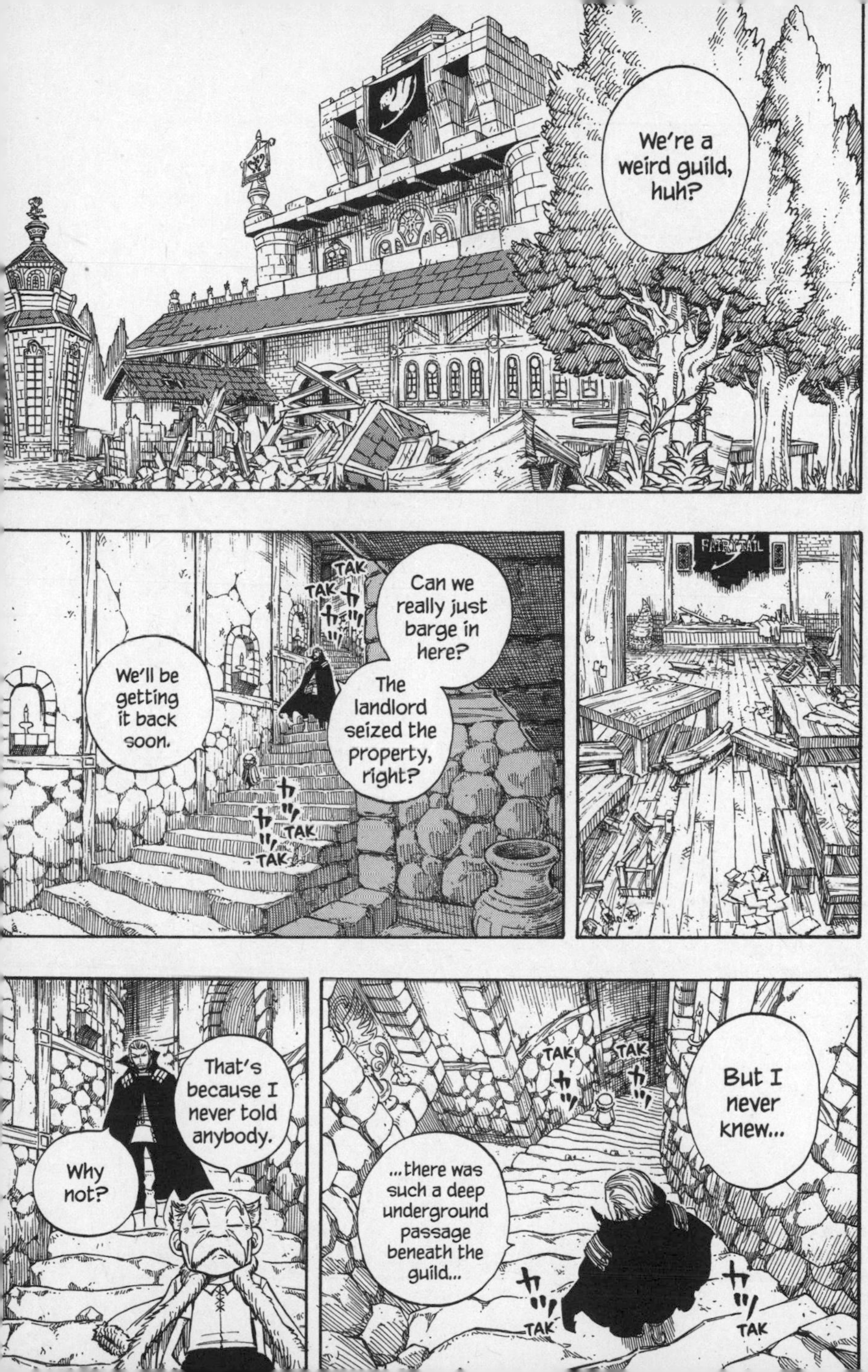
We're a weird guild, huh?
TAK TAK
Can we really just barge in here?
The landlord seized the property, right?
We'll be getting it back soon.
TAK TAK
TAK TAK
But I never knew...
...there was such a deep underground passage beneath the guild...
TAK TAK
That's because I never told anybody.
Why not?

KREEEEEK

Here we go...

?!

Well... You'll see soon enough.

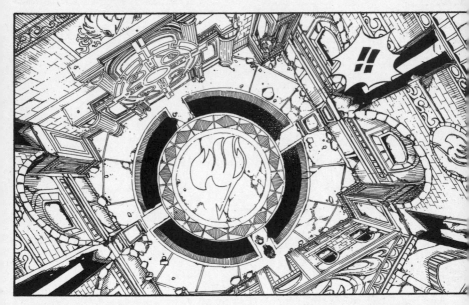

FWSH

FWSH

Wh... What *is* this place...?

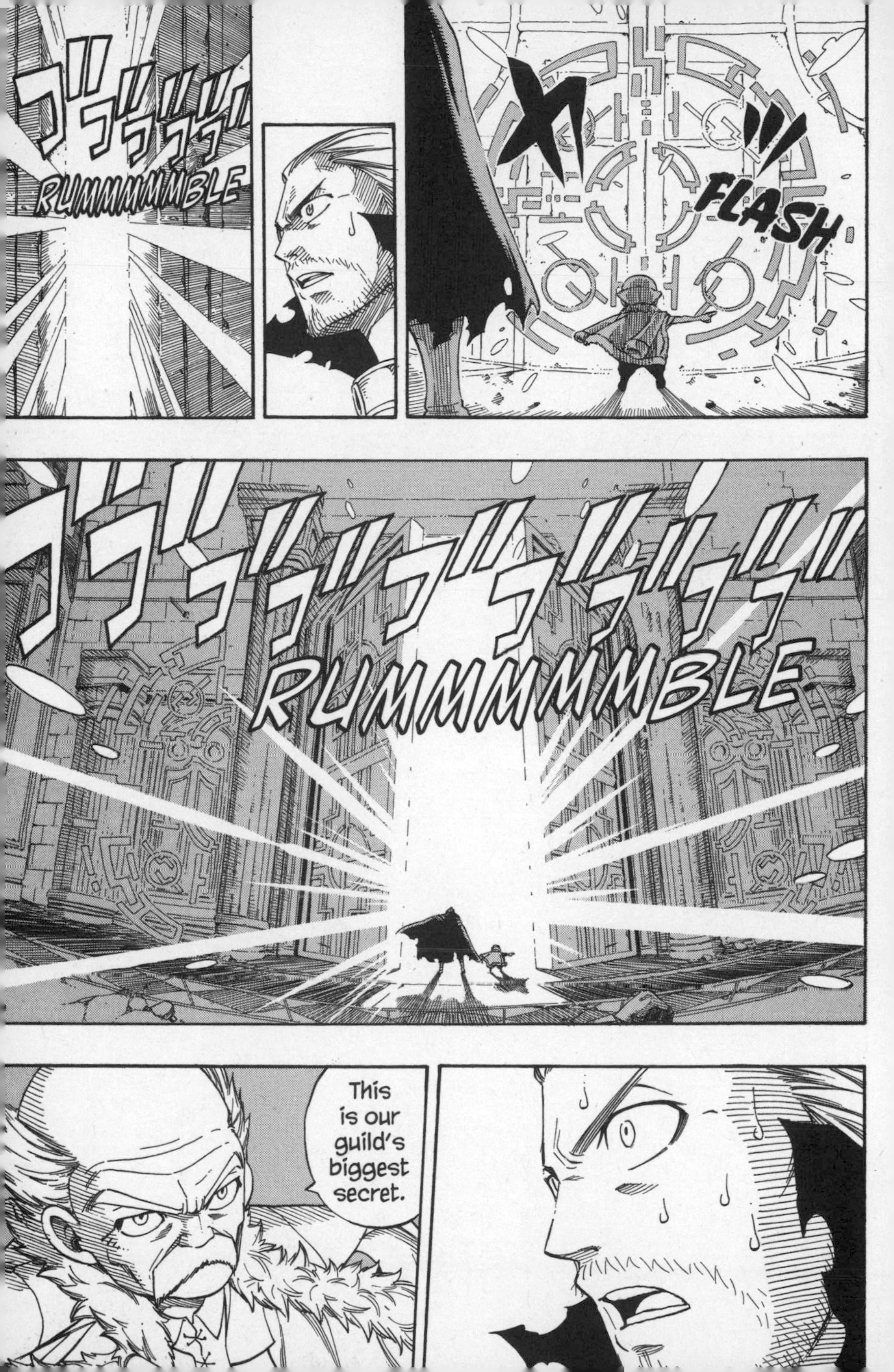
FLASH
RUMMMMMBLE
RUMMMMMMBLE
This is our guild's biggest secret.

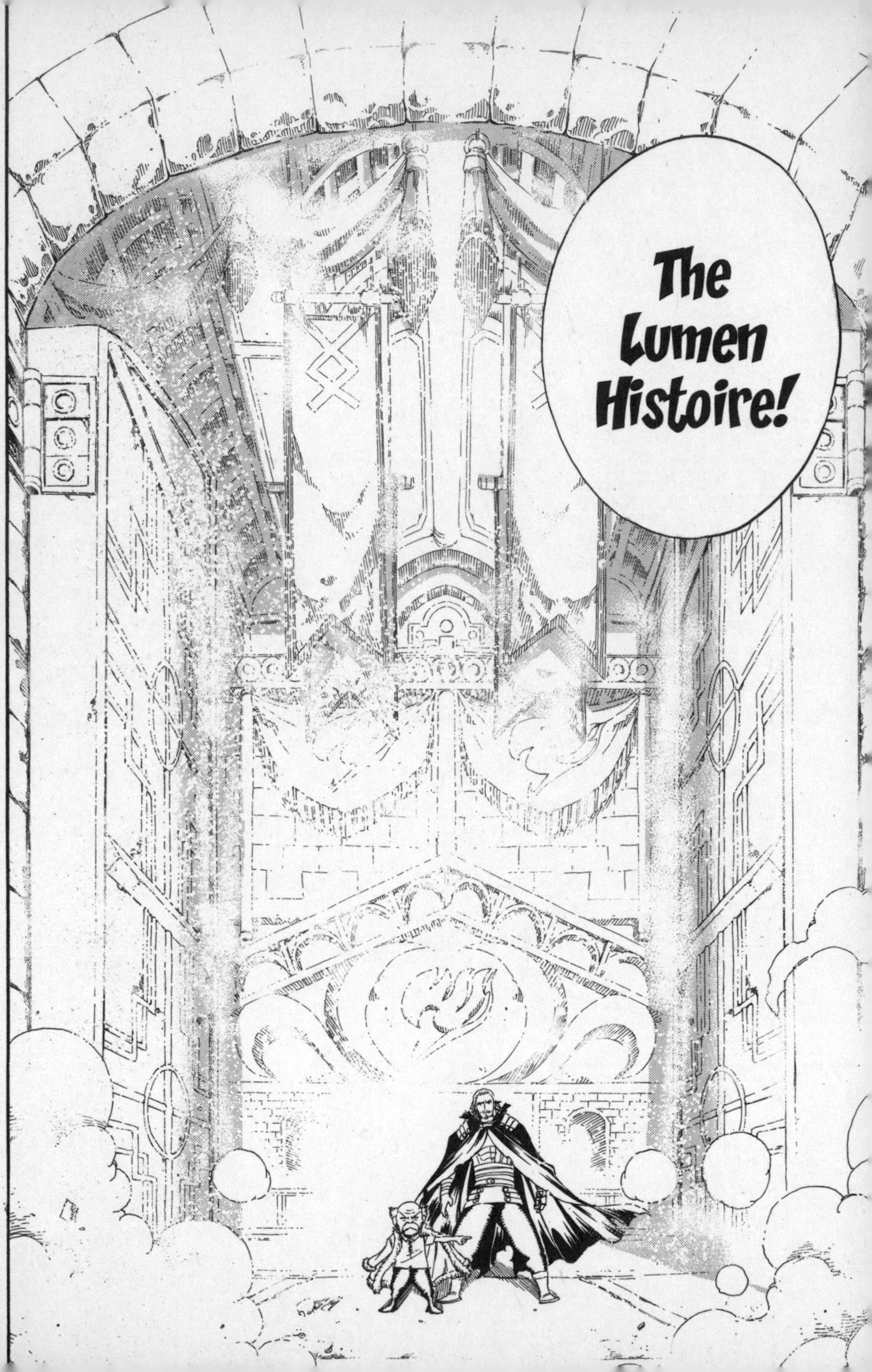
The Lumen Histoire!

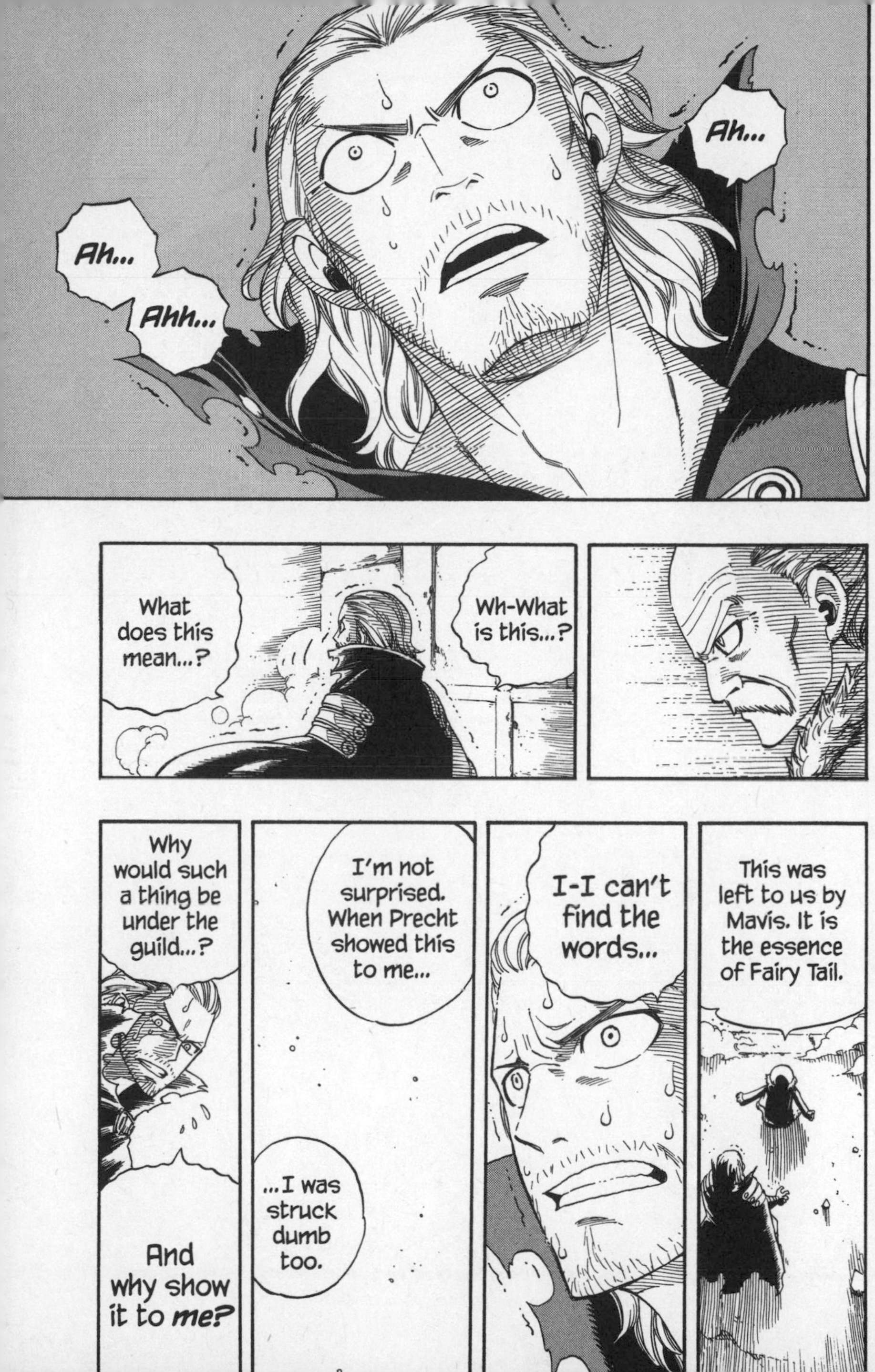
Ah...
Ah...
Ahh...
Wh-What is this...?
What does this mean...?
This was left to us by Mavis. It is the essence of Fairy Tail.
I-I can't find the words...
I'm not surprised. When Precht showed this to me...
...I was struck dumb too.
Why would such a thing be under the guild...?
And why show it to *me?*

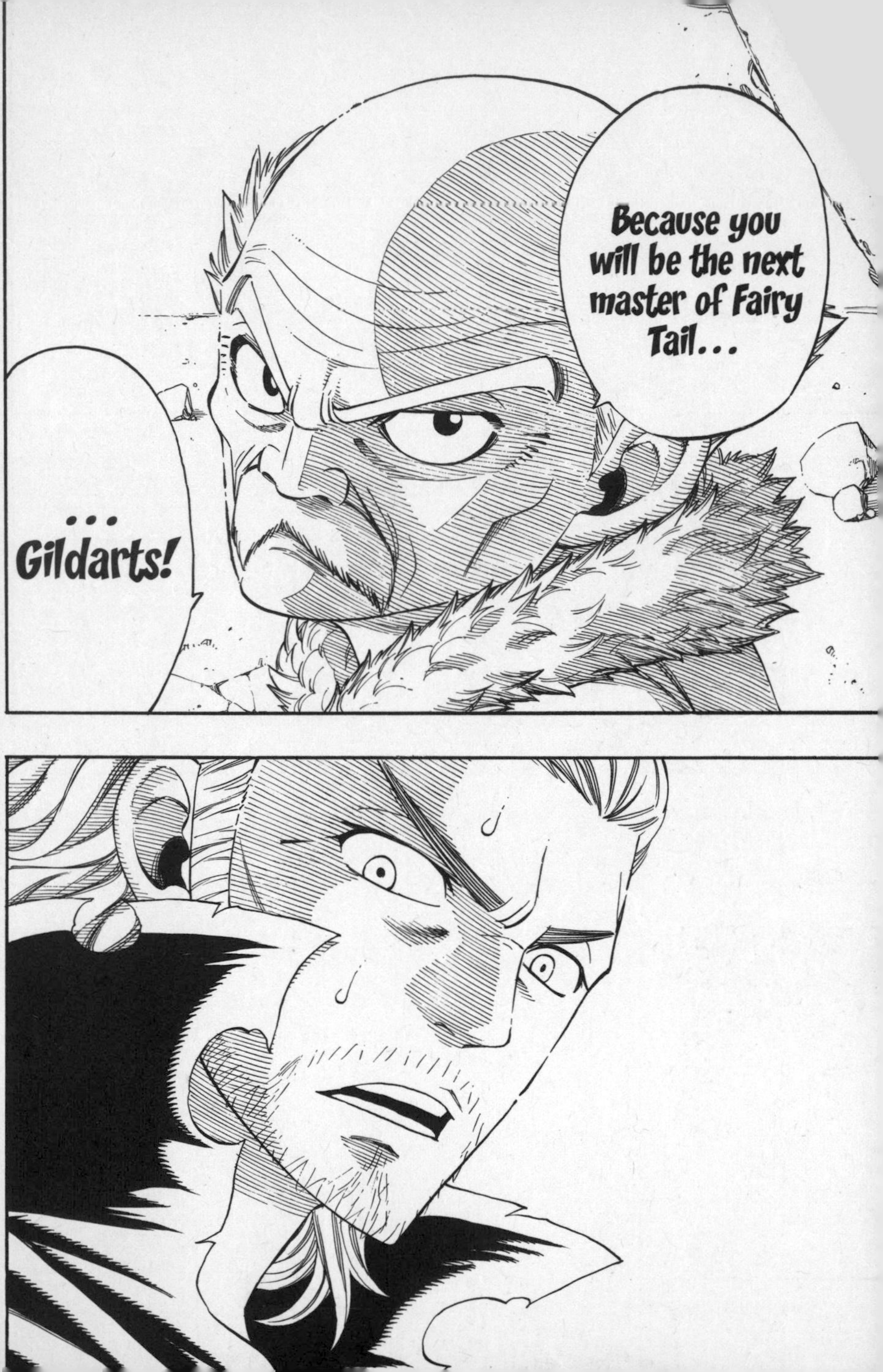
Because you will be the next master of Fairy Tail...
...Gildarts!

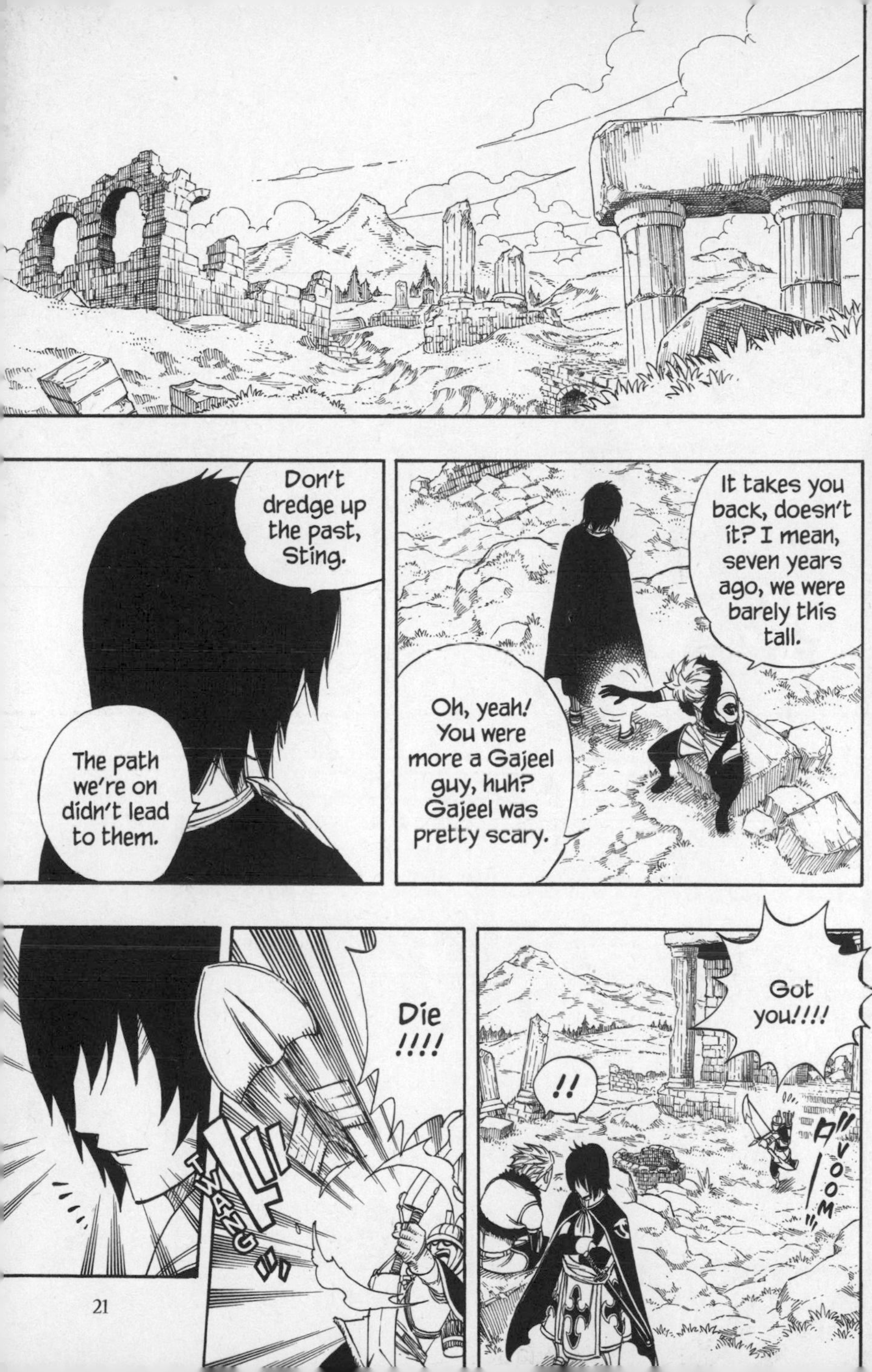
It takes you back, doesn't it? I mean, seven years ago, we were barely this tall.
Oh, yeah! You were more a Gajeel guy, huh? Gajeel was pretty scary.
Don't dredge up the past, Sting.
The path we're on didn't lead to them.
Got you!!!!
!!
VOOM
Die !!!!
TWANG

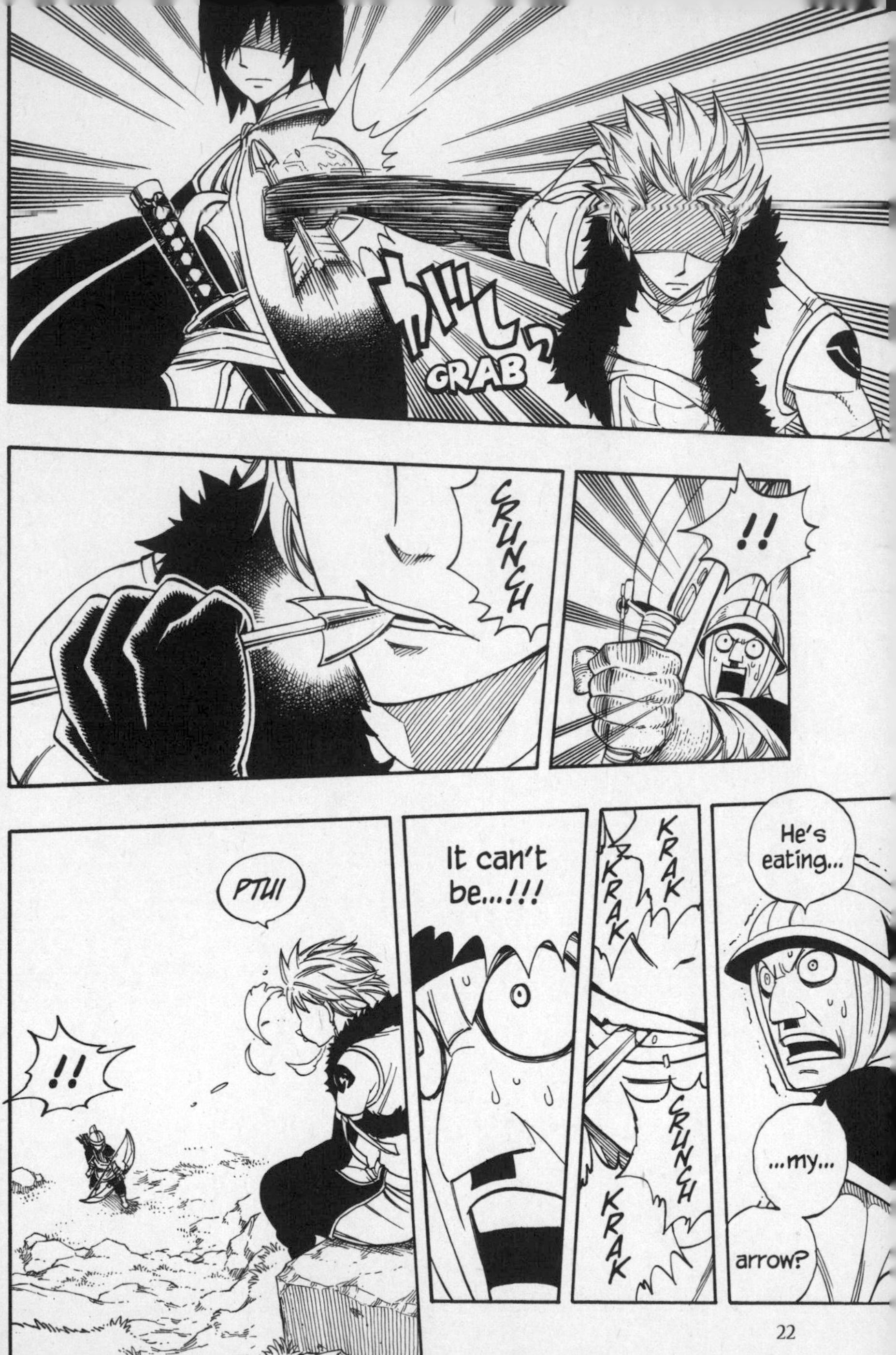
GRAB
!!
CRUNCH
He's eating...
...my...
arrow?
KRAK
KRAK
CRUNCH
KRAK
It can't be...!!!
PTUI
!!

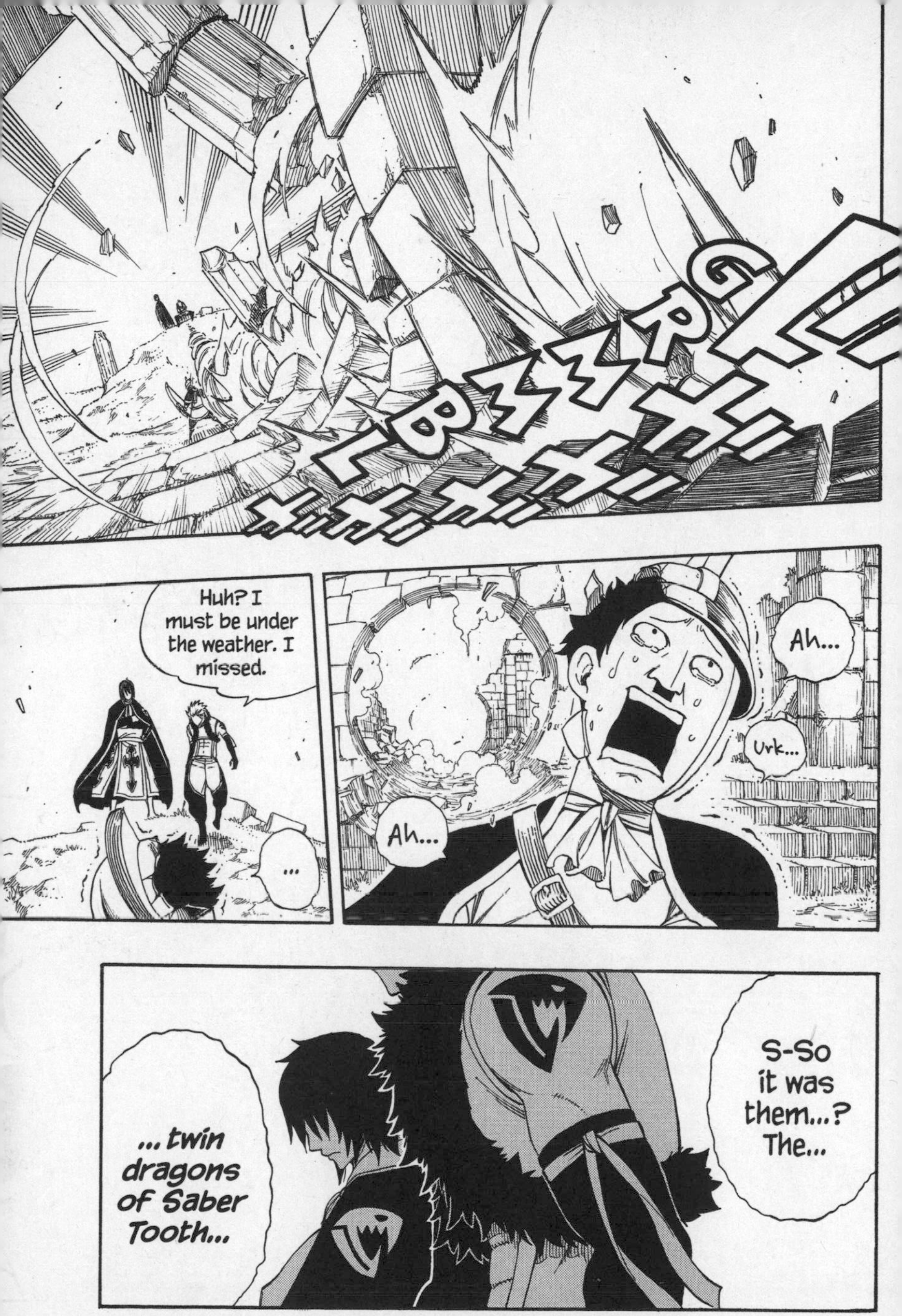
GRMMBL
Ah...
Urk...
Ah...
Huh? I must be under the weather. I missed.
...
S-So it was them...? The...
...twin dragons of Saber Tooth...

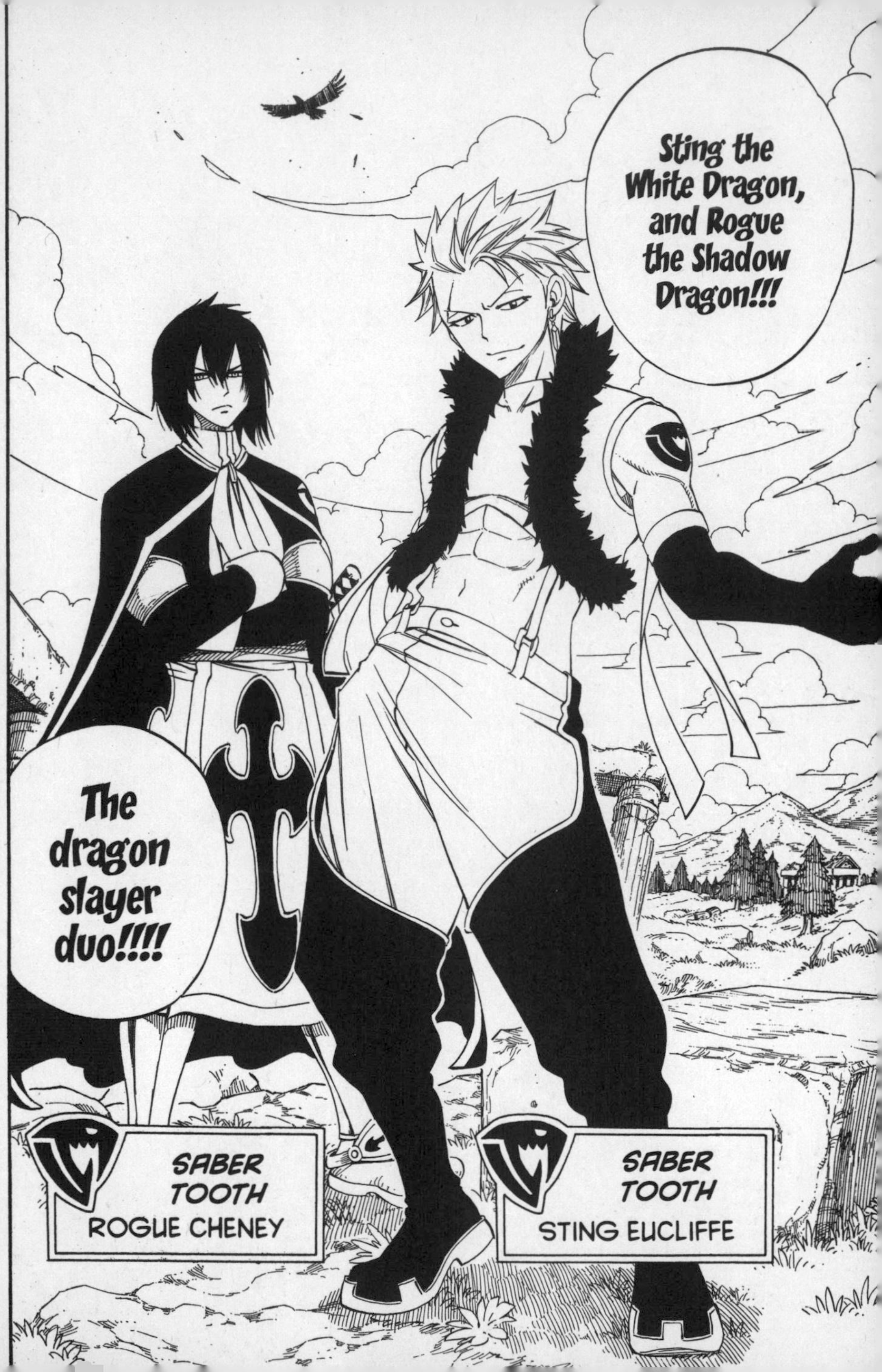
Sting the White Dragon, and Rogue the Shadow Dragon!!!
The dragon slayer duo!!!!
SABER TOOTH
STING EUCLIFFE
SABER TOOTH
ROGUE CHENEY

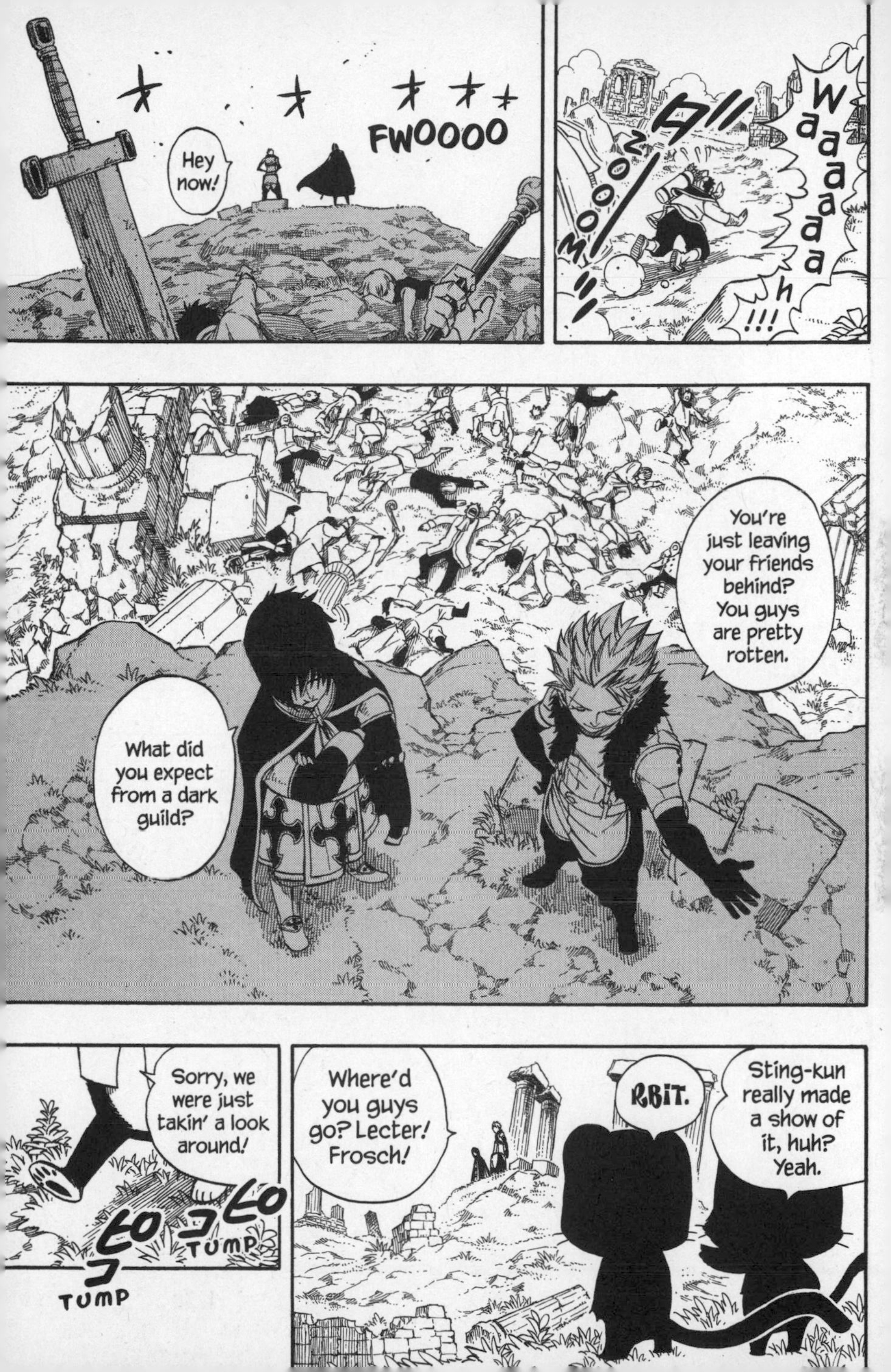
Waaaaaaah!!!
ZOOOOM
Hey now!
FWOOOO
You're just leaving your friends behind? You guys are pretty rotten.
What did you expect from a dark guild?
Sting-kun really made a show of it, huh? Yeah.
RBIT.
Where'd you guys go? Lecter! Frosch!
Sorry, we were just takin' a look around!
TUMP
TUMP

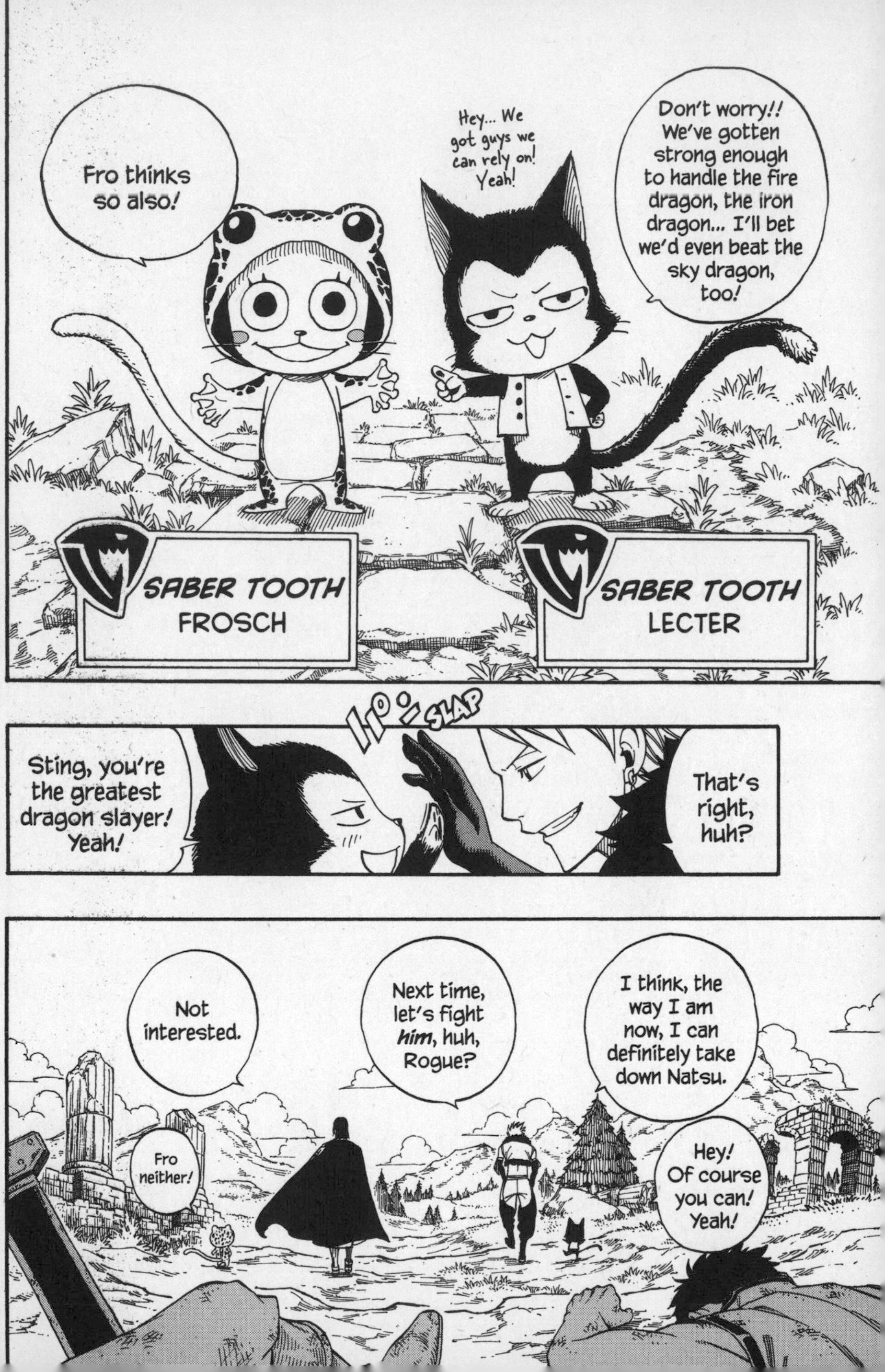
Don't worry!! We've gotten strong enough to handle the fire dragon, the iron dragon... I'll bet we'd even beat the sky dragon, too!
Hey... We got guys we can rely on! Yeah!
Fro thinks so also!
SABER TOOTH
LECTER
SABER TOOTH
FROSCH
SLAP
That's right, huh?
Sting, you're the greatest dragon slayer! Yeah!
I think, the way I am now, I can definitely take down Natsu.
Hey! Of course you can! Yeah!
Next time, let's fight *him*, huh, Rogue?
Not interested.
Fro neither!

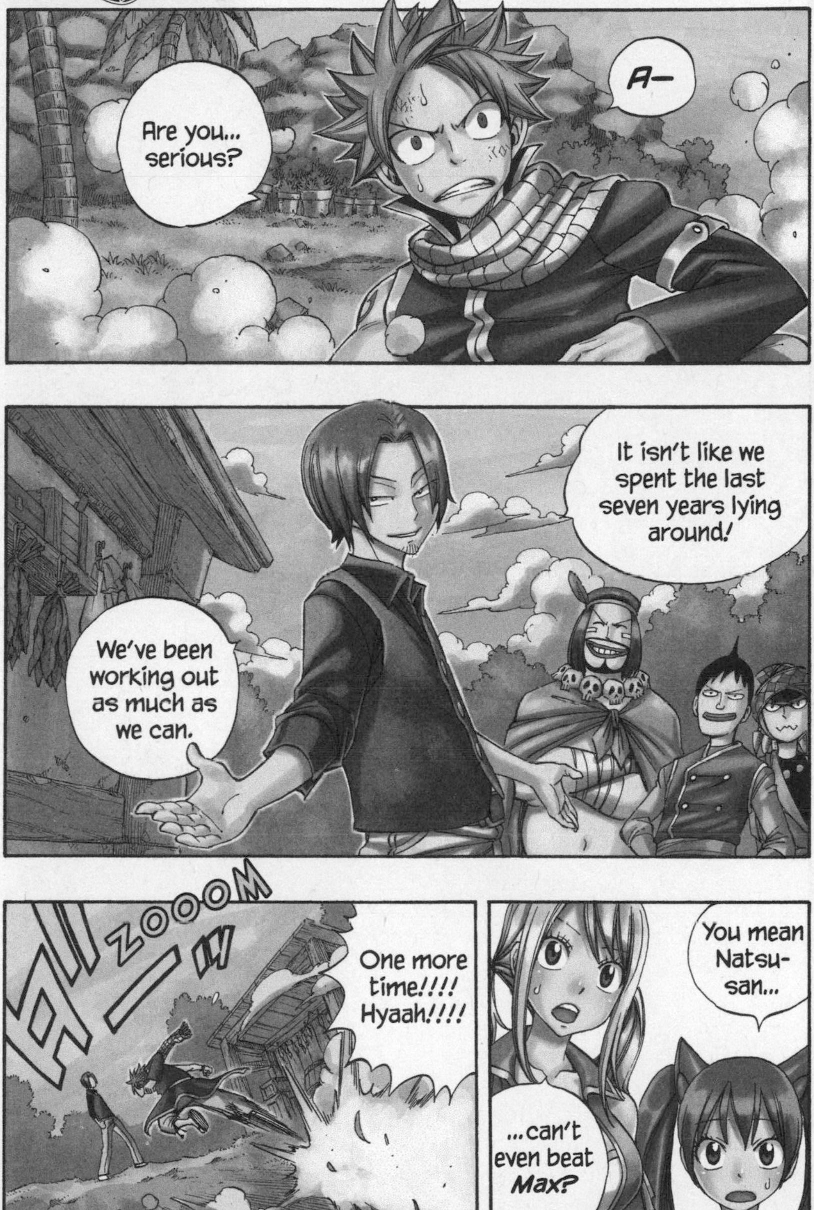
A—
Are you... serious?
It isn't like we spent the last seven years lying around!
We've been working out as much as we can.
You mean Natsu-san...
...can't even beat Max?
One more time!!!! Hyaah!!!!
ZOOOM

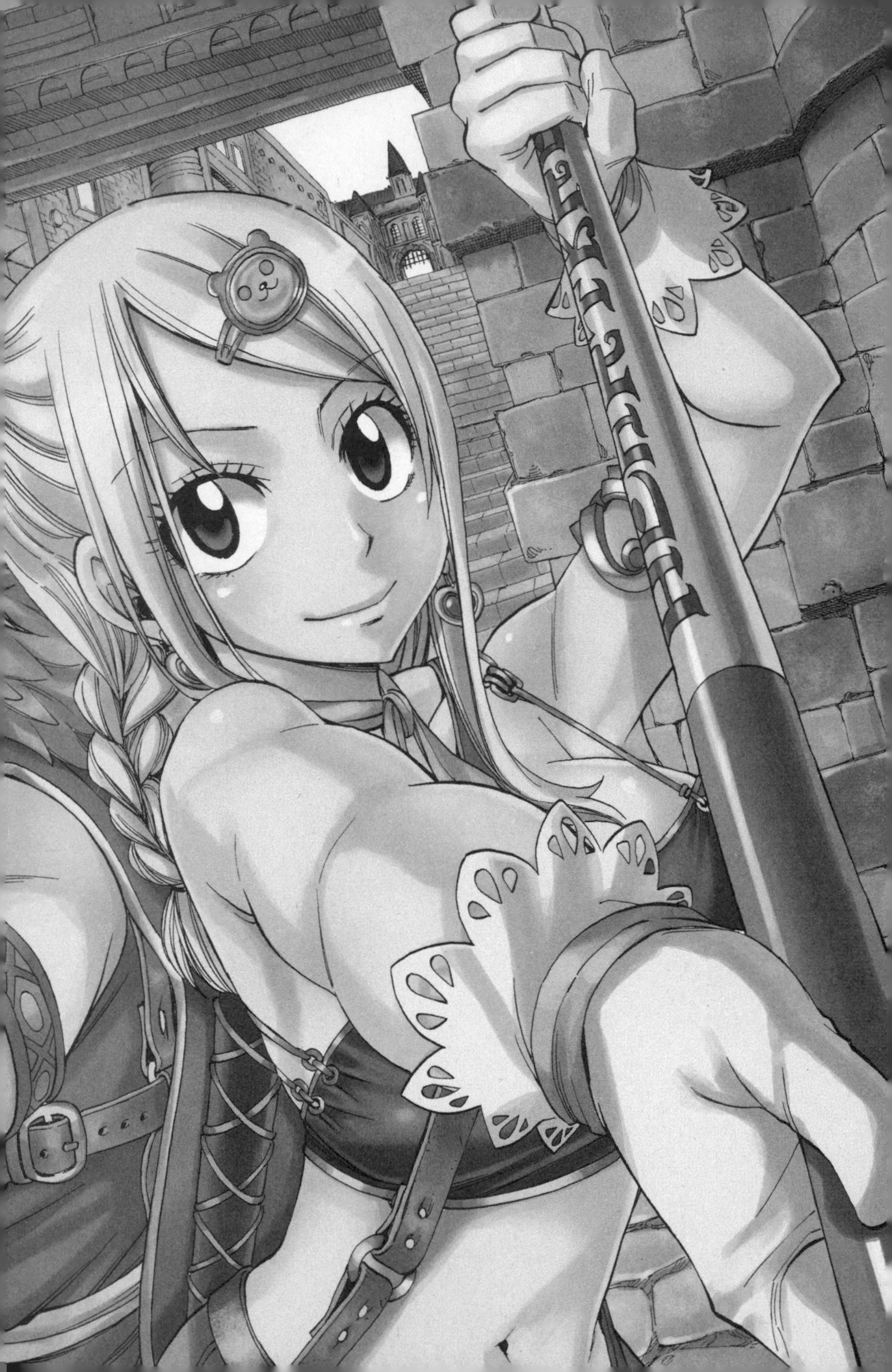

# Chapter 259: Porlyusica

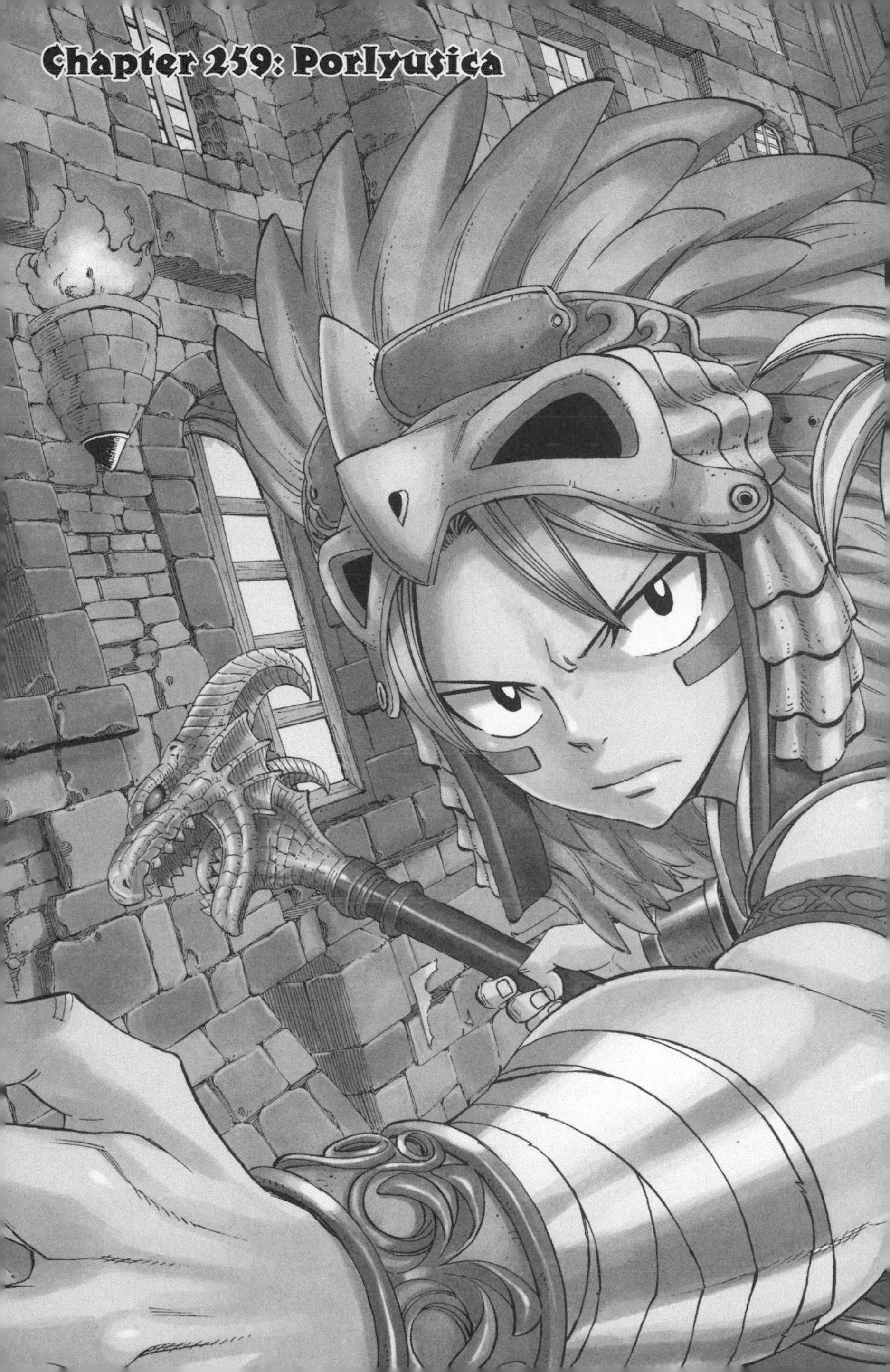

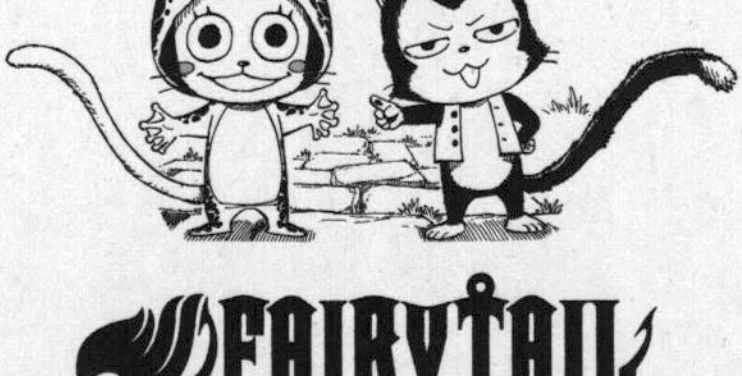

FAIRY TAIL

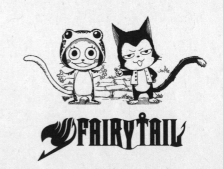

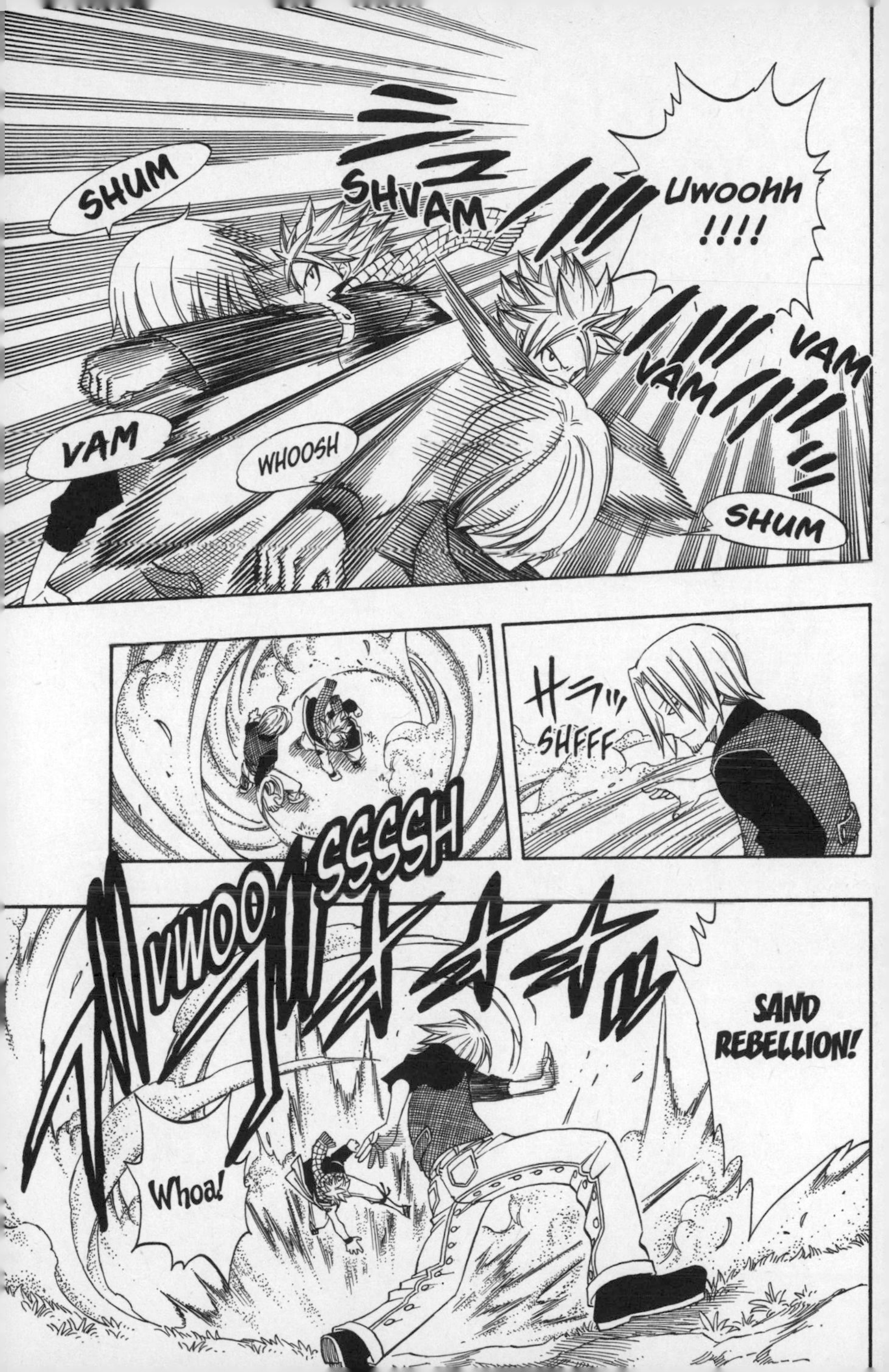
Uwoohh !!!!
SHVAM
SHUM
VAM
VAM
SHUM
WHOOSH
VAM
サラッ
SHFFF
SAND REBELLION!
VWOO
SSSSH
Whoa!

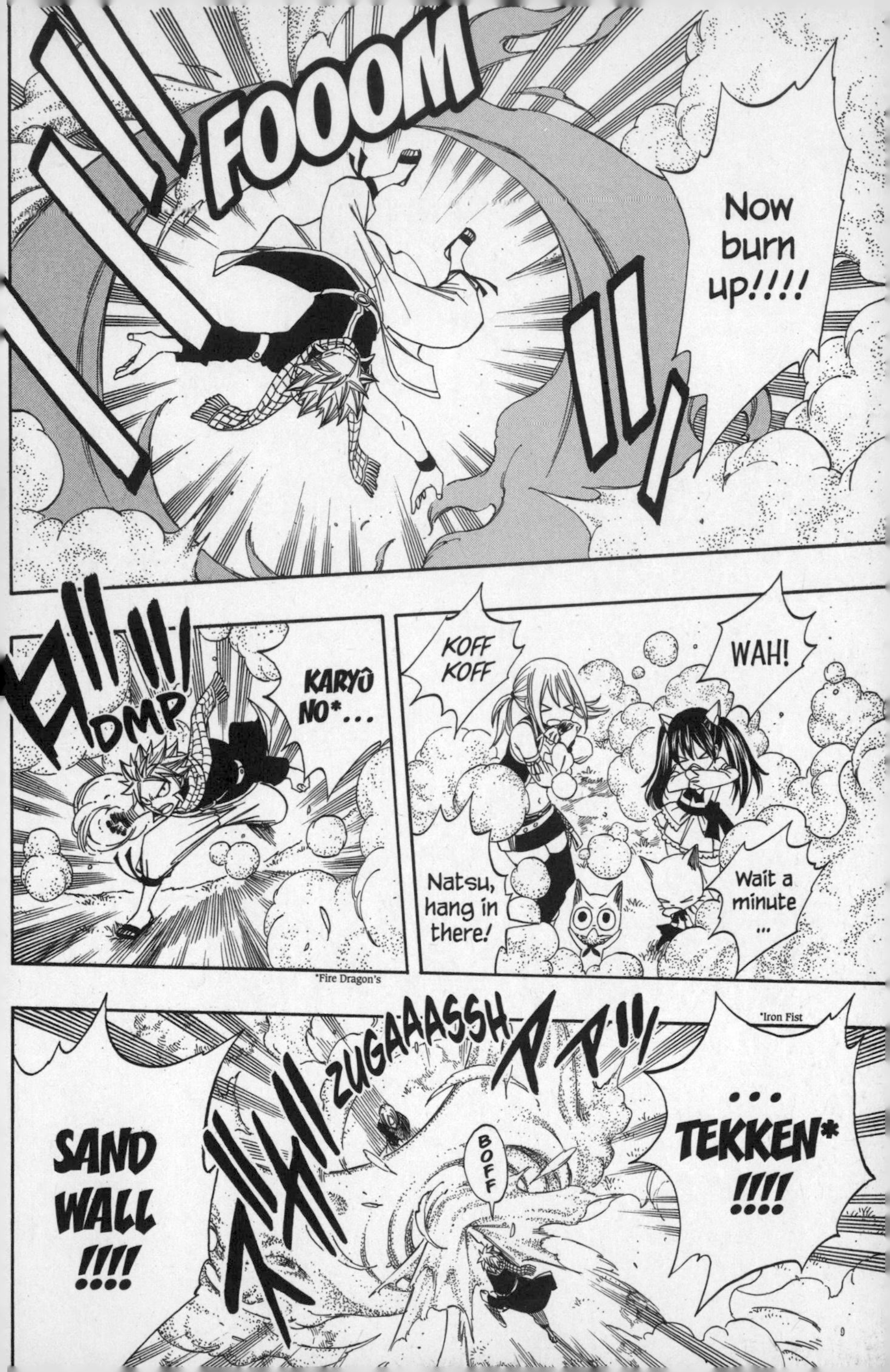
FOOOM
Now burn up!!!!
WAH!
KOFF KOFF
Wait a minute ...
Natsu, hang in there!
KARYÛ NO*...
DMP
... TEKKEN* !!!!
BOFF
ZUGAAASSH
SAND WALL !!!!
*Fire Dragon's
*Iron Fist

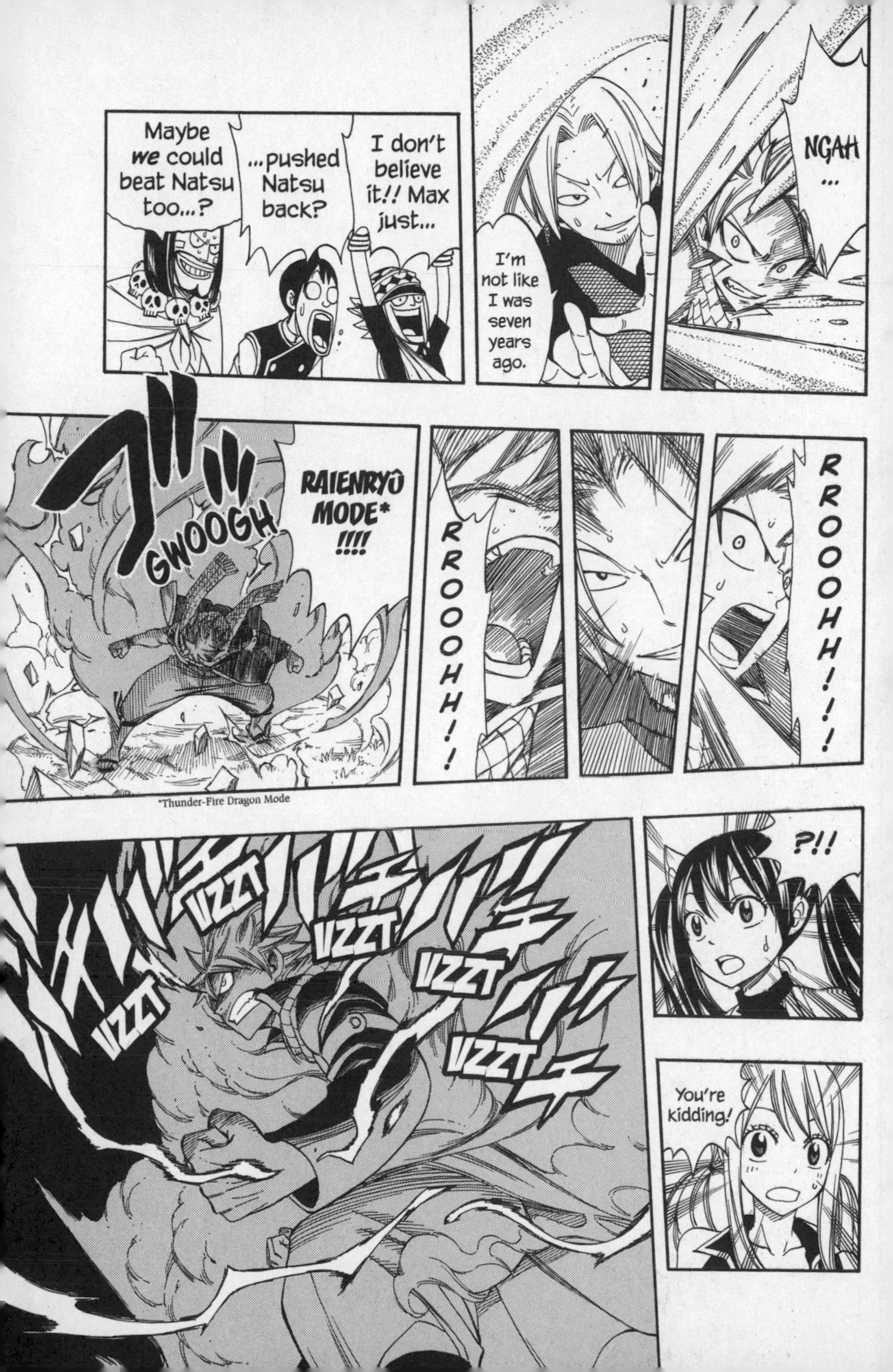
NGAH ...
I'm not like I was seven years ago.
I don't believe it!! Max just...
...pushed Natsu back?
Maybe we could beat Natsu too...?
RROOOHH!!!
RROOOHH!!
RAIENRYŪ MODE* !!!!
GWOOGH
?!!
You're kidding!
VZZT
VZZT
VZZT
VZZT
VZZT
VZZT
*Thunder-Fire Dragon Mode

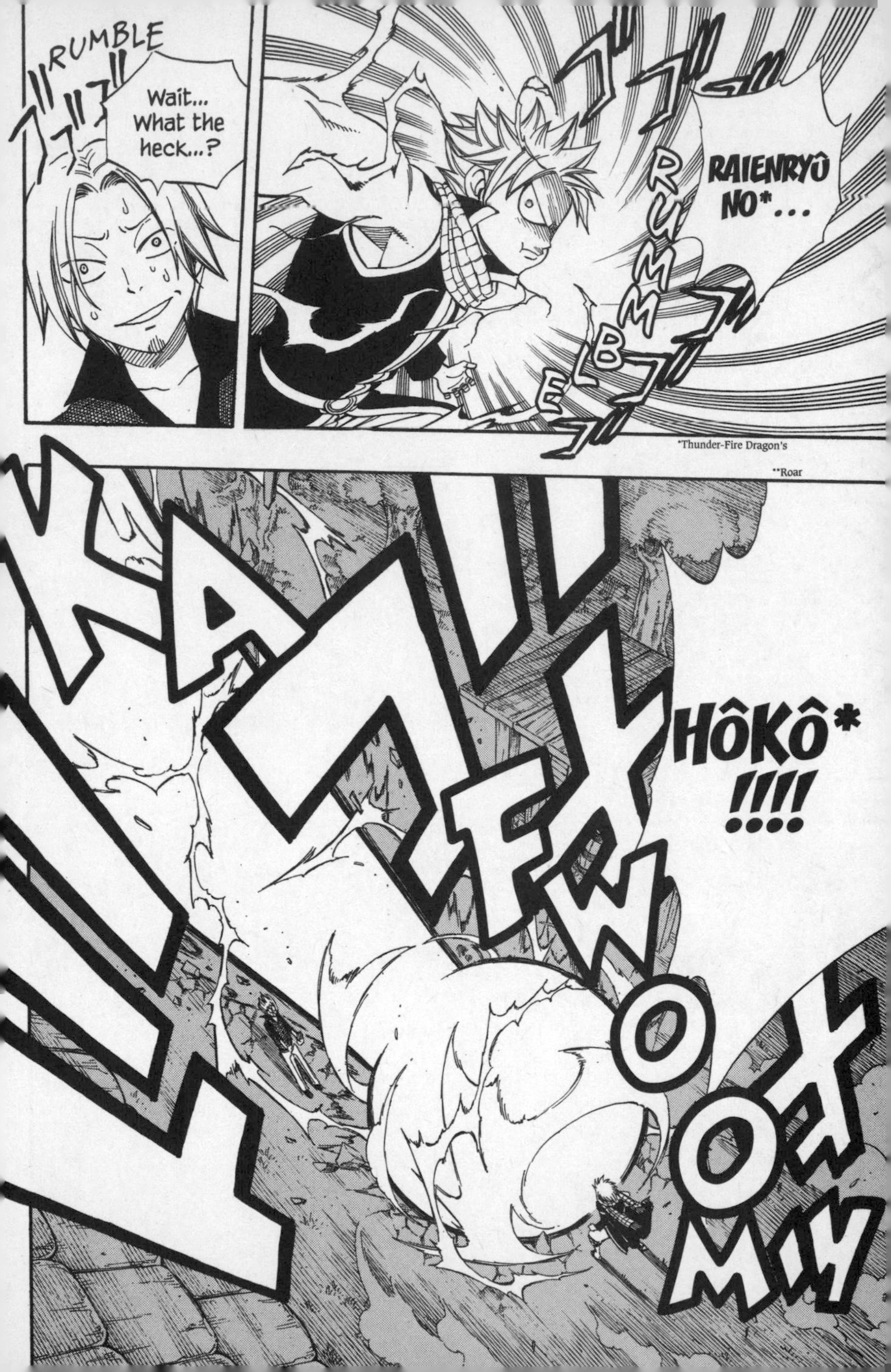
RAIENRYÛ NO*...
RUMMBLE
RUMBLE
Wait... What the heck...?
HÔKÔ* !!!!

*Thunder-Fire Dragon's

**Roar

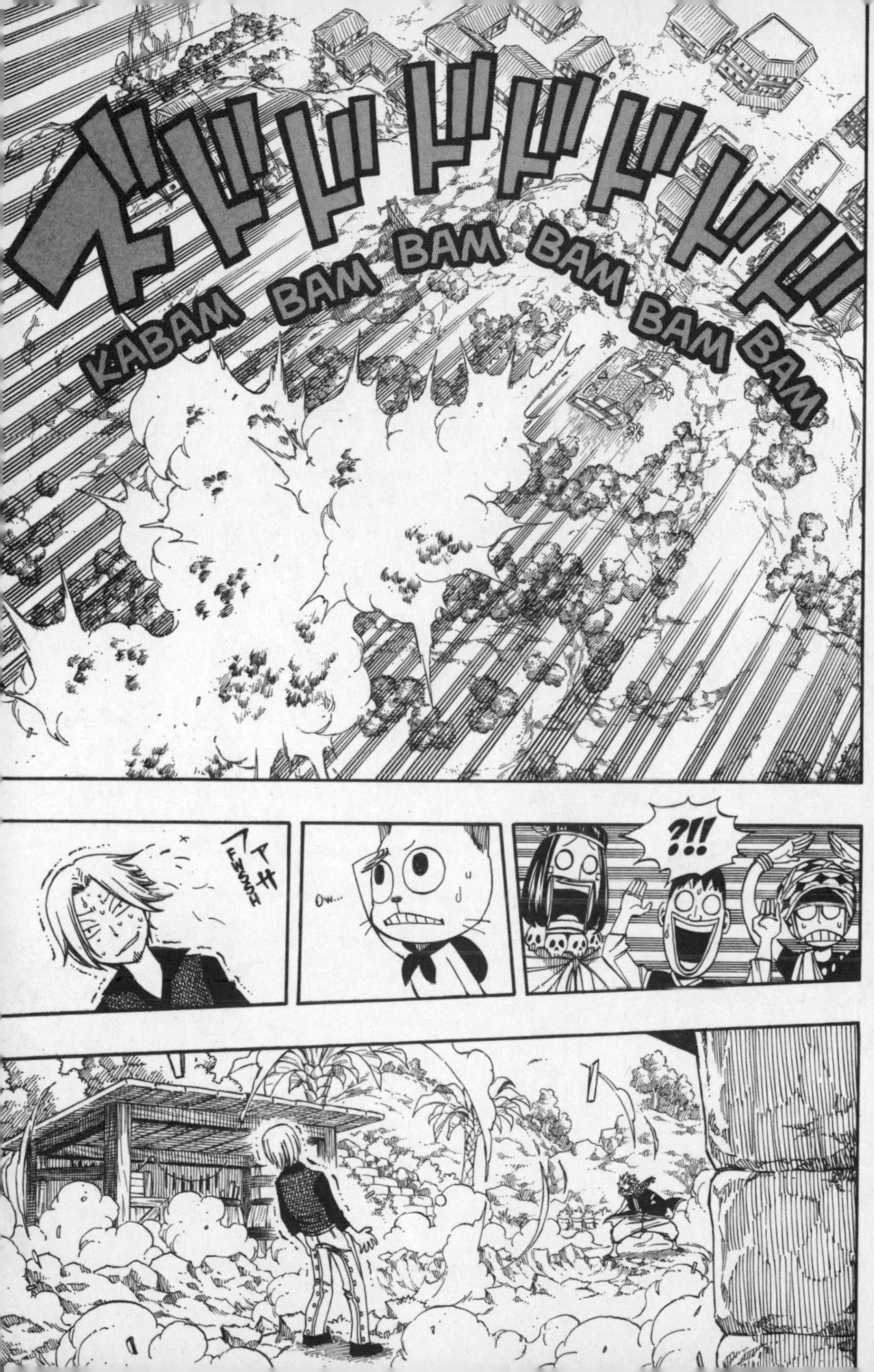
KABAM BAM BAM BAM BAM BAM
?!!
Ow...
FWSSH

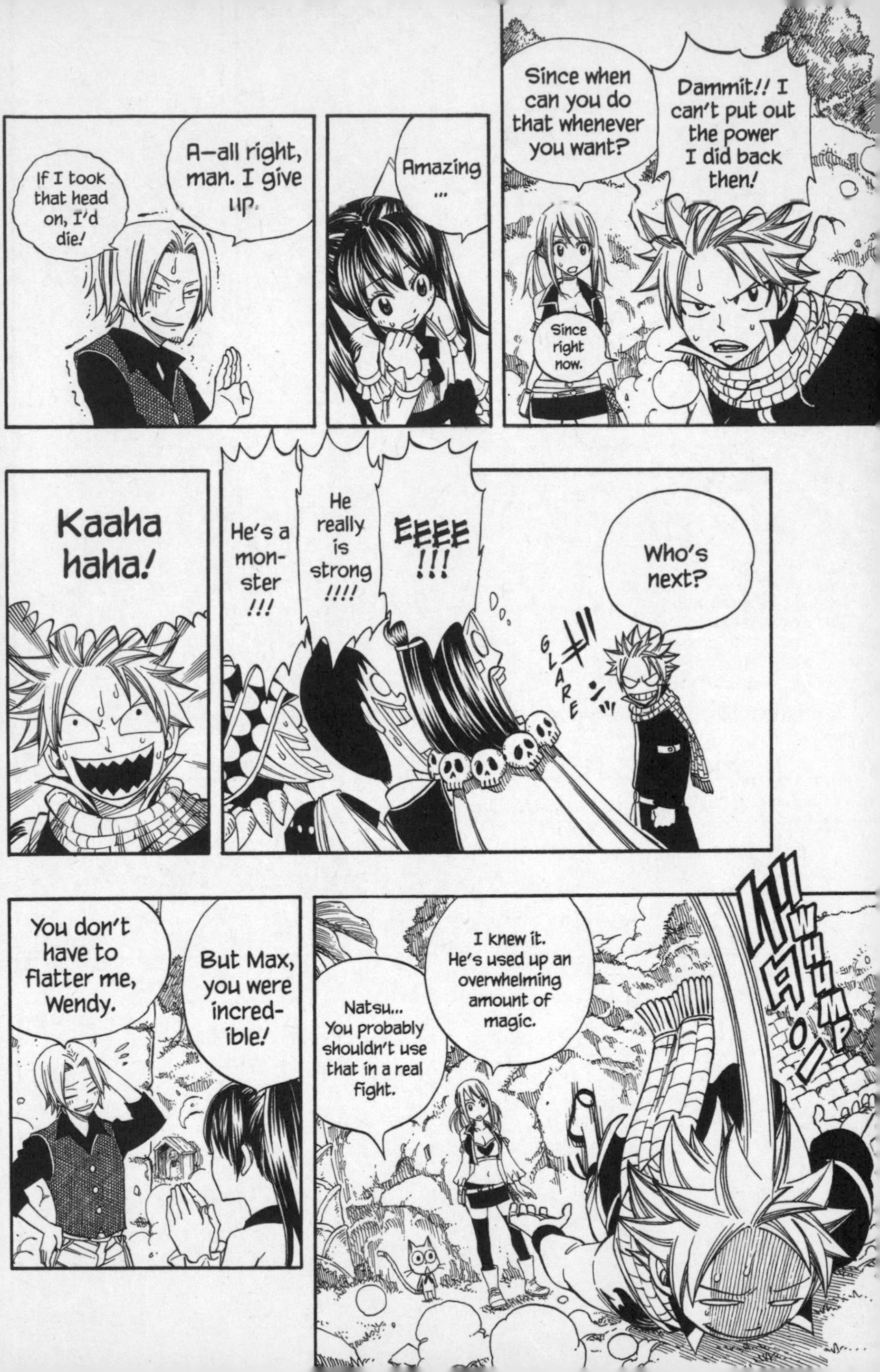
Dammit!! I can't put out the power I did back then!
Since when can you do that whenever you want?
Since right now.
Amazing ...
A—all right, man. I give up.
If I took that head on, I'd die!
Who's next?
GLARE
EEEE !!!
He really is strong !!!!
He's a mon-ster !!!
Kaaha haha!
WHUMP
I knew it. He's used up an overwhelming amount of magic.
Natsu... You probably shouldn't use that in a real fight.
But Max, you were incred-ible!
You don't have to flatter me, Wendy.

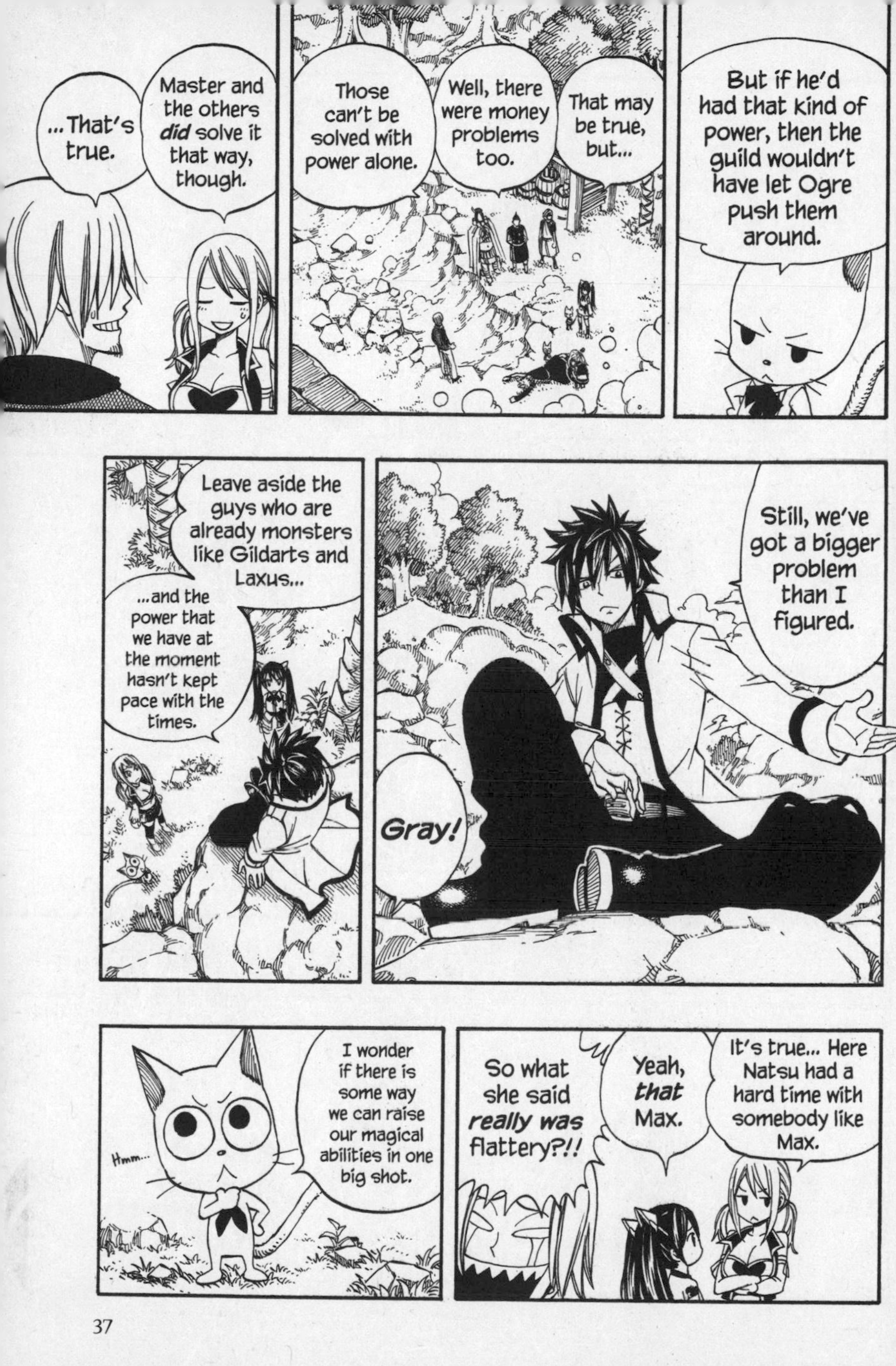
But if he'd had that kind of power, then the guild wouldn't have let Ogre push them around.
That may be true, but...
Well, there were money problems too.
Those can't be solved with power alone.
Master and the others *did* solve it that way, though.
...That's true.
Still, we've got a bigger problem than I figured.
*Gray!*
Leave aside the guys who are already monsters like Gildarts and Laxus...
...and the power that we have at the moment hasn't kept pace with the times.
It's true... Here Natsu had a hard time with somebody like Max.
Yeah, *that* Max.
So what she said *really was* flattery?!!
I wonder if there is some way we can raise our magical abilities in one big shot.
Hmm...

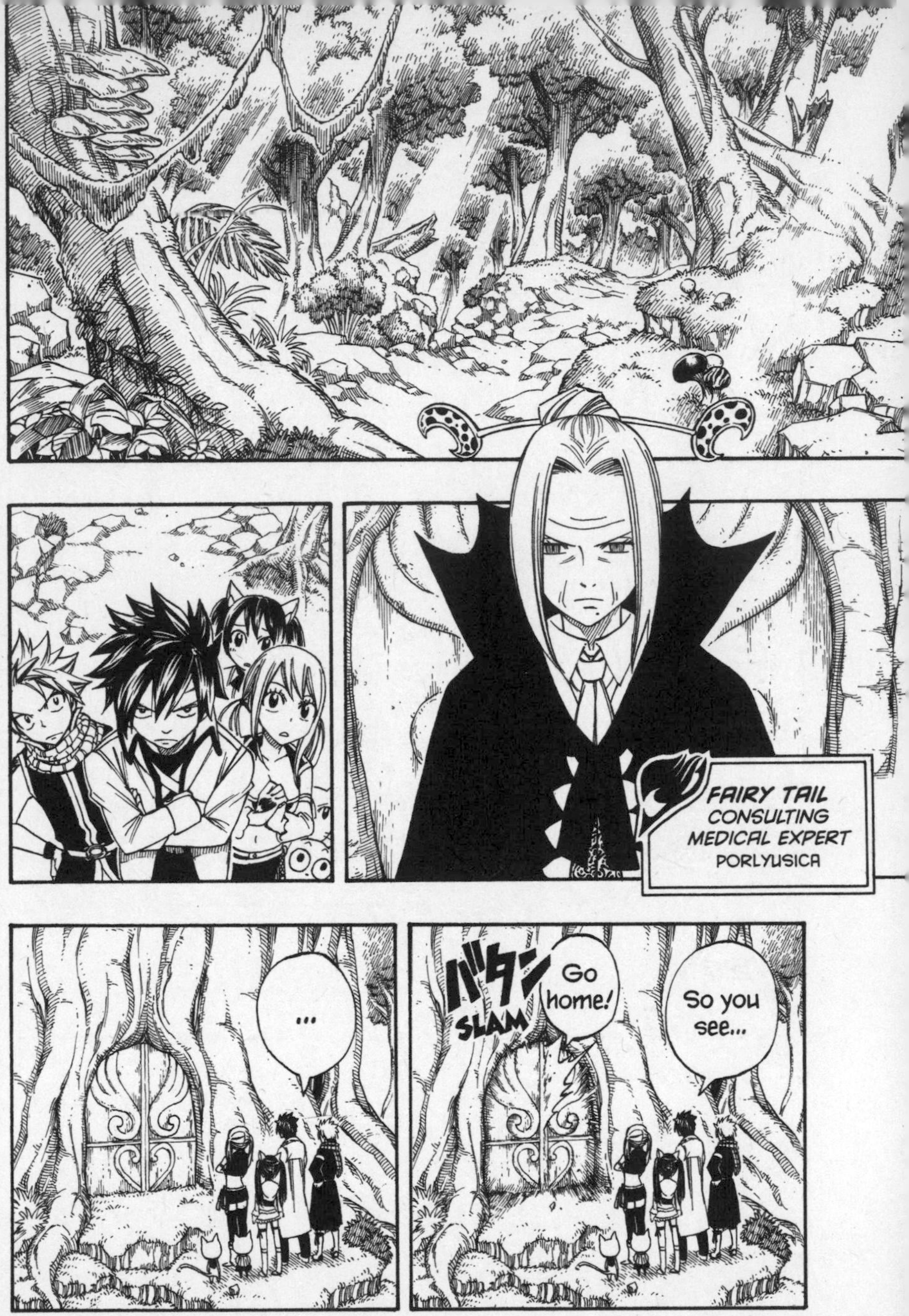
FAIRY TAIL
CONSULTING
MEDICAL EXPERT
PORLYUSICA
So you see...
Go home!
バタン
SLAM
...

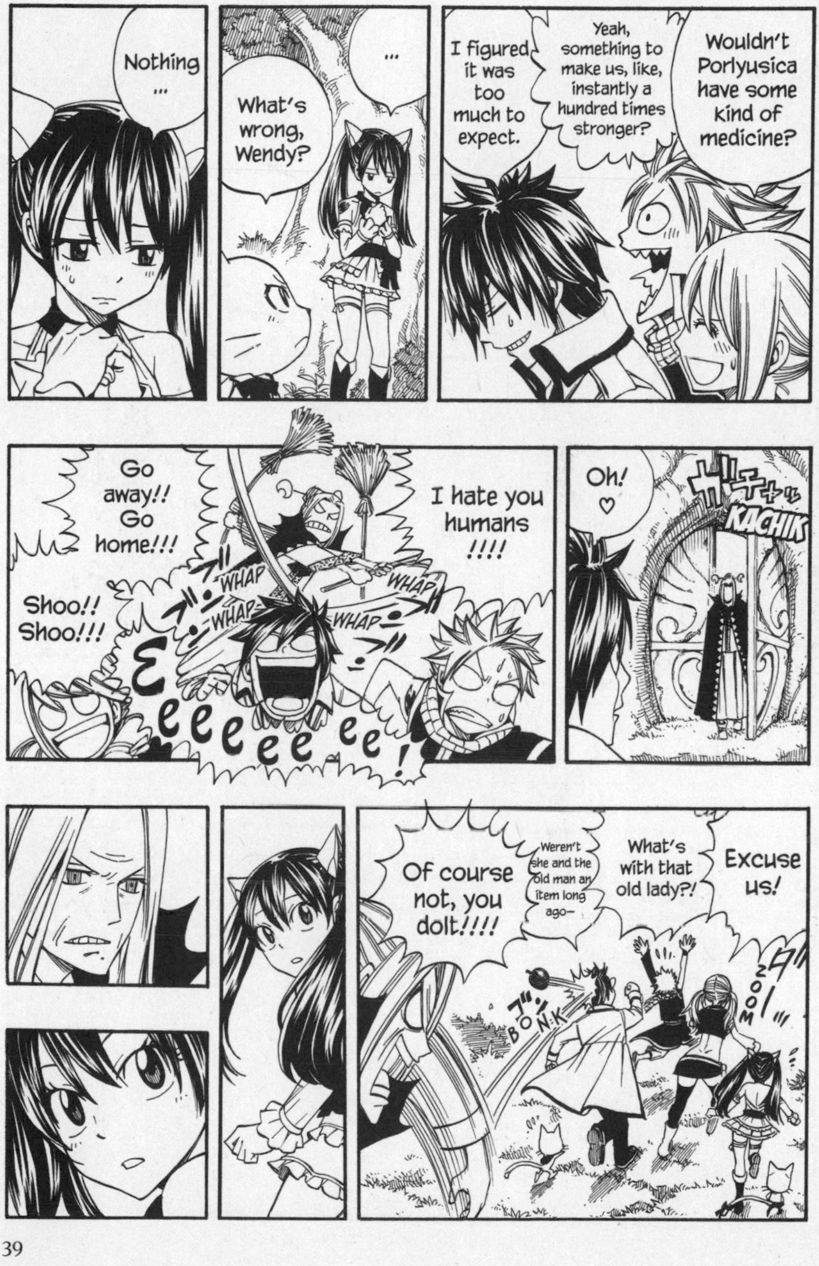

Wouldn't Porlyusica have some kind of medicine?
Yeah, something to make us, like, instantly a hundred times stronger?
I figured it was too much to expect.
...
What's wrong, Wendy?
Nothing ...
Oh! ♥
KACHIK
I hate you humans!!!!
Go away!! Go home!!!
WHAP
WHAP
WHAP
WHAP
Shoo!! Shoo!!!
Eeeeeeee!
Excuse us!
What's with that old lady?!
Weren't she and the old man an item long ago–
Of course not, you dolt!!!!
ZOOM
BONK

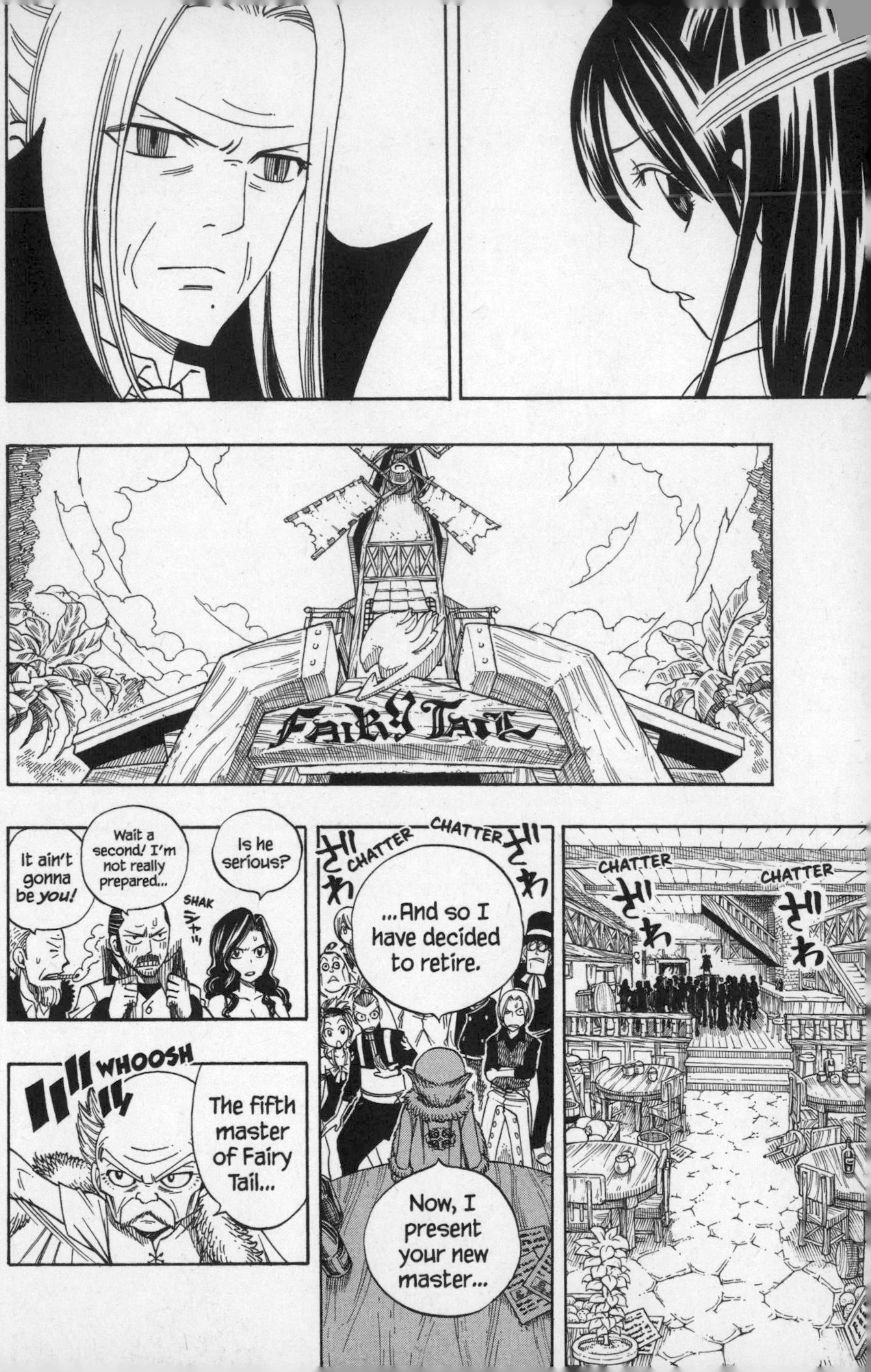

FAIRY TAIL
CHATTER
ざわ
CHATTER
ざわ
CHATTER
ざわ
CHATTER
ざわ
...And so I have decided to retire.
Now, I present your new master...
Is he serious?
Wait a second! I'm not really prepared...
SHAK
It ain't gonna be *you!*
WHOOSH
The fifth master of Fairy Tail...

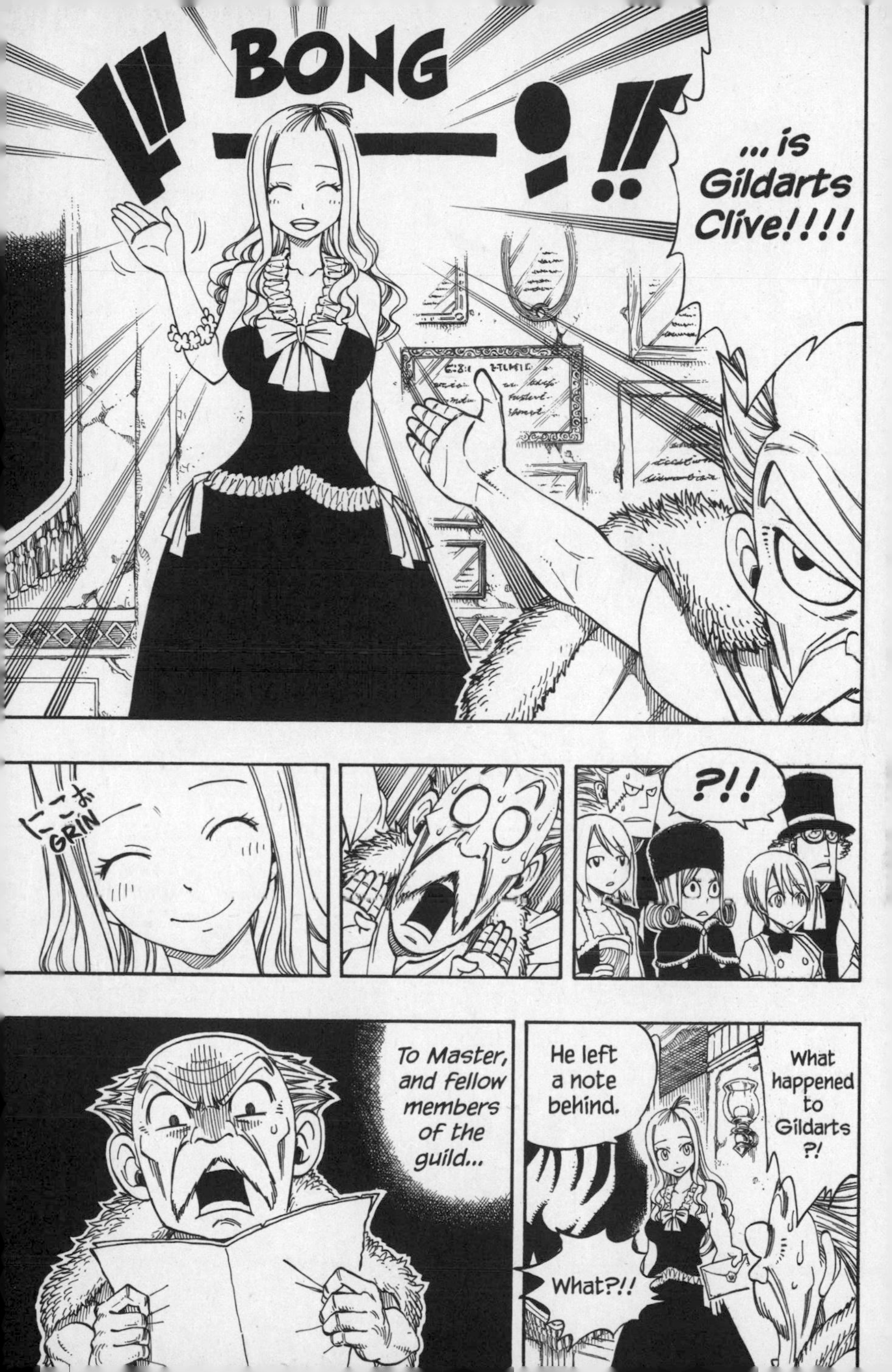
BONG
... is Gildarts Clive!!!!
?!!
GRIN
What happened to Gildarts ?!
He left a note behind.
What?!!
To Master, and fellow members of the guild...

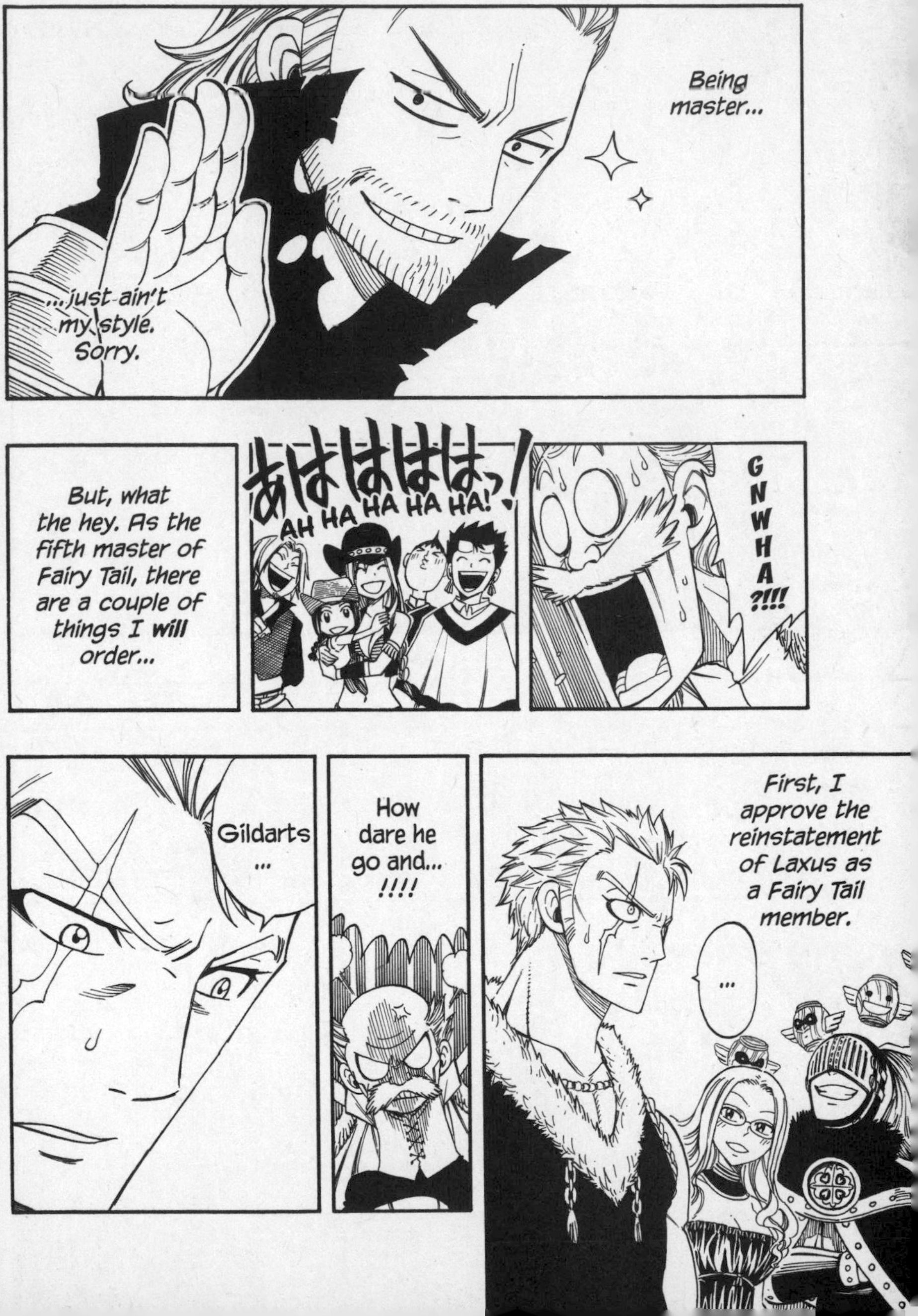
Being master...
...just ain't my style. Sorry.
GNWHA?!!!
あははははっ!
AH HA HA HA HA!
But, what the hey. As the fifth master of Fairy Tail, there are a couple of things I will order...
First, I approve the reinstatement of Laxus as a Fairy Tail member.
...
How dare he go and... !!!!
Gildarts ...

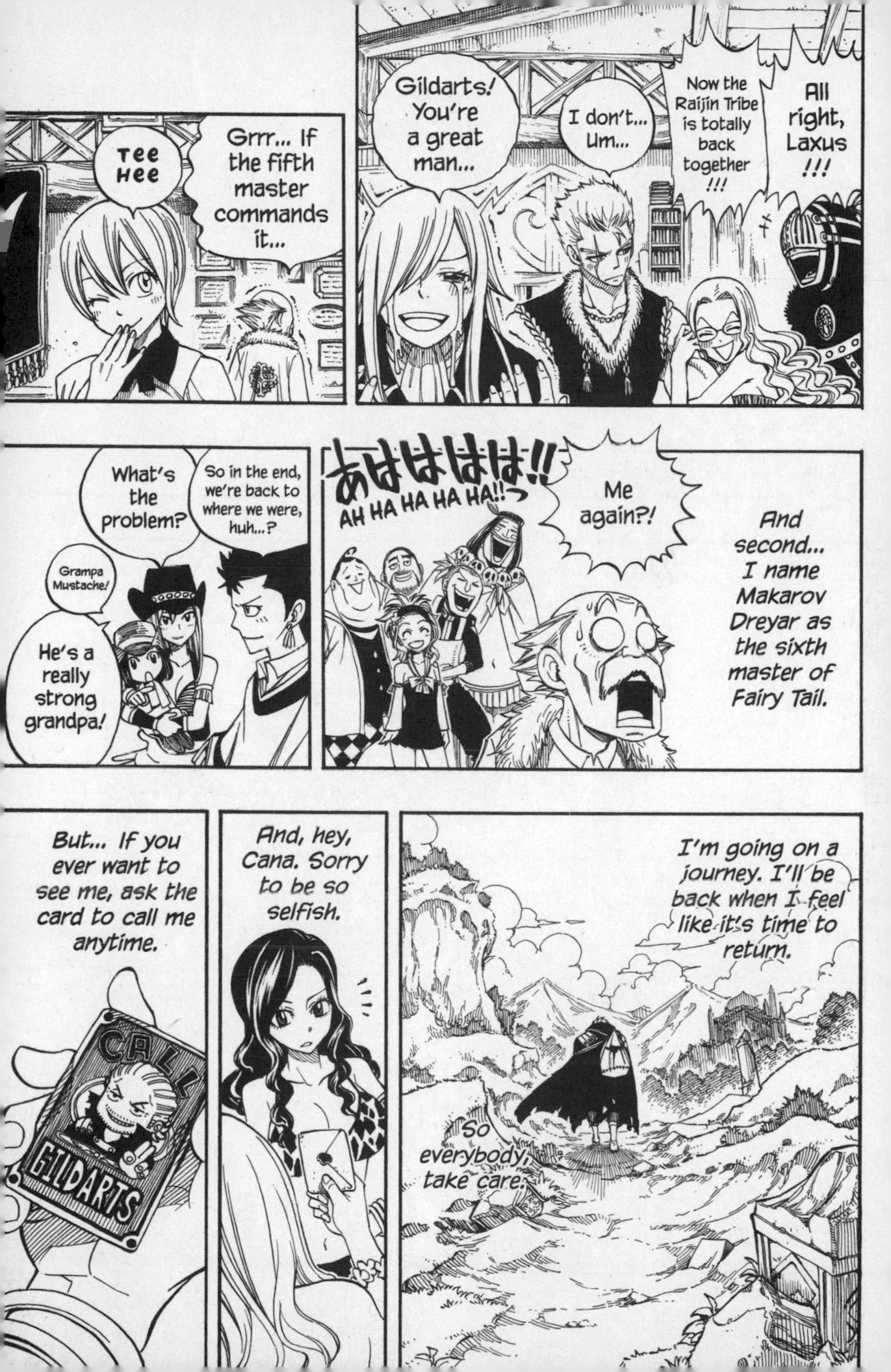
All right, Laxus!!!
Now the Raijin Tribe is totally back together!!!
I don't... Um...
Gildarts! You're a great man...
Grrr... If the fifth master commands it...
Tee Hee
And second... I name Makarov Dreyar as the sixth master of Fairy Tail.
Me again?!
あはははは!!
AH HA HA HA HA!!
So in the end, we're back to where we were, huh...?
What's the problem?
Grampa Mustache!
He's a really strong grandpa!
I'm going on a journey. I'll be back when I feel like it's time to return.
So everybody, take care.
And, hey, Cana. Sorry to be so selfish.
But... If you ever want to see me, ask the card to call me anytime.
CALL
GILDARTS

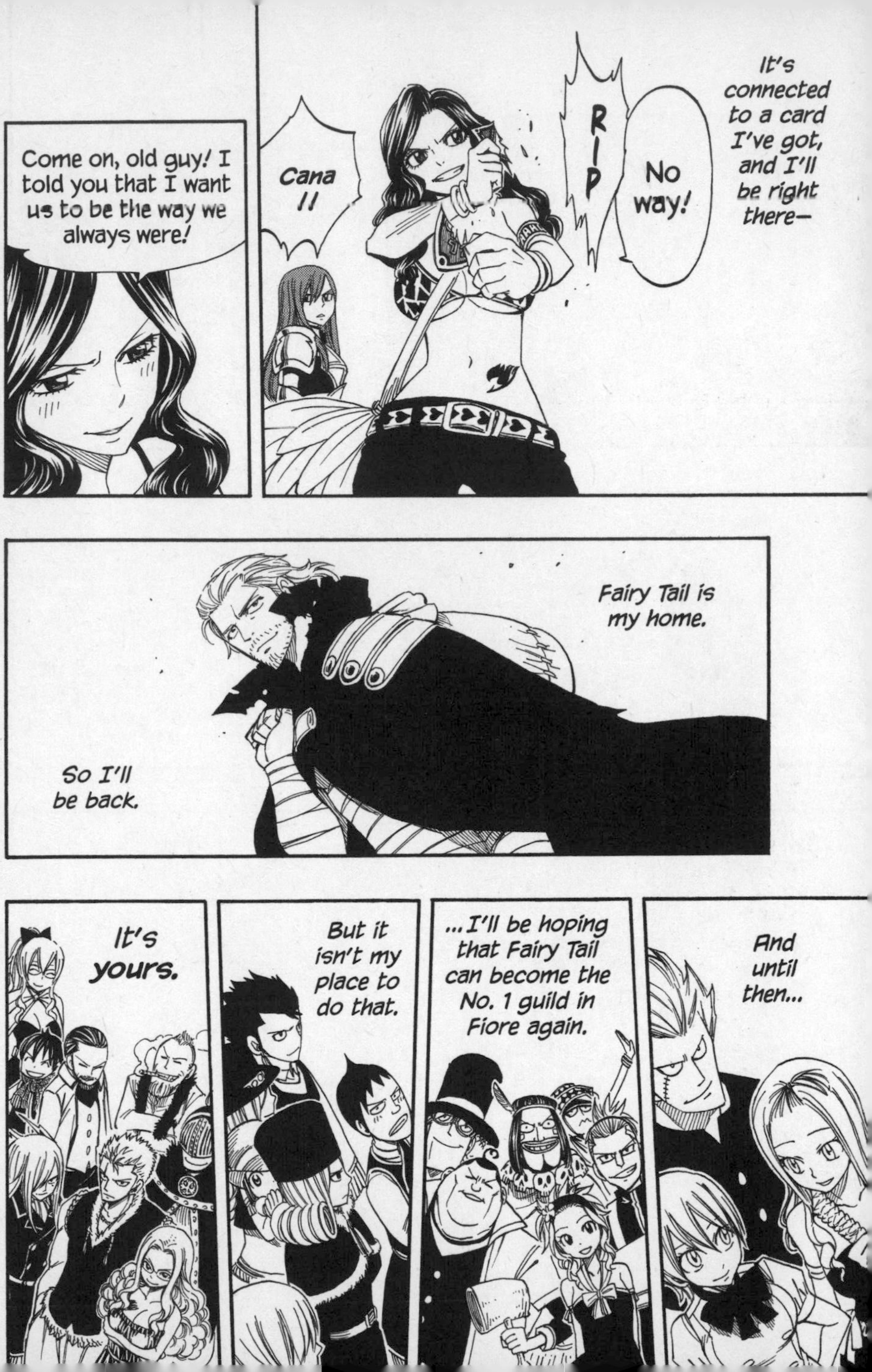
It's connected to a card I've got, and I'll be right there—
No way!
RIP
Cana !!
Come on, old guy! I told you that I want us to be the way we always were!
Fairy Tail is my home.
So I'll be back.
And until then...
...I'll be hoping that Fairy Tail can become the No. 1 guild in Fiore again.
But it isn't my place to do that.
It's yours.

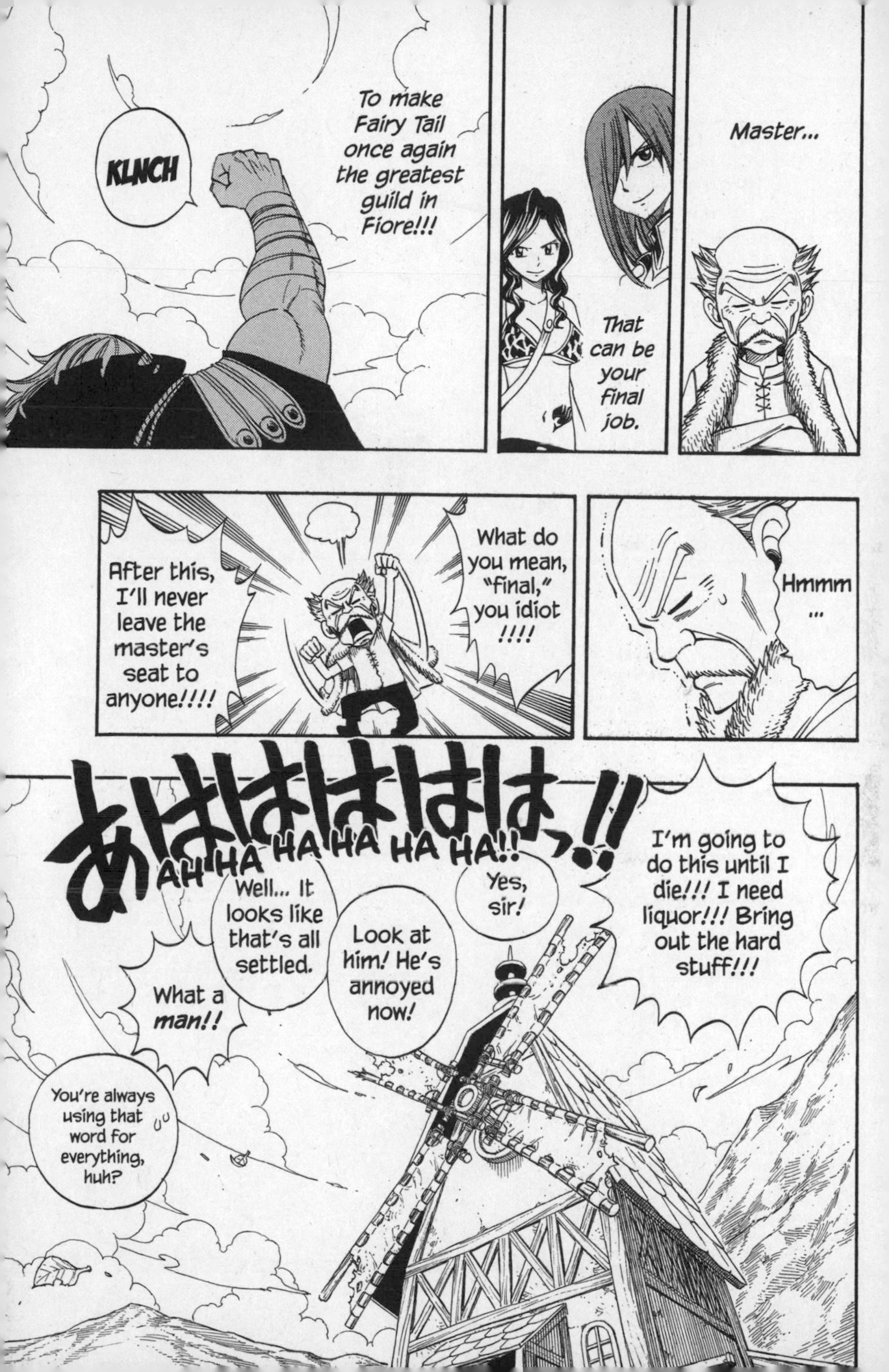

Master...
That can be your final job.
To make Fairy Tail once again the greatest guild in Fiore!!!
KLNCH
Hmmm ...
What do you mean, "final," you idiot !!!!
After this, I'll never leave the master's seat to anyone!!!!
あははははははっ!!
AH HA HA HA HA HA!!
I'm going to do this until I die!!! I need liquor!!! Bring out the hard stuff!!!
Yes, sir!
Look at him! He's annoyed now!
Well... It looks like that's all settled.
What a man!!
You're always using that word for everything, huh?

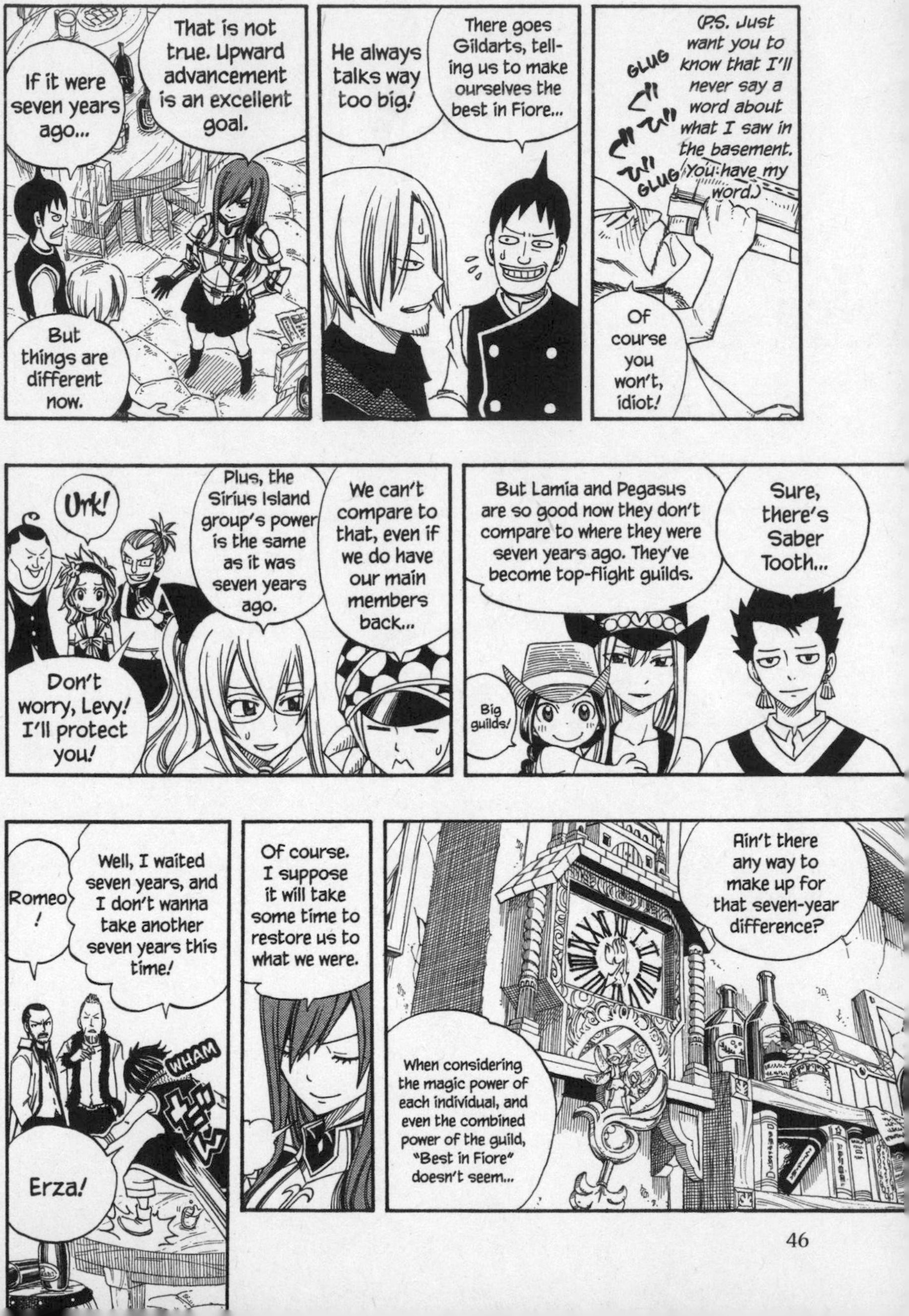
(P.S. Just want you to know that I'll never say a word about what I saw in the basement. You have my word.)
GLUG
GLUG
Of course you won't, idiot!
There goes Gildarts, telling us to make ourselves the best in Fiore...
He always talks way too big!
That is not true. Upward advancement is an excellent goal.
If it were seven years ago...
But things are different now.
Sure, there's Saber Tooth...
But Lamia and Pegasus are so good now they don't compare to where they were seven years ago. They've become top-flight guilds.
Big guilds!
We can't compare to that, even if we do have our main members back...
Plus, the Sirius Island group's power is the same as it was seven years ago.
Urk!
Don't worry, Levy! I'll protect you!
Ain't there any way to make up for that seven-year difference?
When considering the magic power of each individual, and even the combined power of the guild, "Best in Fiore" doesn't seem...
Of course. I suppose it will take some time to restore us to what we were.
Well, I waited seven years, and I don't wanna take another seven years this time!
Romeo!
WHAM
Erza!

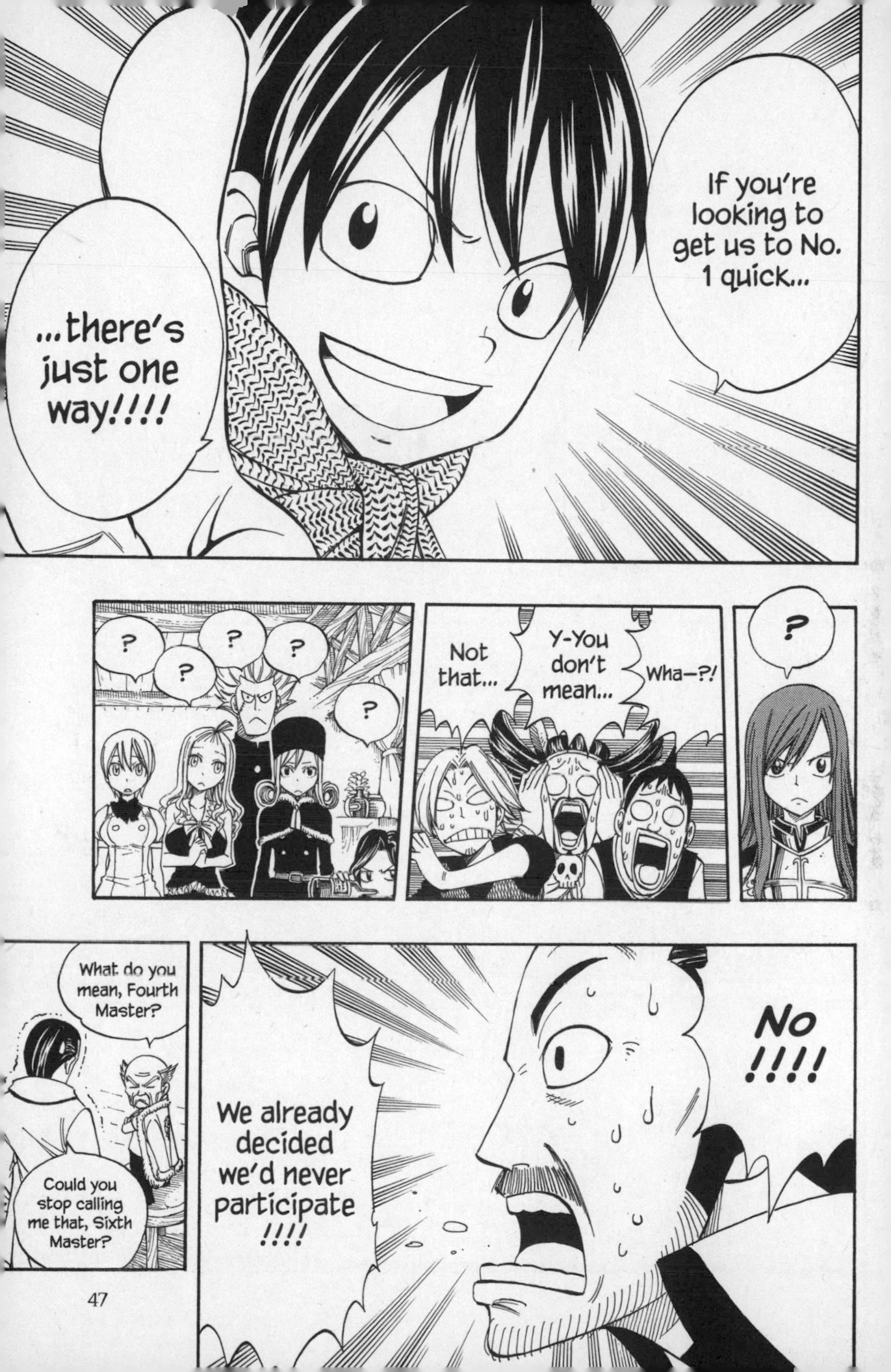

If you're looking to get us to No. 1 quick...
...there's just one way!!!!
?
Wha—?!
Y-You don't mean...
Not that...
?
?
?
?
?
No !!!!
We already decided we'd never participate !!!!
What do you mean, Fourth Master?
Could you stop calling me that, Sixth Master?

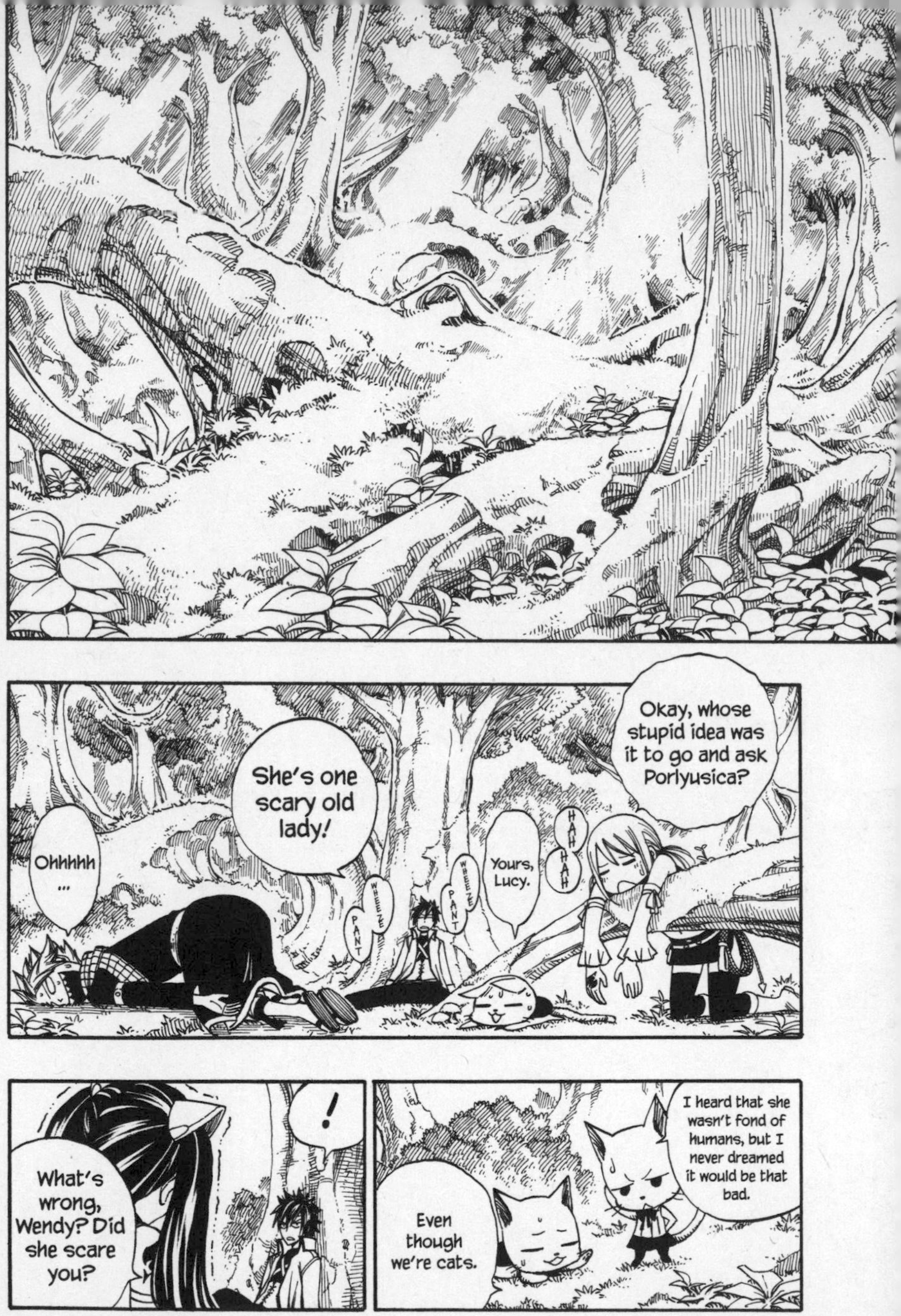
Okay, whose stupid idea was it to go and ask Porlyusica?
HAH HAH
Yours, Lucy.
WHEEZE PANT
She's one scary old lady!
WHEEZE PANT
Ohhhhh ...
I heard that she wasn't fond of humans, but I never dreamed it would be that bad.
Even though we're cats.
!
What's wrong, Wendy? Did she scare you?

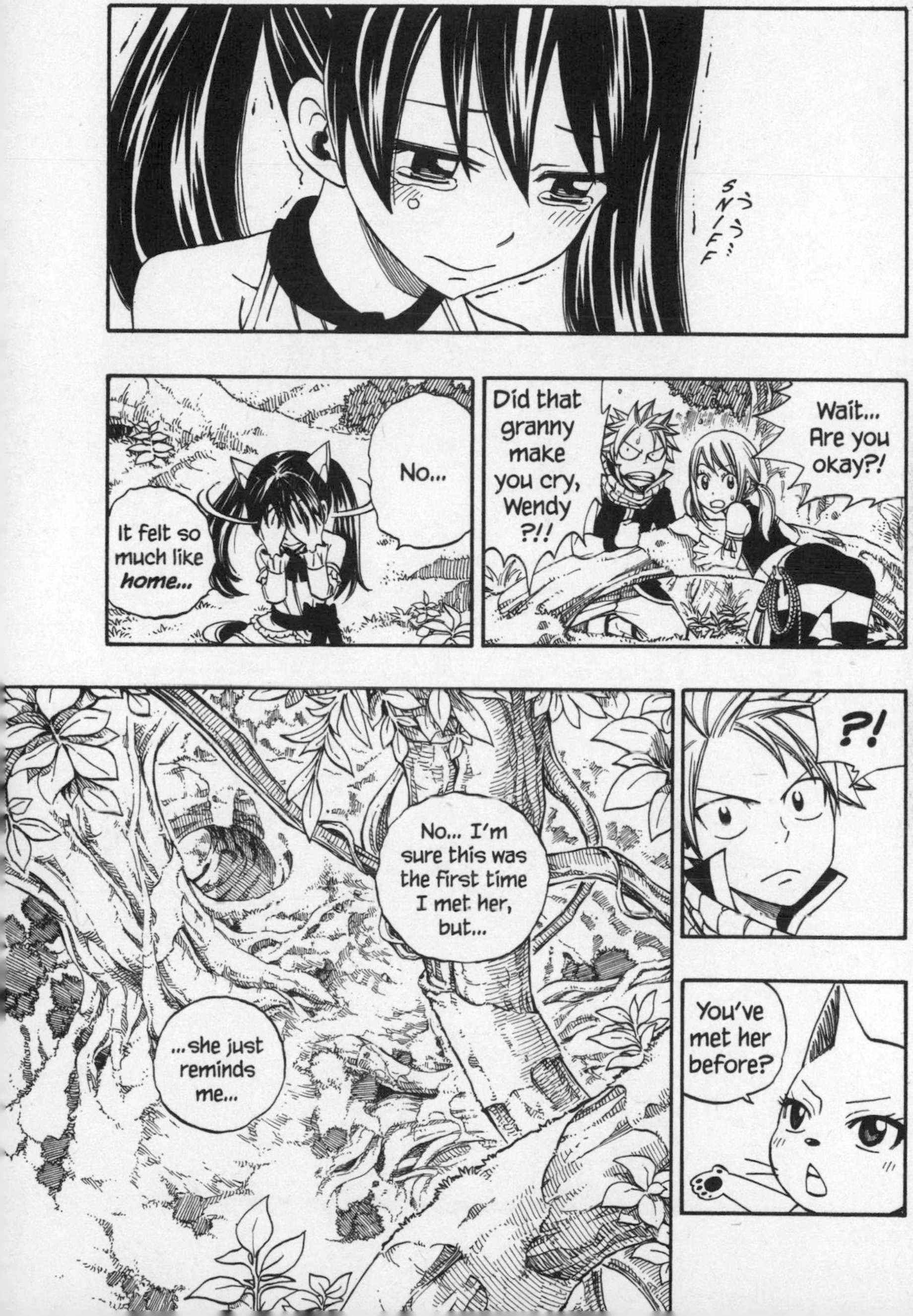
SNIFF
Wait... Are you okay?!
Did that granny make you cry, Wendy?!!
No...
It felt so much like *home*...
?!
You've met her before?
No... I'm sure this was the first time I met her, but...
...she just reminds me...

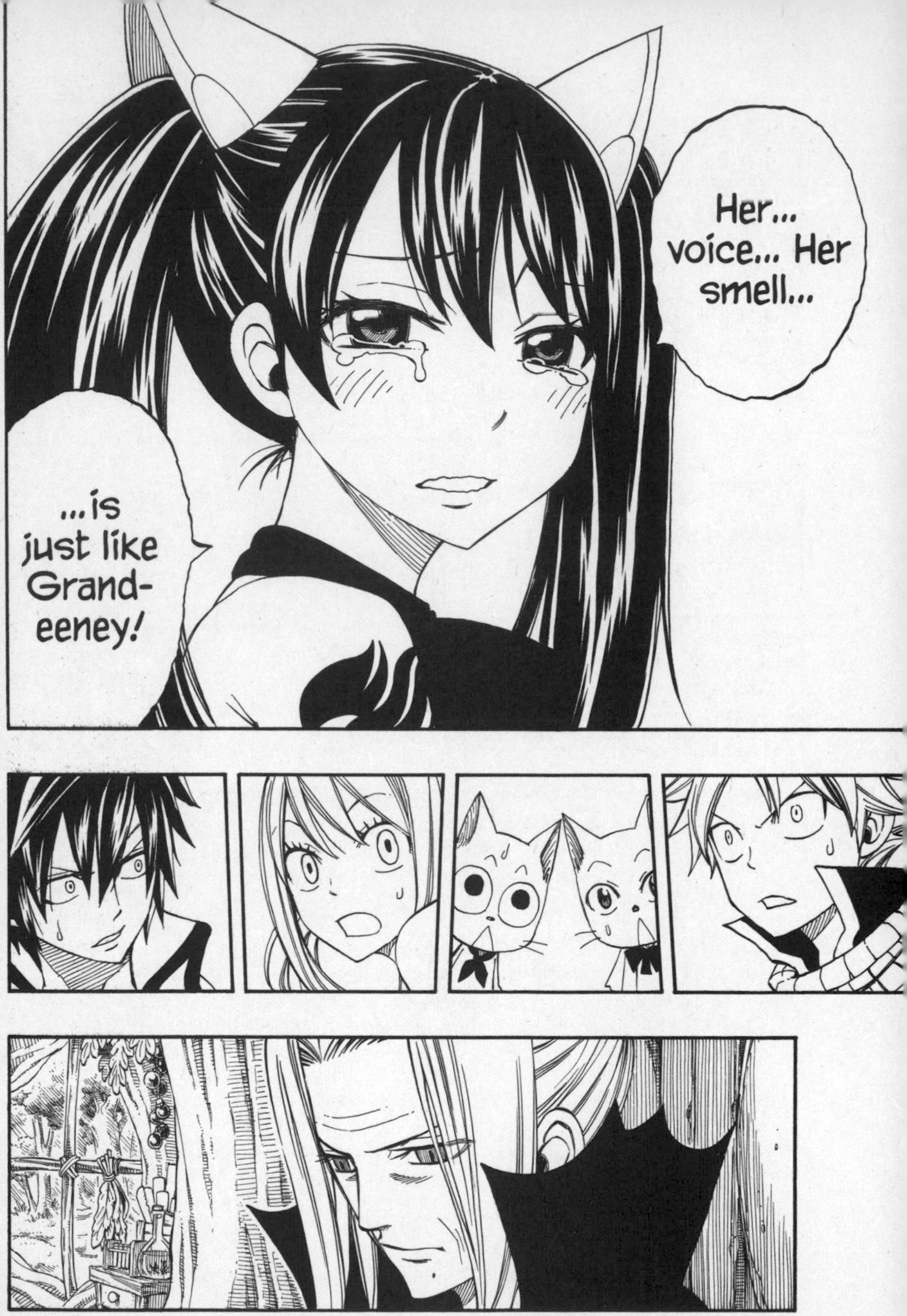
Her... voice... Her smell...
...is just like Grand-eeney!

## FAIRY TAIL

| | | |
|---|---|---|
| **Name:** Alzack Connel | | **Age:** 25 |
| **Magic:** Guns Magic | | |
| **Likes:** Bisca, Asuka | **Dislikes:** Spicy foods | |

# Chapter 260: And We're Going to Aim for the Top

## Remarks

Seven years earlier he fell in love with Bisca, but he could never find the right time to tell her. In X785, they were finally married after Bisca became pregnant. It was Bisca who proposed. Their daughter's name, Asuka, comes from Alzack's "A" sound and Bisca's "ka" sound. He loves his daughter so much that the very sight of her can make his wounds stop hurting, and he brings her to the guild building often. Everyone in the guild loves Asuka. After seven years, his abilities have improved quite a lot, and before the Sirius Island group returned, he was one of the top-class wizards in the guild.

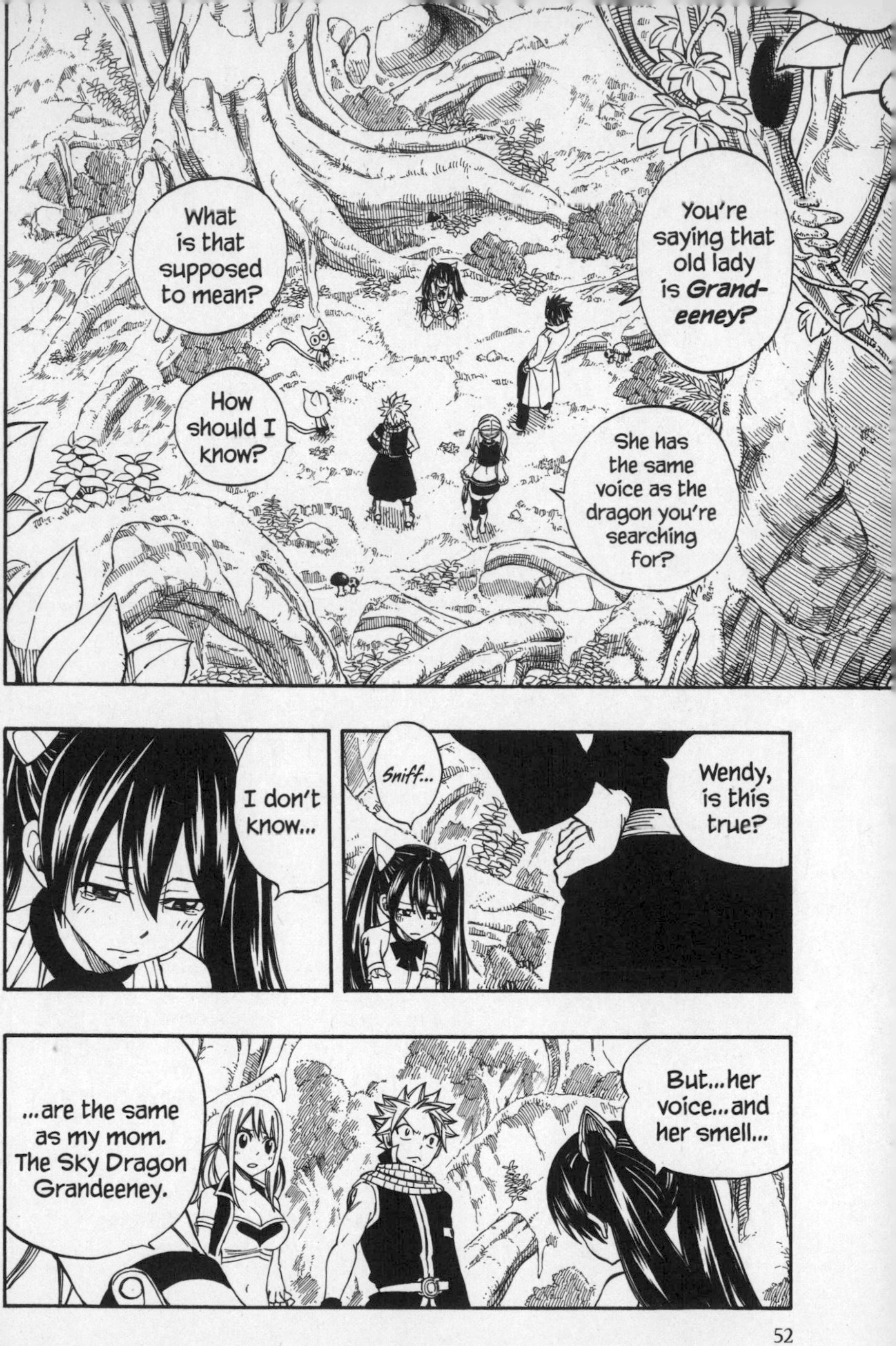
You're saying that old lady is Grandeeney?
She has the same voice as the dragon you're searching for?
What is that supposed to mean?
How should I know?
Wendy, is this true?
Sniff...
I don't know...
But...her voice...and her smell...
...are the same as my mom. The Sky Dragon Grandeeney.

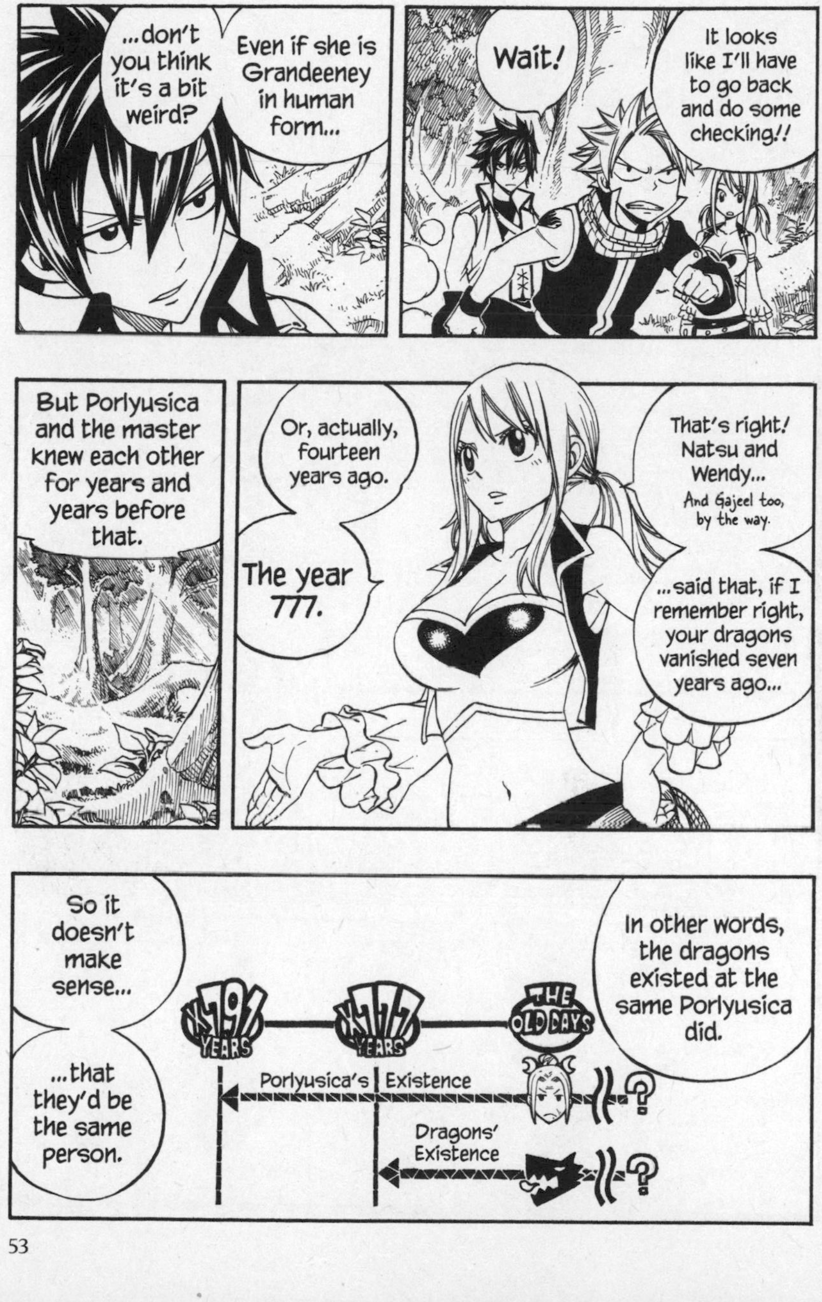
It looks like I'll have to go back and do some checking!!
Wait!
Even if she is Grandeeney in human form...
...don't you think it's a bit weird?
That's right! Natsu and Wendy...
And Gajeel too, by the way.
...said that, if I remember right, your dragons vanished seven years ago...
Or, actually, fourteen years ago.
The year 777.
But Porlyusica and the master knew each other for years and years before that.
In other words, the dragons existed at the same Porlyusica did.
THE OLD DAYS
Porlyusica's Existence
Dragons' Existence
So it doesn't make sense...
...that they'd be the same person.

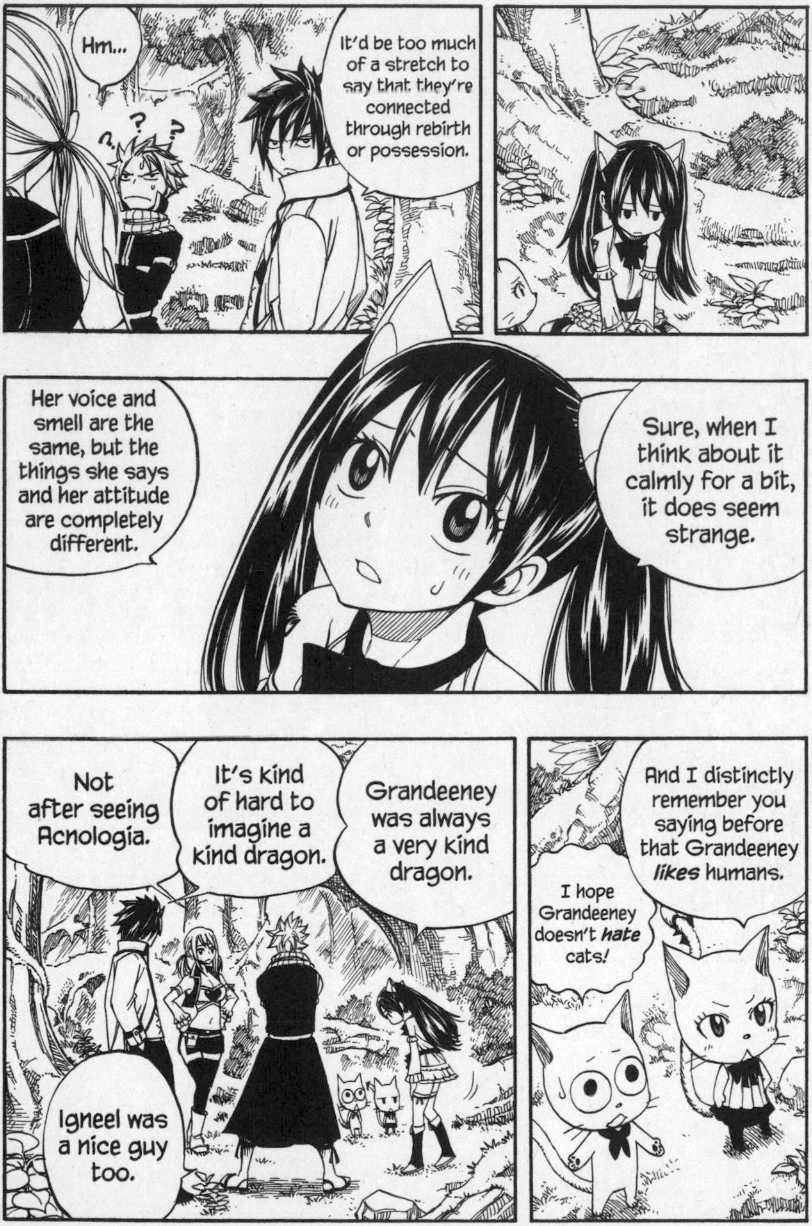
It'd be too much of a stretch to say that they're connected through rebirth or possession.
Hm...
Sure, when I think about it calmly for a bit, it does seem strange.
Her voice and smell are the same, but the things she says and her attitude are completely different.
And I distinctly remember you saying before that Grandeeney *likes* humans.
I hope Grandeeney doesn't *hate* cats!
Grandeeney was always a very kind dragon.
It's kind of hard to imagine a kind dragon.
Not after seeing Acnologia.
Igneel was a nice guy too.

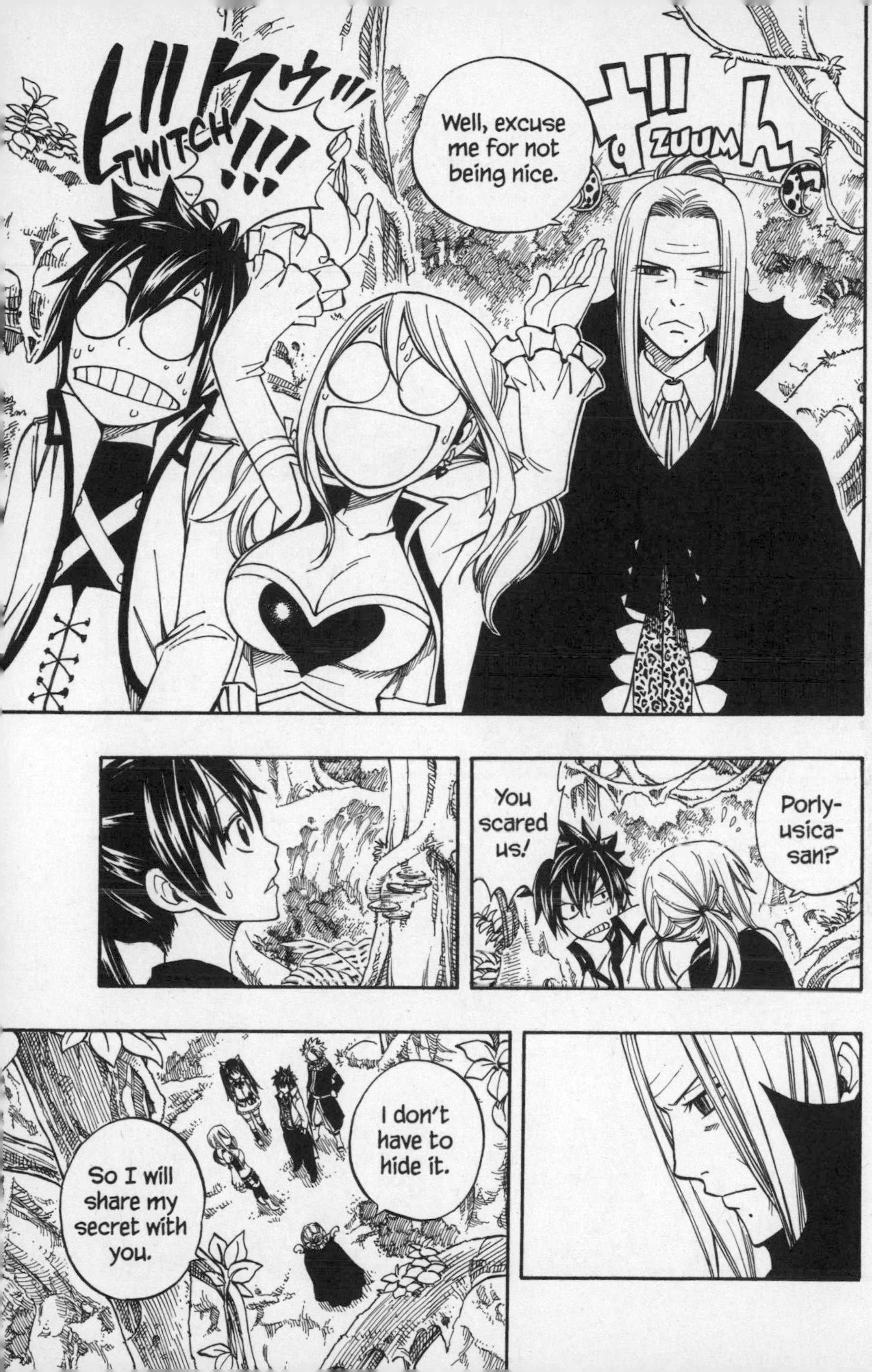
ZUUM
Well, excuse me for not being nice.
TWITCH!!!
Porly-usica-san?
You scared us!
I don't have to hide it.
So I will share my secret with you.

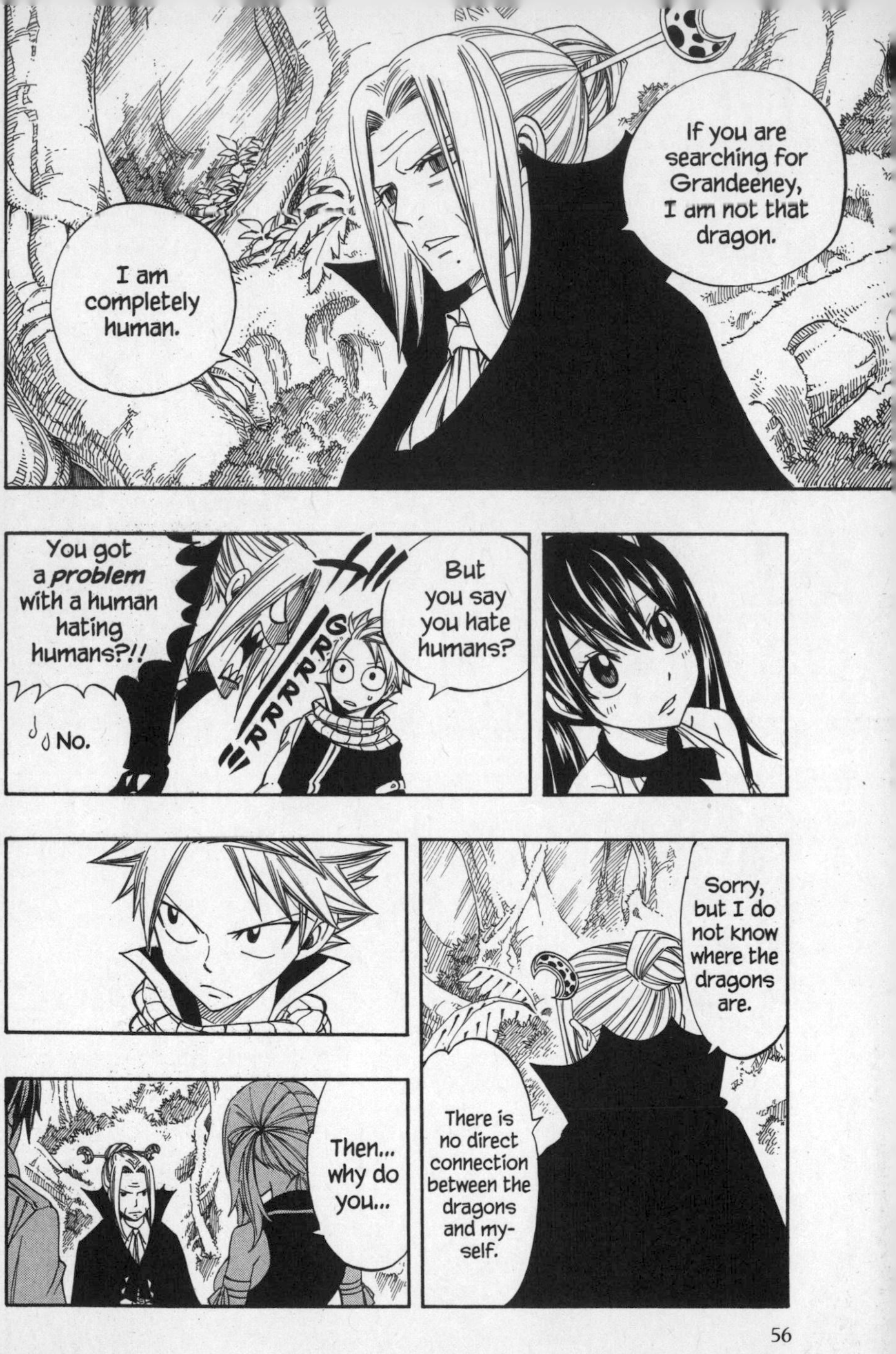
If you are searching for Grandeeney, I am not that dragon.
I am completely human.
But you say you hate humans?
GRRRRRR
You got a *problem* with a human hating humans?!!
No.
Sorry, but I do not know where the dragons are.
There is no direct connection between the dragons and my-self.
Then... why do you...

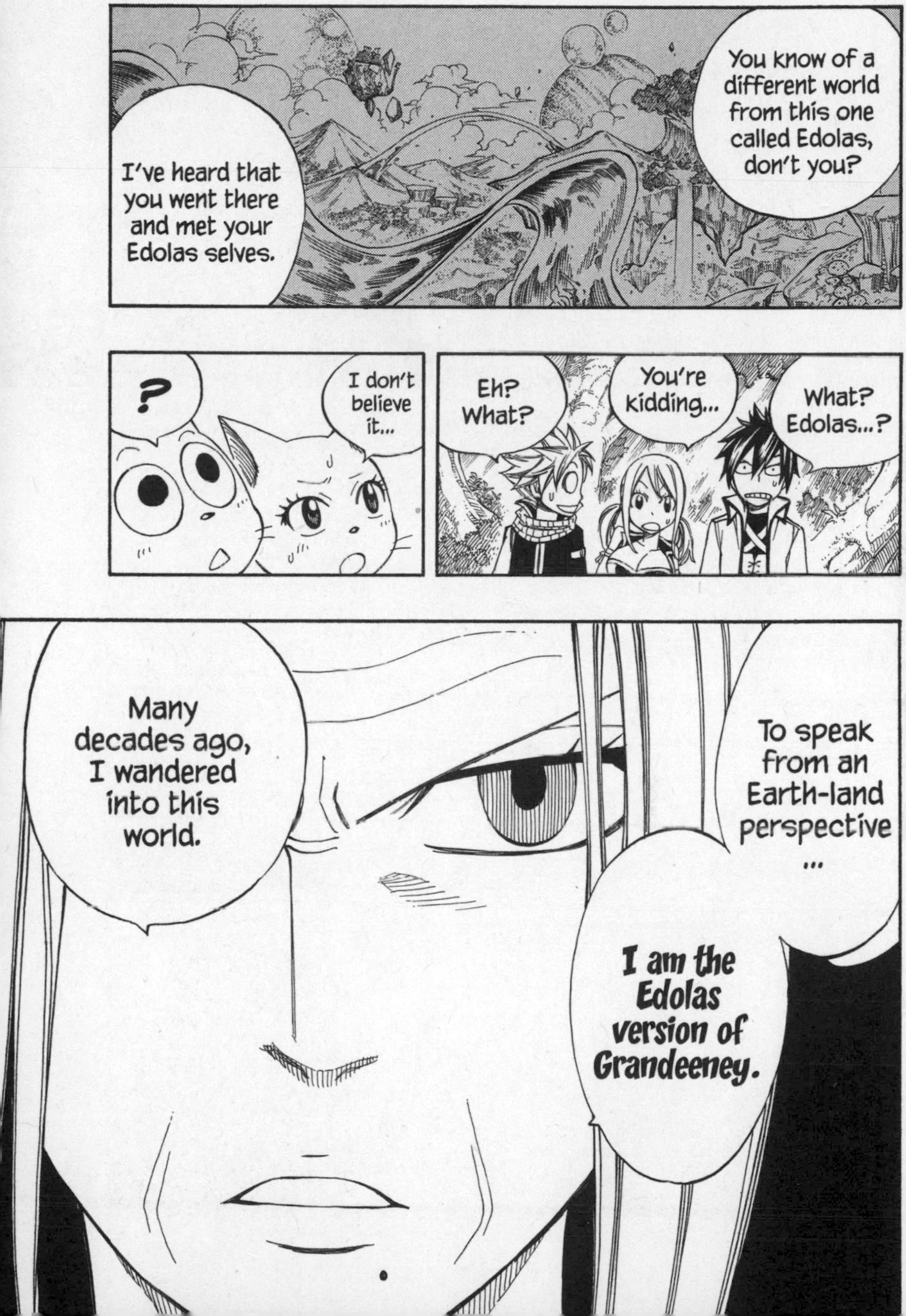
You know of a different world from this one called Edolas, don't you?
I've heard that you went there and met your Edolas selves.
What? Edolas...?
You're kidding...
Eh? What?
I don't believe it...
?
To speak from an Earth-land perspective ...
Many decades ago, I wandered into this world.
I am the Edolas version of Grandeeney.

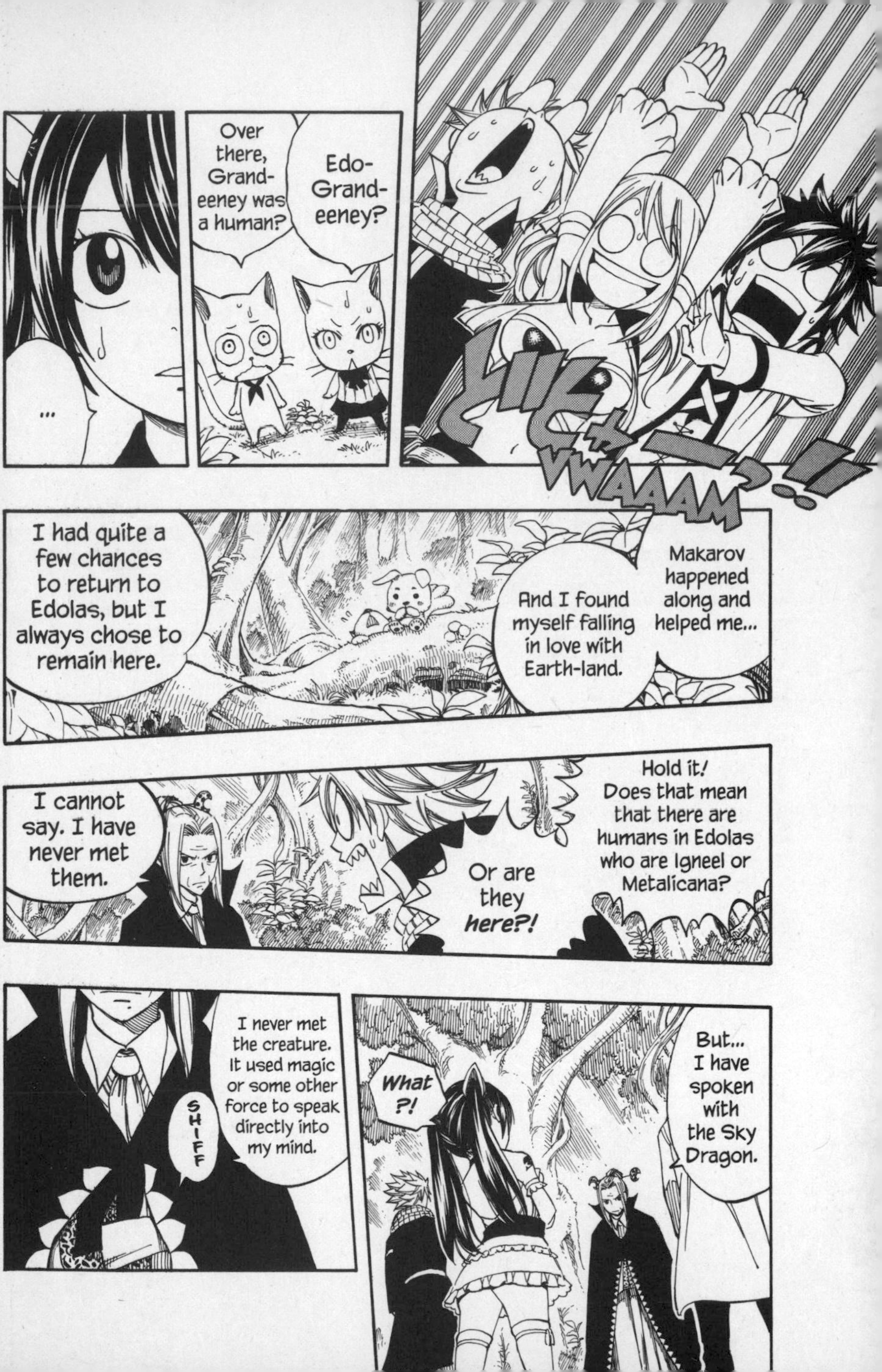
VWAAAM
Edo-Grandeeney?
Over there, Grandeeney was a human?
...
Makarov happened along and helped me...
And I found myself falling in love with Earth-land.
I had quite a few chances to return to Edolas, but I always chose to remain here.
Hold it! Does that mean that there are humans in Edolas who are Igneel or Metalicana?
Or are they *here?!*
I cannot say. I have never met them.
But... I have spoken with the Sky Dragon.
*What?!*
I never met the creature. It used magic or some other force to speak directly into my mind.
SHIFF

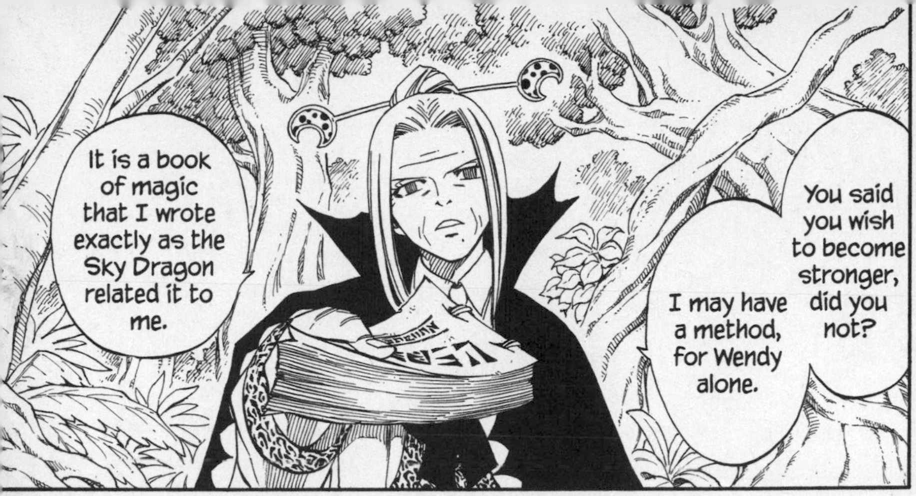
You said you wish to become stronger, did you not?
I may have a method, for Wendy alone.
It is a book of magic that I wrote exactly as the Sky Dragon related it to me.

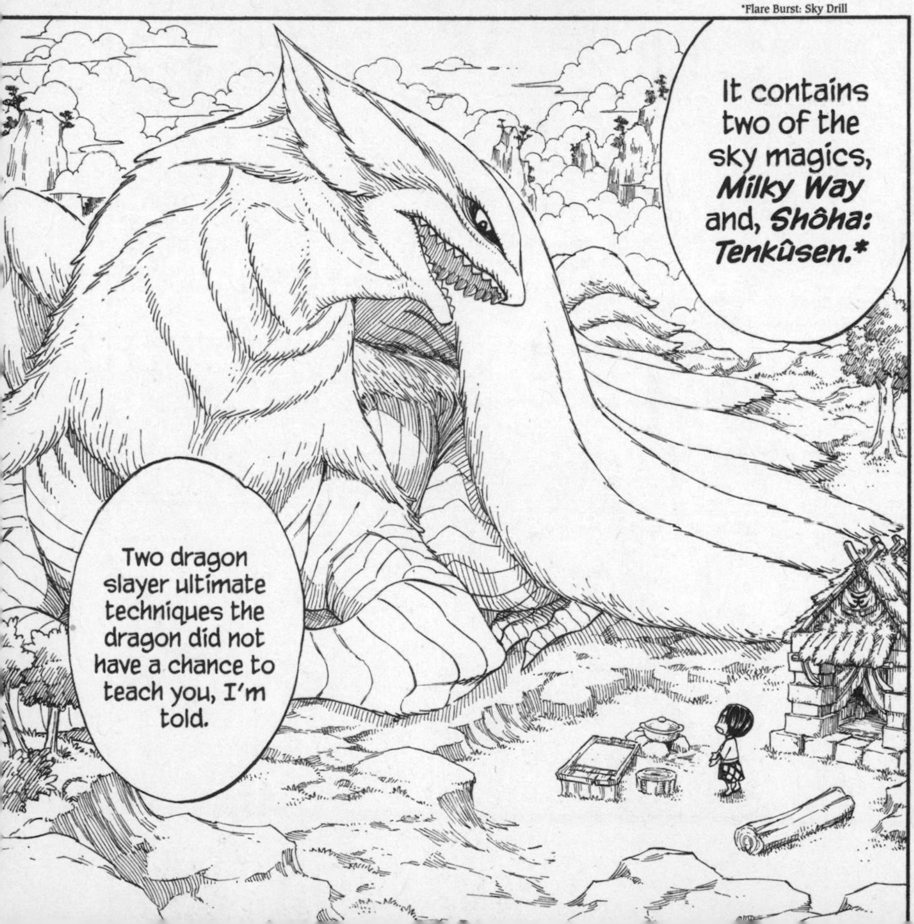
It contains two of the sky magics, *Milky Way* and, *Shôha: Tenkûsen.**
Two dragon slayer ultimate techniques the dragon did not have a chance to teach you, I'm told.

*Flare Burst: Sky Drill

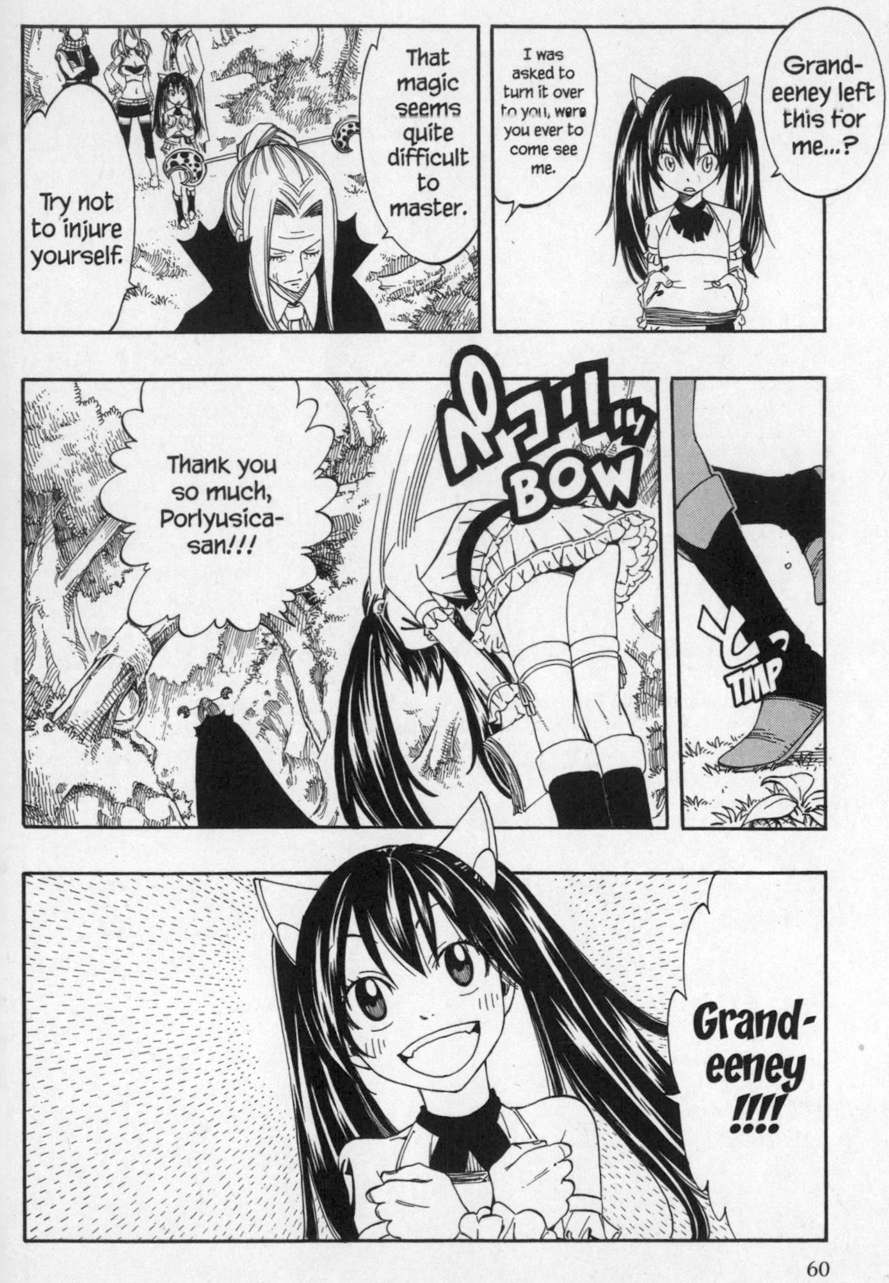
Grand-eeney left this for me...?
I was asked to turn it over to you, were you ever to come see me.
That magic seems quite difficult to master.
Try not to injure yourself.
TMP
BOW
Thank you so much, Porlyusica-san!!!
Grand-eeney!!!!

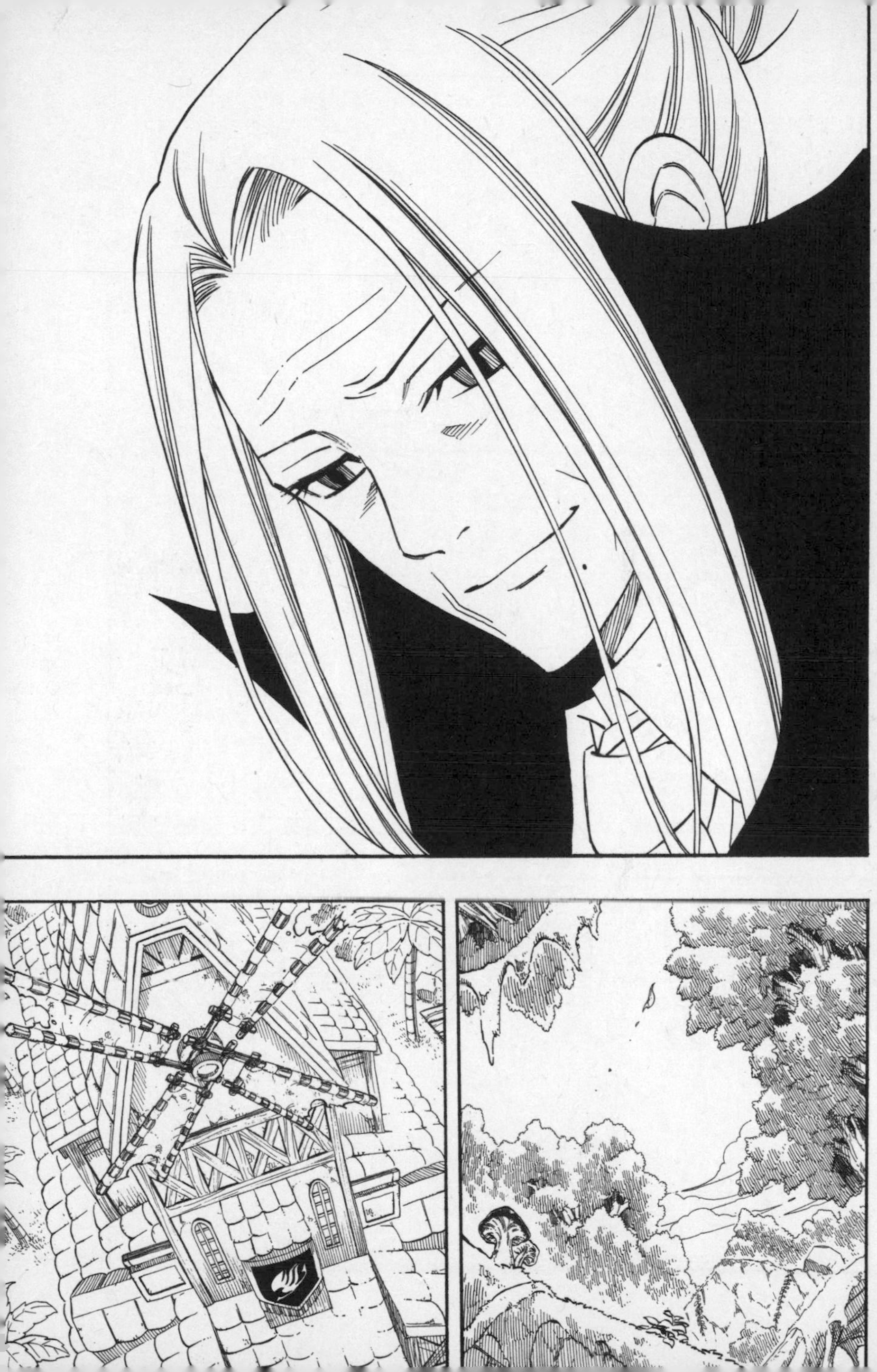

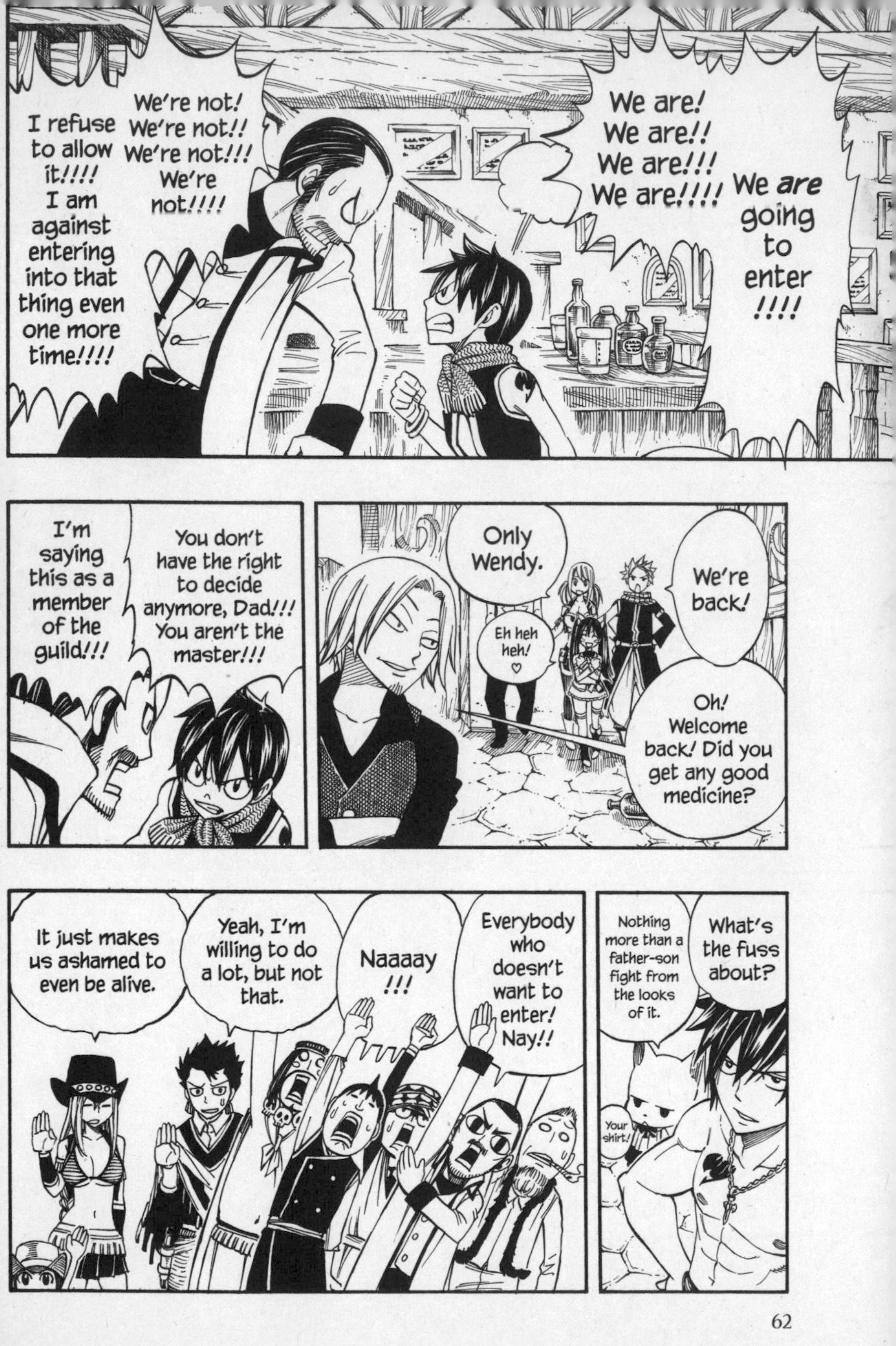
We are going to enter!!!!
We are! We are!! We are!!! We are!!!!
We're not! We're not!! We're not!!! We're not!!!!
I refuse to allow it!!!! I am against entering into that thing even one more time!!!!
We're back!
Only Wendy.
Eh heh heh! ♡
Oh! Welcome back! Did you get any good medicine?
You don't have the right to decide anymore, Dad!!! You aren't the master!!!
I'm saying this as a member of the guild!!!
What's the fuss about?
Nothing more than a father-son fight from the looks of it.
Your shirt!
Everybody who doesn't want to enter! Nay!!
Naaaay!!!
Yeah, I'm willing to do a lot, but not that.
It just makes us ashamed to even be alive.

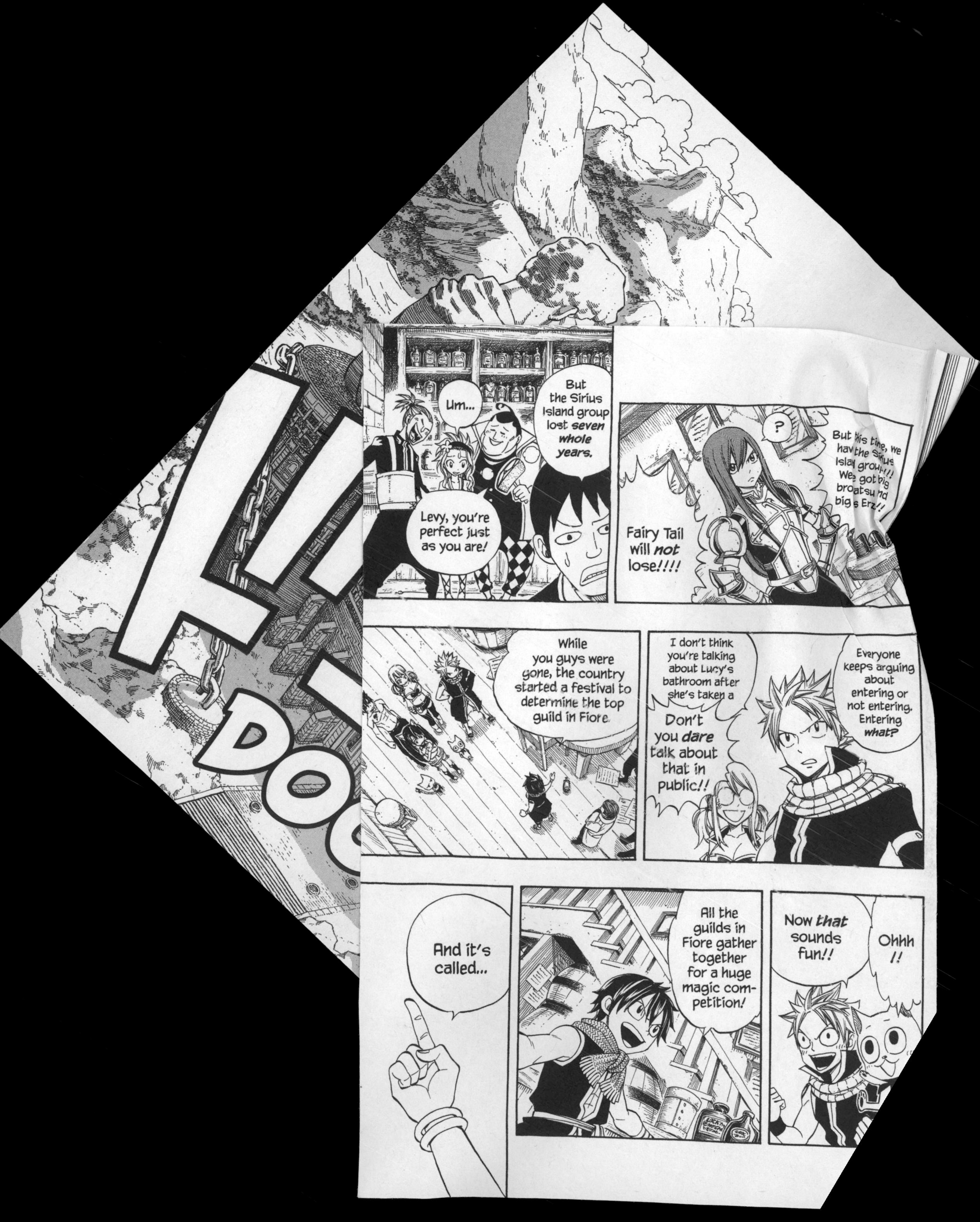
?
But this time, we hav the Sirius Isla group!! We got big bro atsu nd big s Erz!!
Fairy Tail will *not* lose!!!!
But the Sirius Island group lost *seven whole years.*
Um...
Levy, you're perfect just as you are!
Everyone keeps arguing about entering or not entering. Entering *what?*
I don't think you're talking about Lucy's bathroom after she's taken a
Don't you *dare* talk about that in public!!
While you guys were gone, the country started a festival to determine the top guild in Fiore.
Ohhh!!
Now *that* sounds fun!!
All the guilds in Fiore gather together for a huge magic competition!
And it's called...

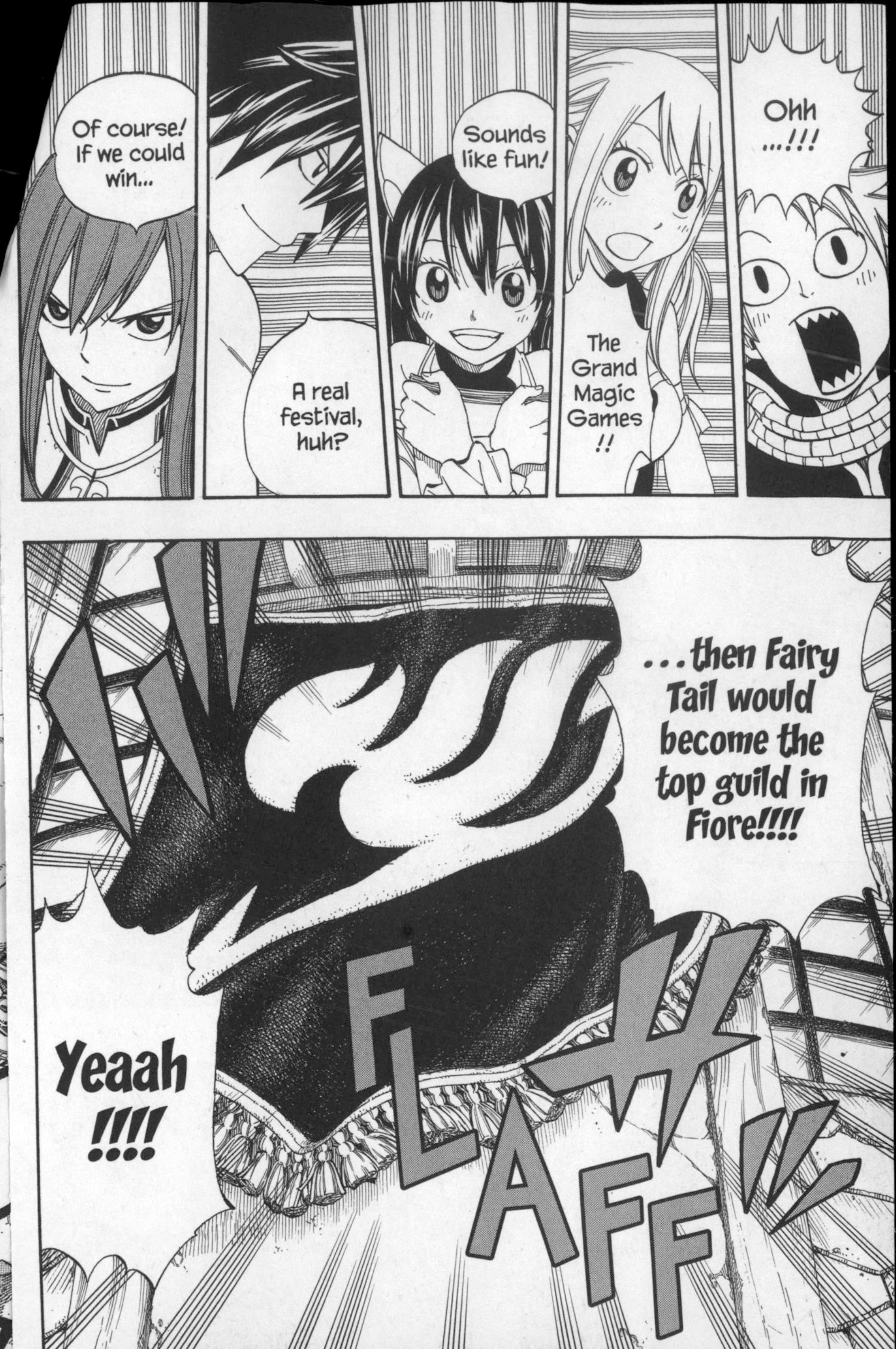
Ohh ...!!!
The Grand Magic Games !!
Sounds like fun!
A real festival, huh?
Of course! If we could win...
...then Fairy Tail would become the top guild in Fiore!!!!
FLAFF!!
Yeaah !!!!
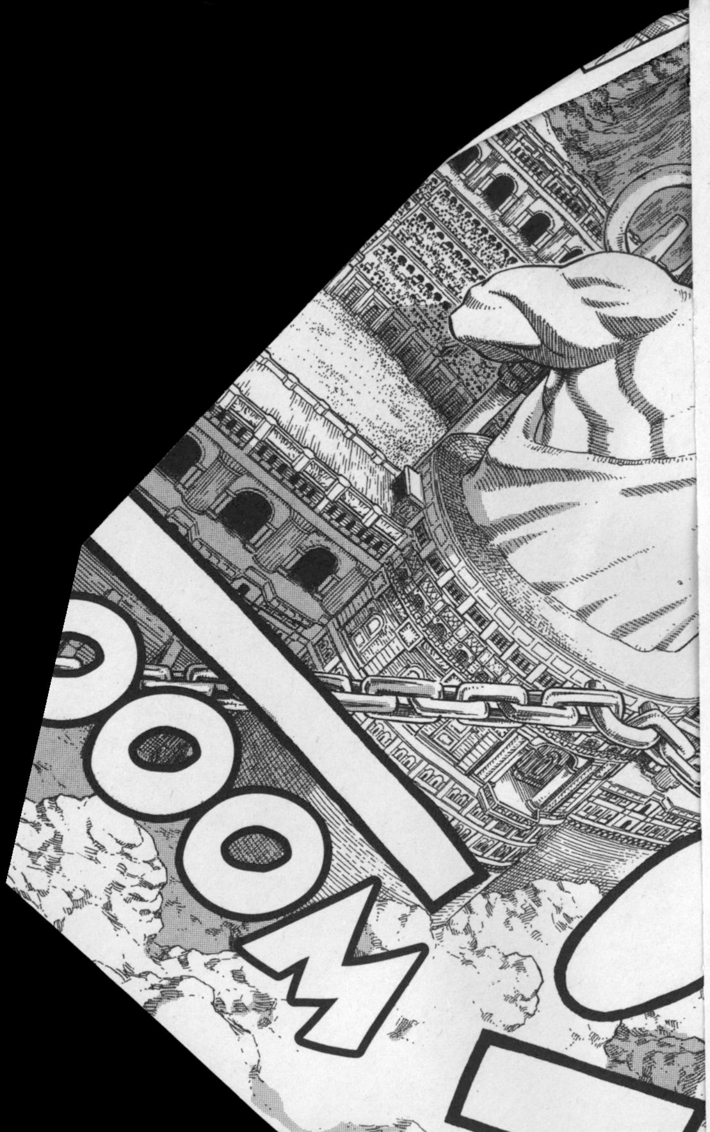
OOOM

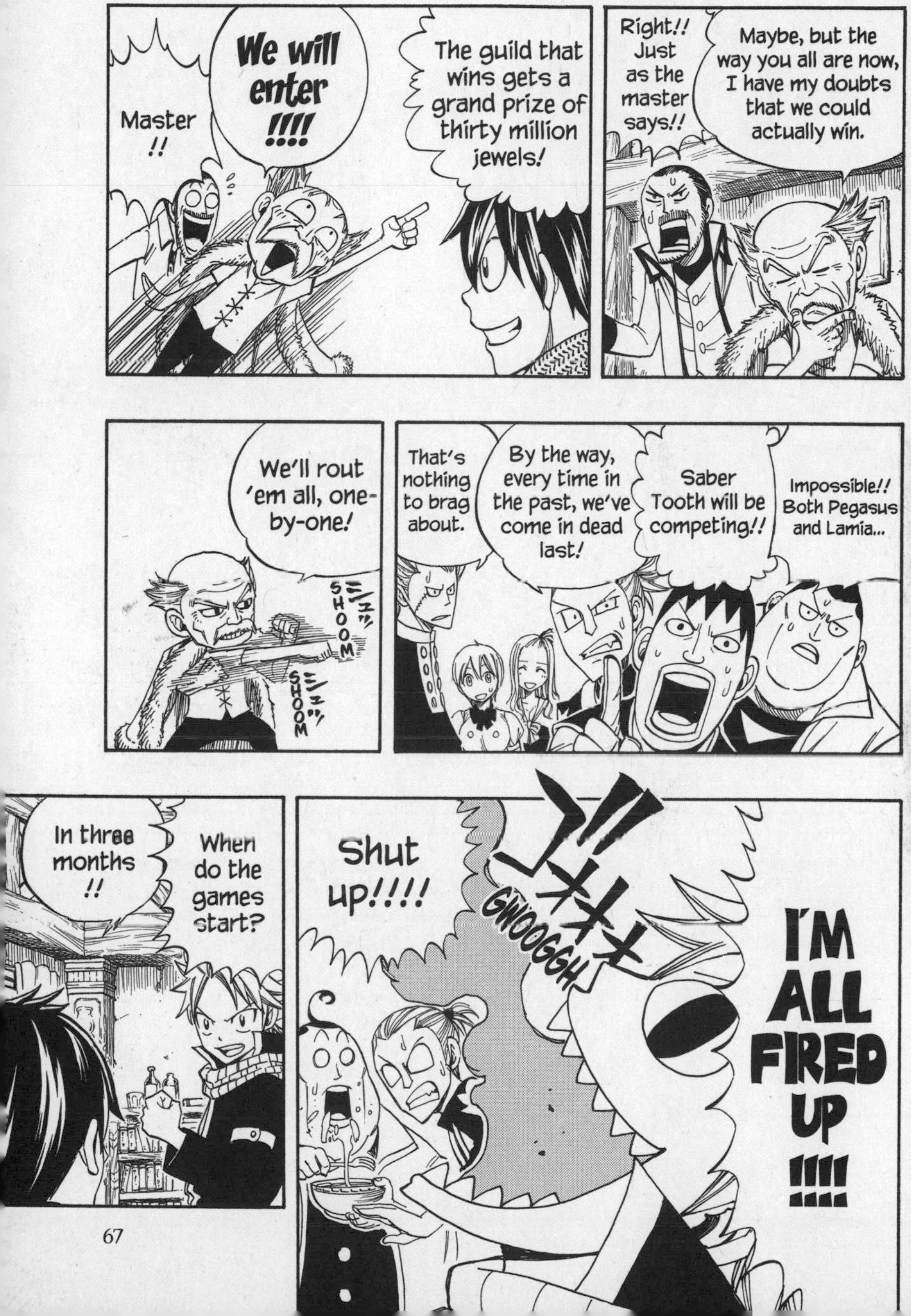
Maybe, but the way you all are now, I have my doubts that we could actually win.
Right!! Just as the master says!!
The guild that wins gets a grand prize of thirty million jewels!
We will enter!!!!
Master!!
Impossible!! Both Pegasus and Lamia...
Saber Tooth will be competing!!
By the way, every time in the past, we've come in dead last!
That's nothing to brag about.
We'll rout 'em all, one-by-one!
SHOOOM
SHOOOM
I'M ALL FIRED UP!!!!
GWOOGGH
Shut up!!!!
When do the games start?
In three months!!

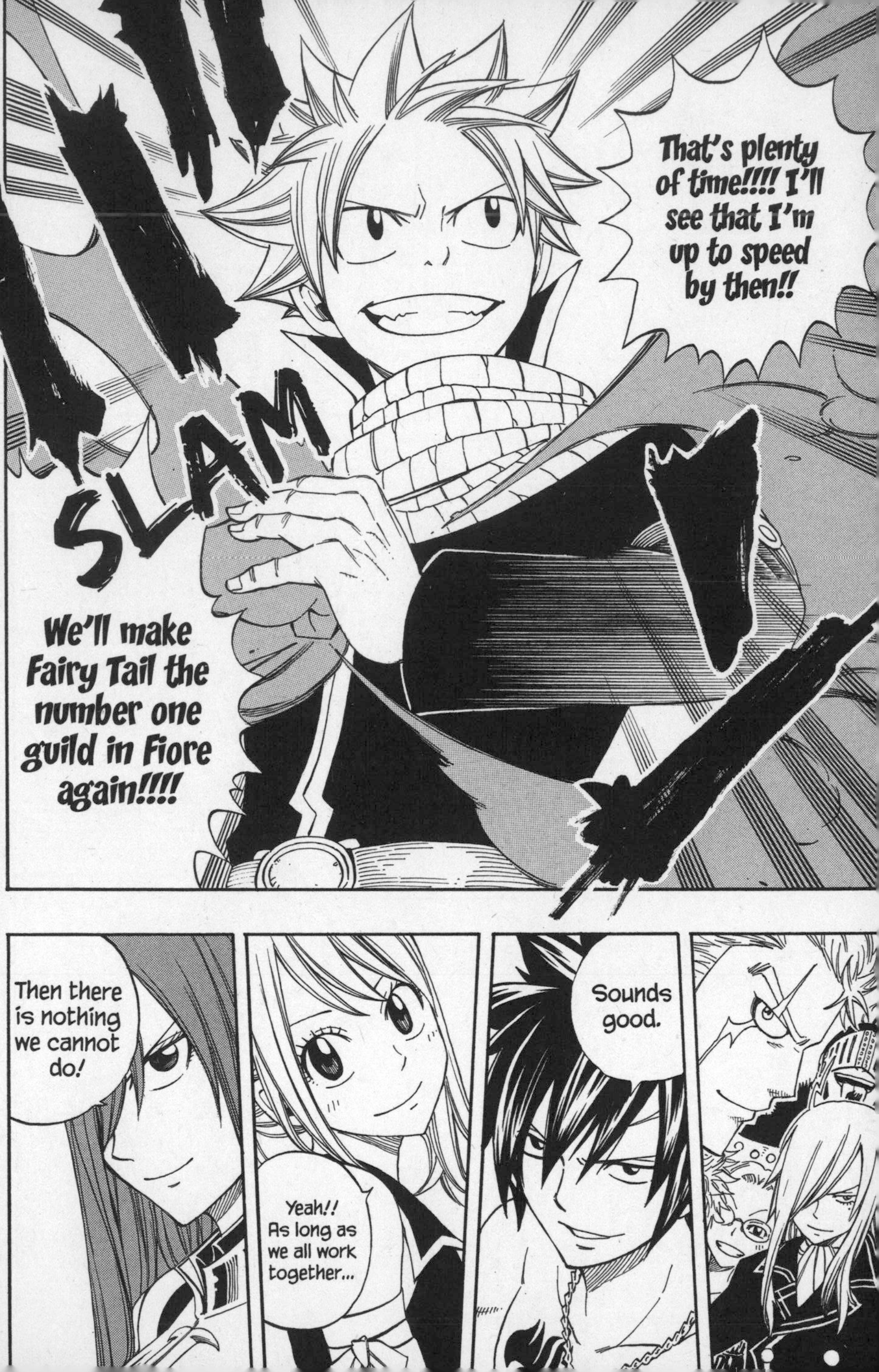
That's plenty of time!!!! I'll see that I'm up to speed by then!!
SLAM
We'll make Fairy Tail the number one guild in Fiore again!!!!
Sounds good.
Yeah!! As long as we all work together...
Then there is nothing we cannot do!

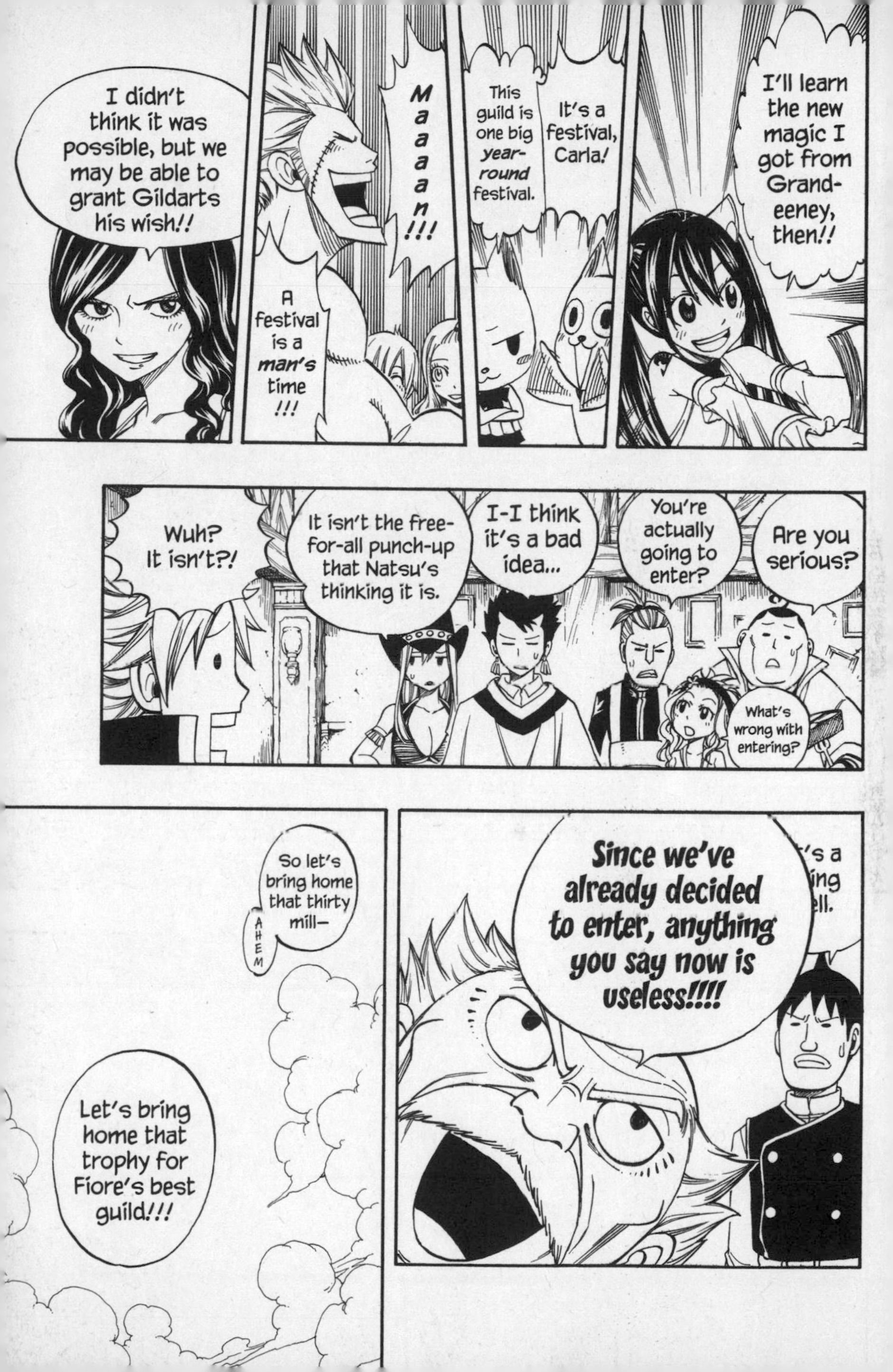
I'll learn the new magic I got from Grandeeney, then!!
It's a festival, Carla!
This guild is one big year-round festival.
Maaaaan!!!
A festival is a man's time!!!
I didn't think it was possible, but we may be able to grant Gildarts his wish!!
Are you serious?
You're actually going to enter?
What's wrong with entering?
I-I think it's a bad idea...
It isn't the free-for-all punch-up that Natsu's thinking it is.
Wuh? It isn't?!
Since we've already decided to enter, anything you say now is useless!!!!
So let's bring home that thirty mill—
AHEM
Let's bring home that trophy for Fiore's best guild!!!

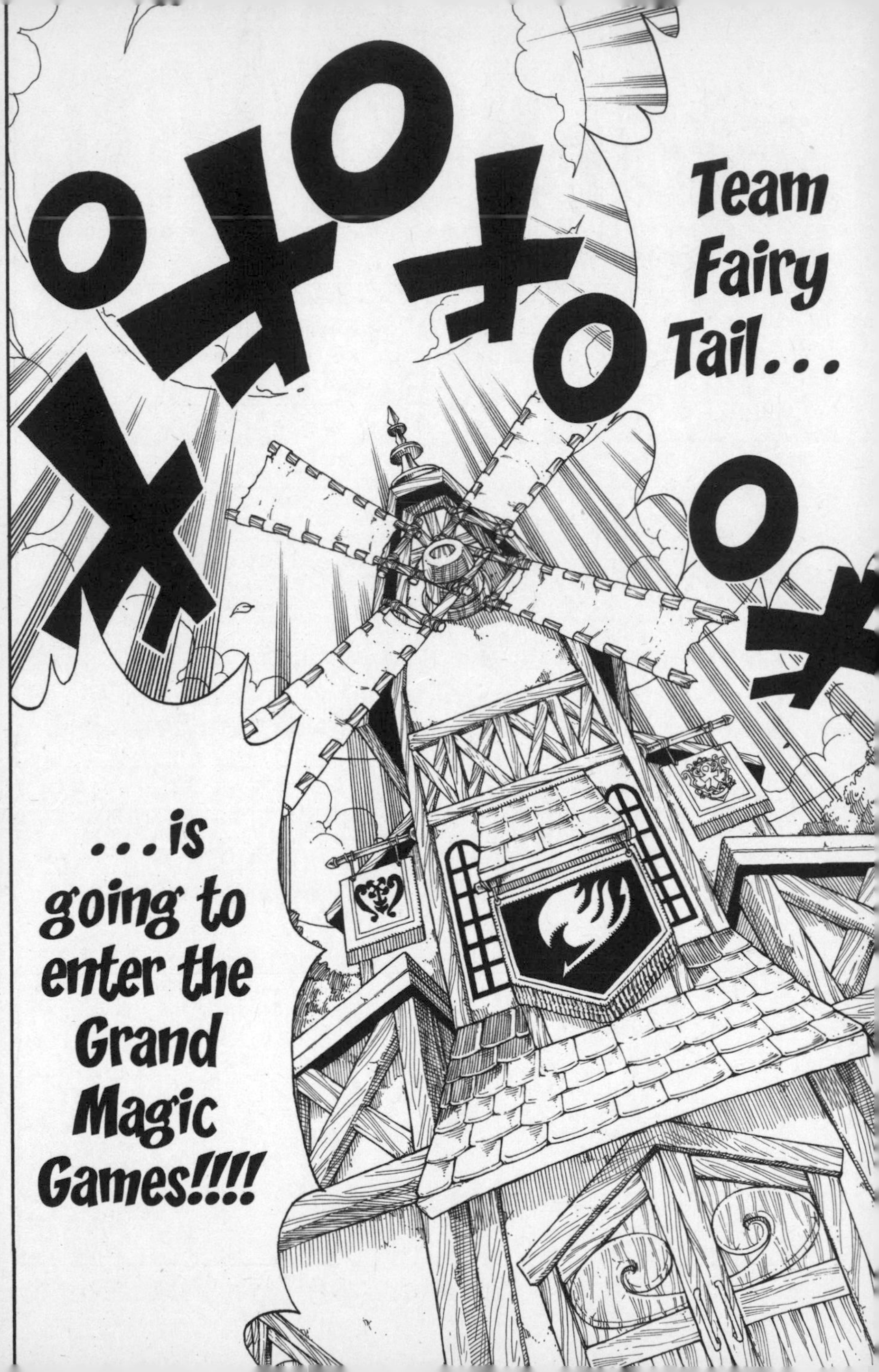
Team Fairy Tail...
...is going to enter the Grand Magic Games!!!!

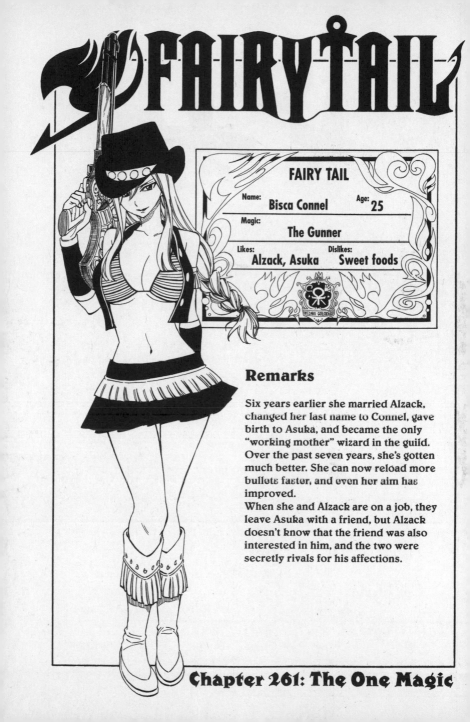

# FAIRY TAIL

## FAIRY TAIL

**Name:** Bisca Connel

**Age:** 25

**Magic:** The Gunner

**Likes:** Alzack, Asuka

**Dislikes:** Sweet foods

### Remarks

Six years earlier she married Alzack, changed her last name to Connel, gave birth to Asuka, and became the only "working mother" wizard in the guild. Over the past seven years, she's gotten much better. She can now reload more bullets faster, and even her aim has improved.

When she and Alzack are on a job, they leave Asuka with a friend, but Alzack doesn't know that the friend was also interested in him, and the two were secretly rivals for his affections.

## Chapter 261: The One Magic

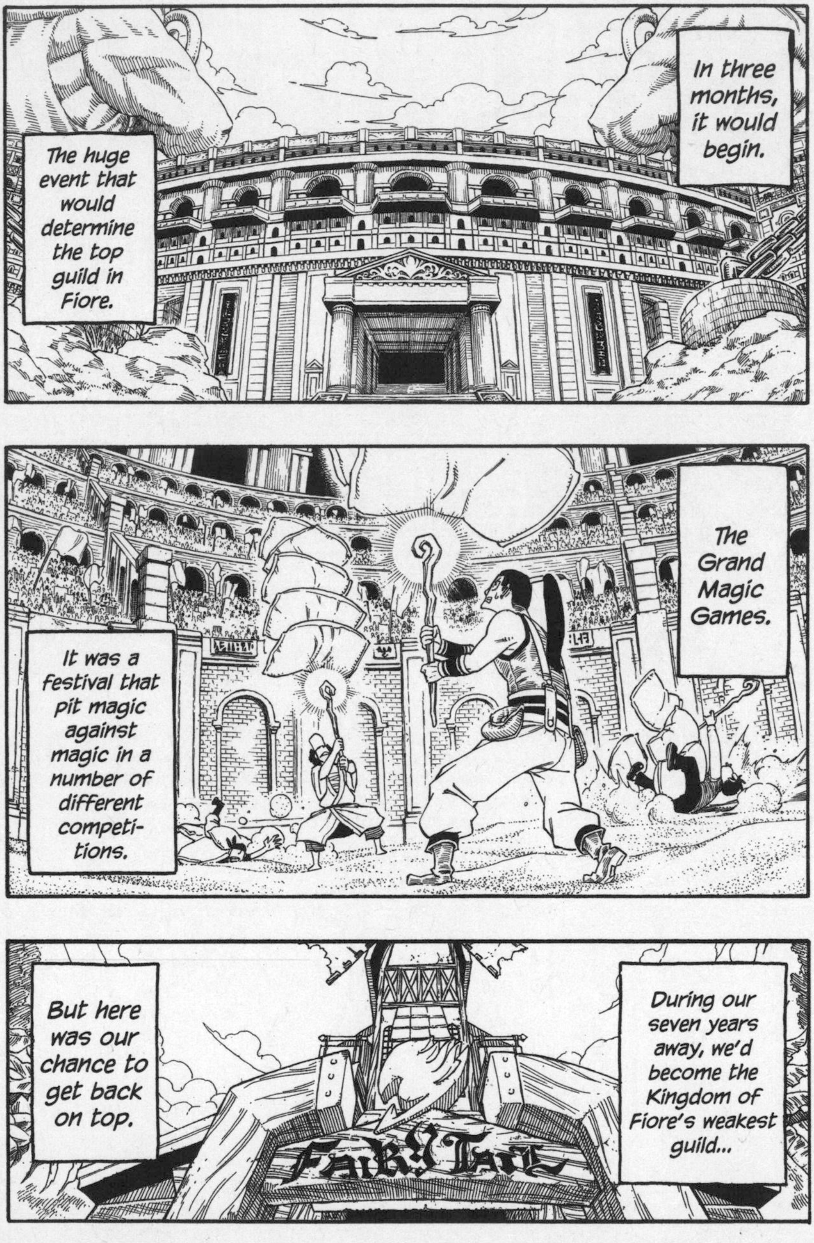
In three months, it would begin.
The huge event that would determine the top guild in Fiore.
The Grand Magic Games.
It was a festival that pit magic against magic in a number of different competitions.
During our seven years away, we'd become the Kingdom of Fiore's weakest guild...
FAIRY TAIL
But here was our chance to get back on top.

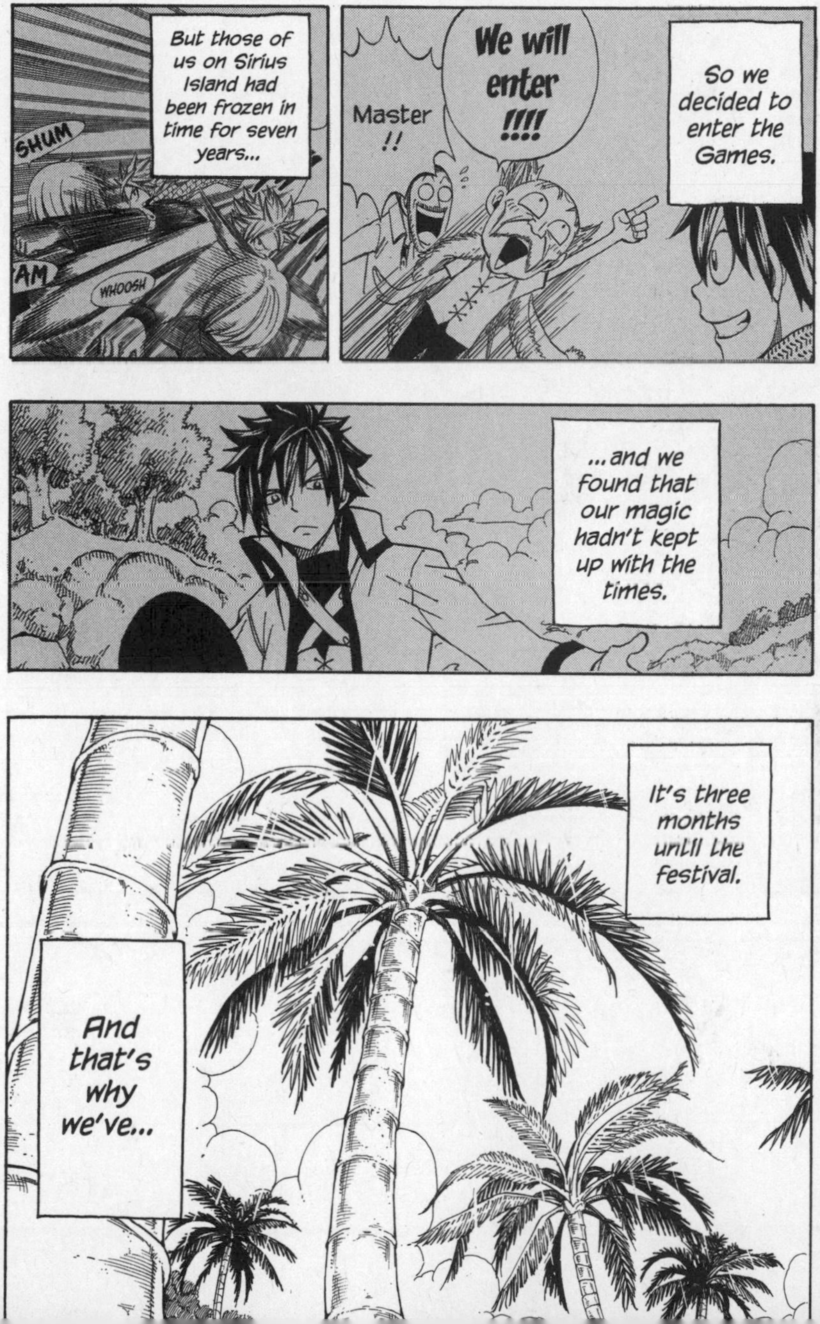
So we decided to enter the Games.
We will enter !!!!
Master !!
But those of us on Sirius Island had been frozen in time for seven years...
SHUM
AM
WHOOSH
...and we found that our magic hadn't kept up with the times.
It's three months until the festival.
And that's why we've...

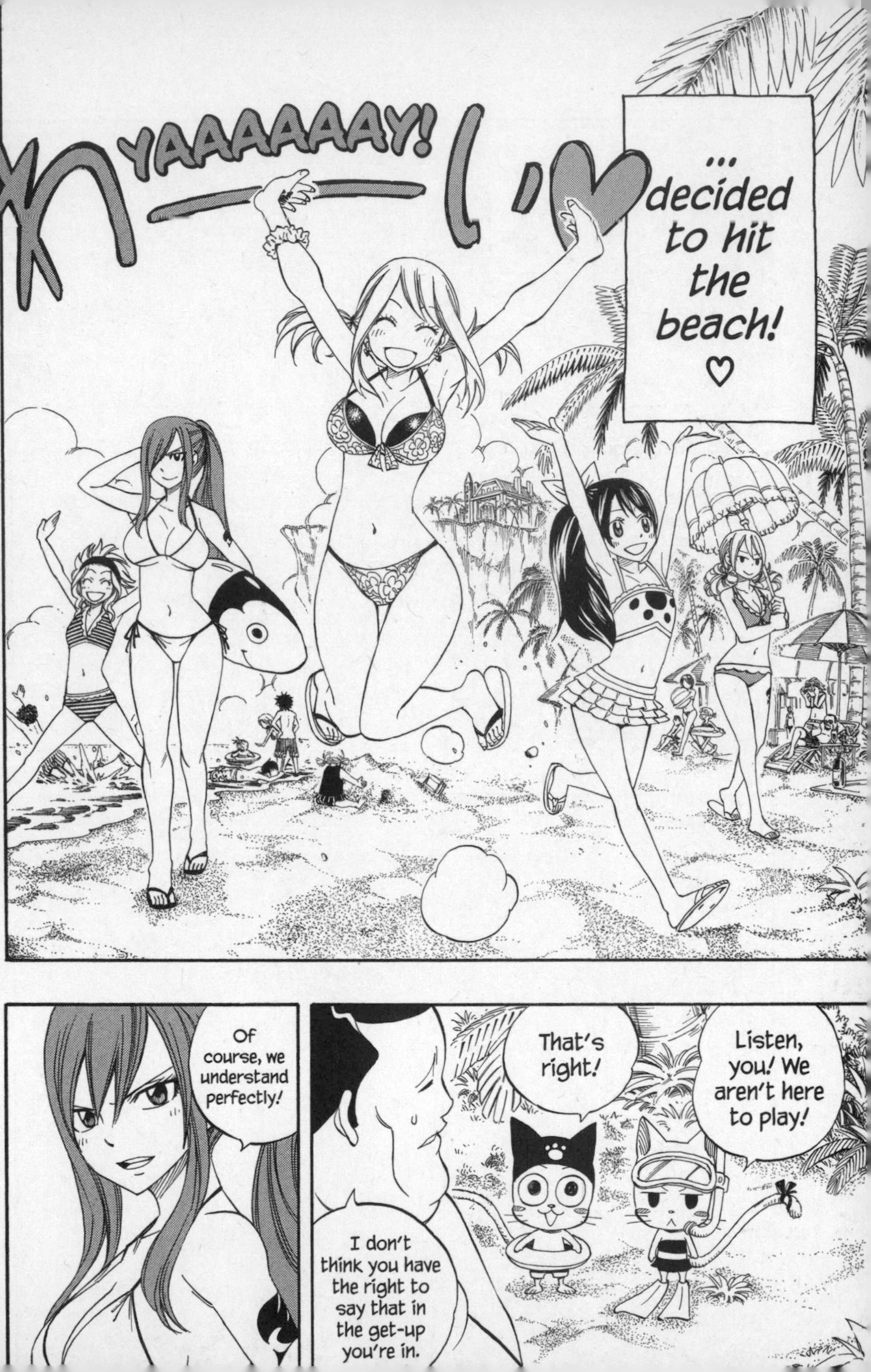
...decided to hit the beach! ♡
YAAAAAAY!
Listen, you! We aren't here to play!
That's right!
I don't think you have the right to say that in the get-up you're in.
Of course, we understand perfectly!

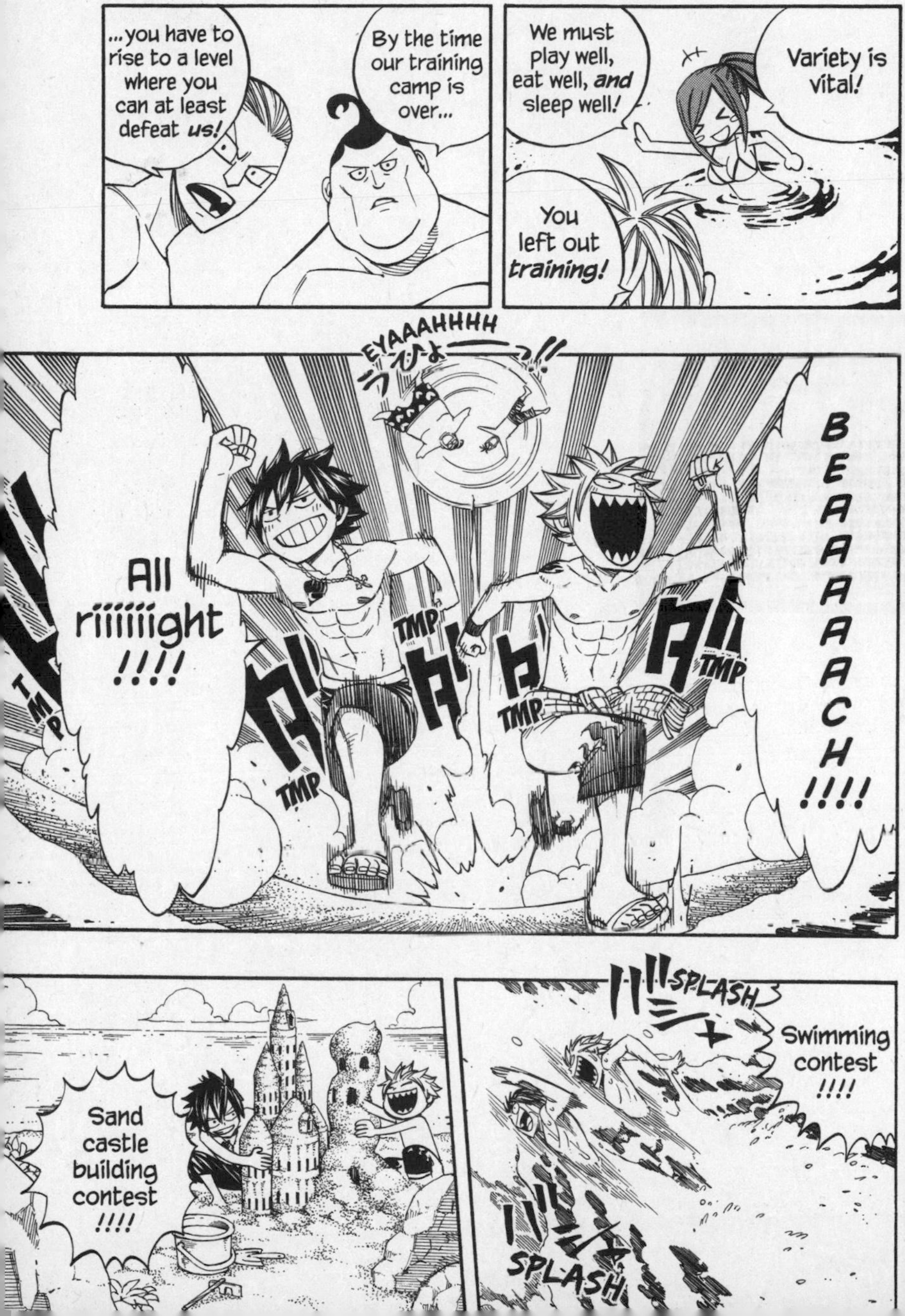
Variety is vital!
We must play well, eat well, and sleep well!
You left out training!
By the time our training camp is over...
...you have to rise to a level where you can at least defeat us!
EYAAAHHHH
BEAAAAAACH!!!!
TMP
TMP
TMP
All riiiiiight!!!!
TMP
TMP
SPLASH
Swimming contest!!!!
SPLASH
Sand castle building contest!!!!

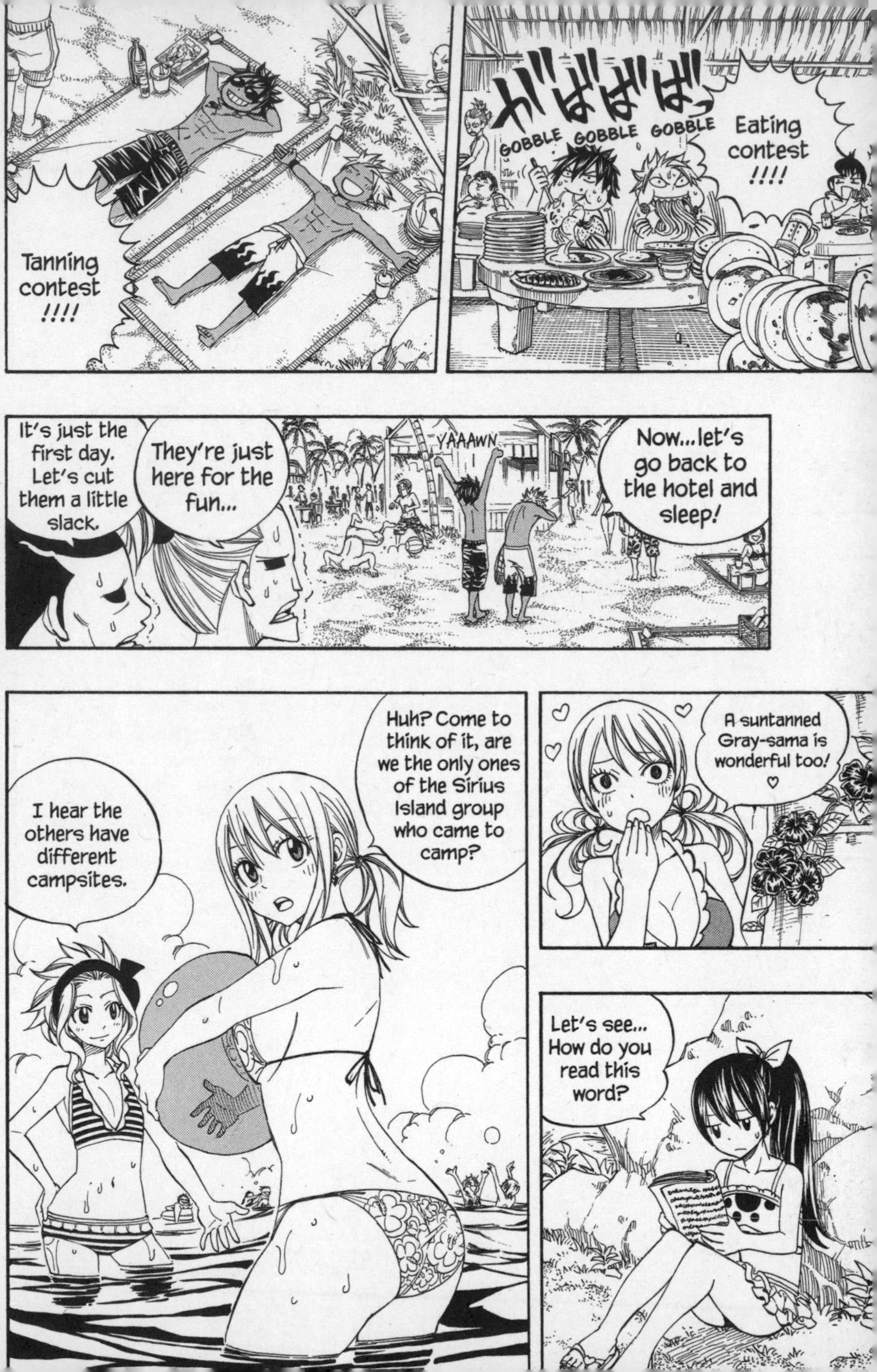
GOBBLE GOBBLE GOBBLE
Eating contest !!!!
Tanning contest !!!!
Now...let's go back to the hotel and sleep!
YAAAWN
They're just here for the fun...
It's just the first day. Let's cut them a little slack.
A suntanned Gray-sama is wonderful too! ♡
Let's see... How do you read this word?
Huh? Come to think of it, are we the only ones of the Sirius Island group who came to camp?
I hear the others have different campsites.

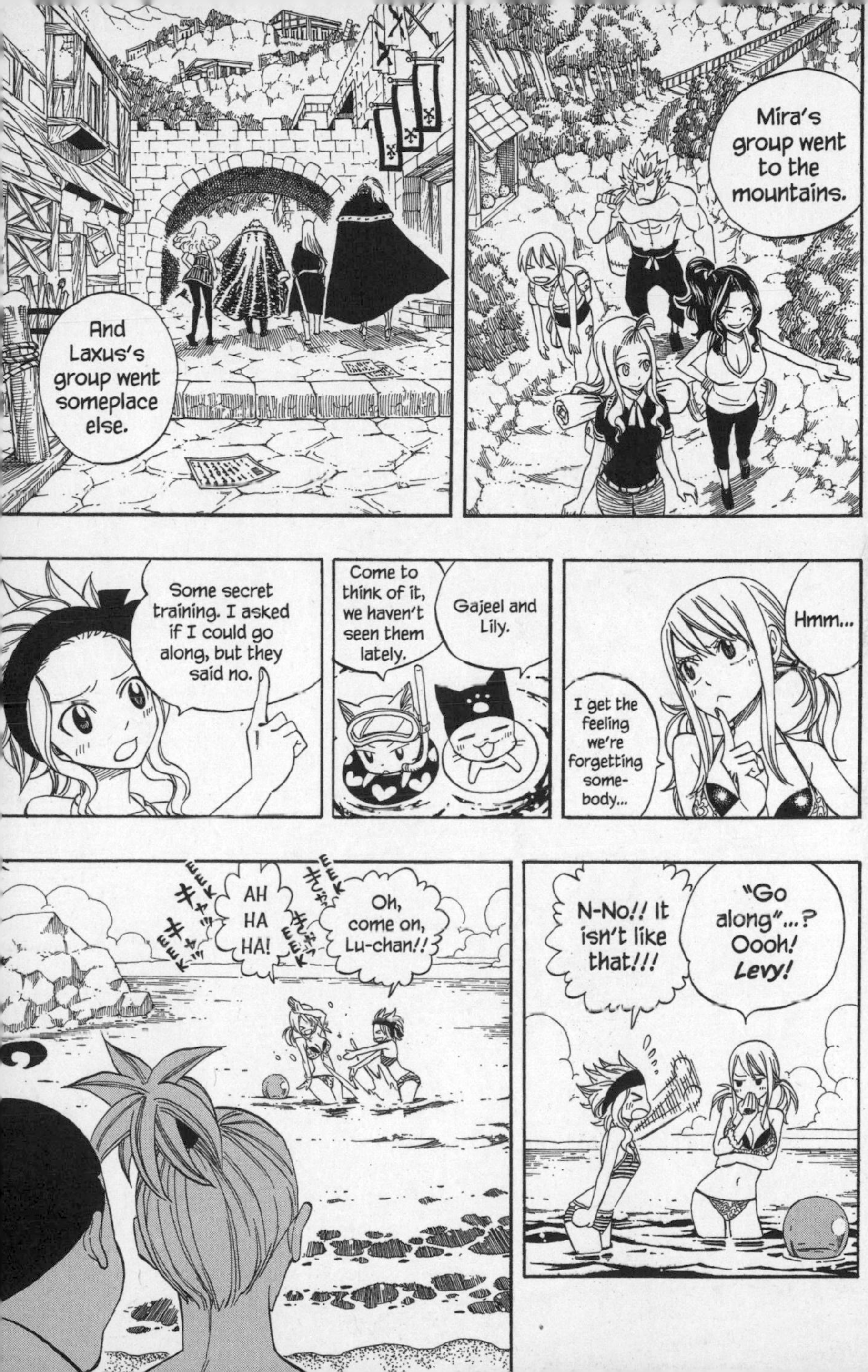
Mira's group went to the mountains.
And Laxus's group went someplace else.
Hmm...
I get the feeling we're forgetting some-body...
Gajeel and Lily.
Come to think of it, we haven't seen them lately.
Some secret training. I asked if I could go along, but they said no.
"Go along"...? Oooh! Levy!
N-No!! It isn't like that!!!
Oh, come on, Lu-chan!!
AH HA HA!
EEK
EEK
EEK
EEK

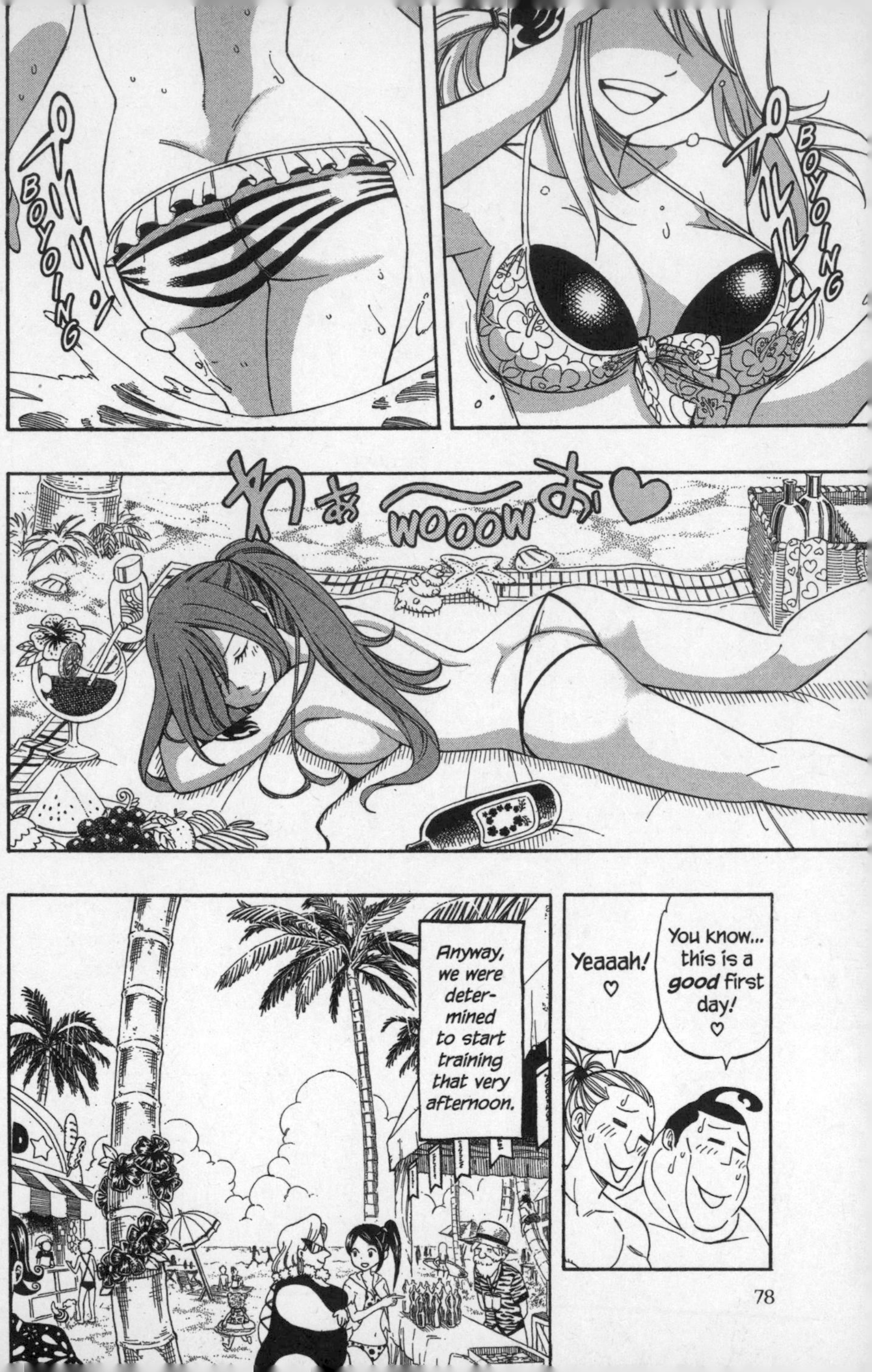
BOYOING
BOYOING
WOOOW
You know... this is a *good* first day! ♡
Yeaaah! ♡
Anyway, we were deter-mined to start training that very afternoon.

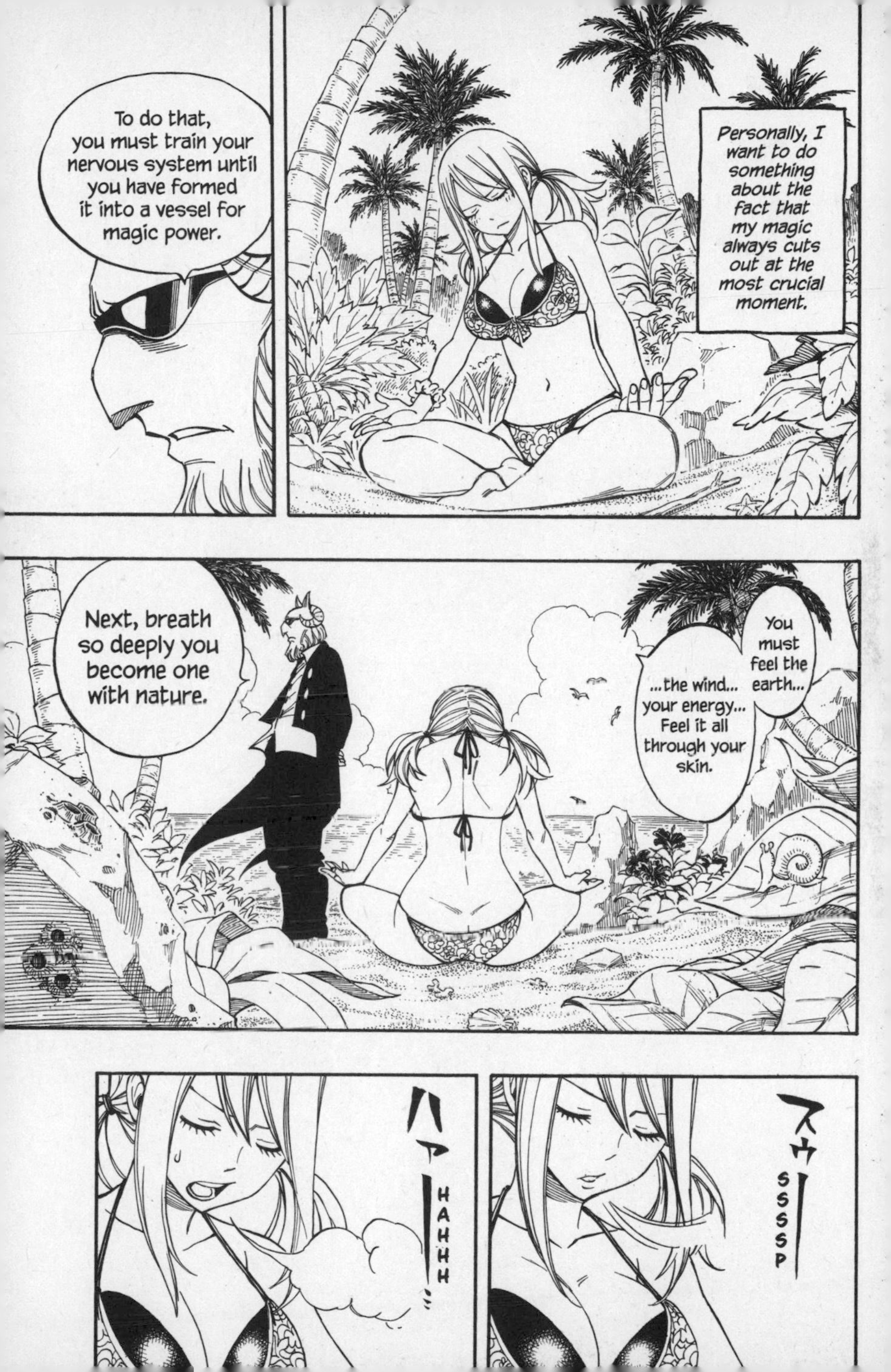
Personally, I want to do something about the fact that my magic always cuts out at the most crucial moment.
To do that, you must train your nervous system until you have formed it into a vessel for magic power.
You must feel the earth...
...the wind... your energy... Feel it all through your skin.
Next, breath so deeply you become one with nature.
スウー
SSSSP
ハァー!!
HAHHH

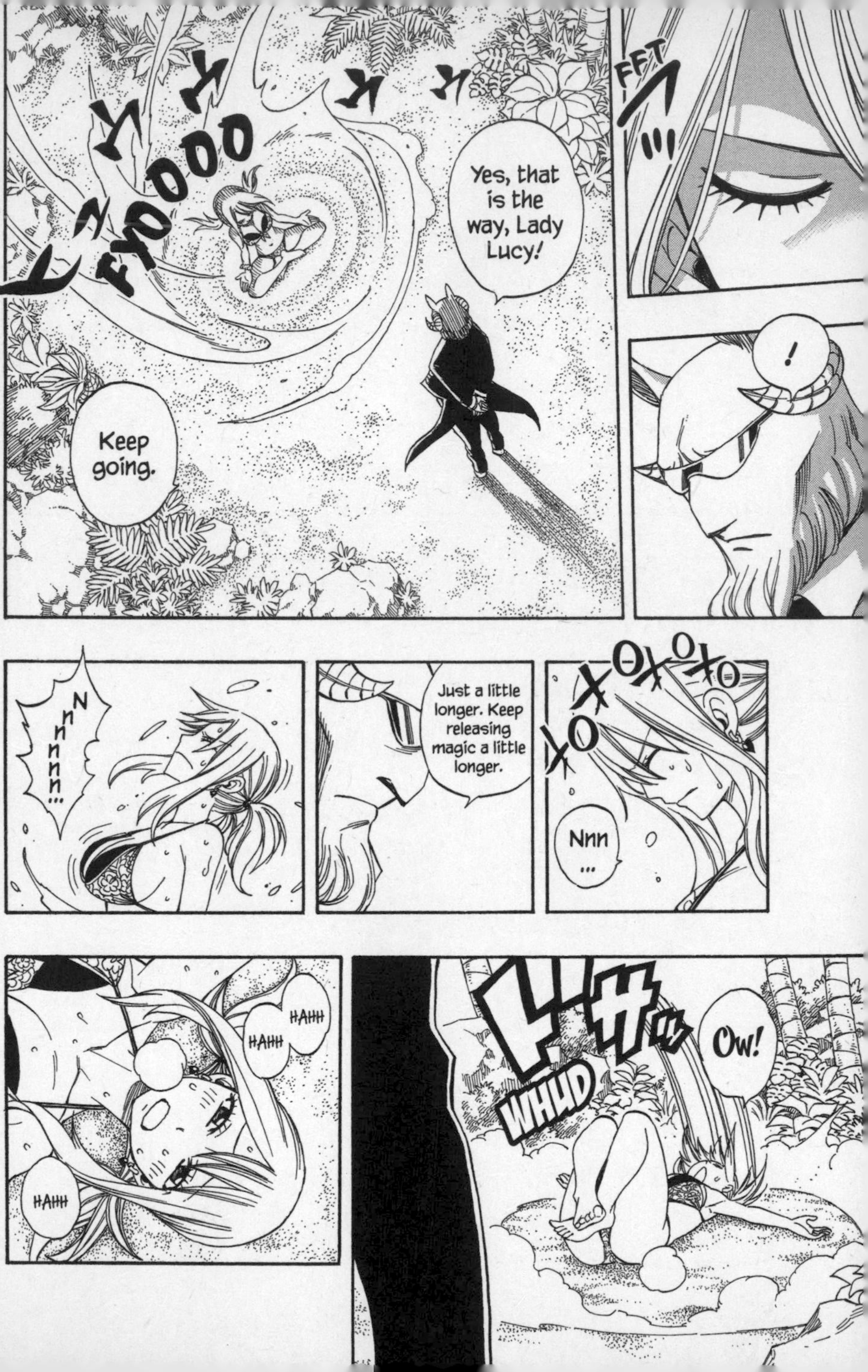
FFT
!
Yes, that is the way, Lady Lucy!
FYOOOO
Keep going.
Nnn ...
Just a little longer. Keep releasing magic a little longer.
Nnnnnn...!!!
WHUD
Ow!
HAHH
HAHH
HAHH

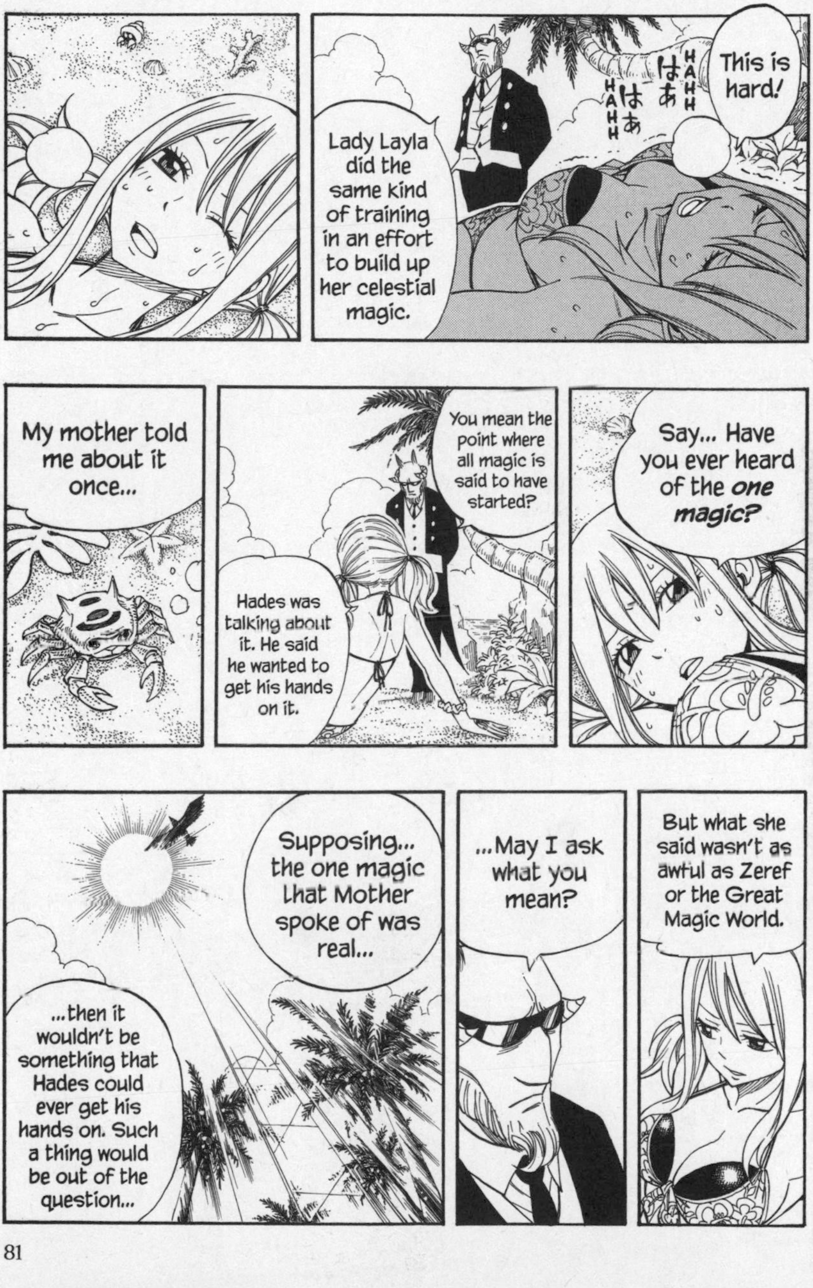
This is hard!
はあ HAHH
はあ HAHH
Lady Layla did the same kind of training in an effort to build up her celestial magic.
Say... Have you ever heard of the *one magic?*
You mean the point where all magic is said to have started?
Hades was talking about it. He said he wanted to get his hands on it.
My mother told me about it once...
But what she said wasn't as awful as Zeref or the Great Magic World.
...May I ask what you mean?
Supposing... the one magic that Mother spoke of was real...
...then it wouldn't be something that Hades could ever get his hands on. Such a thing would be out of the question...

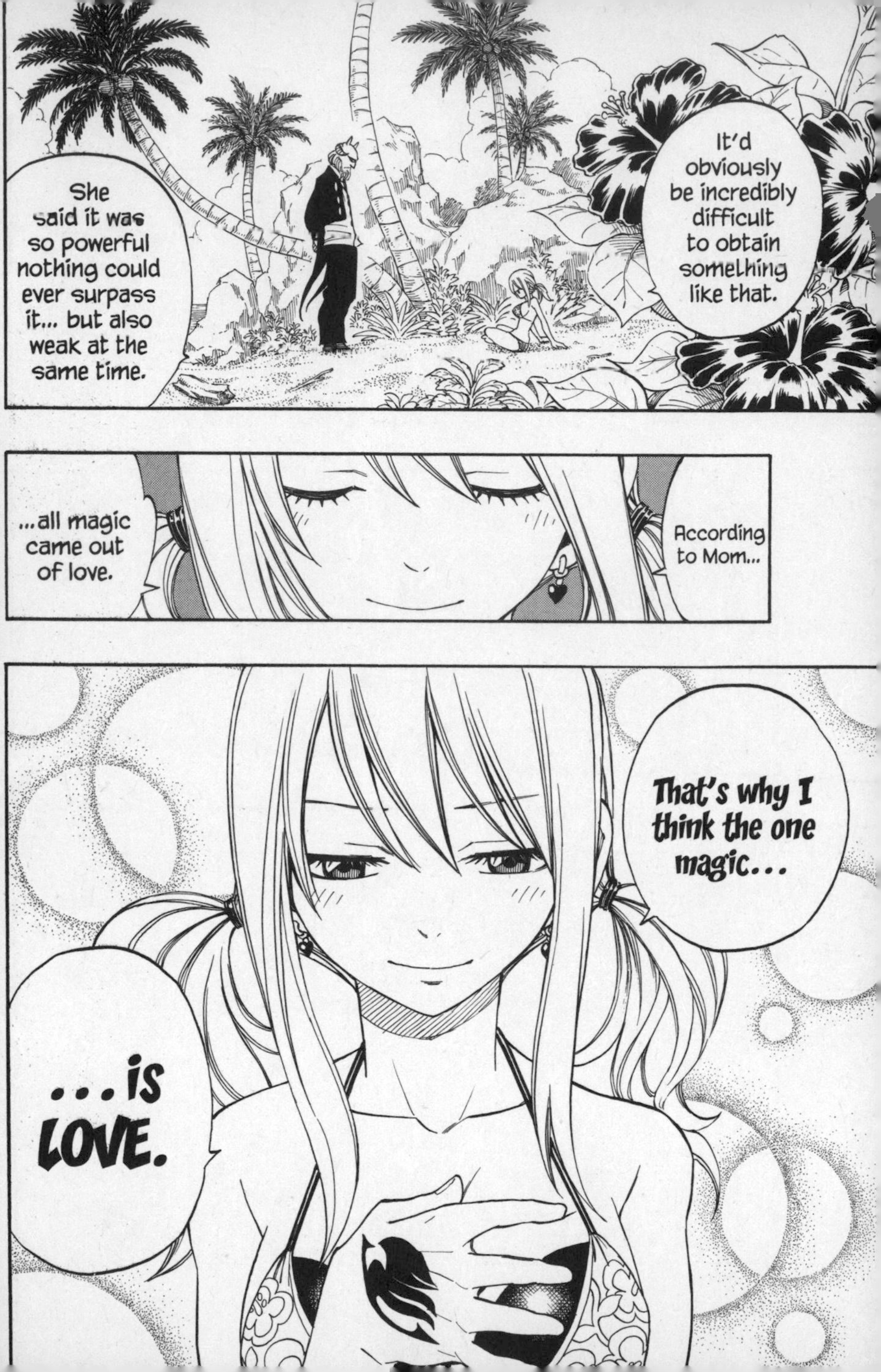
It'd obviously be incredibly difficult to obtain something like that.
She said it was so powerful nothing could ever surpass it... but also weak at the same time.
According to Mom...
...all magic came out of love.
That's why I think the one magic...
...is LOVE.

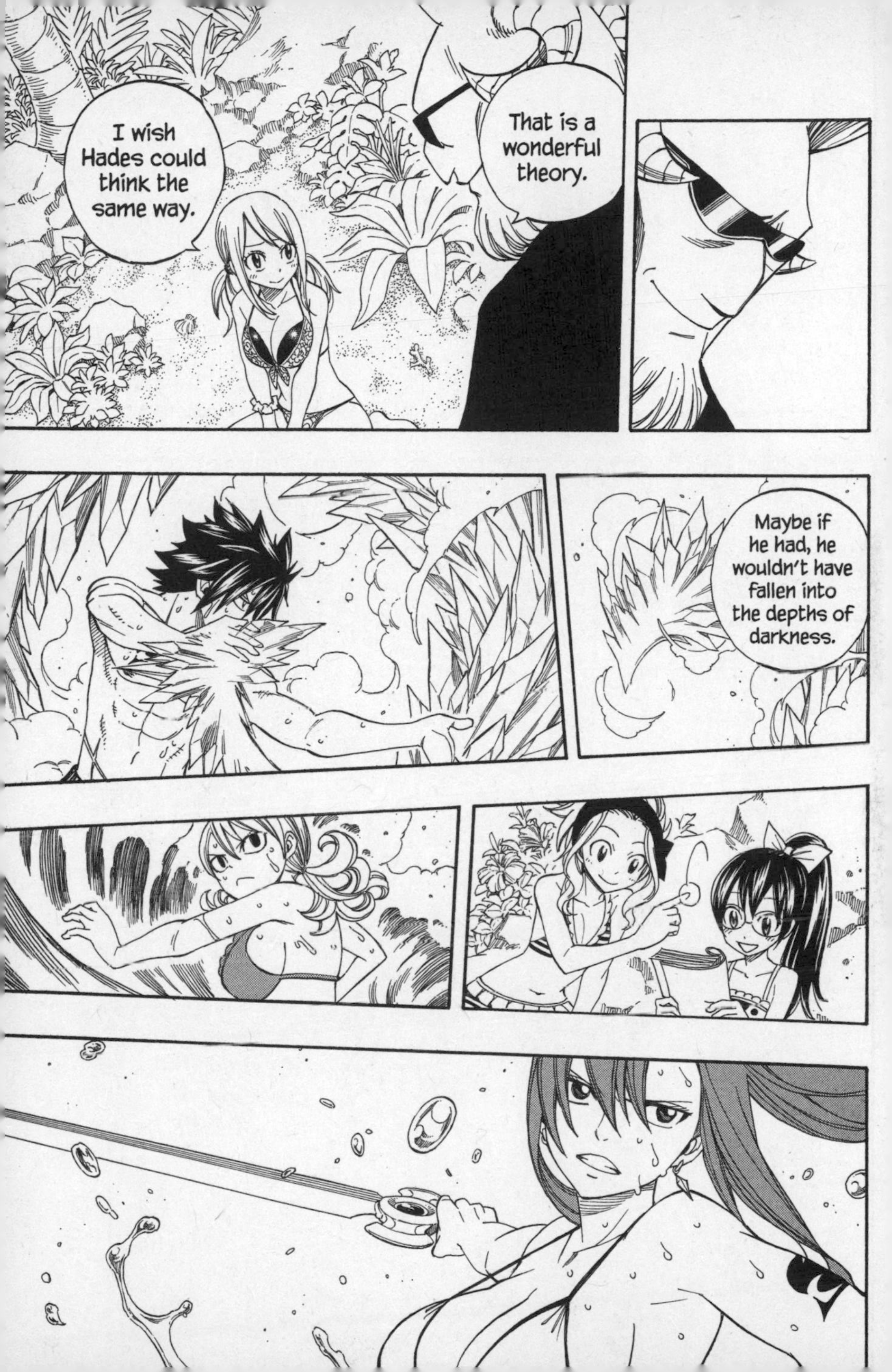
That is a wonderful theory.
I wish Hades could think the same way.
Maybe if he had, he wouldn't have fallen into the depths of darkness.

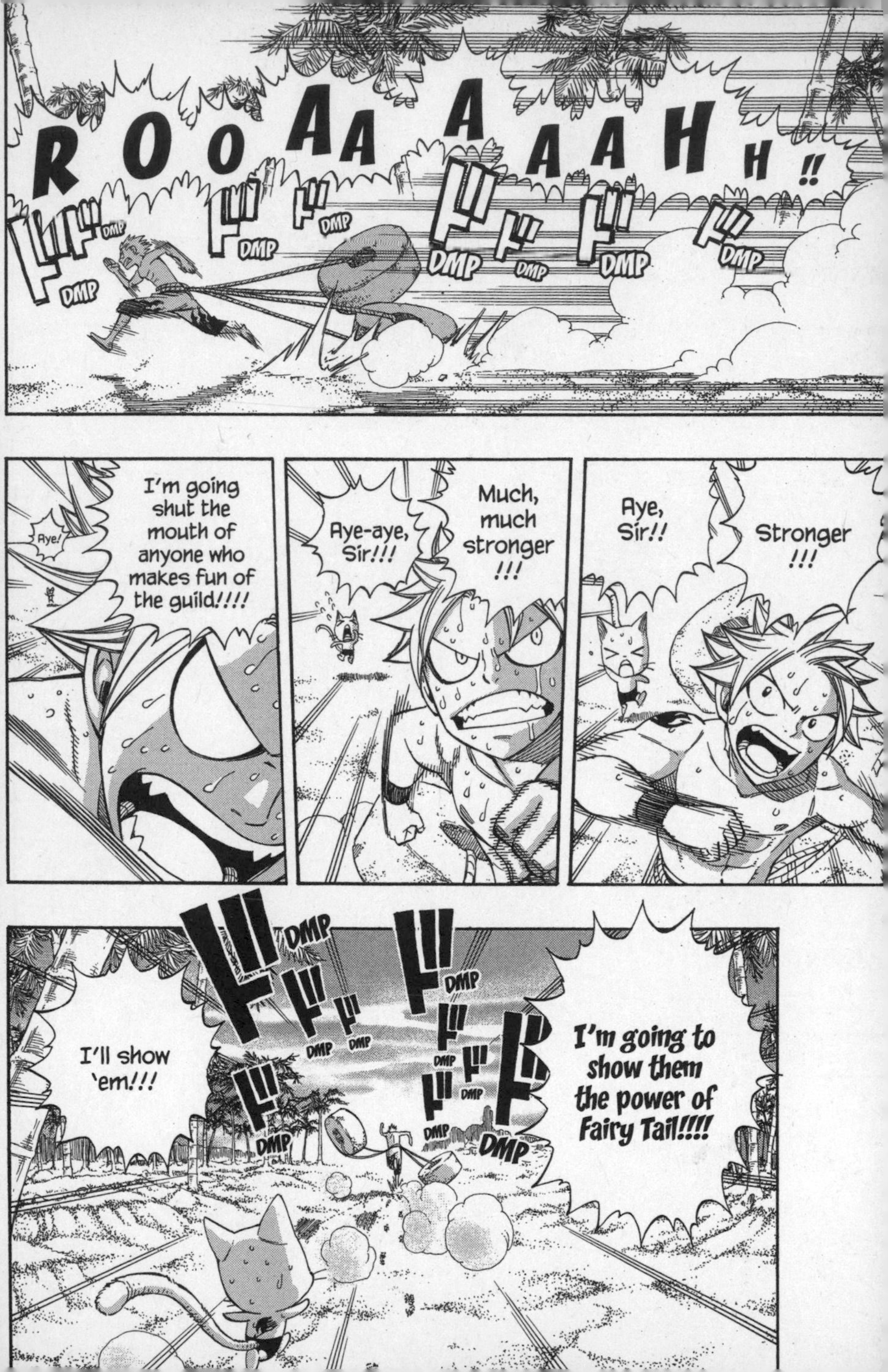
ROOAAAAAHH!!
DMP
DMP
DMP
DMP
DMP
DMP
DMP
DMP
Stronger!!!
Aye, Sir!!
Much, much stronger!!!
Aye-aye, Sir!!!
I'm going shut the mouth of anyone who makes fun of the guild!!!!
Aye!
DMP
DMP
DMP
DMP
DMP
DMP
DMP
DMP
I'm going to show them the power of Fairy Tail!!!!
I'll show 'em!!!

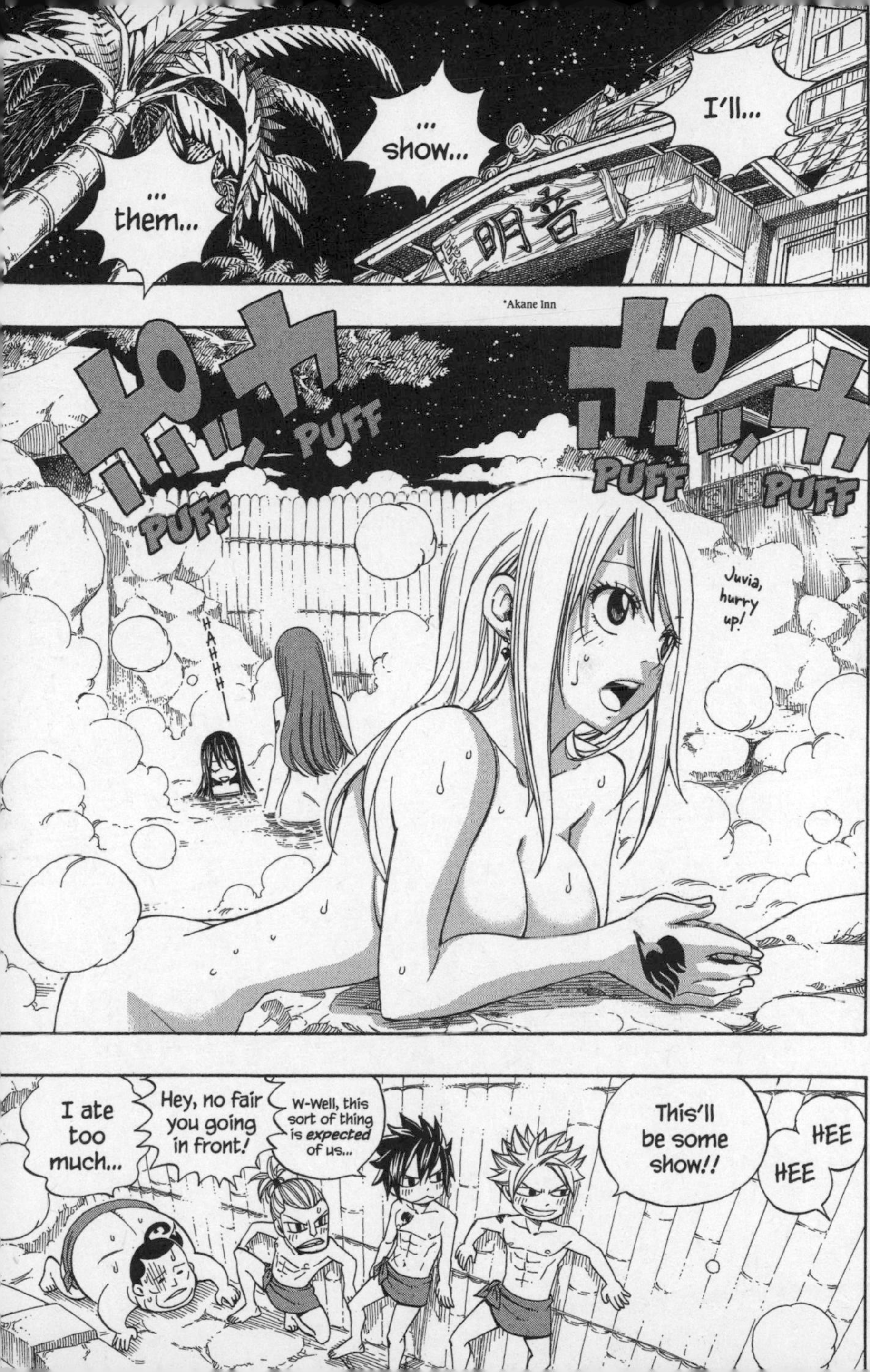
I'll...
... show...
... them...
PUFF PUFF
PUFF PUFF
Juvia, hurry up!
HAHHH
HEE HEE
This'll be some show!!
W-Well, this sort of thing is *expected* of us...
Hey, no fair you going in front!
I ate too much...
*Akane Inn

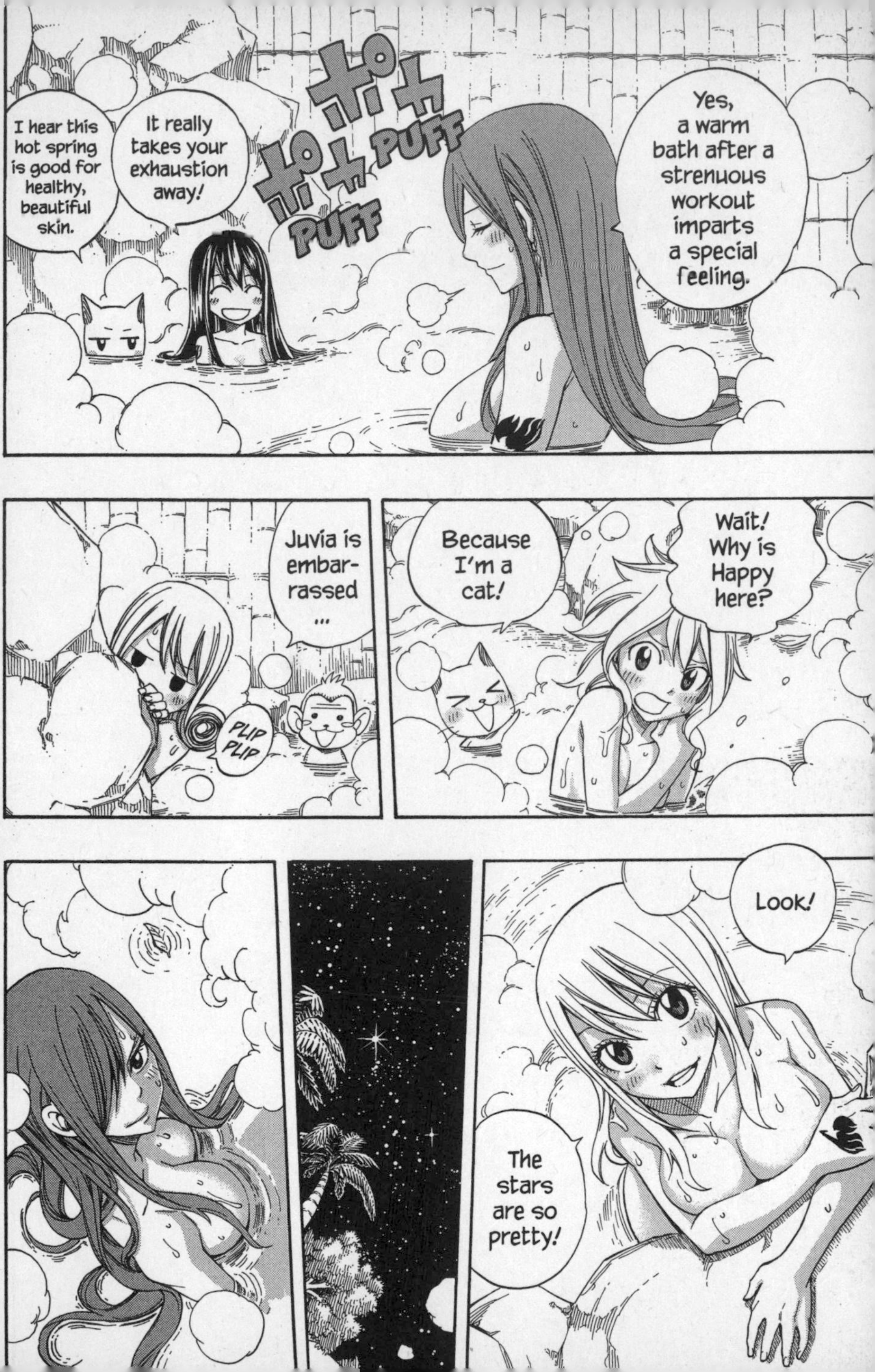
Yes, a warm bath after a strenuous workout imparts a special feeling.
PUFF PUFF
It really takes your exhaustion away!
I hear this hot spring is good for healthy, beautiful skin.
Wait! Why is Happy here?
Because I'm a cat!
Juvia is embar-rassed ...
PLIP PLIP
Look!
The stars are so pretty!

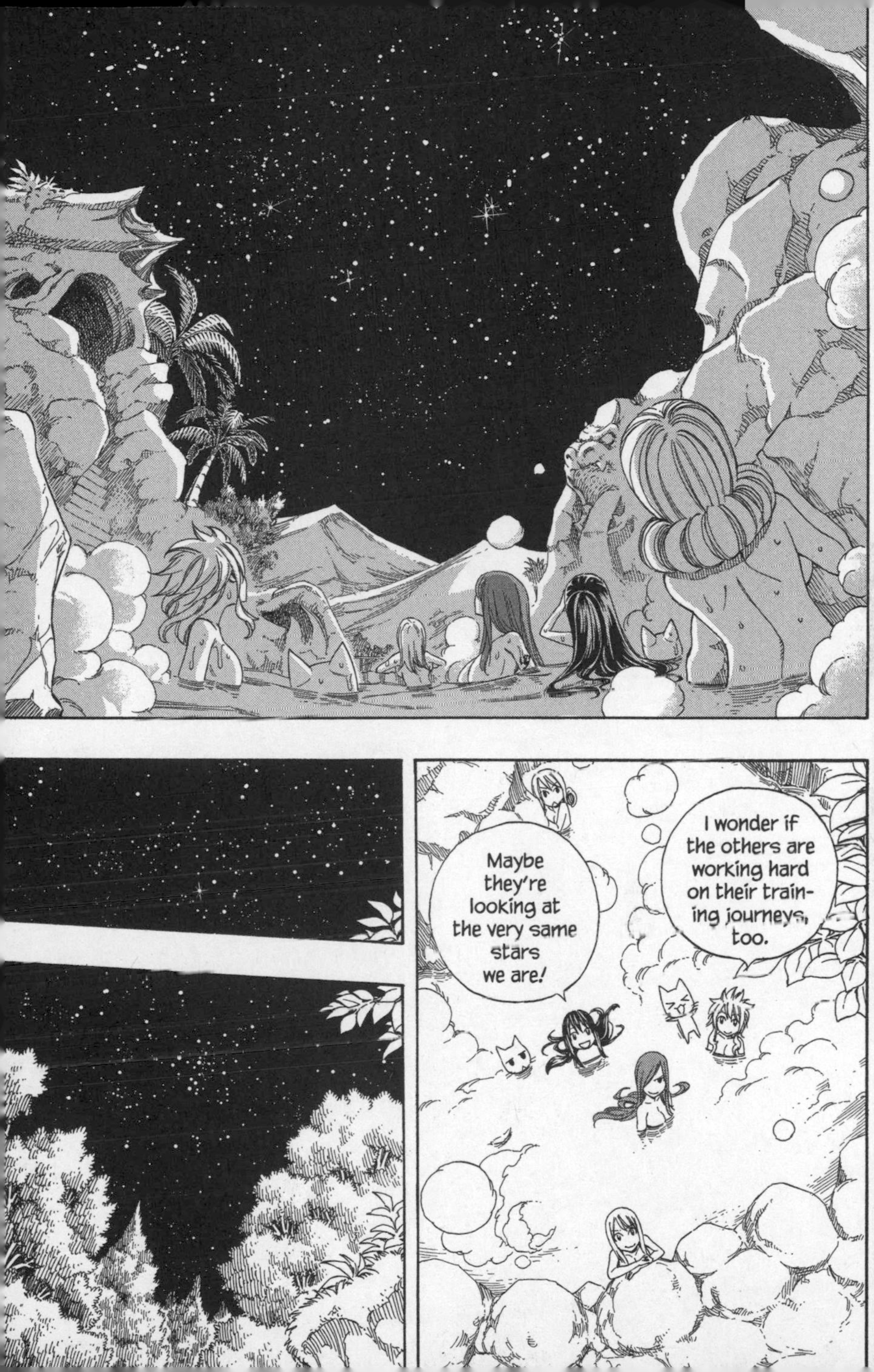
I wonder if the others are working hard on their train-ing journeys, too.
Maybe they're looking at the very same stars we are!

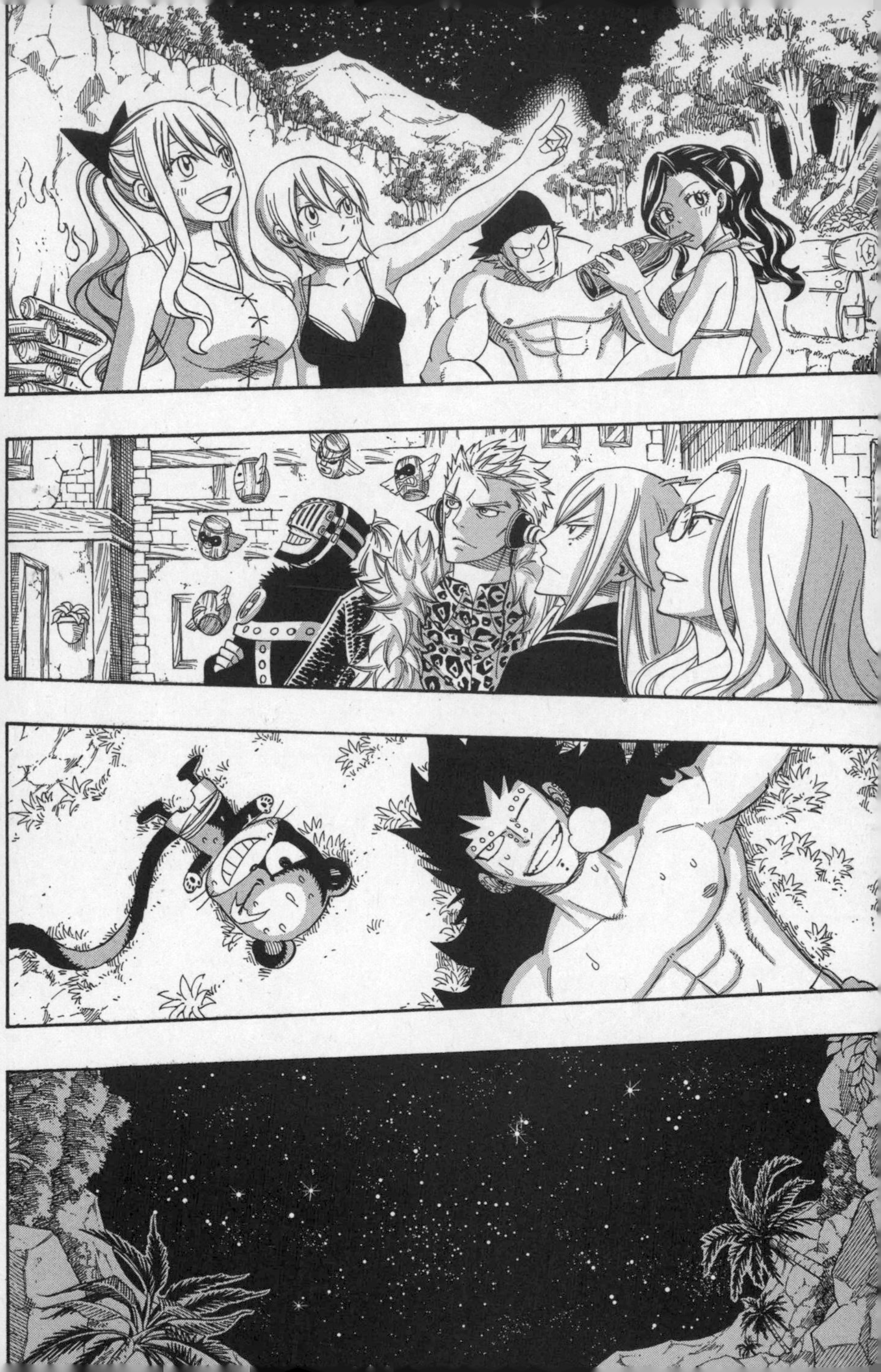

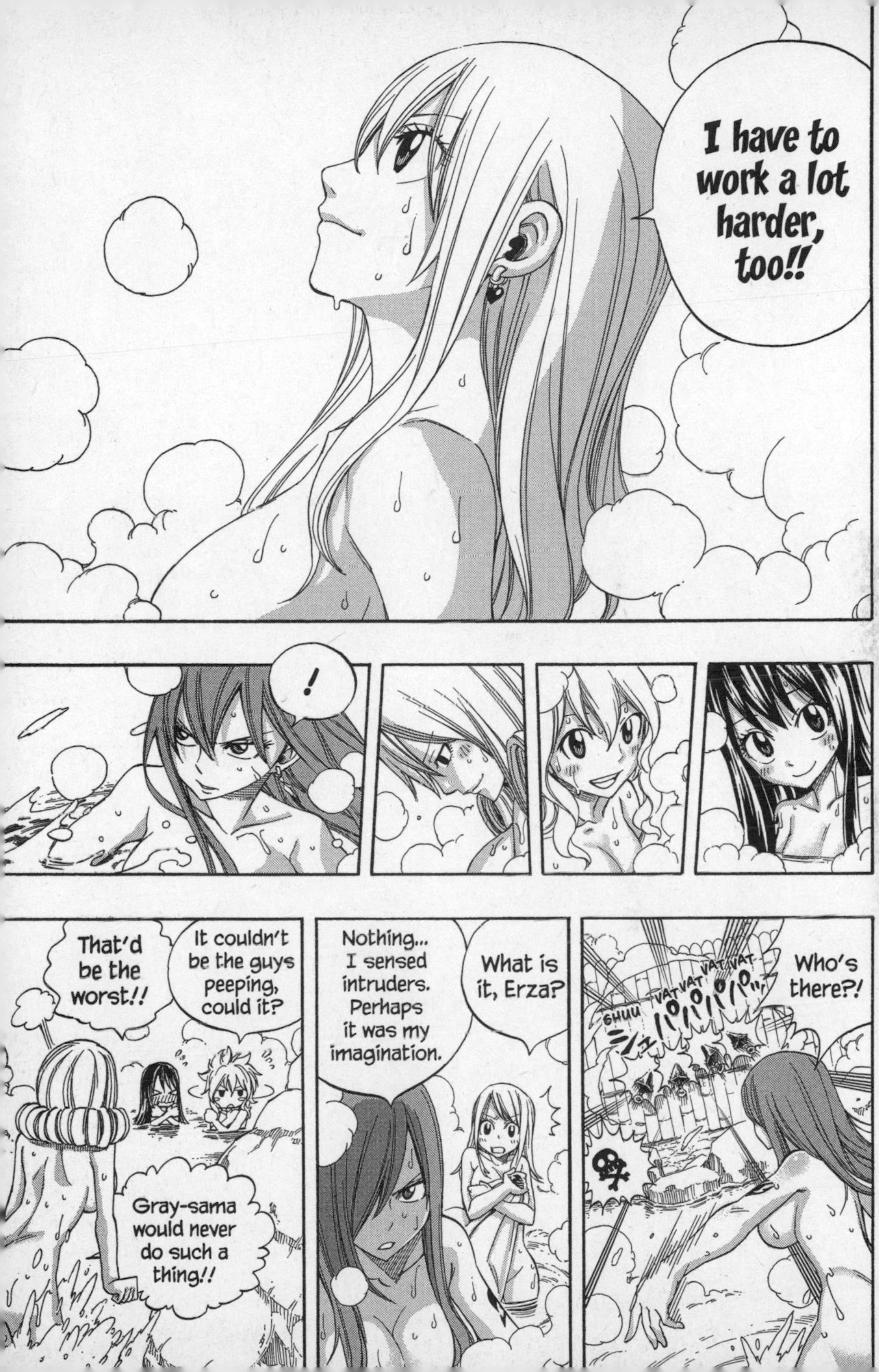
I have to work a lot harder, too!!
!
Who's there?!
VAT VAT VAT VAT
SHUU
What is it, Erza?
Nothing... I sensed intruders. Perhaps it was my imagination.
It couldn't be the guys peeping, could it?
That'd be the worst!!
Gray-sama would never do such a thing!!

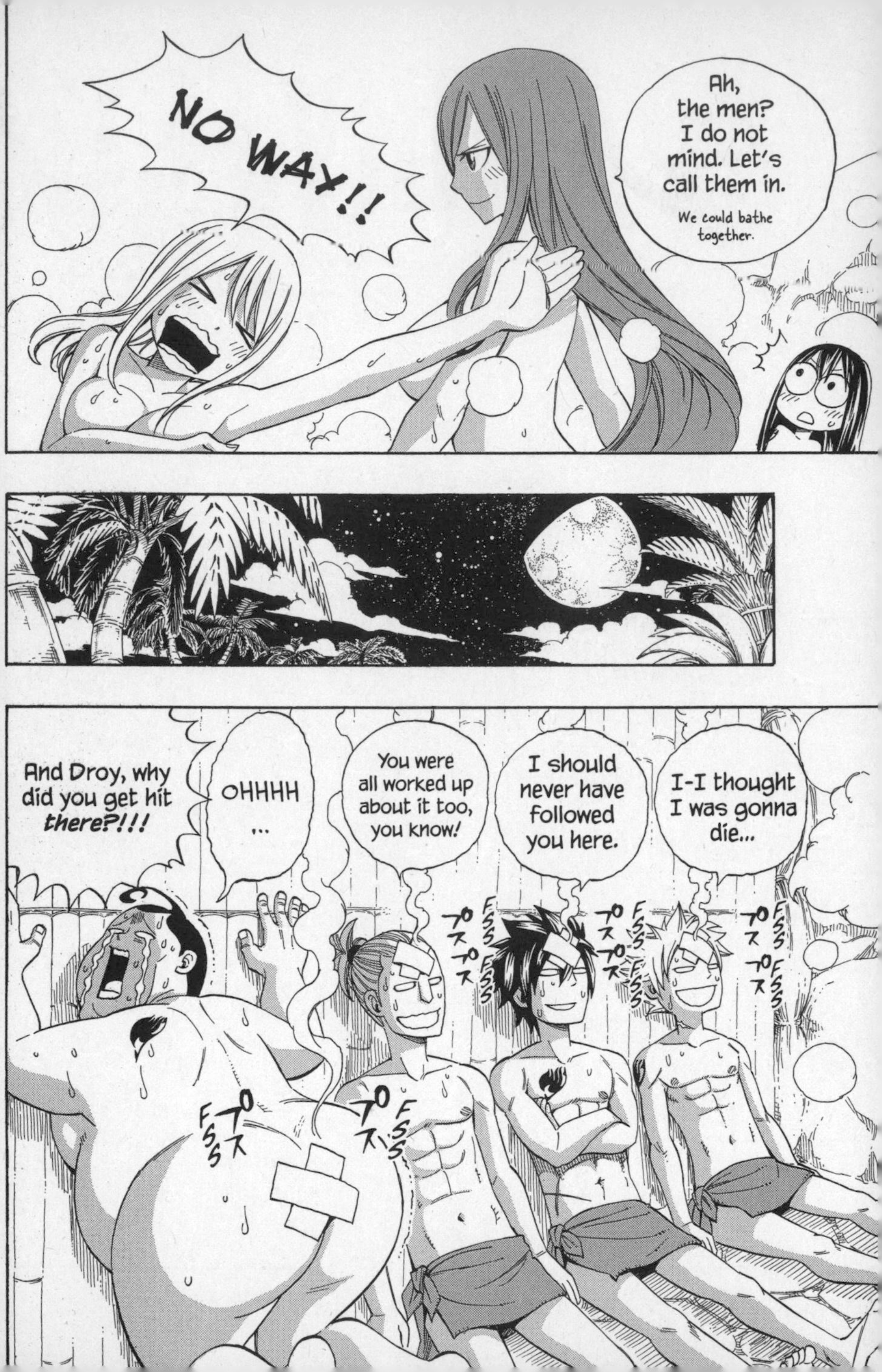
Ah, the men? I do not mind. Let's call them in.
We could bathe together.
NO WAY!!
I-I thought I was gonna die...
FSS FSS
I should never have followed you here.
FSS FSS FSS
You were all worked up about it too, you know!
FSS FSS
OHHHH ...
And Droy, why did you get hit *there?!!!*
FSS

# FAIRY TAIL

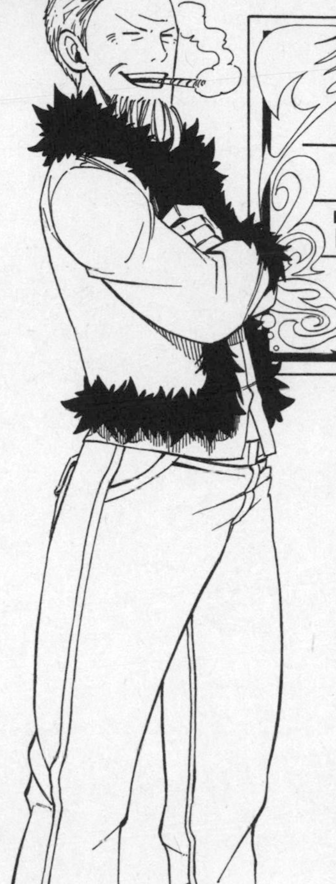

**FAIRY TAIL**

**Name:** Wakaba Mine **Age:** 43

**Magic:** Smoke Magic

**Likes:** Liquor, tabacco, women **Dislikes:** His wife

## Remarks

He was top aide to the fourth master, Macao, for seven years. As such, it could also be said that he was one of those who allowed Fairy Tail's strength to weaken criminally during those years. His tendency toward sexual harassment has angered guild women including Laki and Kinana (guild employees).
He has a daughter about the same age as Romeo, but recently she has not been speaking to him. She has declared that she will join Twilight Ogre when she gets a little bigger, and he was in the midst of doing everything he could to dissuade her when the Sirius Island group returned. Now, a bit of hope has returned to Wakaba's life.

# Chapter 262: Song of the Celestials

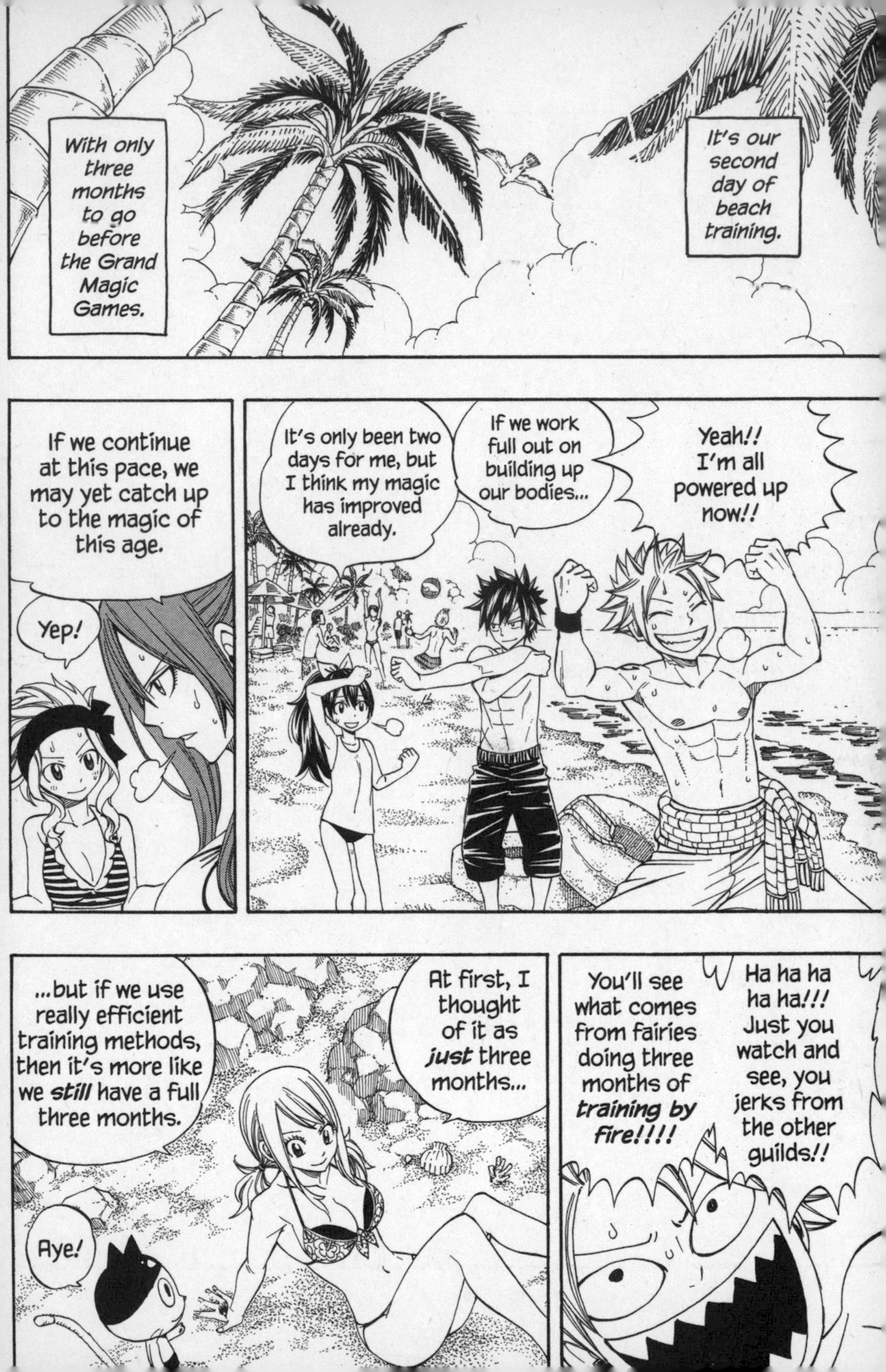

It's our second day of beach training.
With only three months to go before the Grand Magic Games.
Yeah!! I'm all powered up now!!
If we work full out on building up our bodies...
It's only been two days for me, but I think my magic has improved already.
If we continue at this pace, we may yet catch up to the magic of this age.
Yep!
Ha ha ha ha!!! Just you watch and see, you jerks from the other guilds!!
You'll see what comes from fairies doing three months of *training by fire!!!!*
At first, I thought of it as *just* three months...
...but if we use really efficient training methods, then it's more like we *still* have a full three months.
Aye!

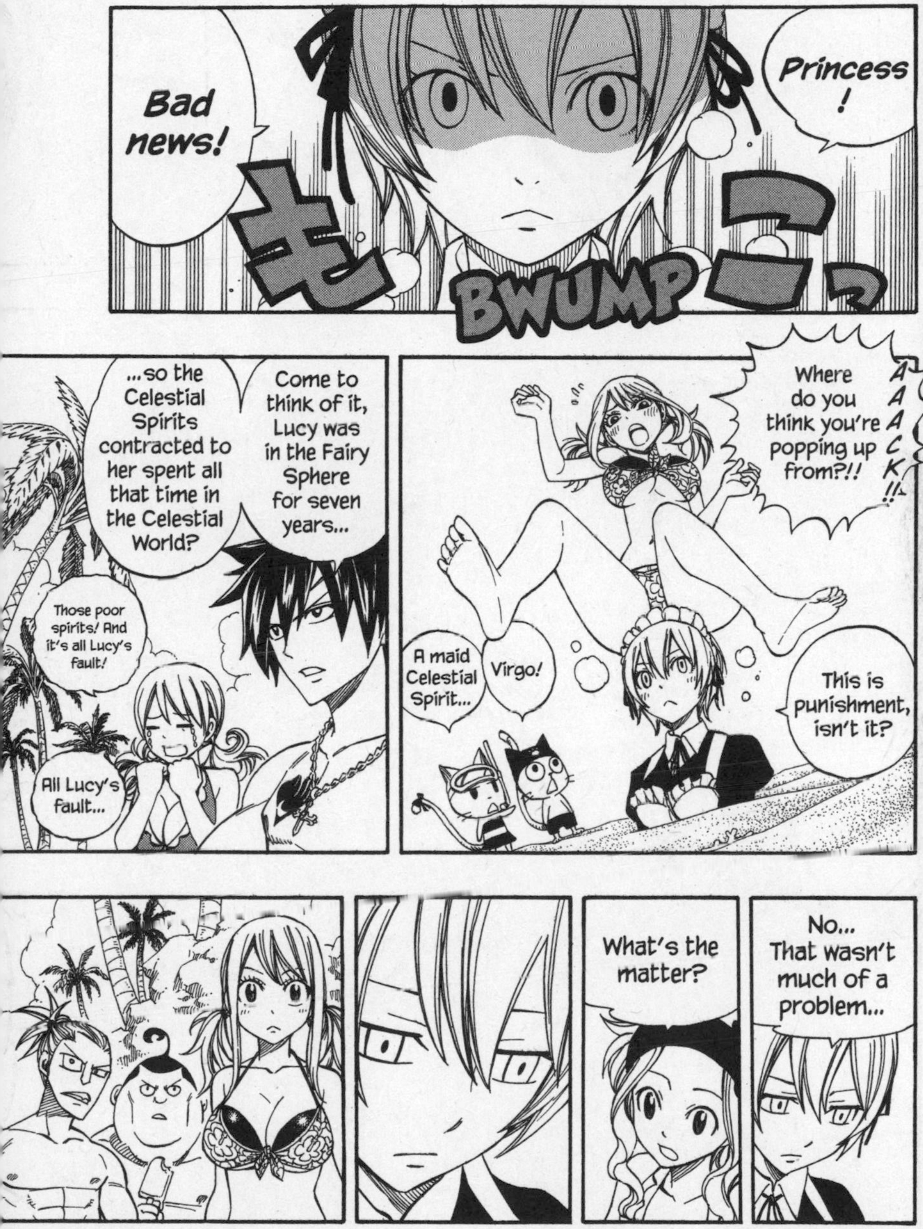

Princess!
Bad news!
BWUMP
Where do you think you're popping up from?!!
AAACK!!
This is punishment, isn't it?
Virgo!
A maid Celestial Spirit...
Come to think of it, Lucy was in the Fairy Sphere for seven years...
...so the Celestial Spirits contracted to her spent all that time in the Celestial World?
Those poor spirits! And it's all Lucy's fault!
All Lucy's fault...
No... That wasn't much of a problem...
What's the matter?

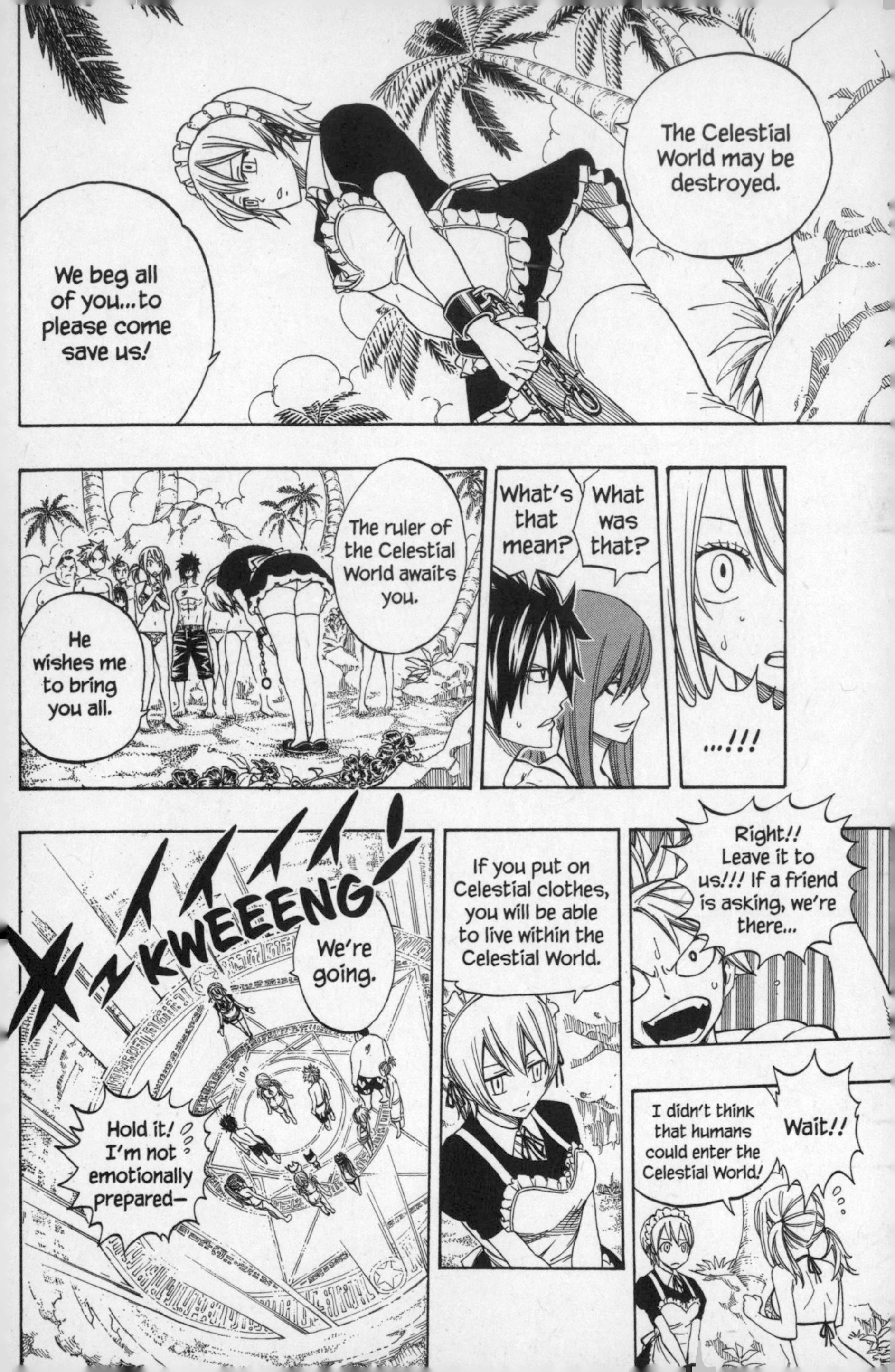
The Celestial World may be destroyed.
We beg all of you...to please come save us!
...!!!
What was that?
What's that mean?
The ruler of the Celestial World awaits you.
He wishes me to bring you all.
Right!! Leave it to us!!! If a friend is asking, we're there...
Wait!!
I didn't think that humans could enter the Celestial World!
If you put on Celestial clothes, you will be able to live within the Celestial World.
KWEEENG!
We're going.
Hold it! I'm not emotionally prepared—

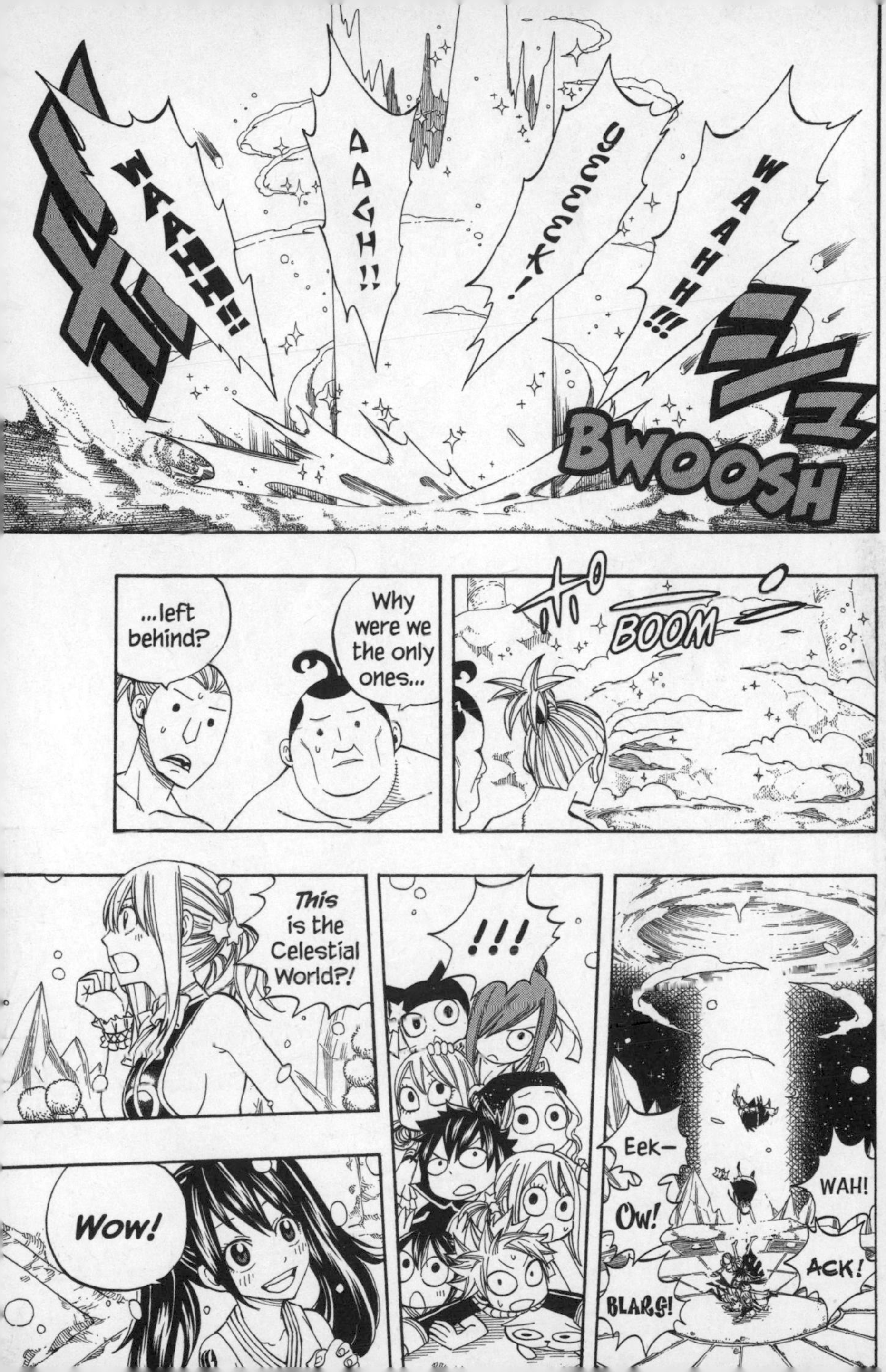

WAAHH!!!
YEOWWWK!
AAGH!!
WAAHH!!!
BWOOSH
BOOM
Why were we the only ones...
...left behind?
Eek–
WAH!
OW!
ACK!
BLARG!
!!!
This is the Celestial World?!
WOW!

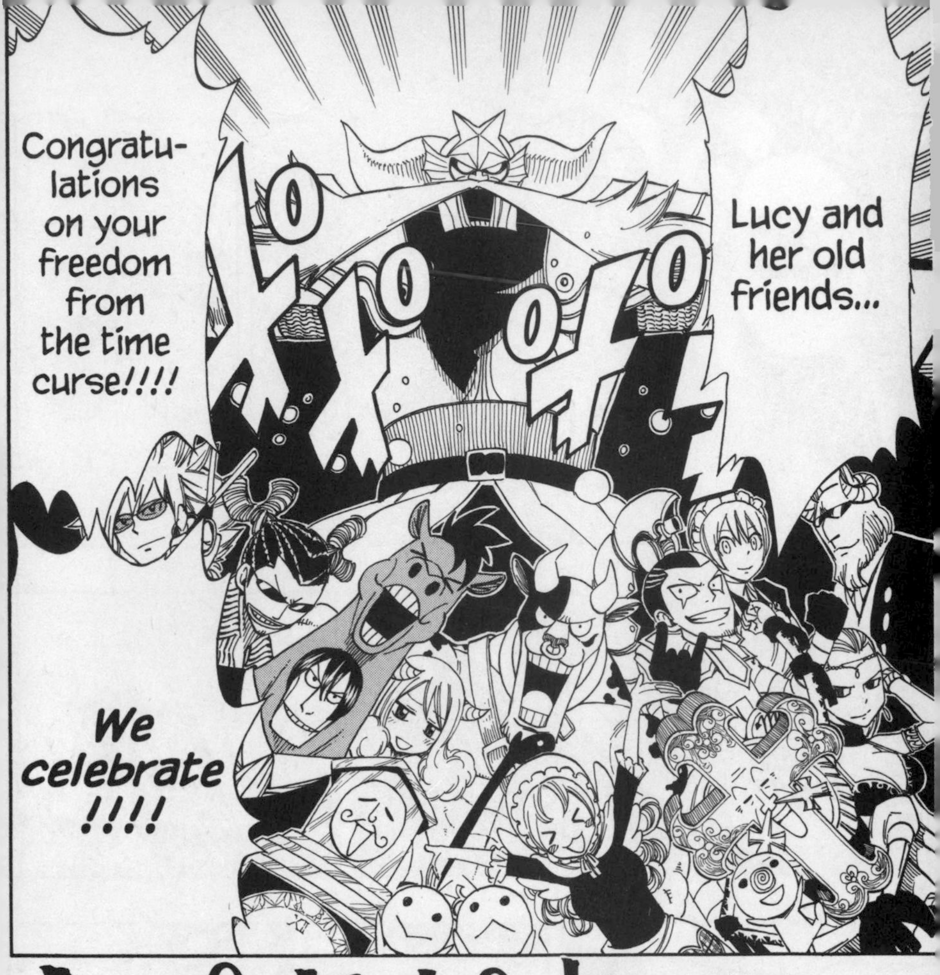
Lucy and her old friends...
Congratulations on your freedom from the time curse!!!!
We celebrate !!!!

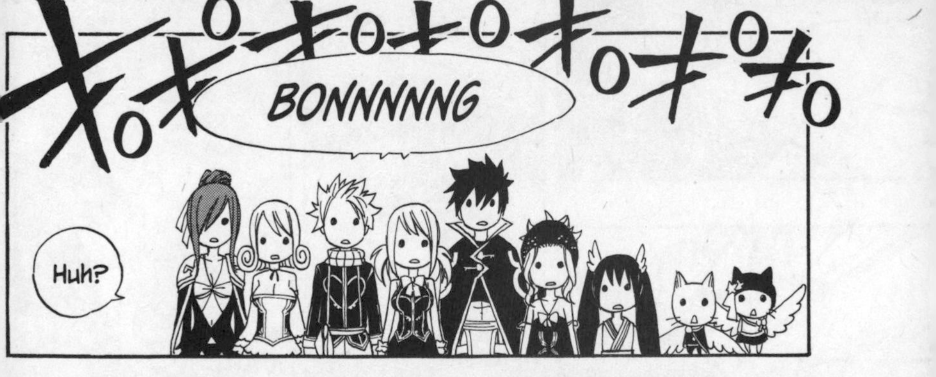
BONNNNNG
Huh?

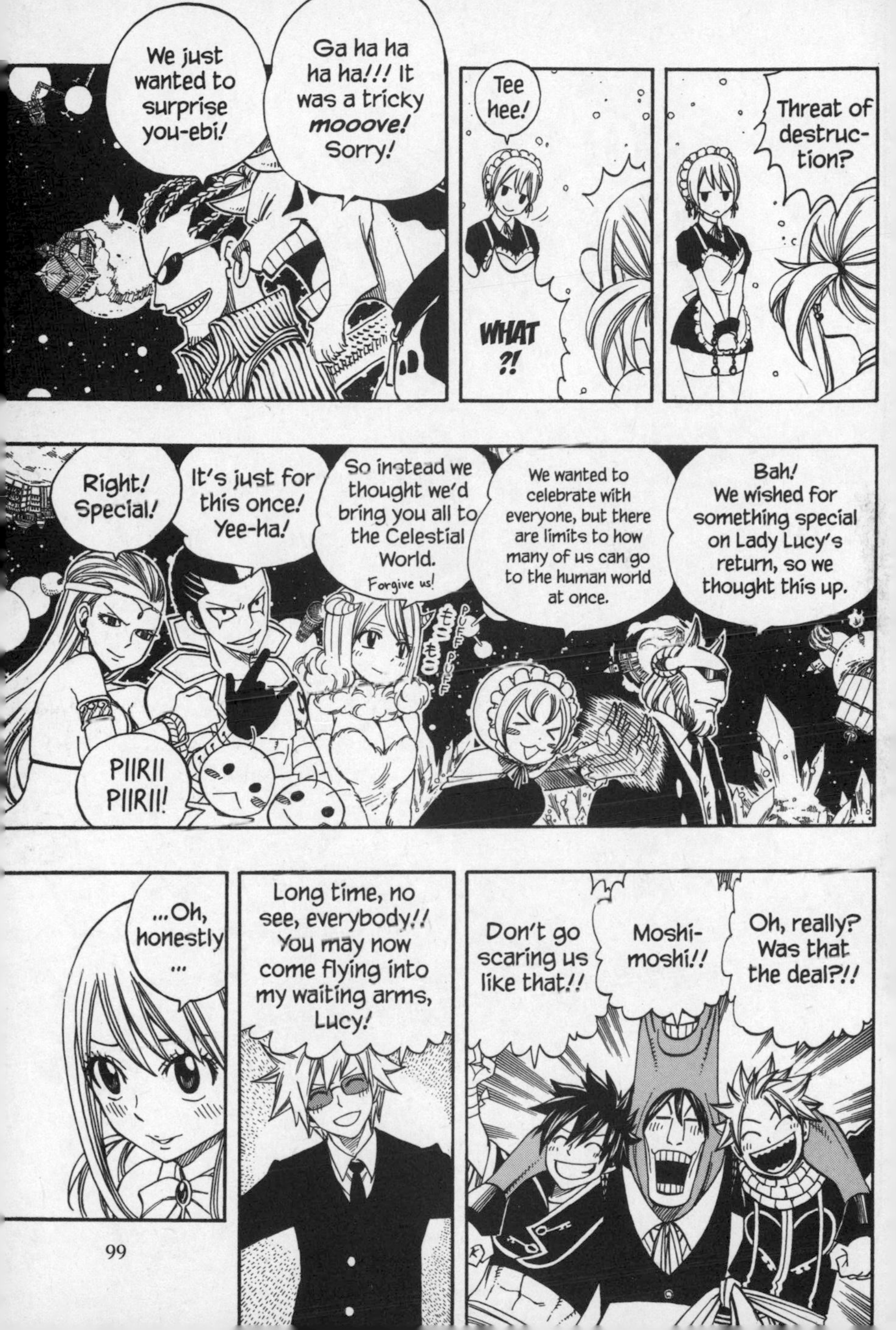
Threat of destruction?
Tee hee!
WHAT ?!
Ga ha ha ha ha!!! It was a tricky *mooove!* Sorry!
We just wanted to surprise you-ebi!
Bah! We wished for something special on Lady Lucy's return, so we thought this up.
We wanted to celebrate with everyone, but there are limits to how many of us can go to the human world at once.
So instead we thought we'd bring you all to the Celestial World.
Forgive us!
PUFF PUFF
It's just for this once! Yee-ha!
Right! Special!
PIIRII PIIRII!
Oh, really? Was that the deal?!!
Moshi-moshi!!
Don't go scaring us like that!!
Long time, no see, everybody!! You may now come flying into my waiting arms, Lucy!
...Oh, honestly...

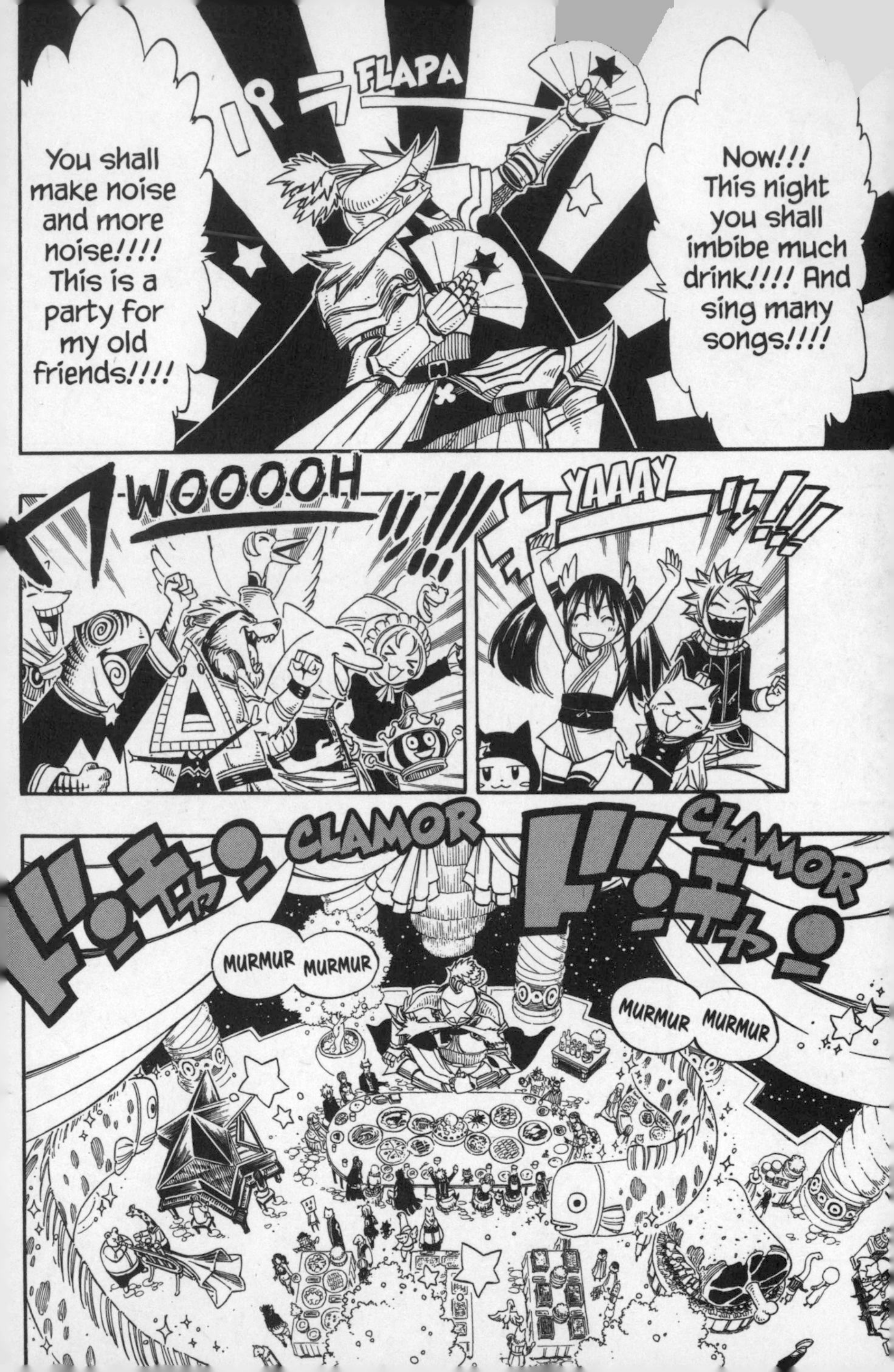
FLAPA
Now!!! This night you shall imbibe much drink!!!! And sing many songs!!!!
You shall make noise and more noise!!!! This is a party for my old friends!!!!
YAAAY
WOOOOH
CLAMOR
CLAMOR
MURMUR MURMUR
MURMUR MURMUR

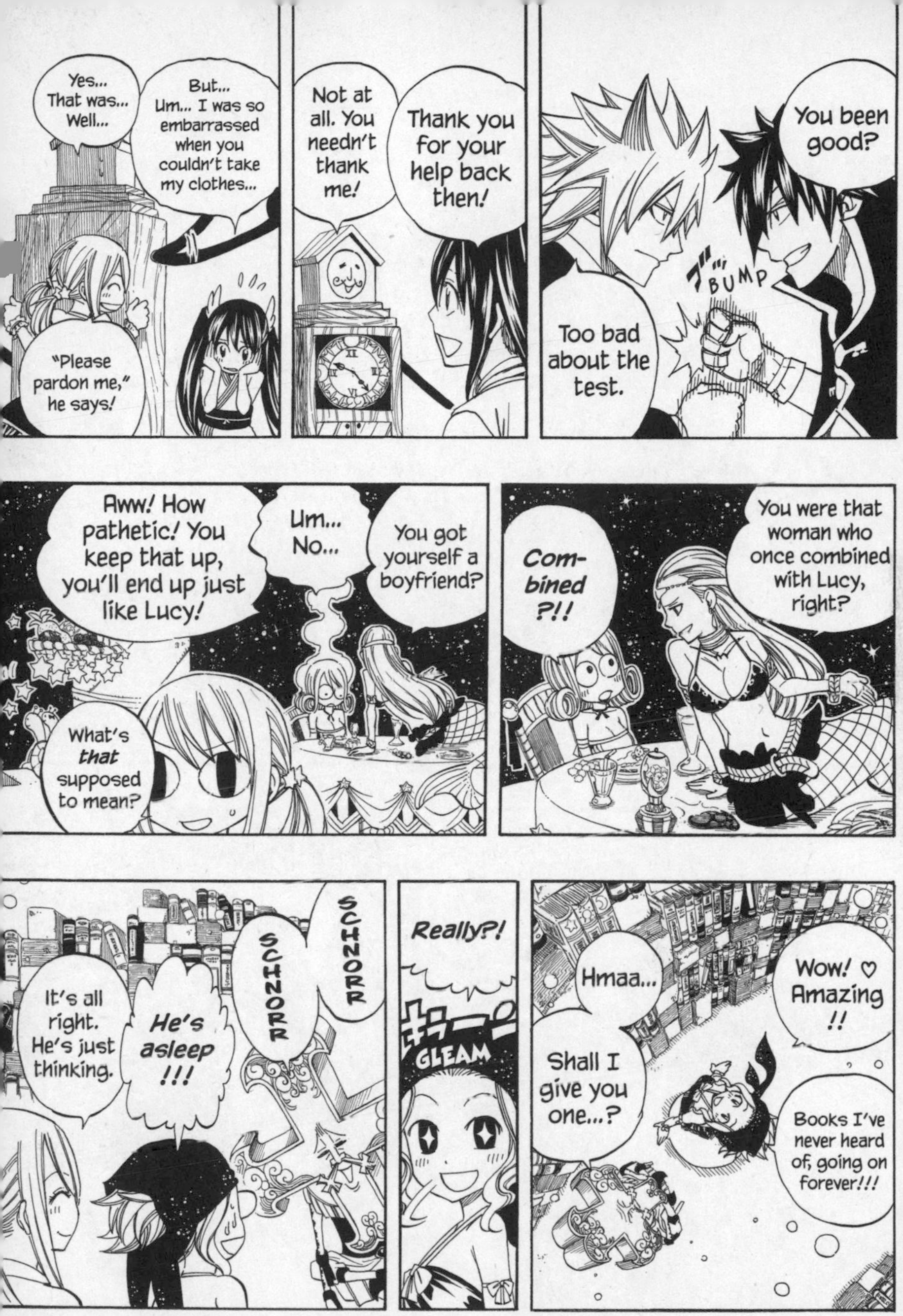
You been good?
BUMP
Too bad about the test.
Thank you for your help back then!
Not at all. You needn't thank me!
But... Um... I was so embarrassed when you couldn't take my clothes...
Yes... That was... Well...
"Please pardon me," he says!
You were that woman who once combined with Lucy, right?
Com-bined?!!
You got yourself a boyfriend?
Um... No...
Aww! How pathetic! You keep that up, you'll end up just like Lucy!
What's *that* supposed to mean?
Wow! ♡ Amazing!!
Books I've never heard of, going on forever!!!
Hmaa...
Shall I give you one...?
Really?!
GLEAM
SCHNORR
SCHNORR
*He's asleep!!!*
It's all right. He's just thinking.

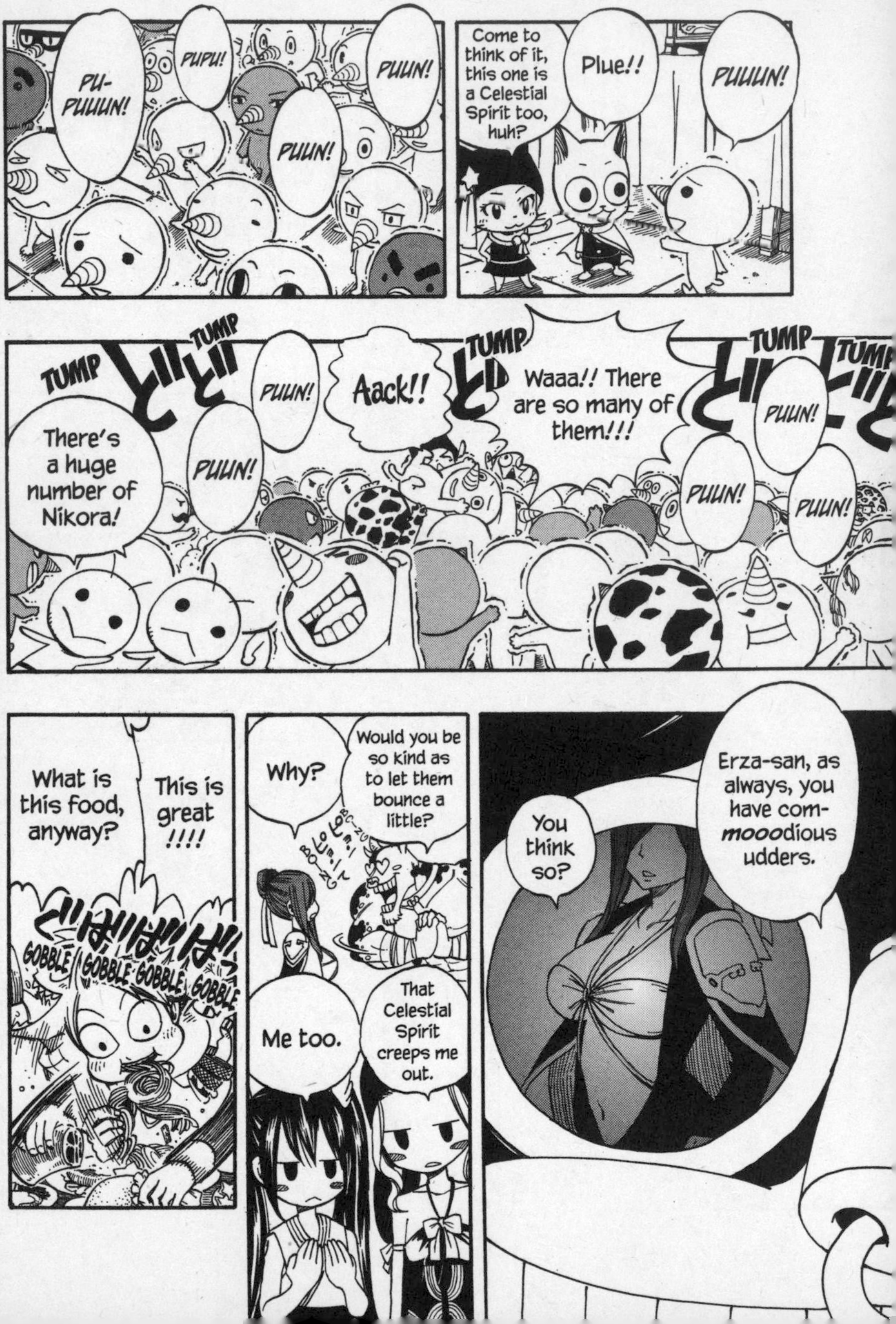
PUUUN!
Plue!!
Come to think of it, this one is a Celestial Spirit too, huh?
PUUN!
PUUN!
PUPU!
PU-PUUUN!
TUMP
TUMP
PUUN!
PUUN!
PUUN!
Waaa!! There are so many of them!!!
TUMP
Aack!!
PUUN!
TUMP
TUMP
PUUN!
There's a huge number of Nikora!
Erza-san, as always, you have com-*mooo*dious udders.
You think so?
Would you be so kind as to let them bounce a little?
Why?
That Celestial Spirit creeps me out.
Me too.
This is great!!!!
What is this food, anyway?
GOBBLE
GOBBLE
GOBBLE
GOBBLE

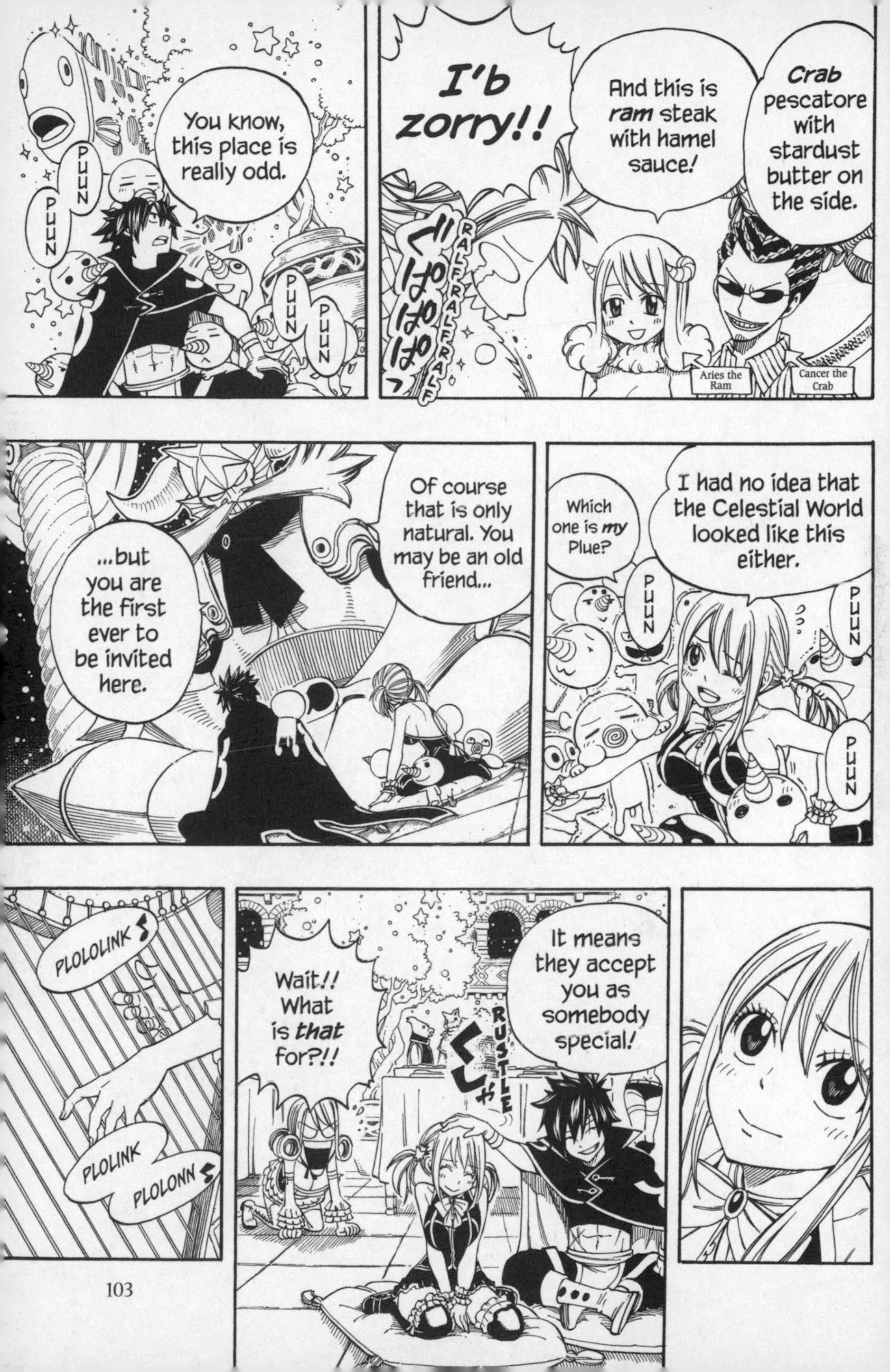
Crab pescatore with stardust butter on the side.
And this is ram steak with hamel sauce!
Cancer the Crab
Aries the Ram
I'b zorry!!
RALFRALFRALF
You know, this place is really odd.
PUUN
PUUN
PUUN
PUUN
I had no idea that the Celestial World looked like this either.
PUUN
Which one is my Plue?
PUUN
PUUN
Of course that is only natural. You may be an old friend...
...but you are the first ever to be invited here.
It means they accept you as somebody special!
RUSTLE
Wait!! What is that for?!!
PLOLOLINK
PLOLINK
PLOLONN

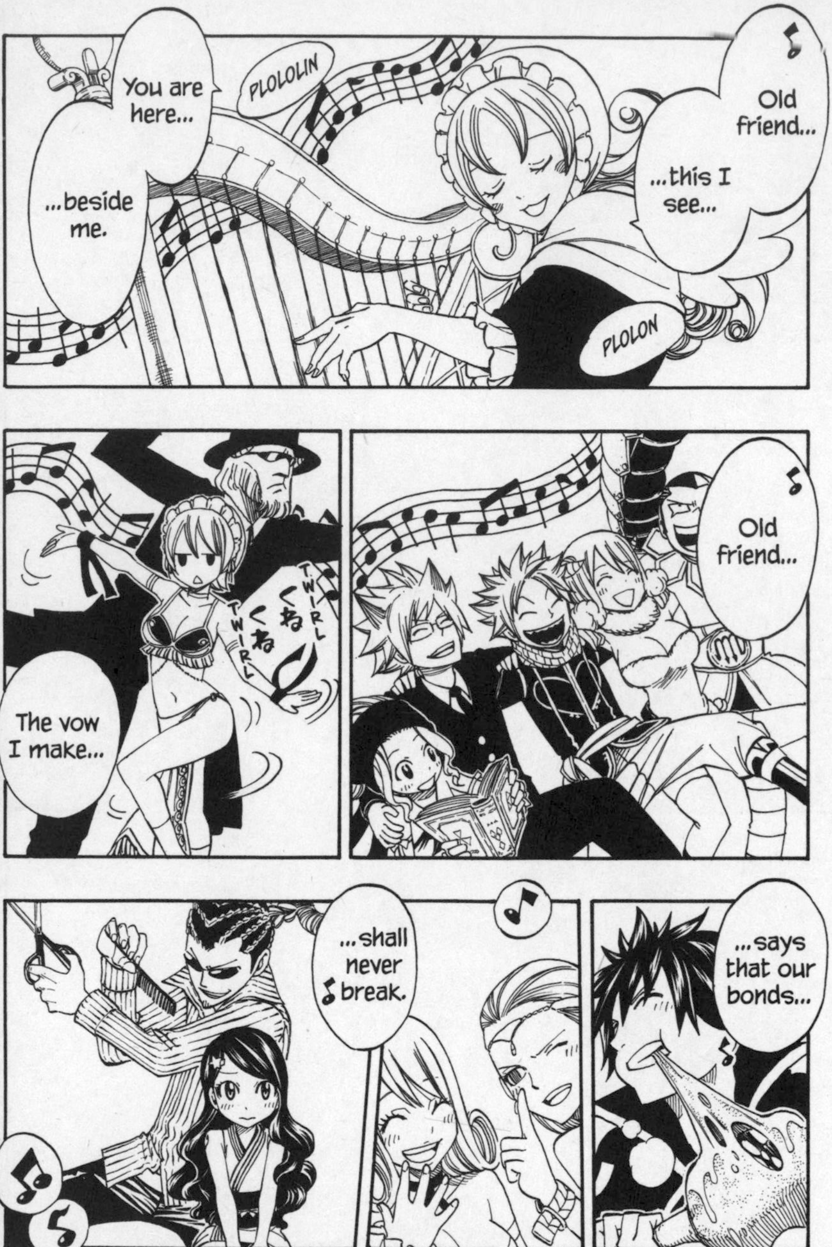
Old friend...
...this I see...
PLOLOLIN
You are here...
...beside me.
PLOLON
Old friend...
TWIRL
くねくね
TWIRL
The vow I make...
...says that our bonds...
...shall never break.

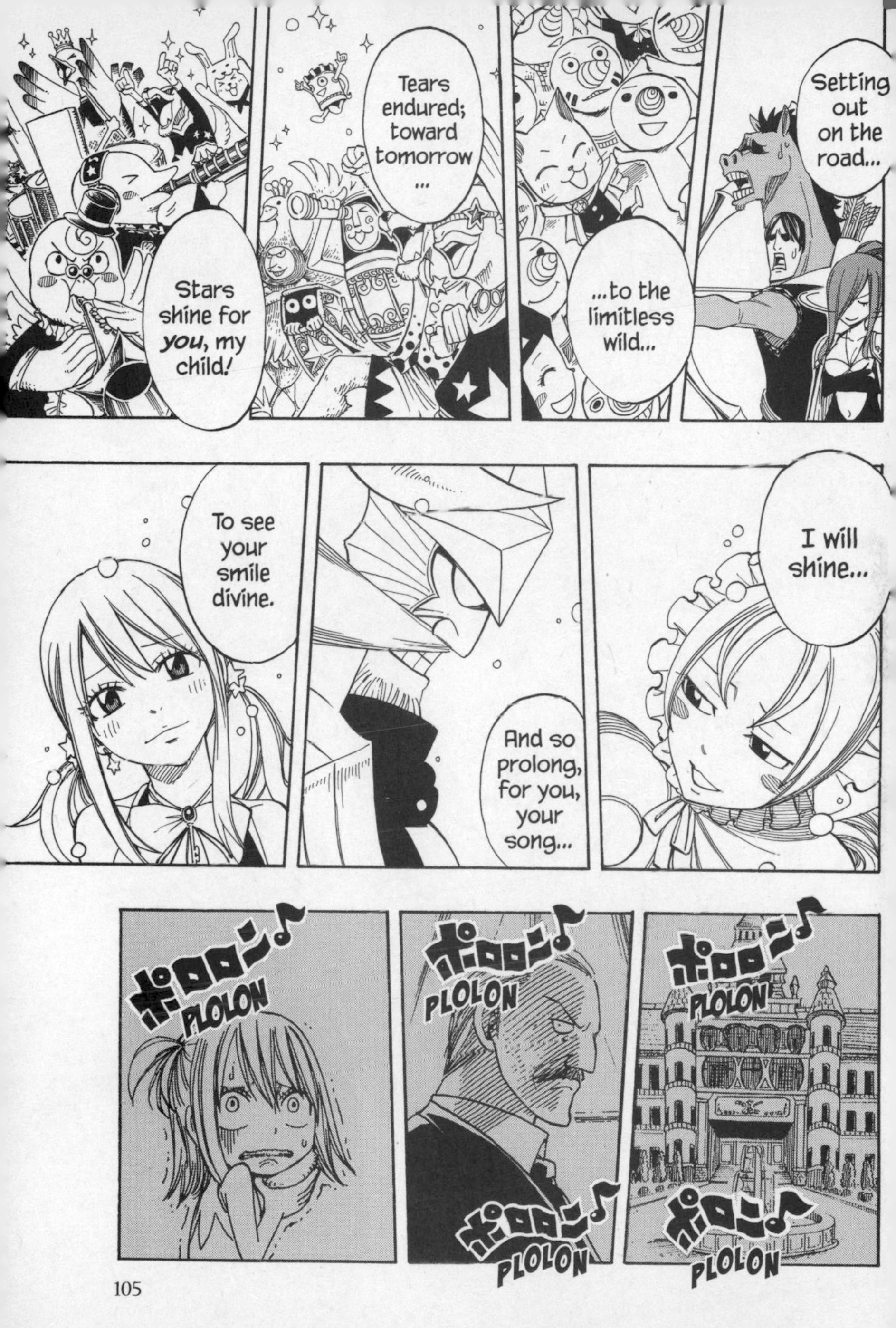
Setting out on the road...
...to the limitless wild...
Tears endured; toward tomorrow ...
Stars shine for *you*, my child!
I will shine...
And so prolong, for you, your song...
To see your smile divine.
PLOLON
PLOLON
PLOLON
PLOLON
PLOLON

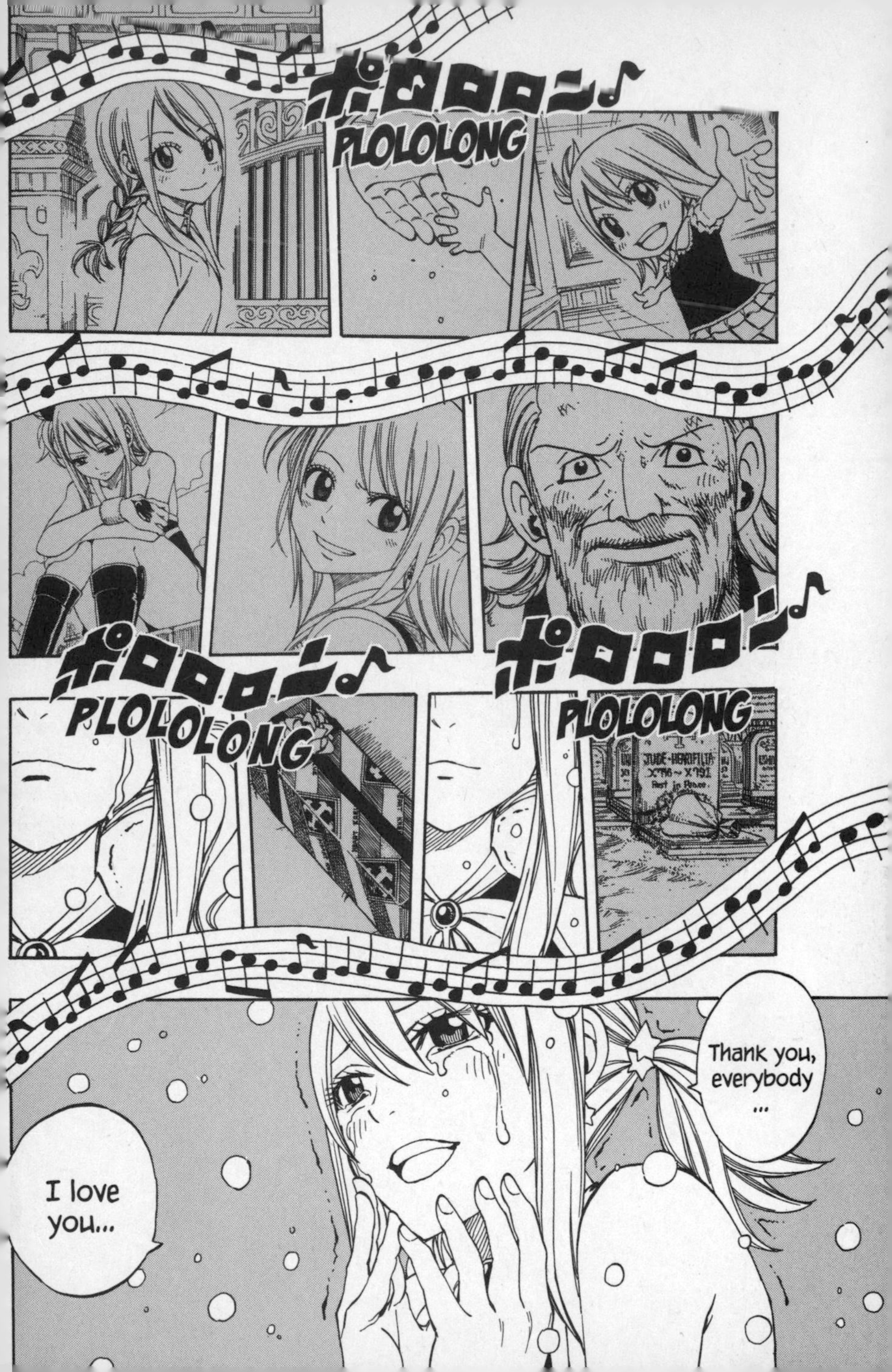
ポロロロン♪
PLOLOLONG
ポロロロン♪
PLOLOLONG
ポロロロン♪
PLOLOLONG
Thank you, everybody ...
I love you...

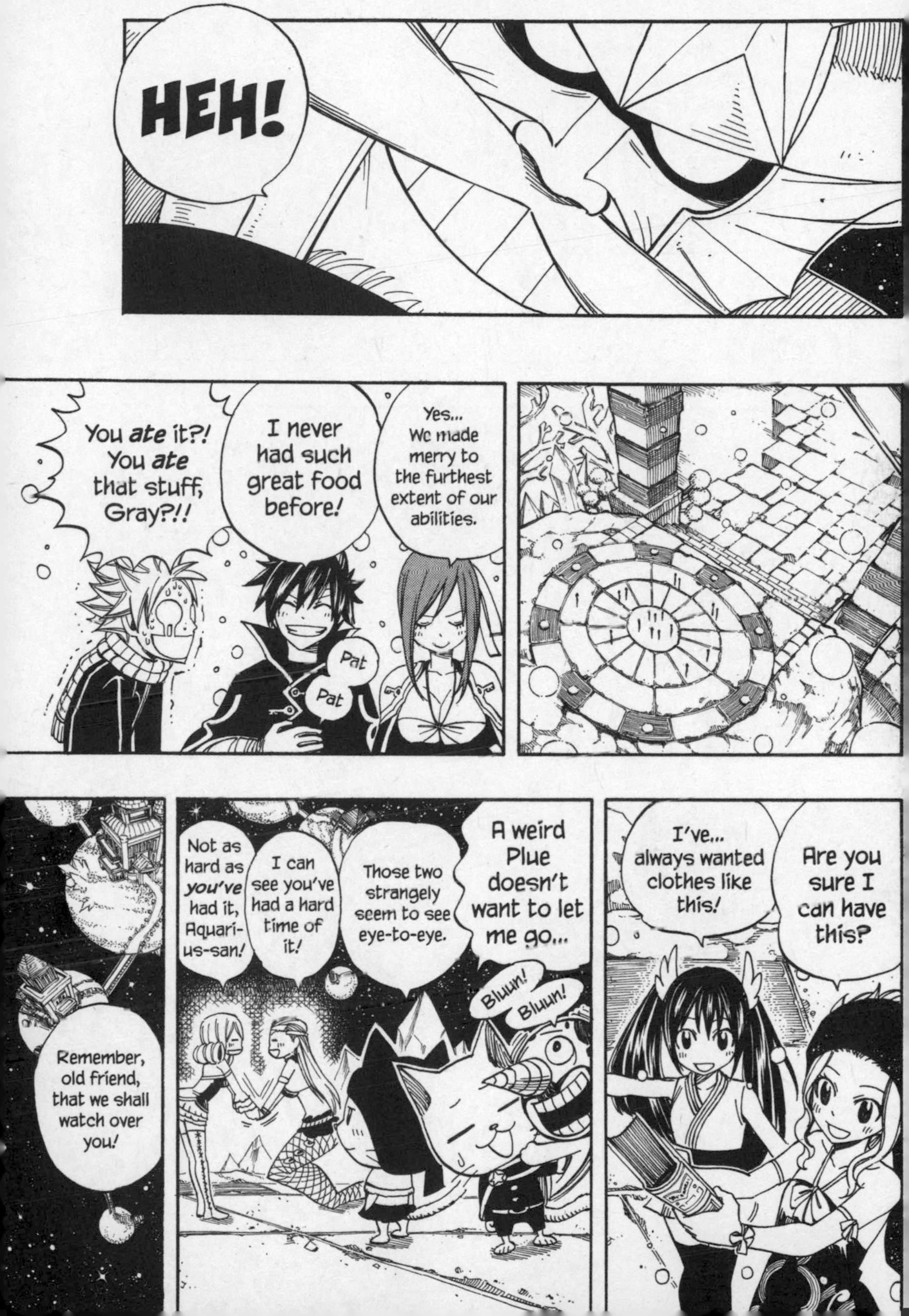
HEH!
Yes... We made merry to the furthest extent of our abilities.
I never had such great food before!
You *ate* it?! You *ate* that stuff, Gray?!!
Pat
Pat
Are you sure I can have this?
I've... always wanted clothes like this!
A weird Plue doesn't want to let me go...
Bluun! Bluun!
Those two strangely seem to see eye-to-eye.
I can see you've had a hard time of it!
Not as hard as *you've* had it, Aquari-us-san!
Remember, old friend, that we shall watch over you!

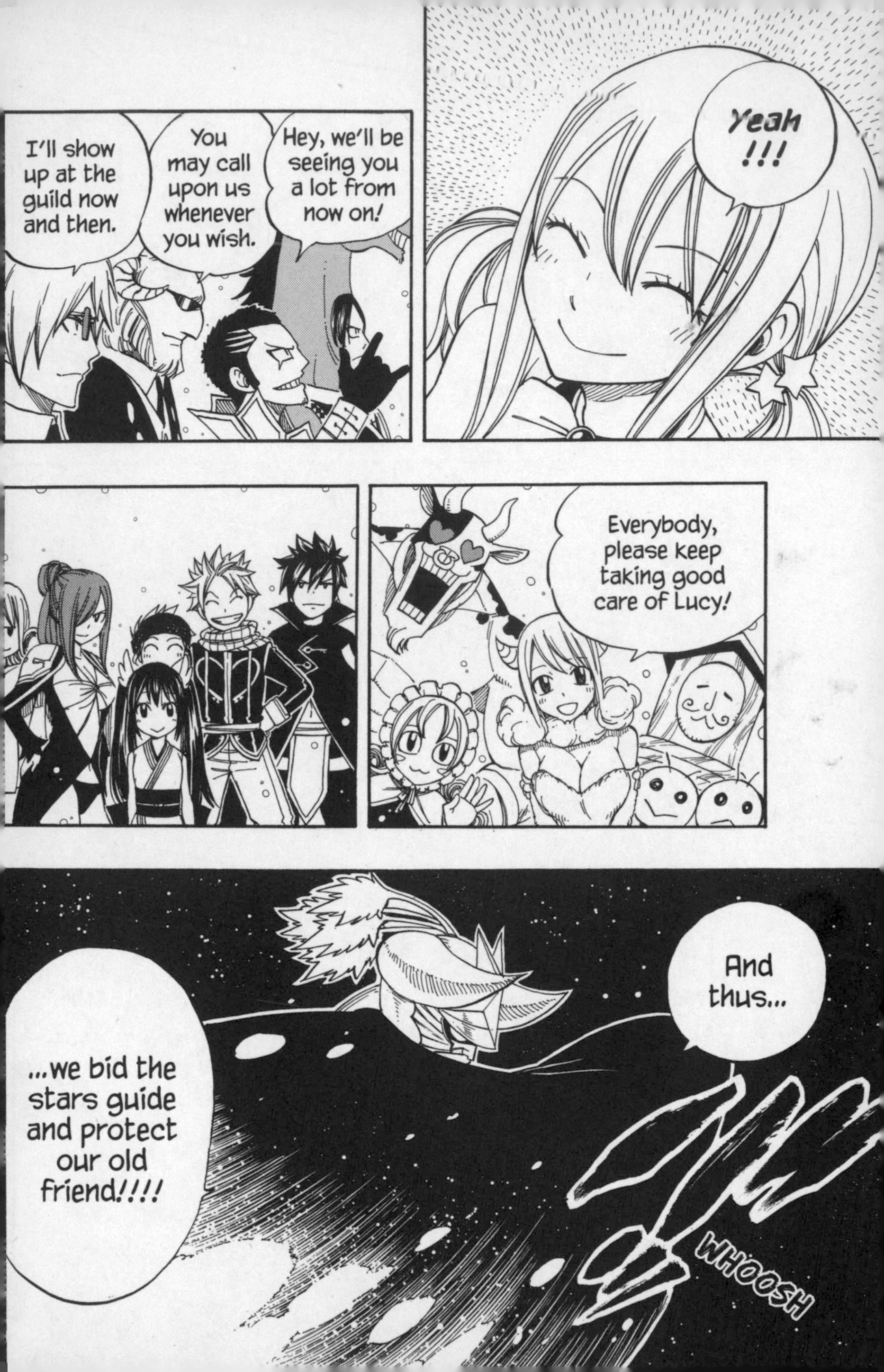
Yeah!!!
Hey, we'll be seeing you a lot from now on!
You may call upon us whenever you wish.
I'll show up at the guild now and then.
Everybody, please keep taking good care of Lucy!
And thus...
...we bid the stars guide and protect our old friend!!!!
WHOOSH

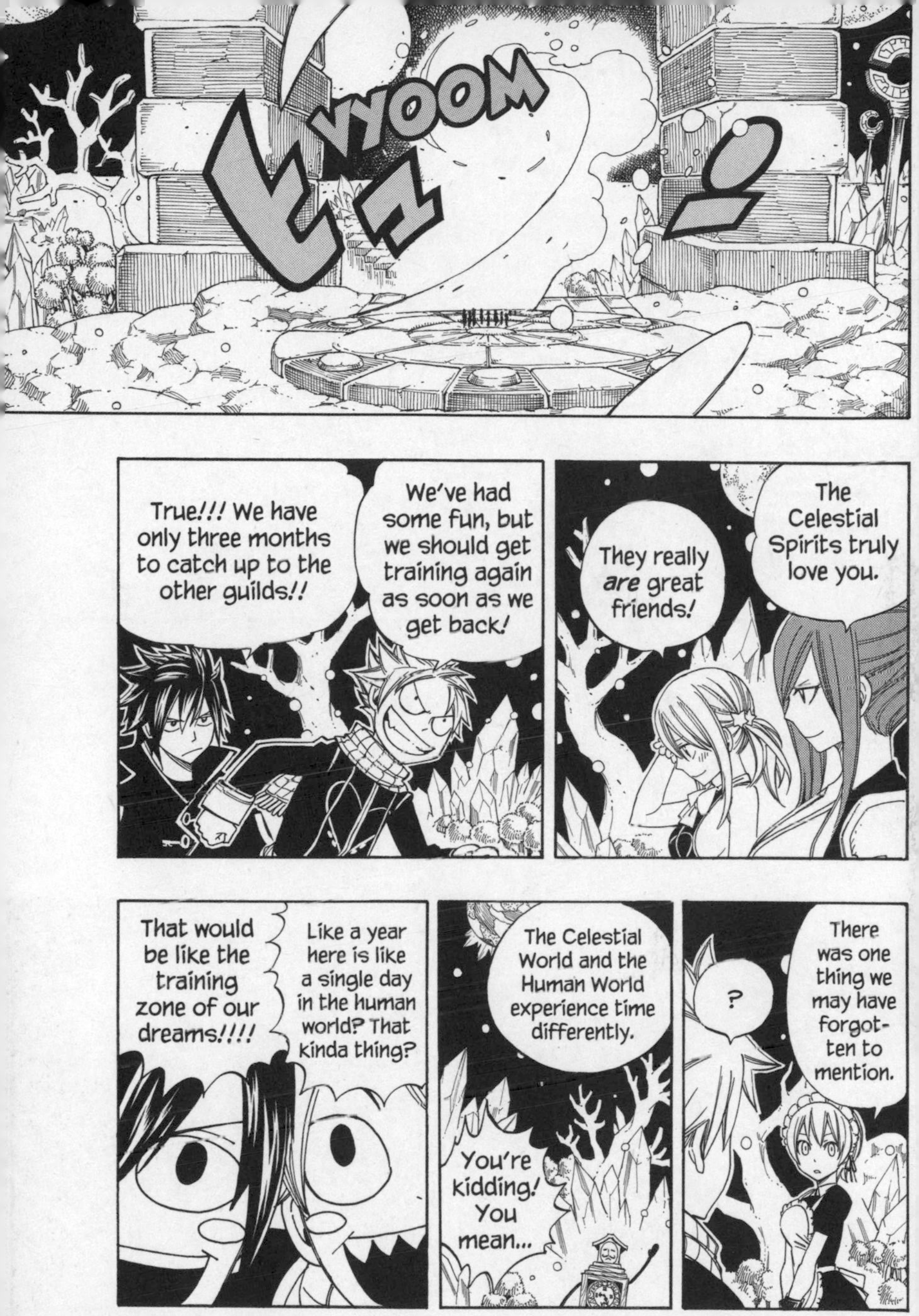
VYOOM
!
The Celestial Spirits truly love you.
They really *are* great friends!
We've had some fun, but we should get training again as soon as we get back!
True!!! We have only three months to catch up to the other guilds!!
There was one thing we may have forgotten to mention.
?
The Celestial World and the Human World experience time differently.
You're kidding! You mean...
Like a year here is like a single day in the human world? That kinda thing?
That would be like the training zone of our dreams!!!!

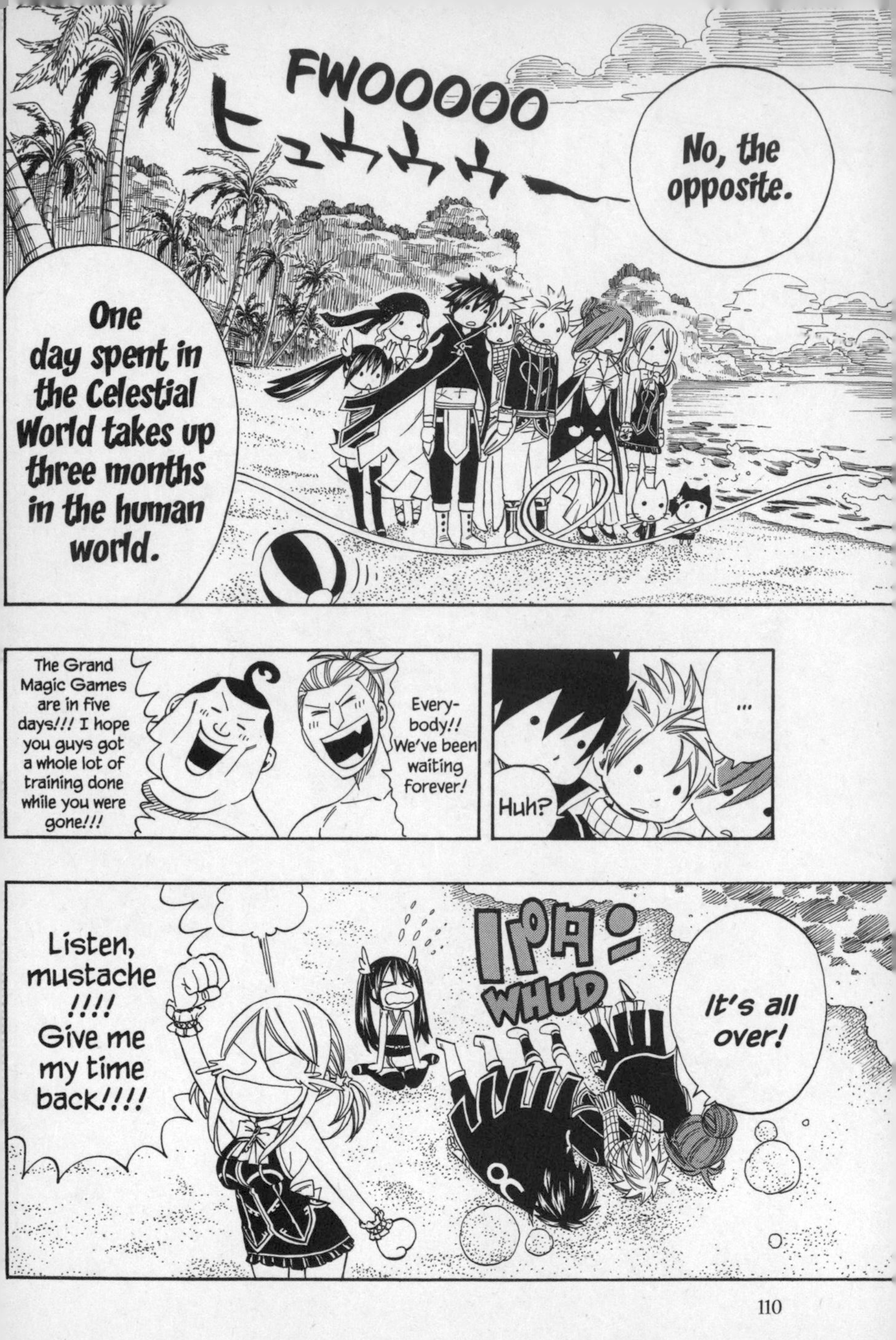
FWOOOOO
ヒュゥゥゥー
No, the opposite.
One day spent in the Celestial World takes up three months in the human world.
...
Huh?
Every-body!! We've been waiting forever!
The Grand Magic Games are in five days!!! I hope you guys got a whole lot of training done while you were gone!!!
It's all over!
WHUD
Listen, mustache!!!! Give me my time back!!!!

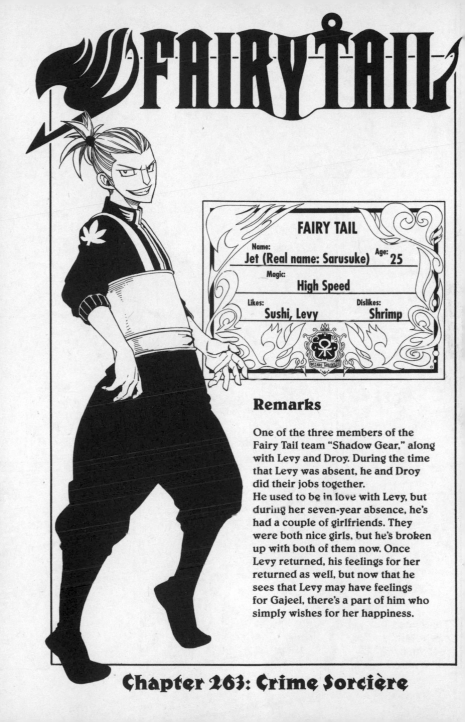

# FAIRY TAIL

## FAIRY TAIL

**Name:**
Jet (Real name: Sarusuke)   **Age:** 25

**Magic:**
High Speed

**Likes:**
Sushi, Levy

**Dislikes:**
Shrimp

## Remarks

One of the three members of the
Fairy Tail team "Shadow Gear," along
with Levy and Droy. During the time
that Levy was absent, he and Droy
did their jobs together.
He used to be in love with Levy, but
during her seven-year absence, he's
had a couple of girlfriends. They
were both nice girls, but he's broken
up with both of them now. Once
Levy returned, his feelings for her
returned as well, but now that he
sees that Levy may have feelings
for Gajeel, there's a part of him who
simply wishes for her happiness.

## Chapter 263: Crime Sorcière

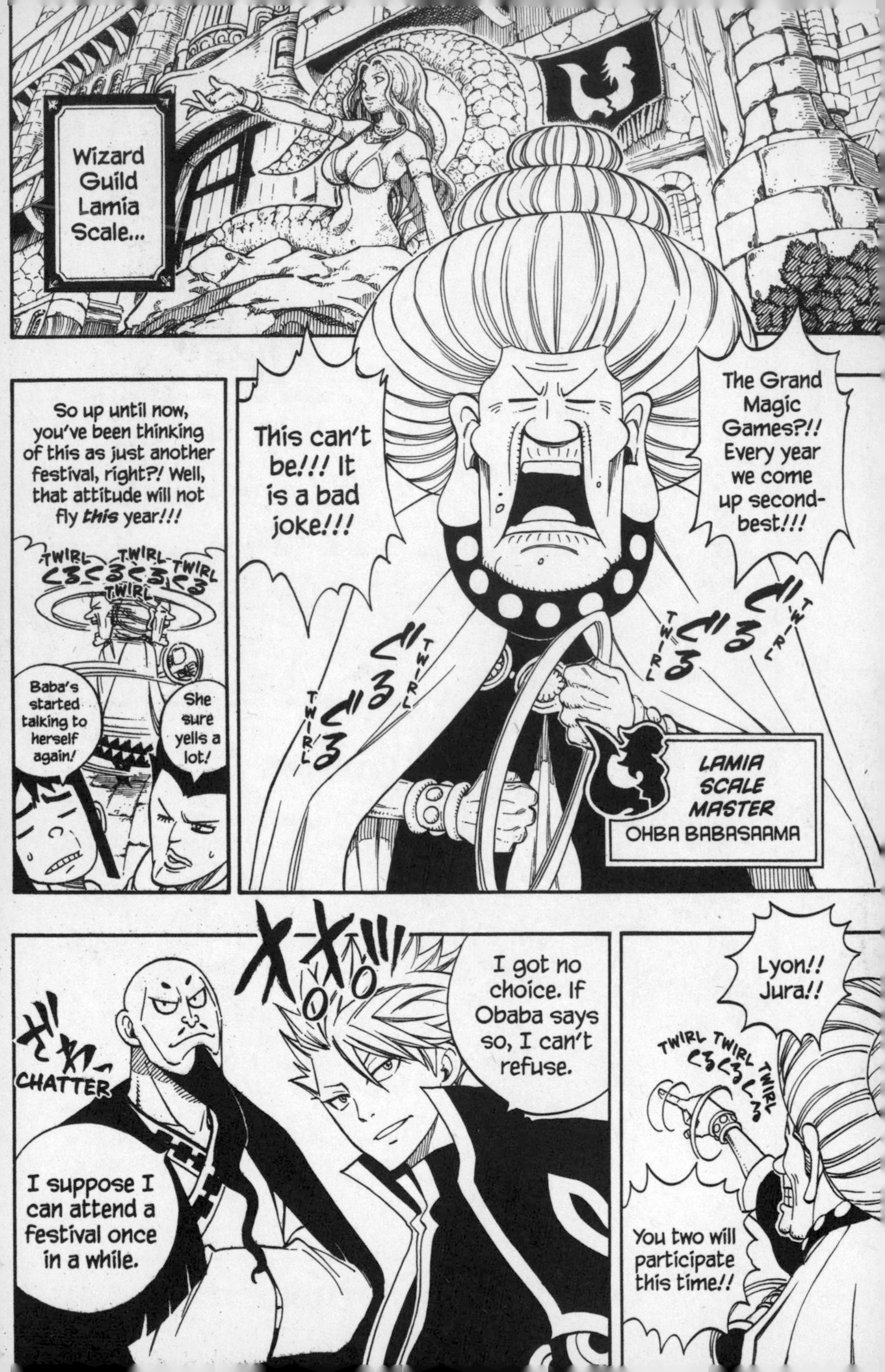
Wizard Guild Lamia Scale...
The Grand Magic Games?!! Every year we come up second-best!!!
This can't be!!! It is a bad joke!!!
TWIRL TWIRL TWIRL TWIRL
LAMIA SCALE MASTER
OHBA BABASAAMA
So up until now, you've been thinking of this as just another festival, right?! Well, that attitude will not fly *this* year!!!
TWIRL TWIRL TWIRL TWIRL
She sure yells a lot!
Baba's started talking to herself again!
Lyon!! Jura!!
TWIRL TWIRL TWIRL
You two will participate this time!!
I got no choice. If Obaba says so, I can't refuse.
CHATTER
I suppose I can attend a festival once in a while.

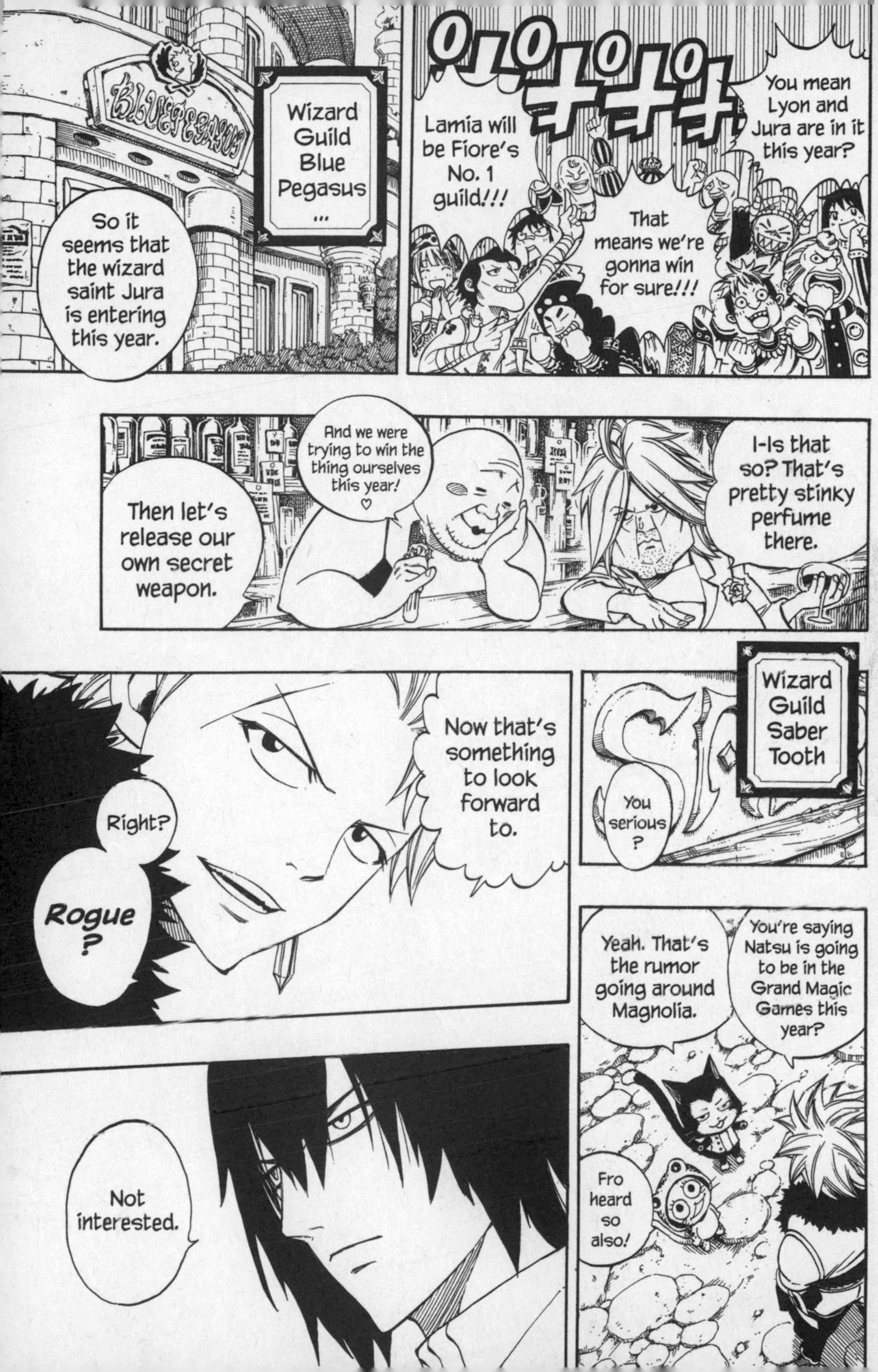
You mean Lyon and Jura are in it this year?
Lamia will be Fiore's No. 1 guild!!!
That means we're gonna win for sure!!!
Wizard Guild Blue Pegasus ...
BLUE PEGASUS
So it seems that the wizard saint Jura is entering this year.
I-Is that so? That's pretty stinky perfume there.
And we were trying to win the thing ourselves this year! ♡
Then let's release our own secret weapon.
Wizard Guild Saber Tooth
You serious?
You're saying Natsu is going to be in the Grand Magic Games this year?
Yeah. That's the rumor going around Magnolia.
Fro heard so also!
Now that's something to look forward to.
Right?
Rogue?
Not interested.

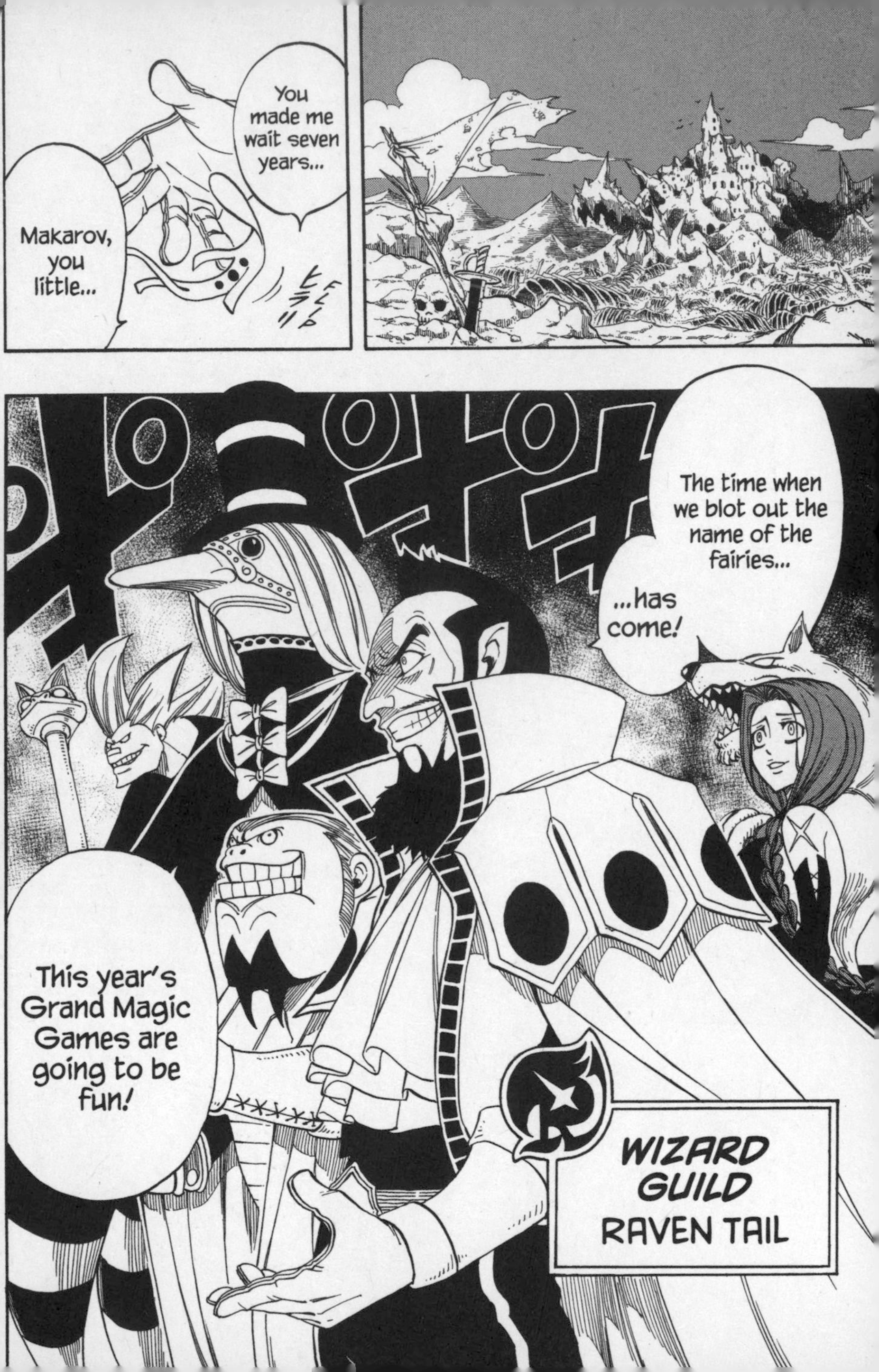
You made me wait seven years...
Makarov, you little...
The time when we blot out the name of the fairies...
...has come!
This year's Grand Magic Games are going to be fun!
WIZARD GUILD RAVEN TAIL

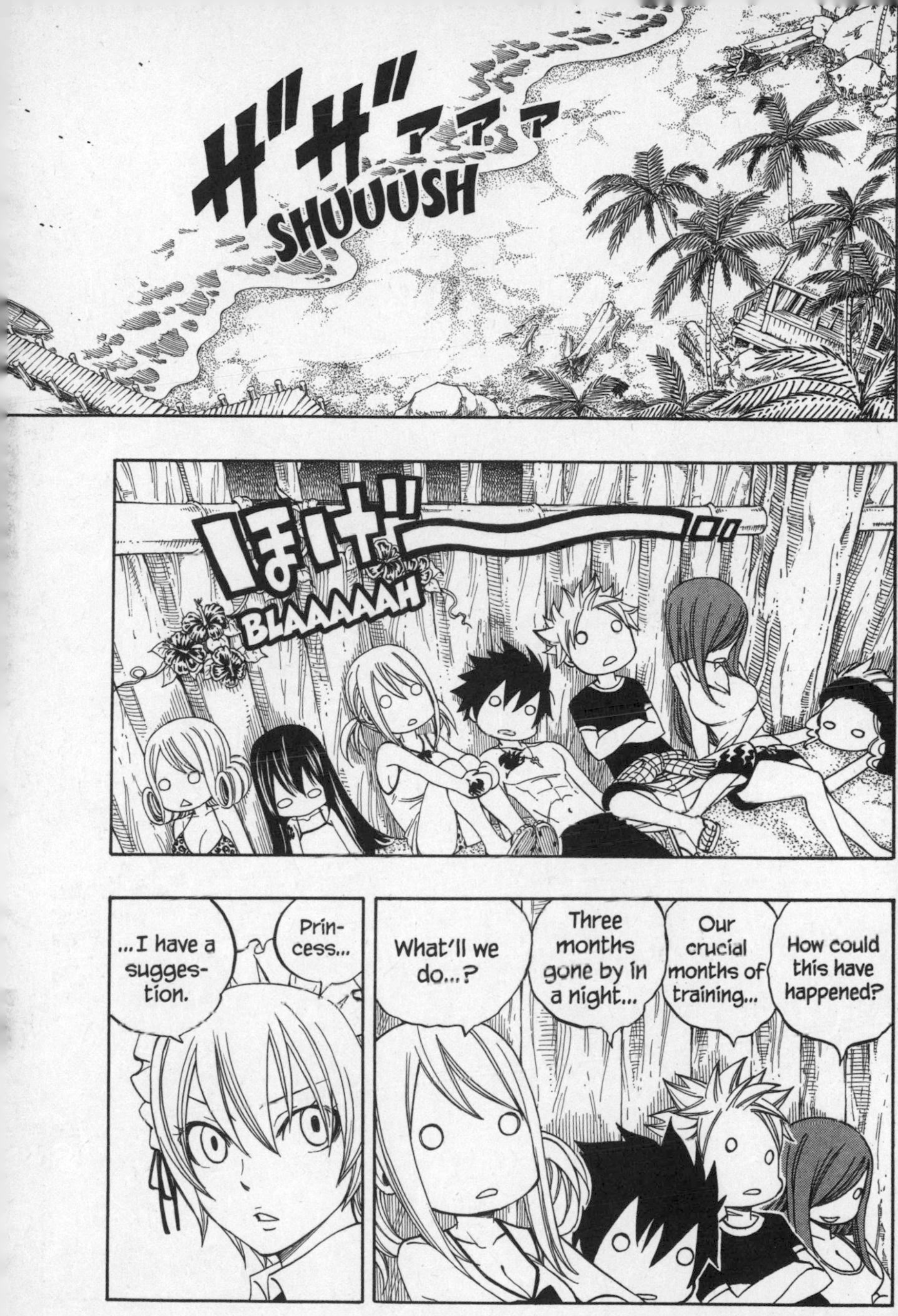
ザザァァァ
SHUUUSH
ほげー
BLAAAAAH
How could this have happened?
Our crucial months of training...
Three months gone by in a night...
What'll we do...?
Prin-cess...
...I have a sugges-tion.

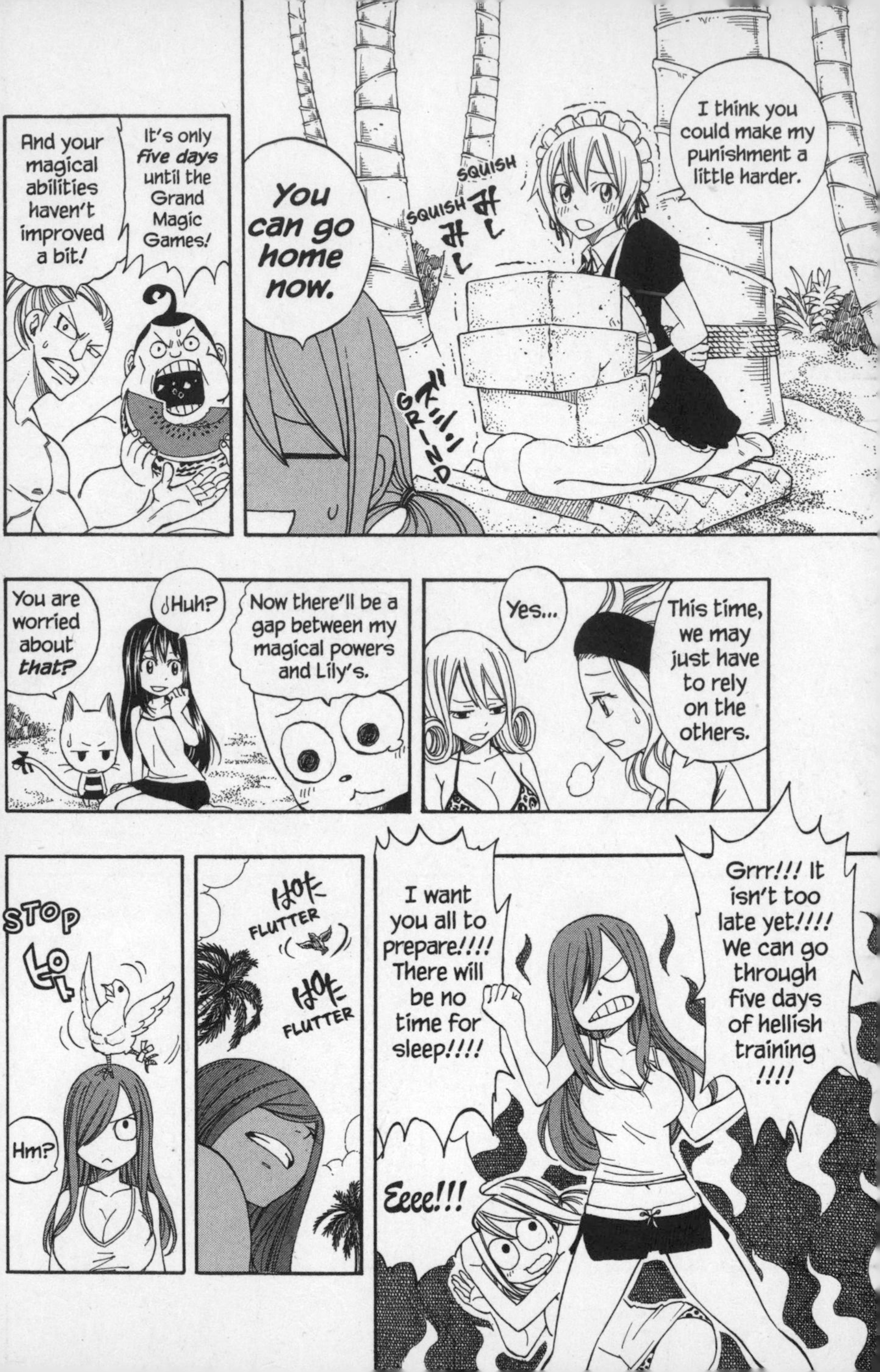
I think you could make my punishment a little harder.
SQUISH みし
SQUISH みし
GRIND
You can go home now.
It's only *five days* until the Grand Magic Games!
And your magical abilities haven't improved a bit!
This time, we may just have to rely on the others.
Yes...
Now there'll be a gap between my magical powers and Lily's.
Huh?
You are worried about that?
Grrr!!! It isn't too late yet!!!! We can go through five days of hellish training!!!!
I want you all to prepare!!!! There will be no time for sleep!!!!
Eeee!!!
FLUTTER
FLUTTER
STOP
Hm?

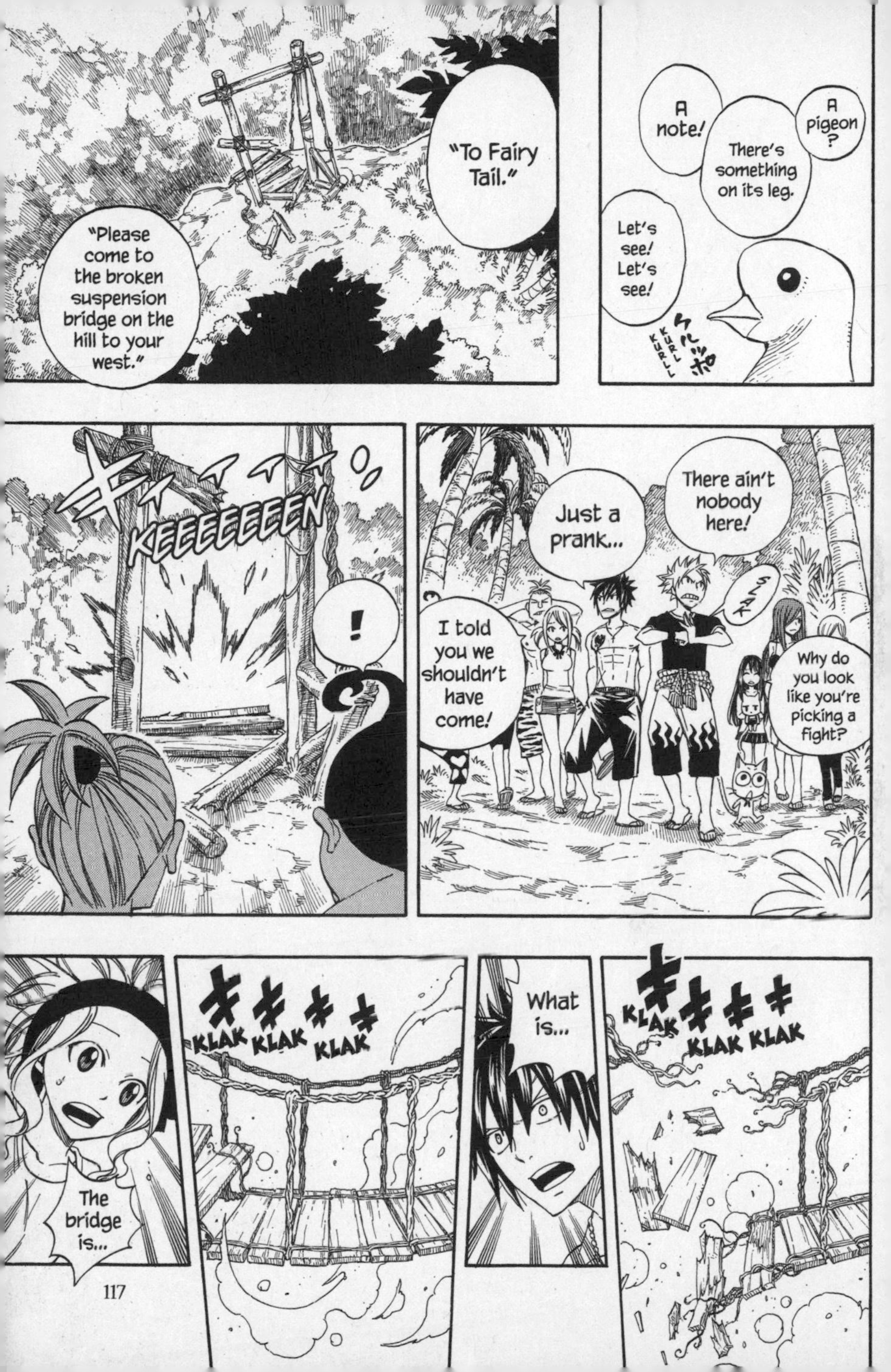
A pigeon?
There's something on its leg.
A note!
Let's see! Let's see!
KURLL KURL
"To Fairy Tail."
"Please come to the broken suspension bridge on the hill to your west."
There ain't nobody here!
Just a prank...
SLAK
Why do you look like you're picking a fight?
I told you we shouldn't have come!
KEEEEEEEN
!
KLAK KLAK KLAK KLAK
What is...
KLAK KLAK KLAK
The bridge is...

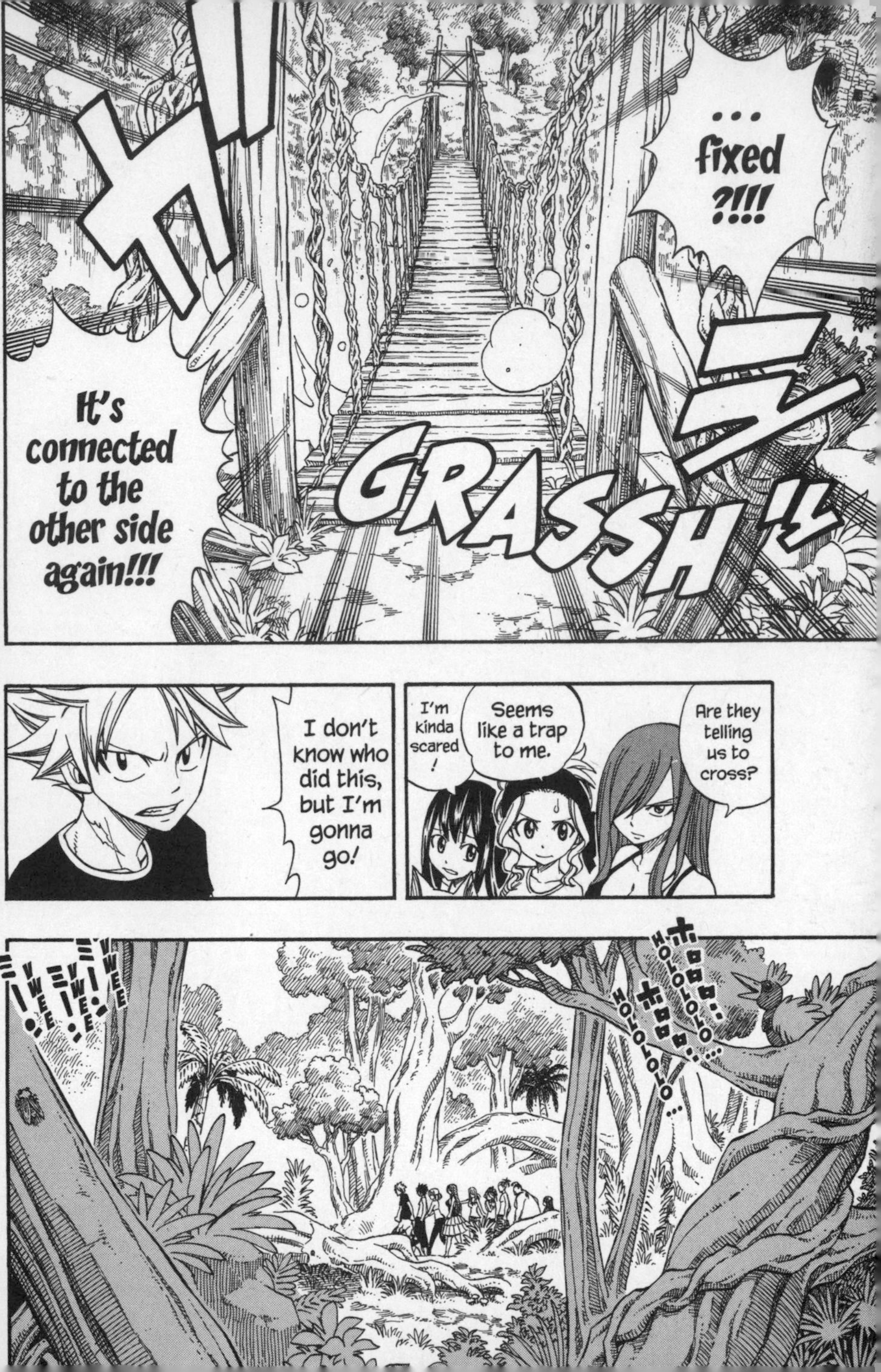

... fixed ?!!!
GRASSH!!
It's connected to the other side again!!!
Are they telling us to cross?
Seems like a trap to me.
I'm kinda scared!
I don't know who did this, but I'm gonna go!
HOLOLOLO...
HOLOLOLO...
VWEE...
VWEE...
VWEE

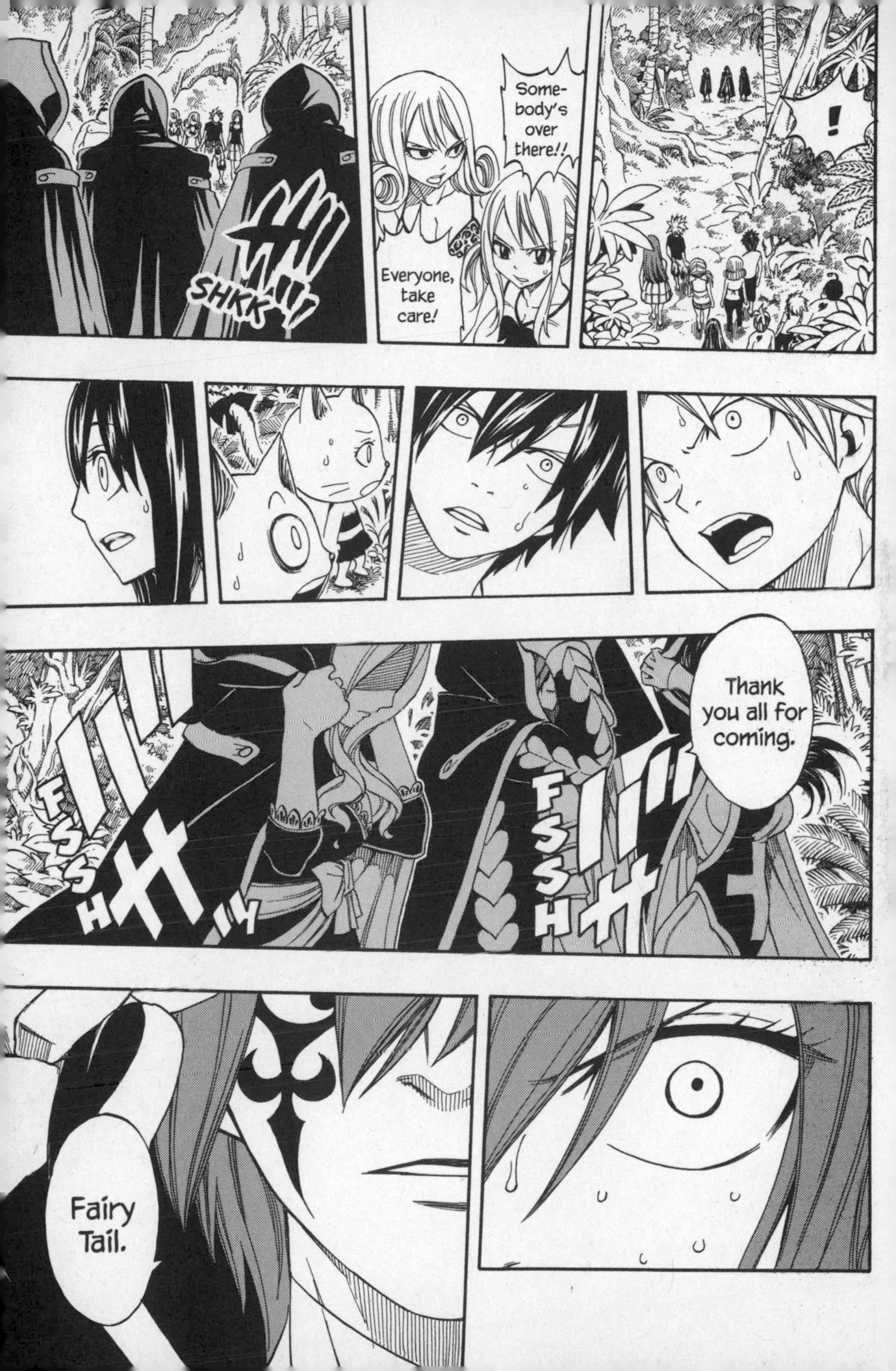
!
Somebody's over there!!
Everyone, take care!
SHKK
Thank you all for coming.
FSSH
FSSH
Fairy Tail.

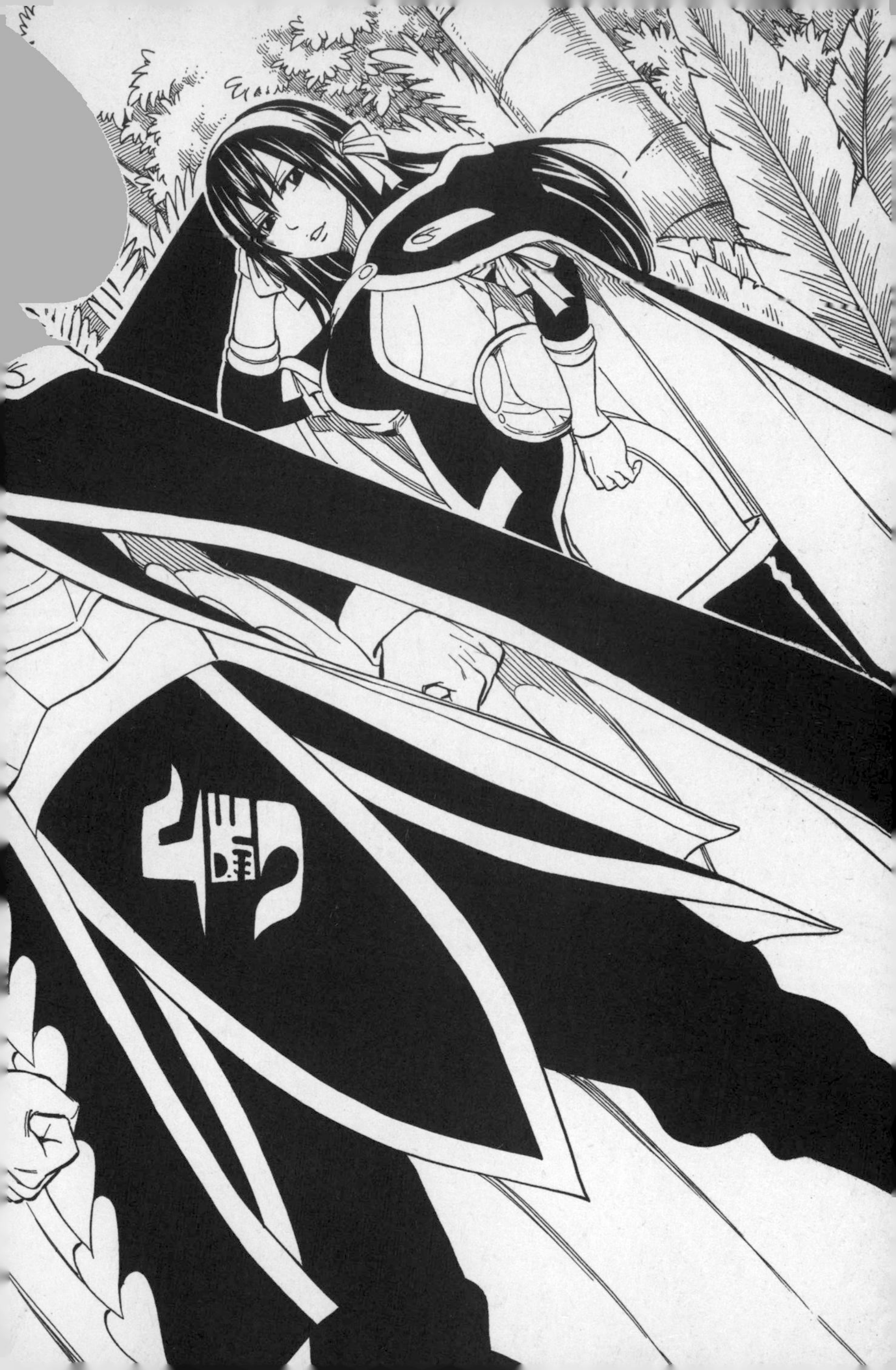

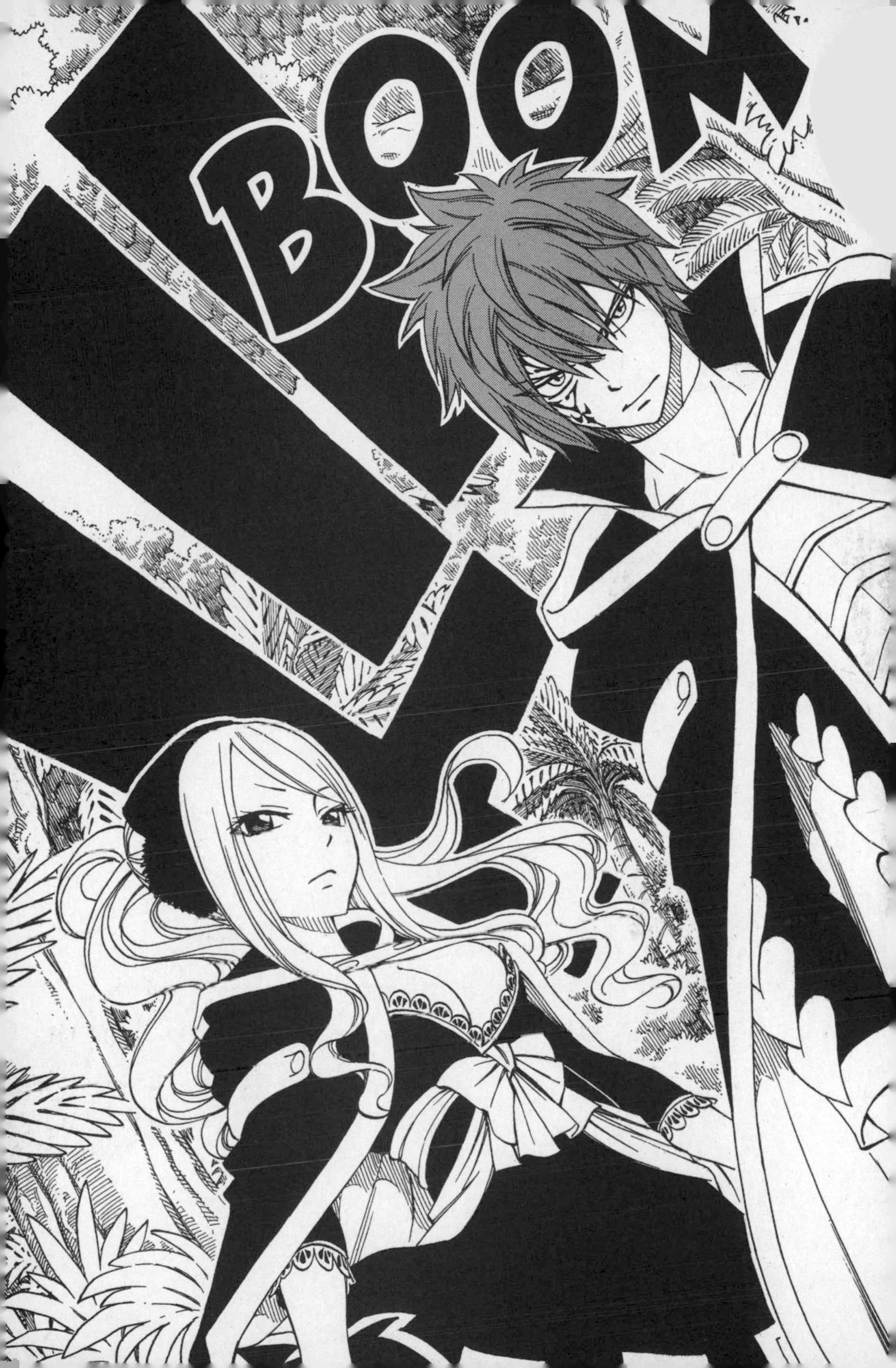
BOOM

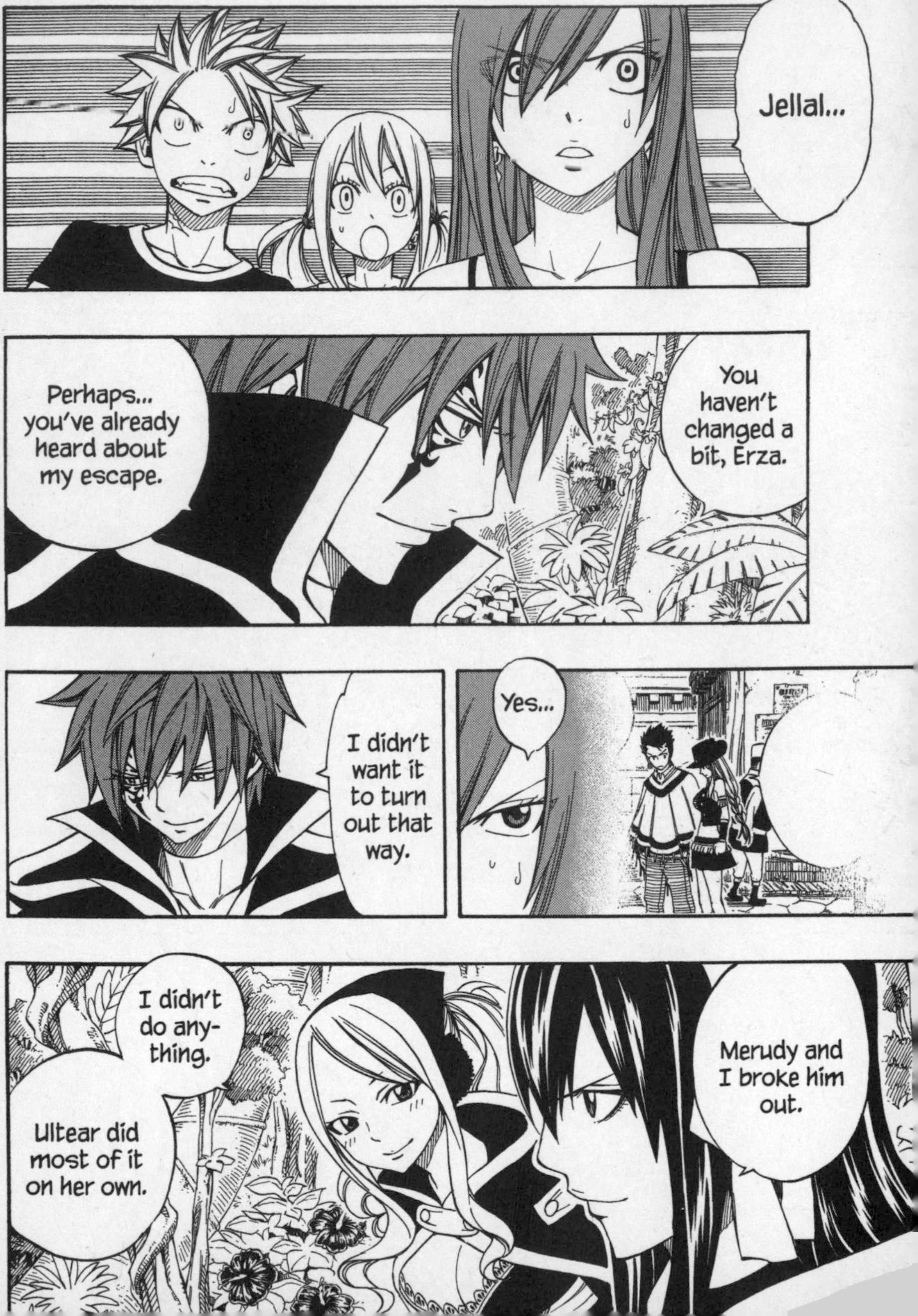
Jellal...
You haven't changed a bit, Erza.
Perhaps... you've already heard about my escape.
Yes...
I didn't want it to turn out that way.
Merudy and I broke him out.
I didn't do any-thing.
Ultear did most of it on her own.

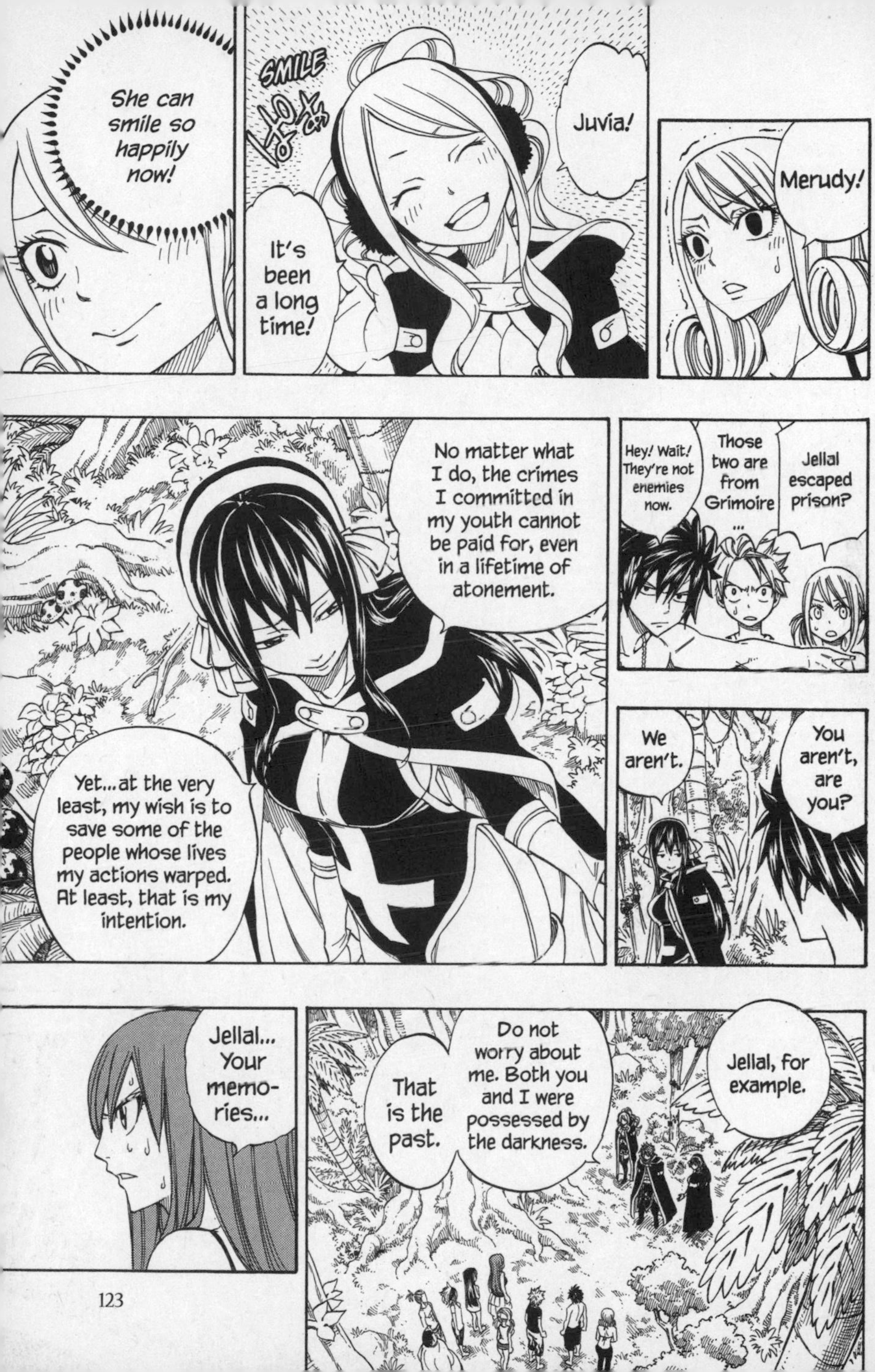

Merudy!
Juvia!
SMILE
It's been a long time!
She can smile so happily now!
Jellal escaped prison?
Those two are from Grimoire...
Hey! Wait! They're not enemies now.
You aren't, are you?
We aren't.
No matter what I do, the crimes I committed in my youth cannot be paid for, even in a lifetime of atonement.
Yet...at the very least, my wish is to save some of the people whose lives my actions warped. At least, that is my intention.
Jellal, for example.
Do not worry about me. Both you and I were possessed by the darkness.
That is the past.
Jellal... Your memories...

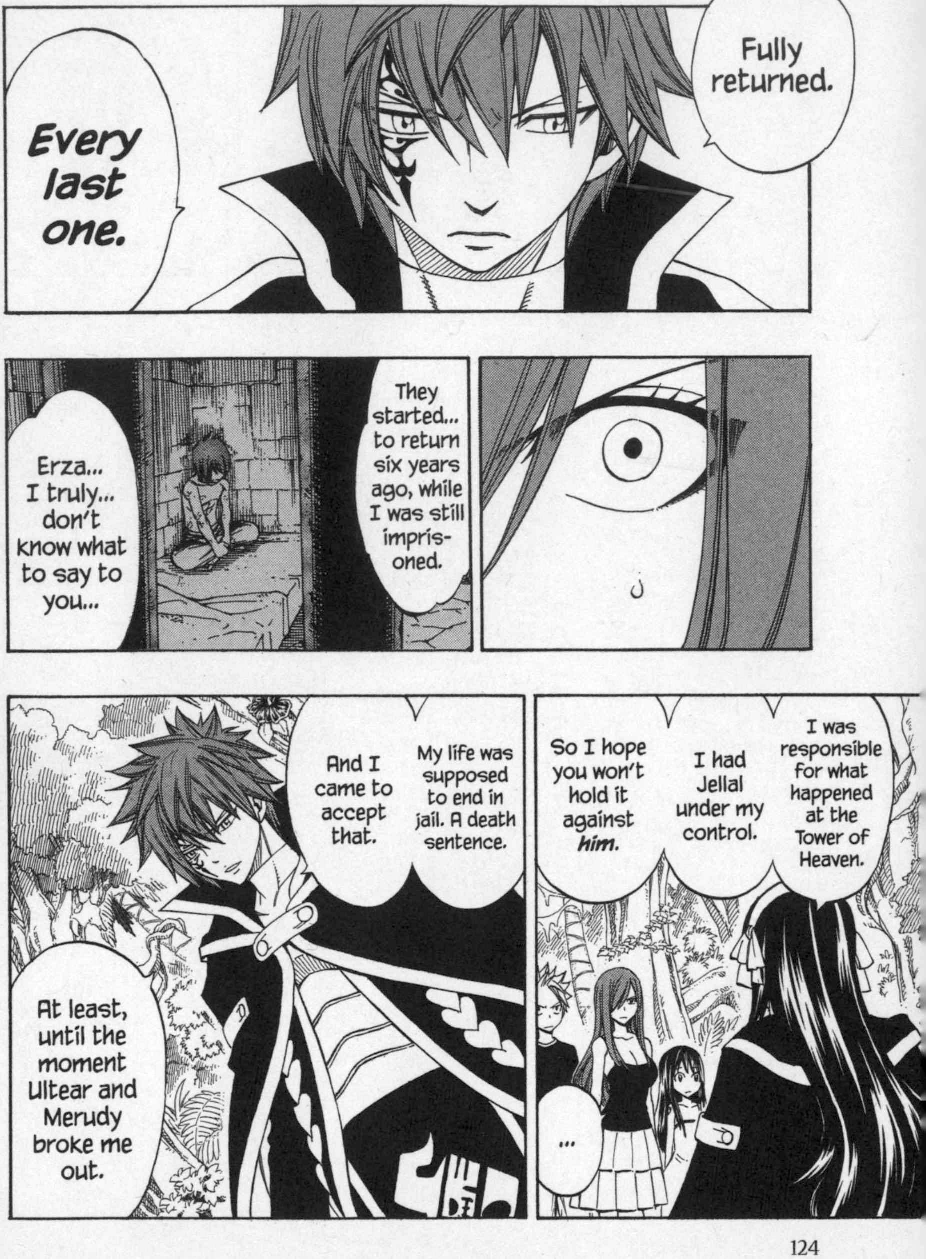
Fully returned.
*Every last one.*
They started... to return six years ago, while I was still impris- oned.
Erza... I truly... don't know what to say to you...
I was responsible for what happened at the Tower of Heaven.
I had Jellal under my control.
So I hope you won't hold it against *him.*
...
My life was supposed to end in jail. A death sentence.
And I came to accept that.
At least, until the moment Ultear and Merudy broke me out.

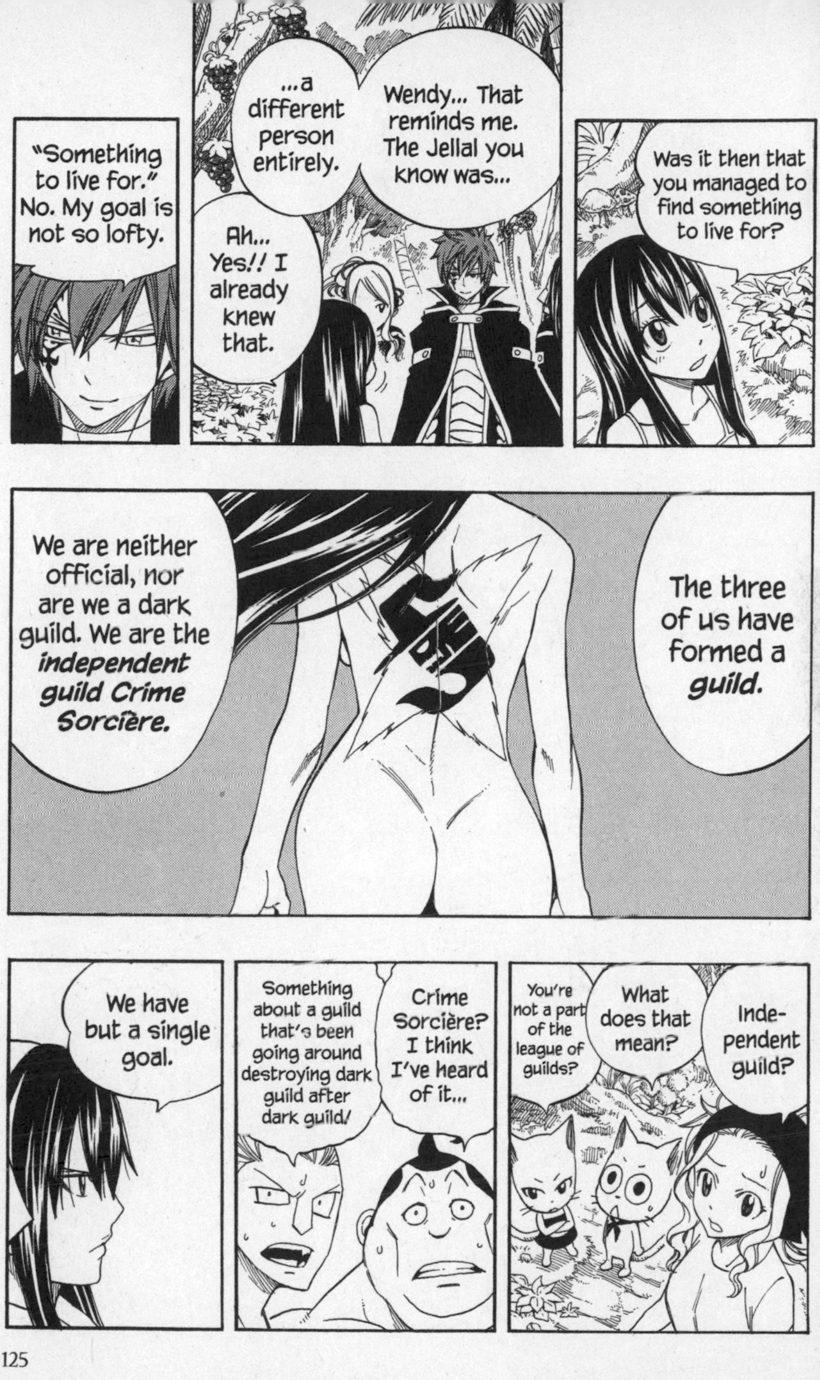
Was it then that you managed to find something to live for?
Wendy... That reminds me. The Jellal you know was...
...a different person entirely.
Ah... Yes!! I already knew that.
"Something to live for." No. My goal is not so lofty.
The three of us have formed a *guild.*
We are neither official, nor are we a dark guild. We are the *independent guild Crime Sorcière.*
Inde-pendent guild?
What does that mean?
You're not a part of the league of guilds?
Crime Sorcière? I think I've heard of it...
Something about a guild that's been going around destroying dark guild after dark guild!
We have but a single goal.

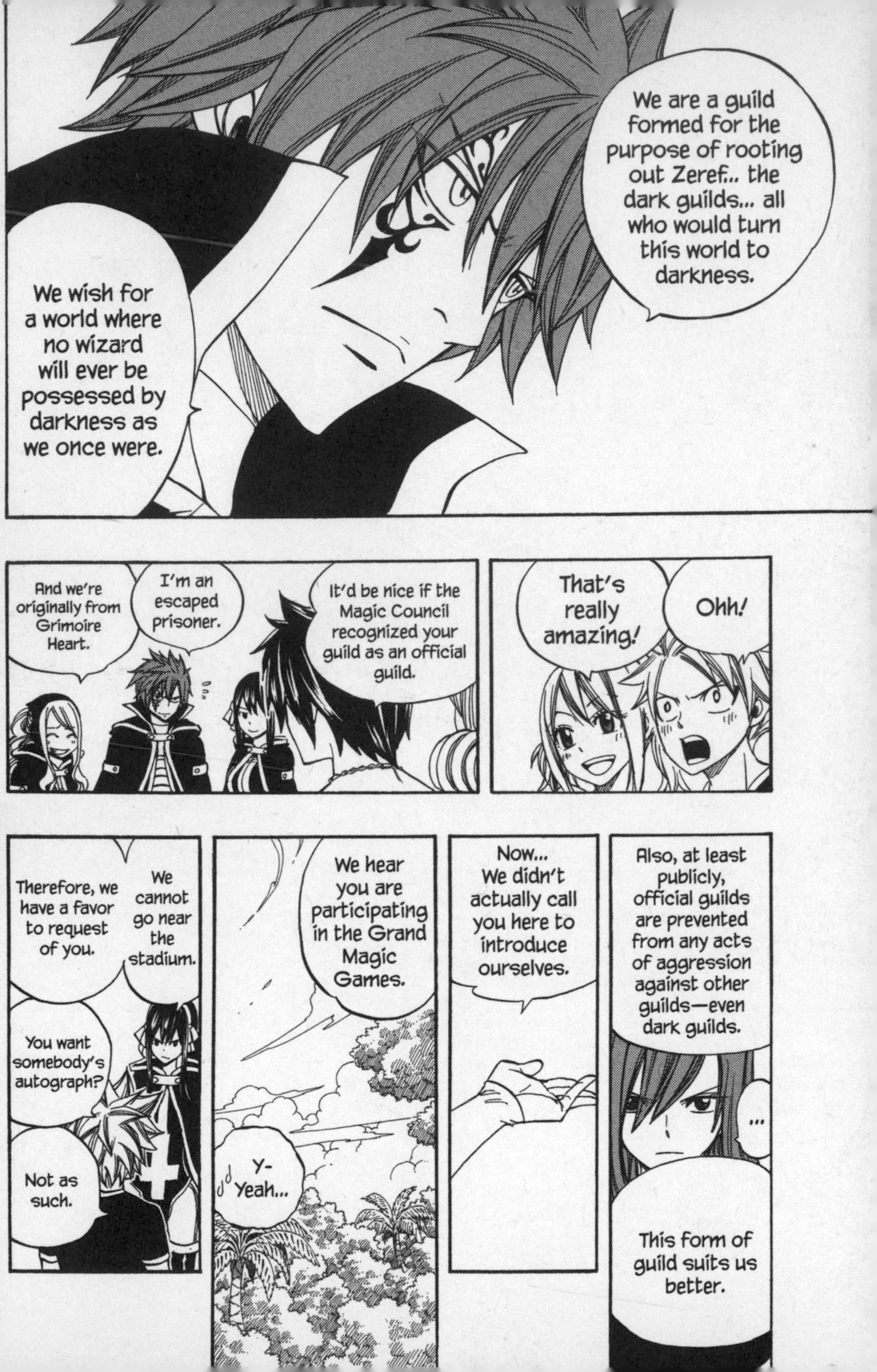
We are a guild formed for the purpose of rooting out Zeref... the dark guilds... all who would turn this world to darkness.
We wish for a world where no wizard will ever be possessed by darkness as we once were.
Ohh!
That's really amazing!
It'd be nice if the Magic Council recognized your guild as an official guild.
I'm an escaped prisoner.
And we're originally from Grimoire Heart.
Also, at least publicly, official guilds are prevented from any acts of aggression against other guilds—even dark guilds.
...
This form of guild suits us better.
Now... We didn't actually call you here to introduce ourselves.
We hear you are participating in the Grand Magic Games.
Y-Yeah...
We cannot go near the stadium.
Therefore, we have a favor to request of you.
You want somebody's autograph?
Not as such.

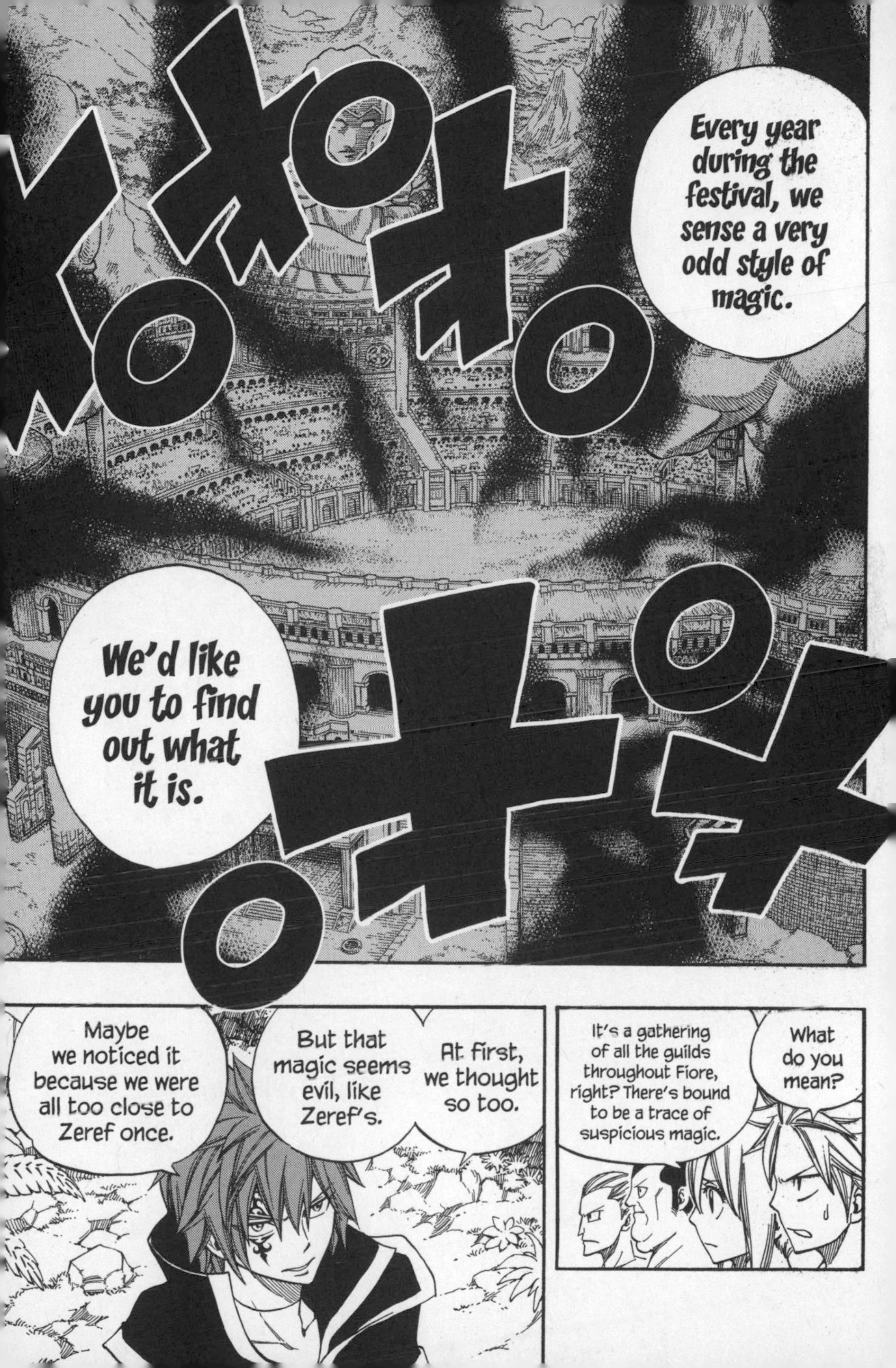
Every year during the festival, we sense a very odd style of magic.
We'd like you to find out what it is.
What do you mean?
It's a gathering of all the guilds throughout Fiore, right? There's bound to be a trace of suspicious magic.
At first, we thought so too.
But that magic seems evil, like Zeref's.
Maybe we noticed it because we were all too close to Zeref once.

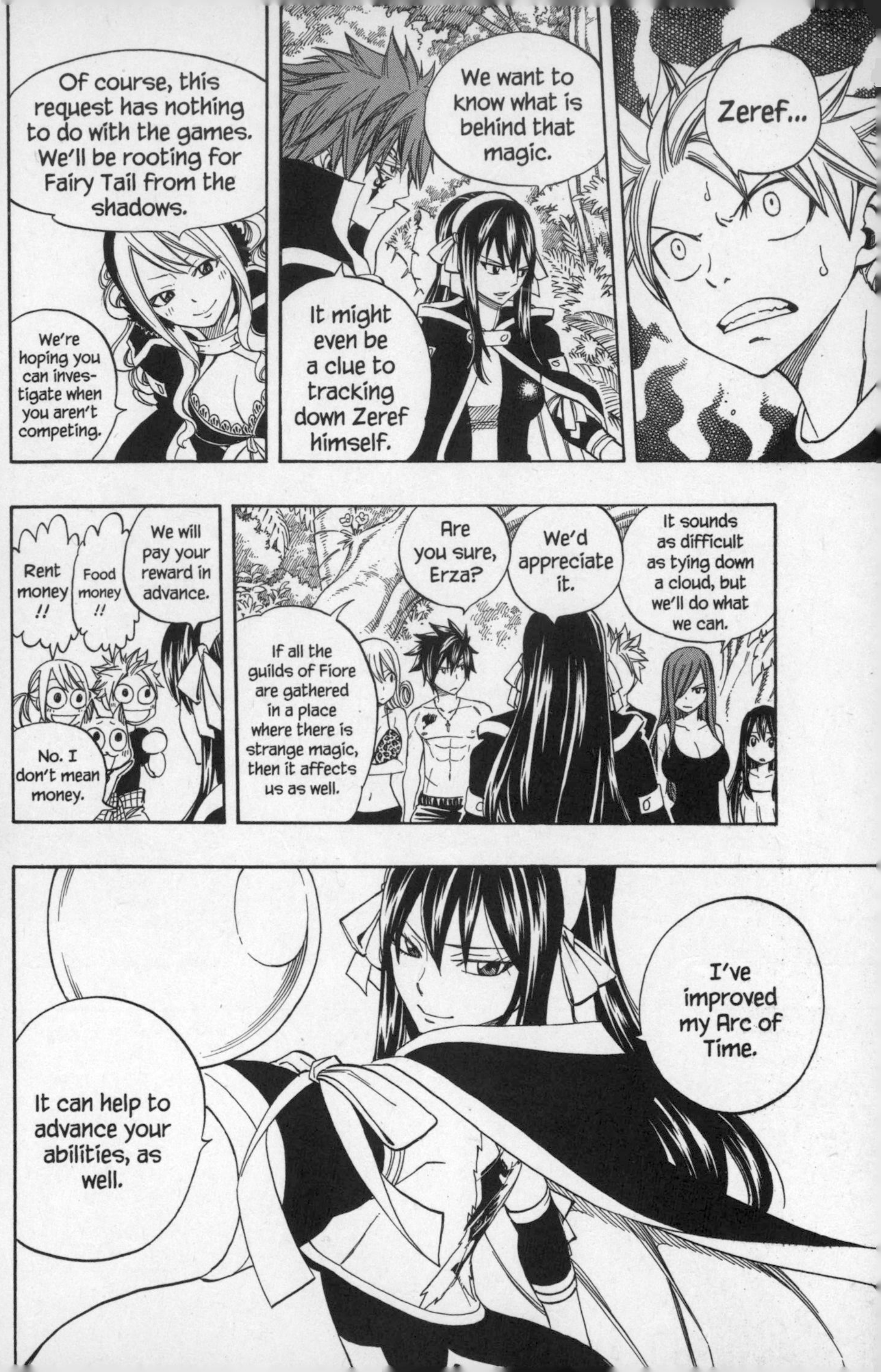
Zeref...
We want to know what is behind that magic.
It might even be a clue to tracking down Zeref himself.
Of course, this request has nothing to do with the games. We'll be rooting for Fairy Tail from the shadows.
We're hoping you can investigate when you aren't competing.
It sounds as difficult as tying down a cloud, but we'll do what we can.
We'd appreciate it.
Are you sure, Erza?
If all the guilds of Fiore are gathered in a place where there is strange magic, then it affects us as well.
We will pay your reward in advance.
Food money !!
Rent money !!
No. I don't mean money.
I've improved my Arc of Time.
It can help to advance your abilities, as well.

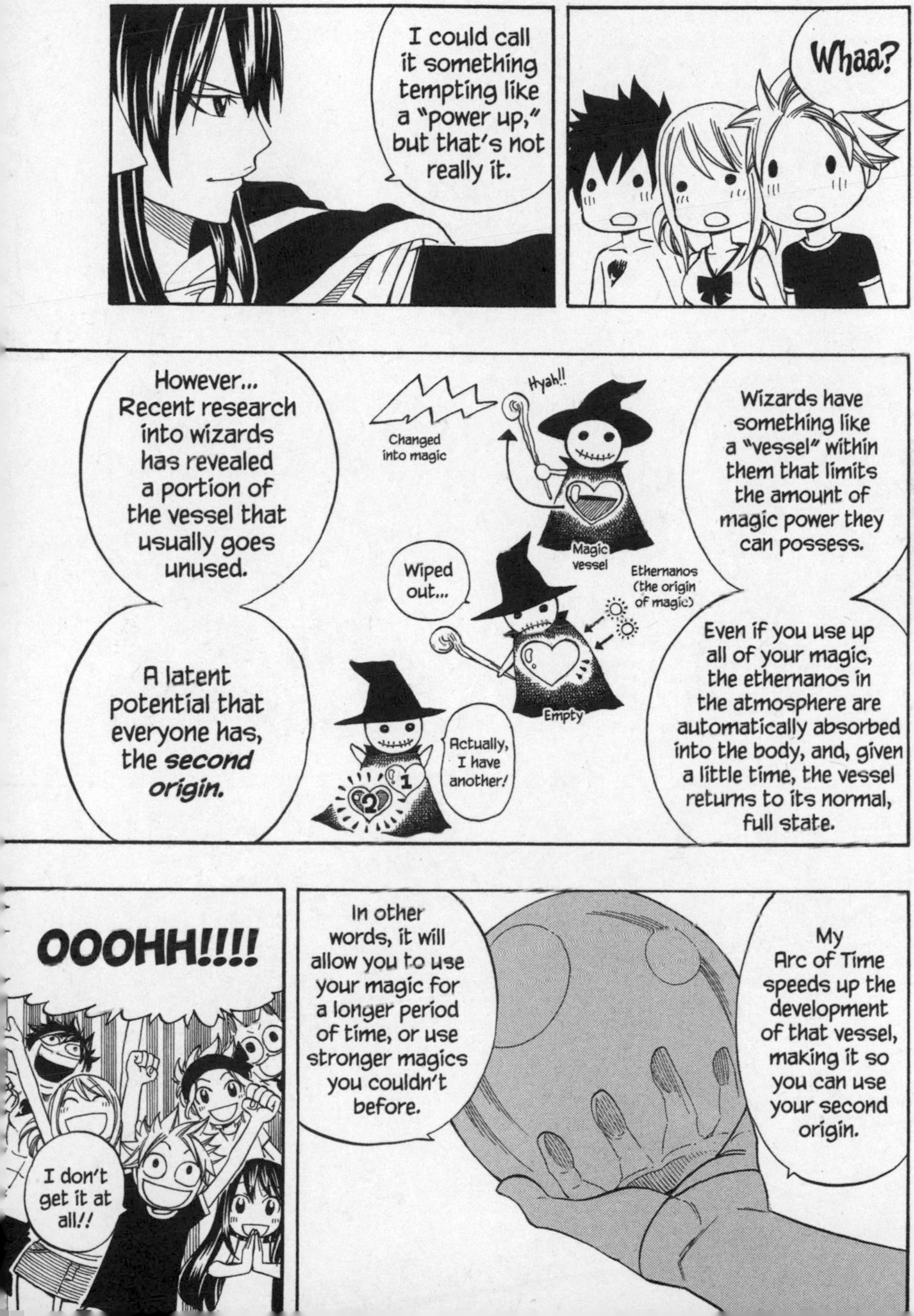
Whaa?
I could call it something tempting like a "power up," but that's not really it.
Wizards have something like a "vessel" within them that limits the amount of magic power they can possess.
Even if you use up all of your magic, the ethernanos in the atmosphere are automatically absorbed into the body, and, given a little time, the vessel returns to its normal, full state.
Hyah!!
Changed into magic
Magic vessel
Ethernanos (the origin of magic)
Wiped out...
Empty
Actually, I have another!
1
2
However... Recent research into wizards has revealed a portion of the vessel that usually goes unused.
A latent potential that everyone has, the *second origin.*
My Arc of Time speeds up the development of that vessel, making it so you can use your second origin.
In other words, it will allow you to use your magic for a longer period of time, or use stronger magics you couldn't before.
OOOHH!!!!
I don't get it at all!!

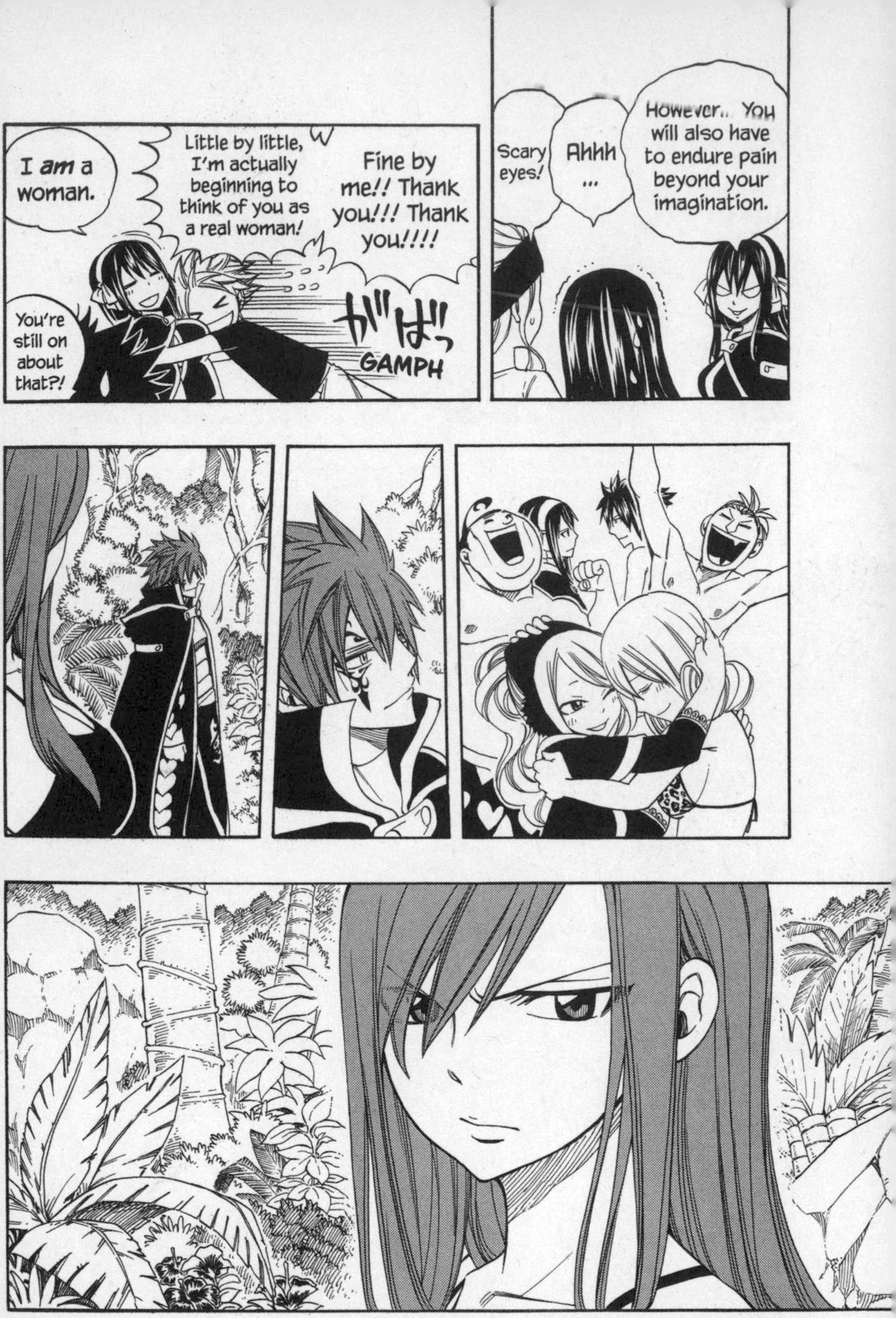
However... You will also have to endure pain beyond your imagination.
Ahhh ...
Scary eyes!
Fine by me!! Thank you!!! Thank you!!!!
Little by little, I'm actually beginning to think of you as a real woman!
I *am* a woman.
がばっ
GAMPH
You're still on about that?!

# FAIRY TAIL

## FAIRY TAIL

**Name:** Droy    **Age:** 25

**Magic:** Plant

**Likes:** Food    **Dislikes:** Spiders

### Remarks

Seven years ago, he was a thin wizard, but he awakened his love of food, and his body type changed before anybody noticed. During the period when his partner Jet had his girlfriends, he would try to act strong, saying, "Steak is my love interest!" to everyone who would listen. But his frustration resulted only in more weight gain. He fell in love a number of times, but when he tried to ask them out, they would always reject him. Now that Levy is back, his old feelings for her have returned, but he's also noticed that Levy may have fallen for Gajeel, and seeing that has resulted only in more weight gain.

## Chapter 264: Only the Amount of Time Lost

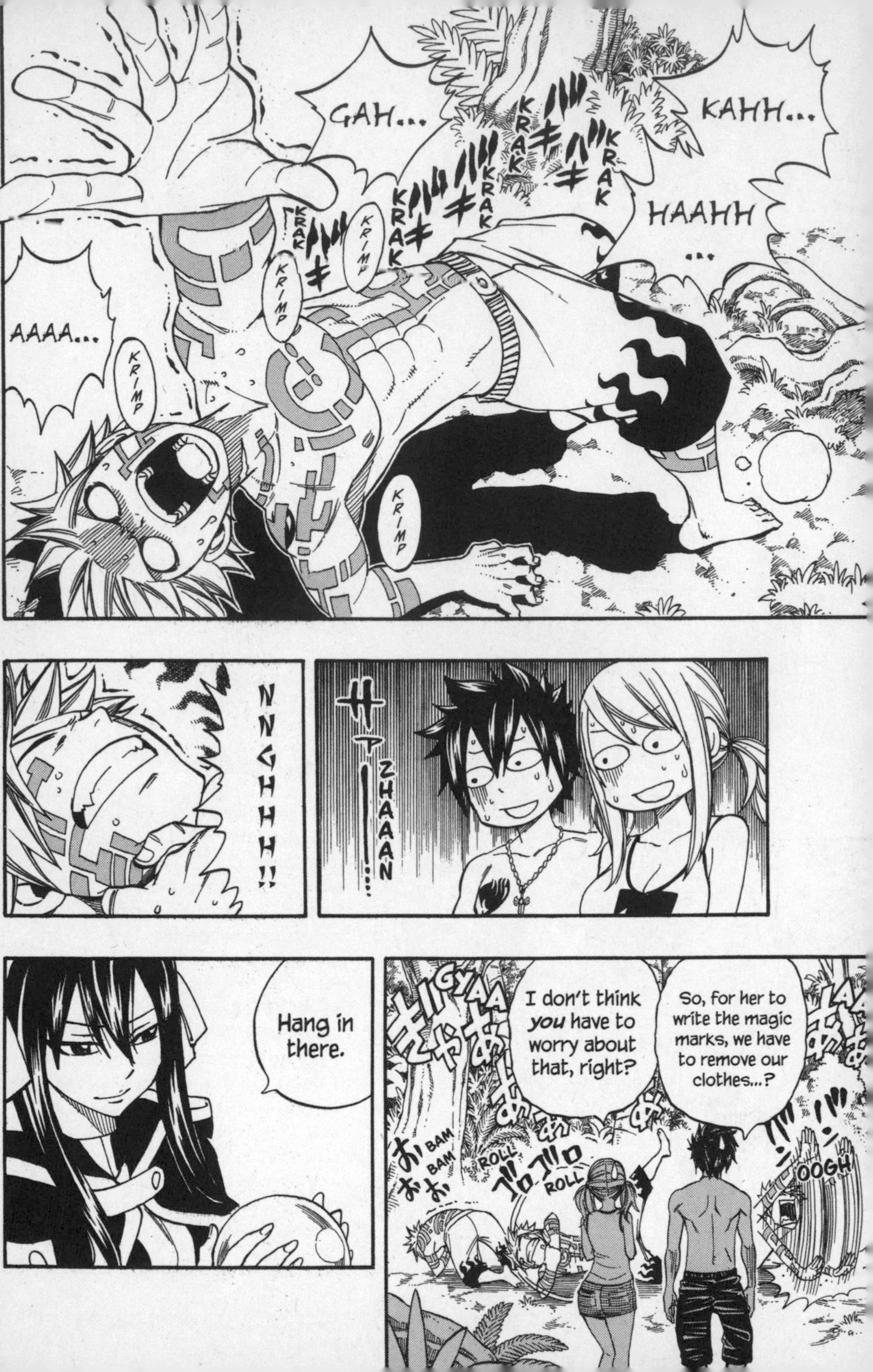
KAHH...
HAAHH...
KRAK KRAK KRAK KRAK KRAK
GAH...
KRIMP KRIMP KRIMP KRIMP
AAAA...
ZHAAAAN...
NNGHHHH!!
OOGH
So, for her to write the magic marks, we have to remove our clothes...?
I don't think *you* have to worry about that, right?
GYAA
BAM BAM
ROLL ROLL
Hang in there.

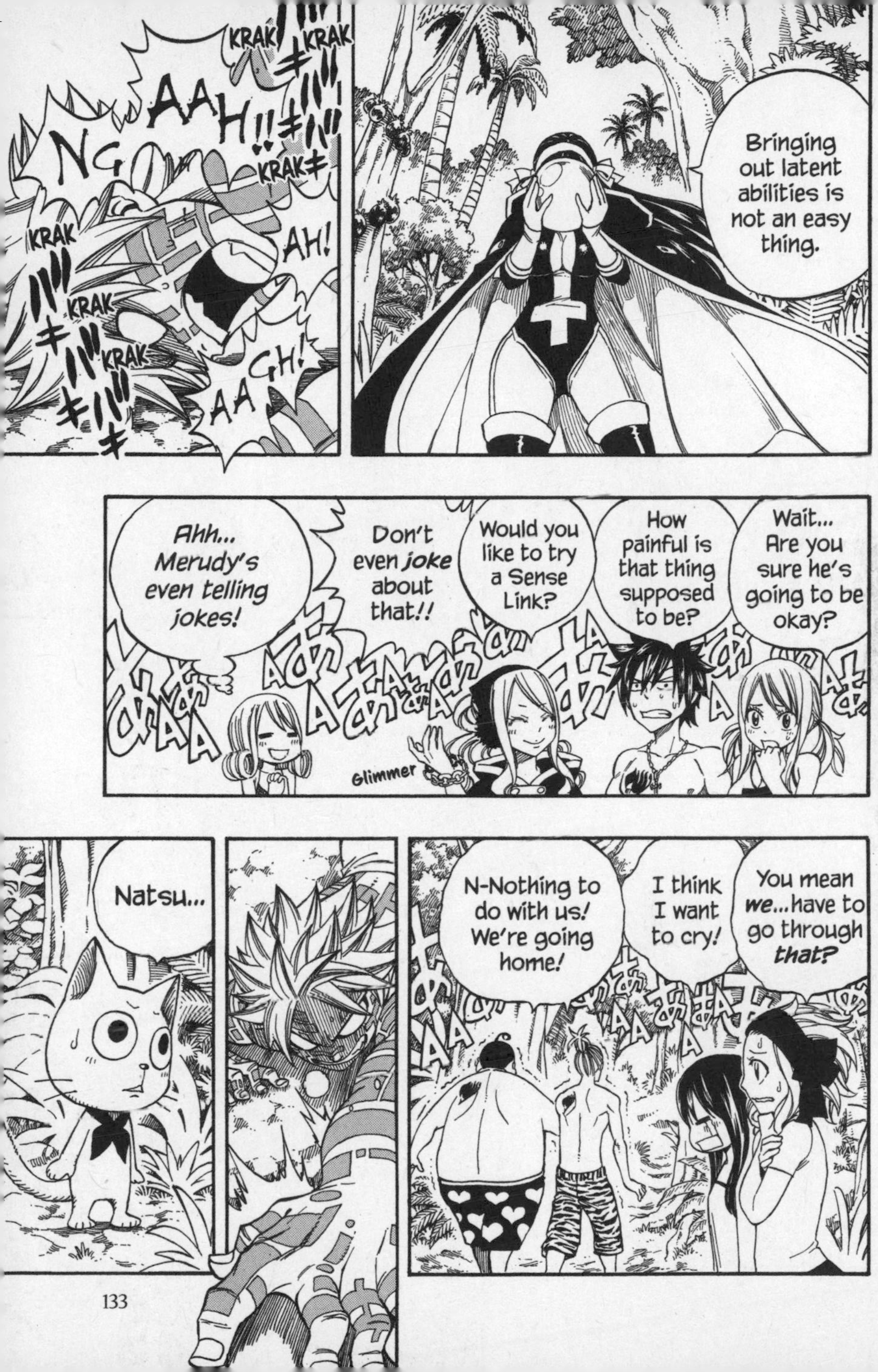
Bringing out latent abilities is not an easy thing.
KRAK
KRAK
AAH!!
NG
KRAK
AH!
KRAK
KRAK
KRAK
AAGH!
Wait... Are you sure he's going to be okay?
How painful is that thing supposed to be?
Would you like to try a Sense Link?
Don't even *joke* about that!!
Ahh... Merudy's even telling jokes!
Glimmer
You mean *we*...have to go through *that*?
I think I want to cry!
N-Nothing to do with us! We're going home!
Natsu...

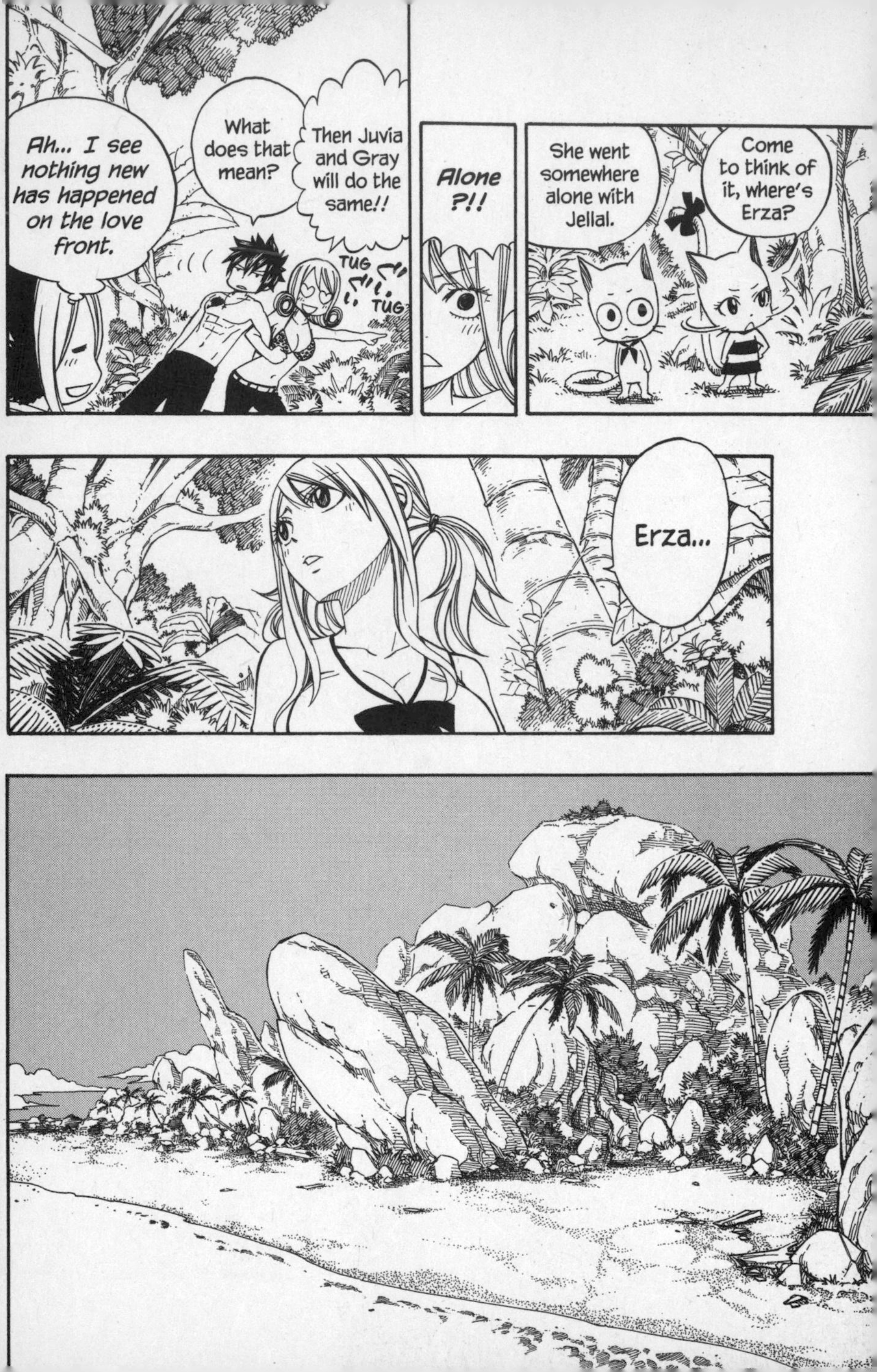
Come to think of it, where's Erza?
She went somewhere alone with Jellal.
Alone ?!!
Then Juvia and Gray will do the same!!
What does that mean?
TUG TUG
Ah... I see nothing new has happened on the love front.
Erza...

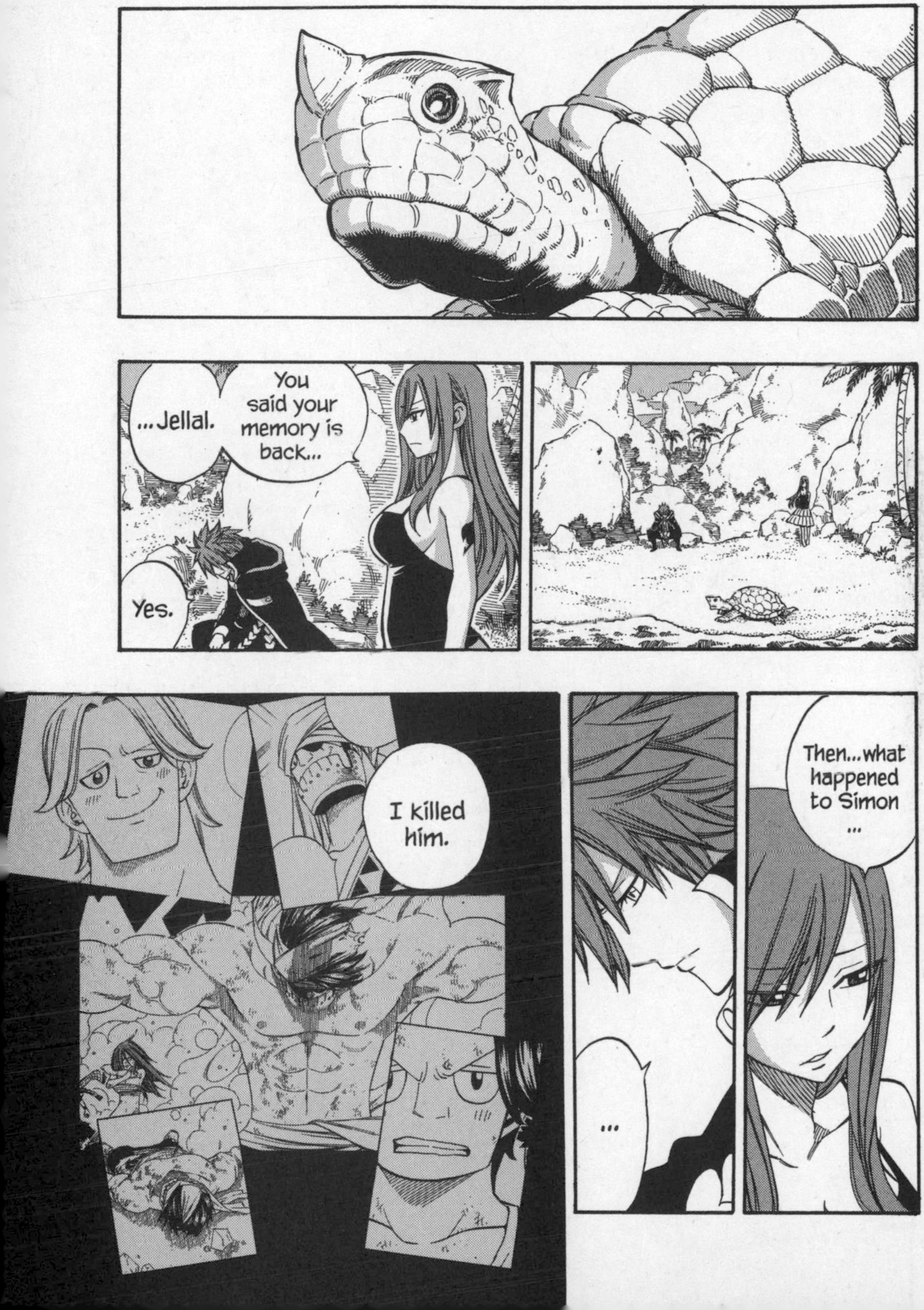
...Jellal.
You said your memory is back...
Yes.
Then...what happened to Simon ...
...
I killed him.

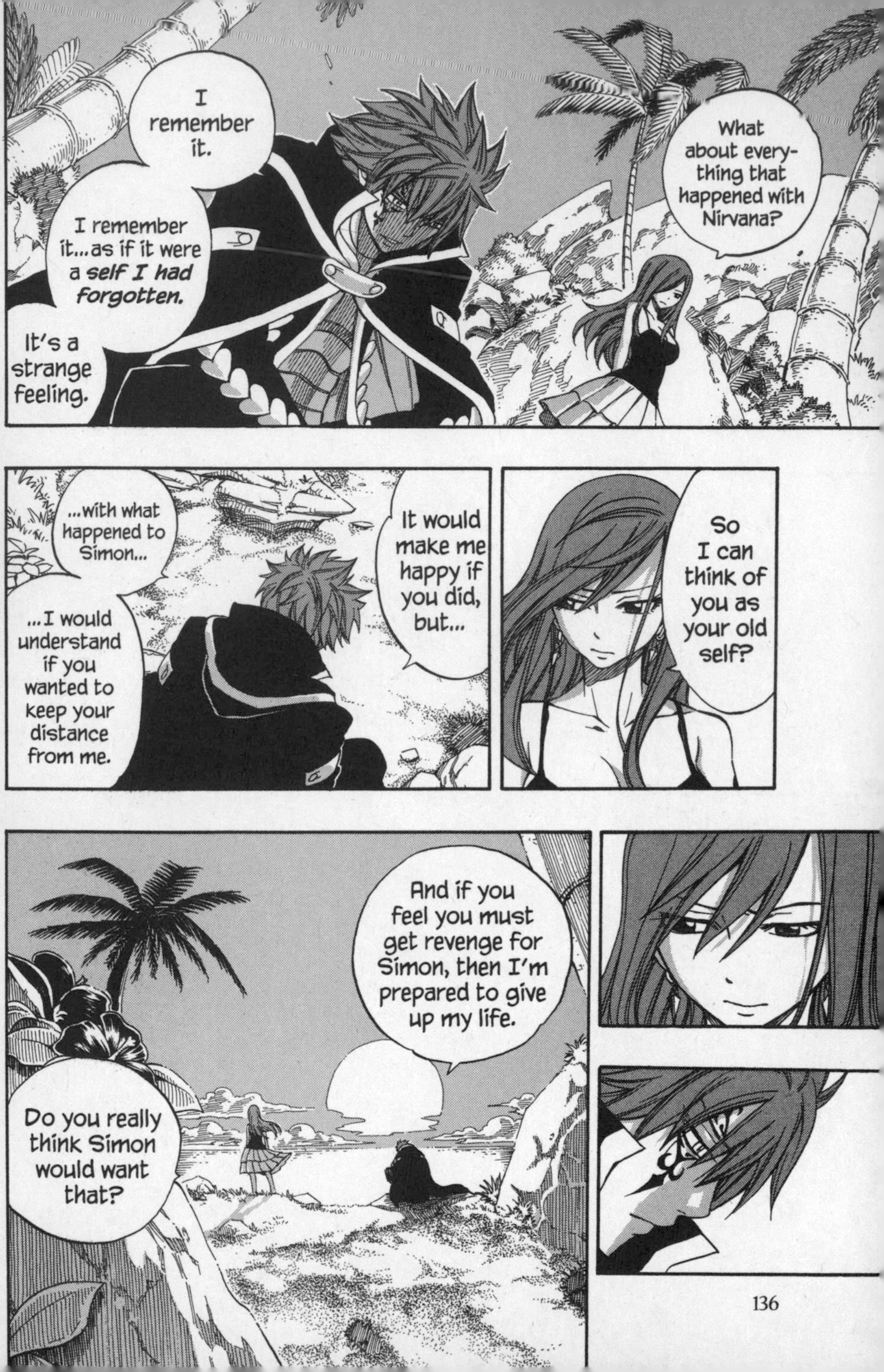
What about every-thing that happened with Nirvana?
I remember it.
I remember it...as if it were a *self I had forgotten.*
It's a strange feeling.
So I can think of you as your old self?
It would make me happy if you did, but...
...with what happened to Simon...
...I would understand if you wanted to keep your distance from me.
And if you feel you must get revenge for Simon, then I'm prepared to give up my life.
Do you really think Simon would want that?

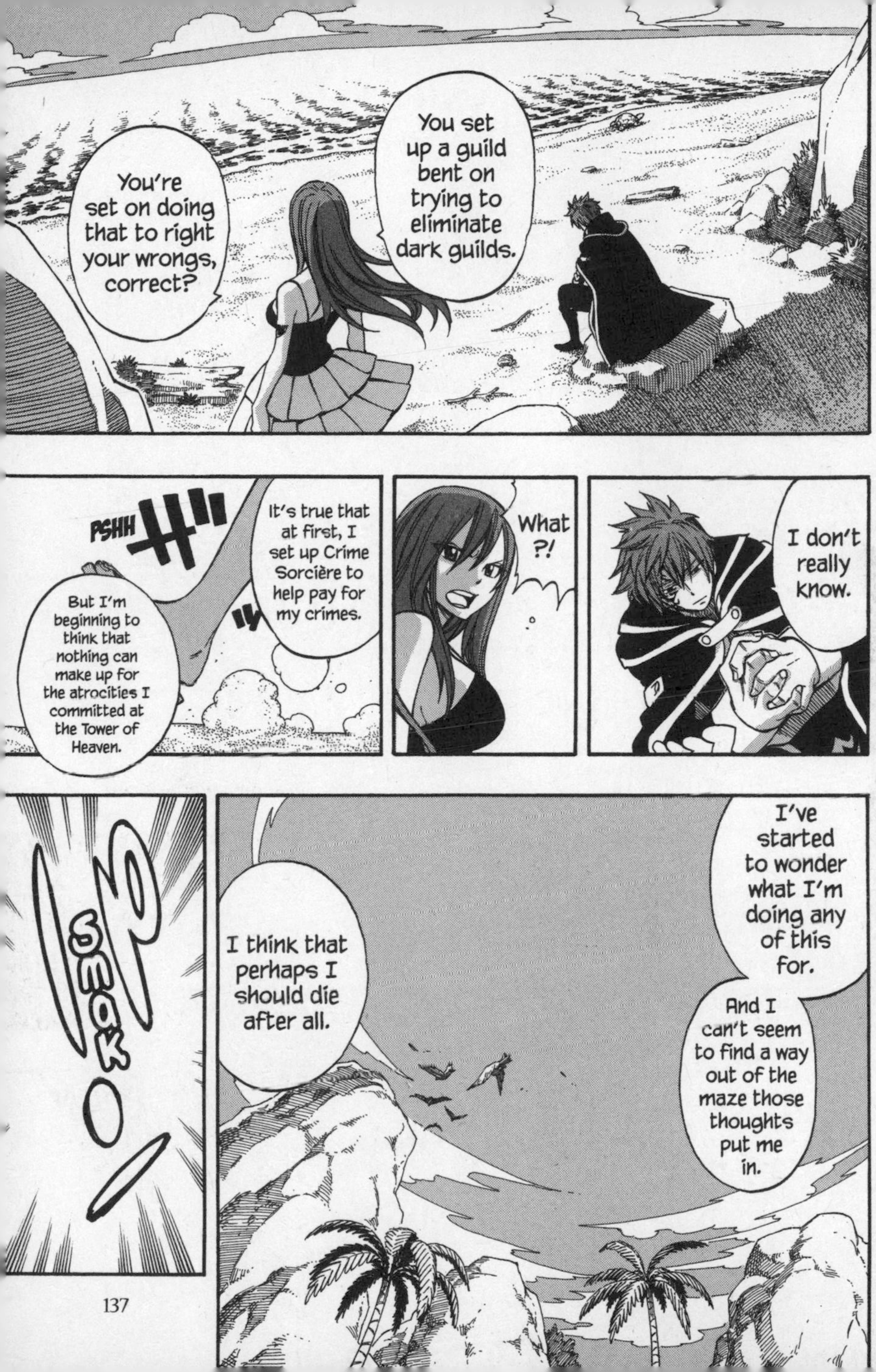
You set up a guild bent on trying to eliminate dark guilds.
You're set on doing that to right your wrongs, correct?
I don't really know.
What ?!
It's true that at first, I set up Crime Sorcière to help pay for my crimes.
PSHH
But I'm beginning to think that nothing can make up for the atrocities I committed at the Tower of Heaven.
I've started to wonder what I'm doing any of this for.
And I can't seem to find a way out of the maze those thoughts put me in.
I think that perhaps I should die after all.
SMAK

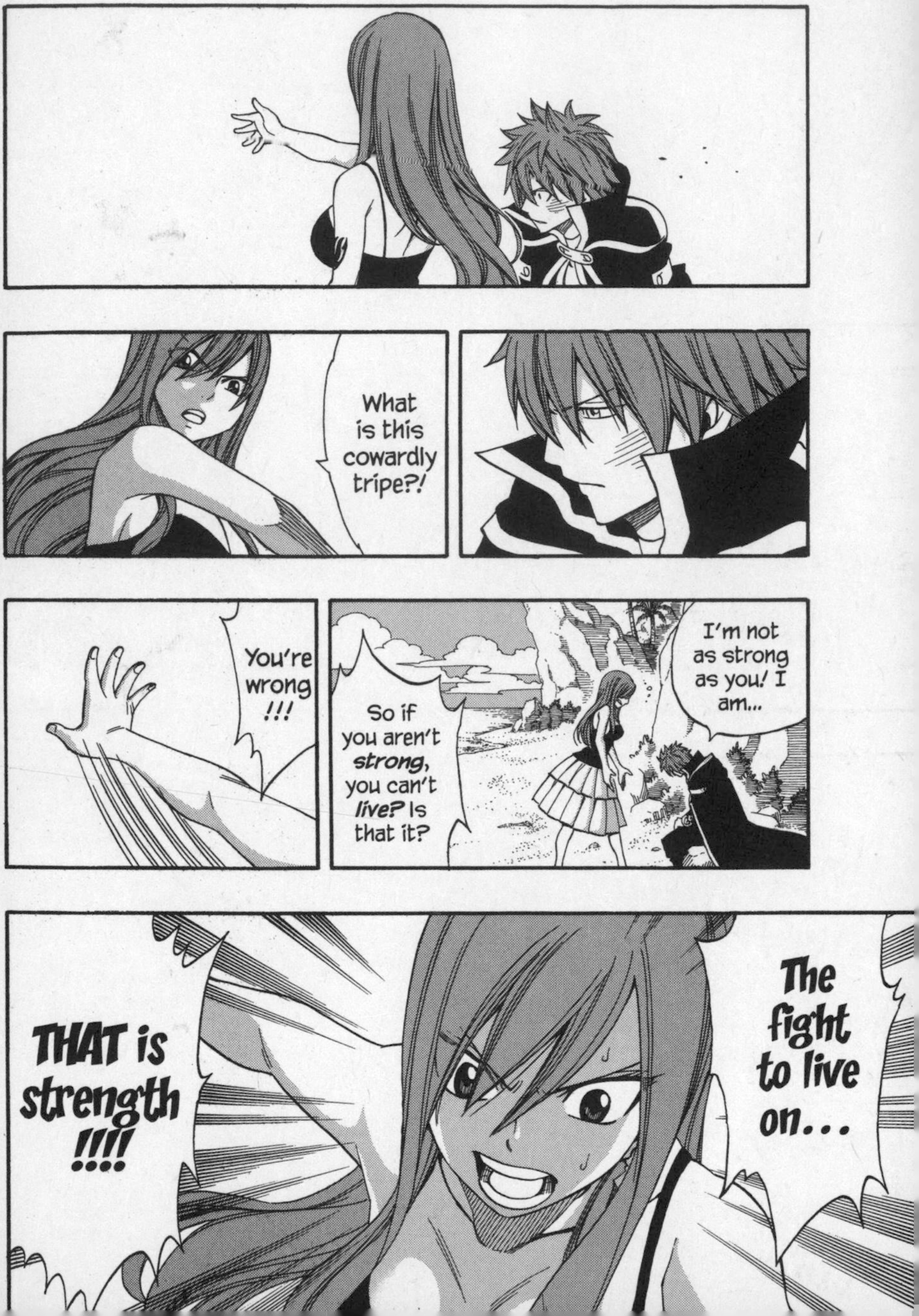
What is this cowardly tripe?!
I'm not as strong as you! I am...
So if you aren't *strong*, you can't *live?* Is that it?
You're wrong!!!
The fight to live on...
THAT is strength!!!!

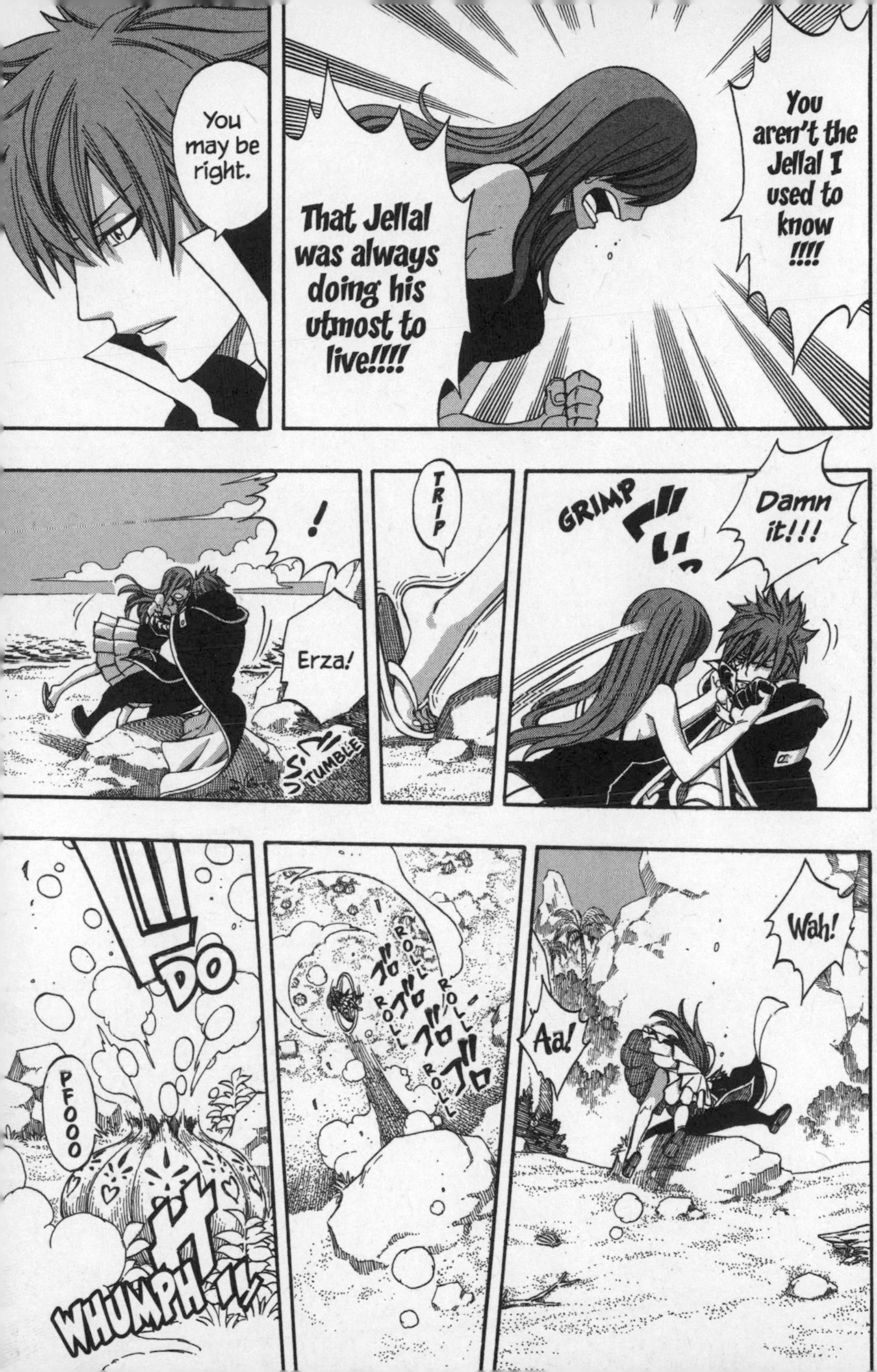
You aren't the Jellal I used to know !!!!
That Jellal was always doing his utmost to live!!!!
You may be right.
Damn it!!!
GRIMP
TRIP
!
Erza!
TUMBLE
Wah!
Aa!
ROLL
ROLL
ROLL
ROLL
DO
PFOOO
WHUMPH!!

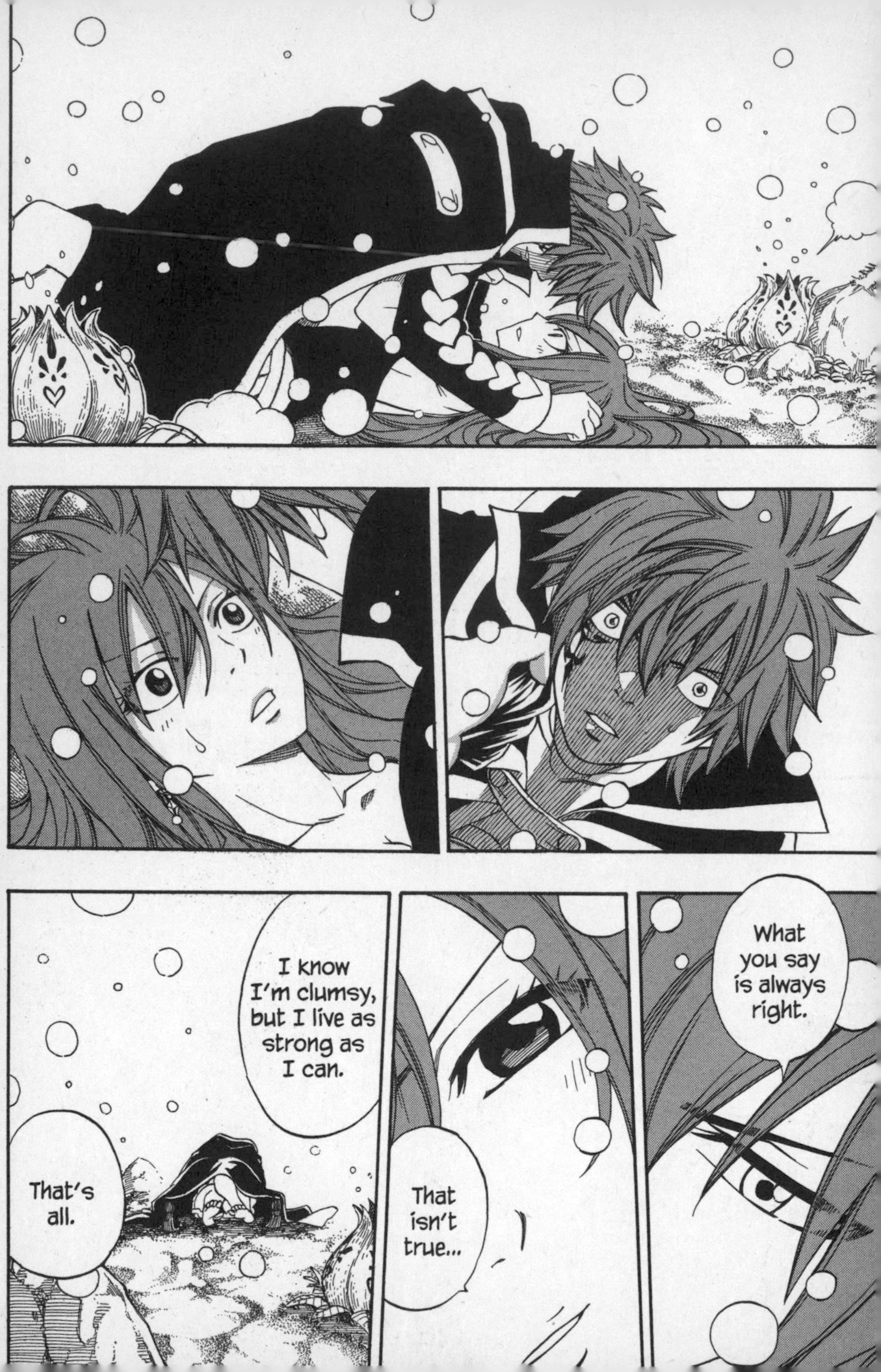
What you say is always right.
That isn't true...
I know I'm clumsy, but I live as strong as I can.
That's all.

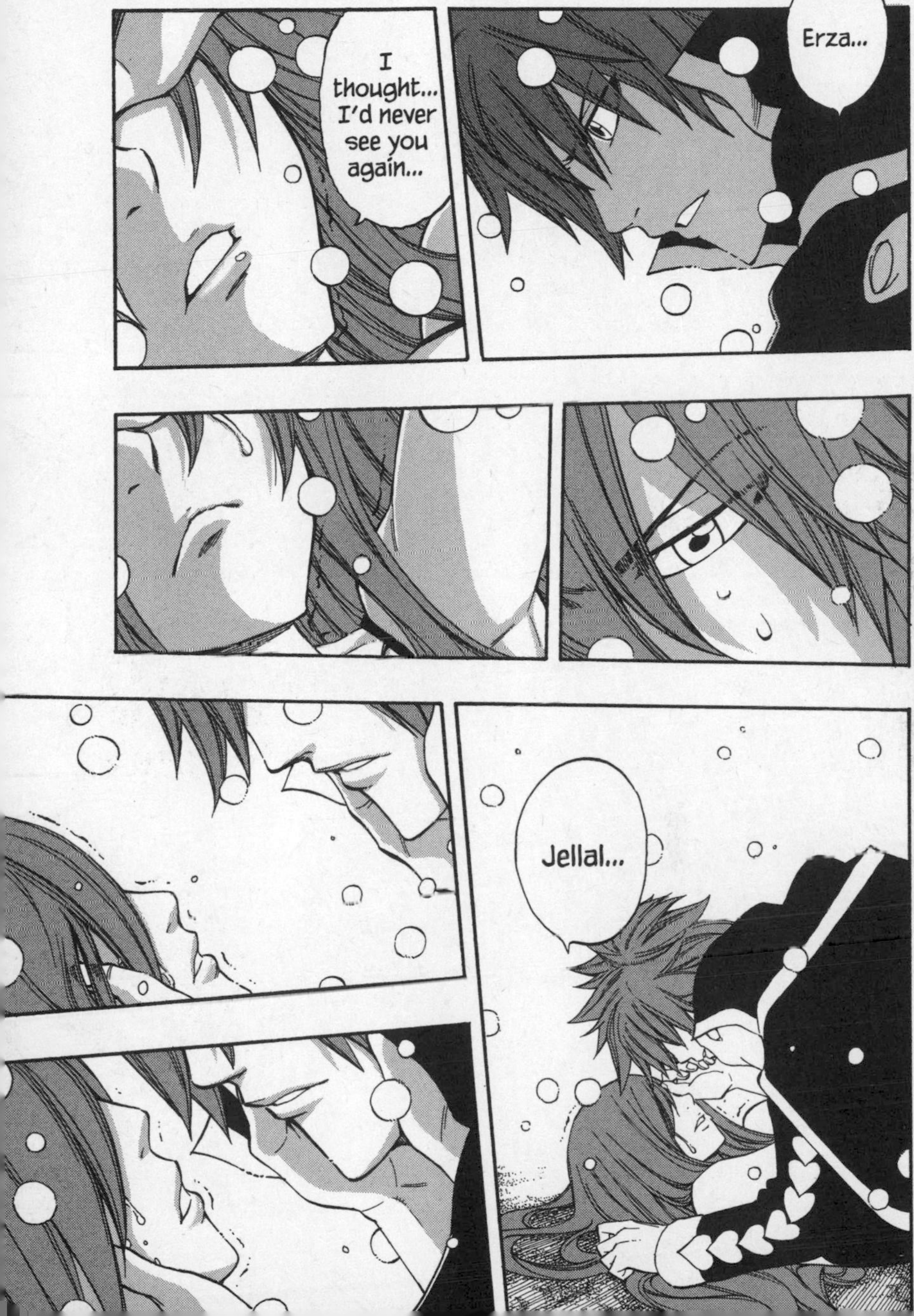
Erza...
I thought... I'd never see you again...
Jellal...

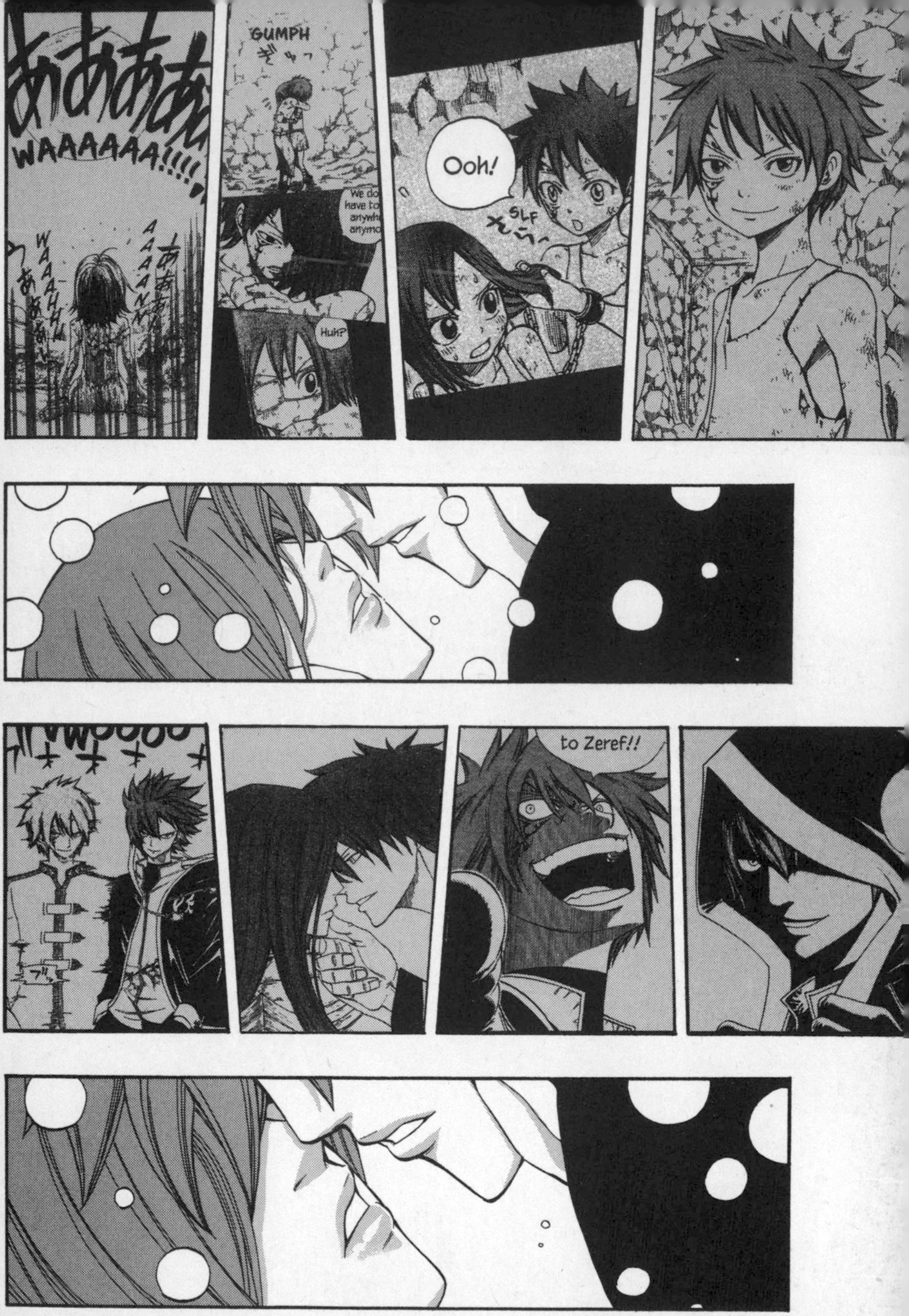
Ooh!
SLF
GUMPH
Huh?
WAAAAAA!!!!
to Zeref!!

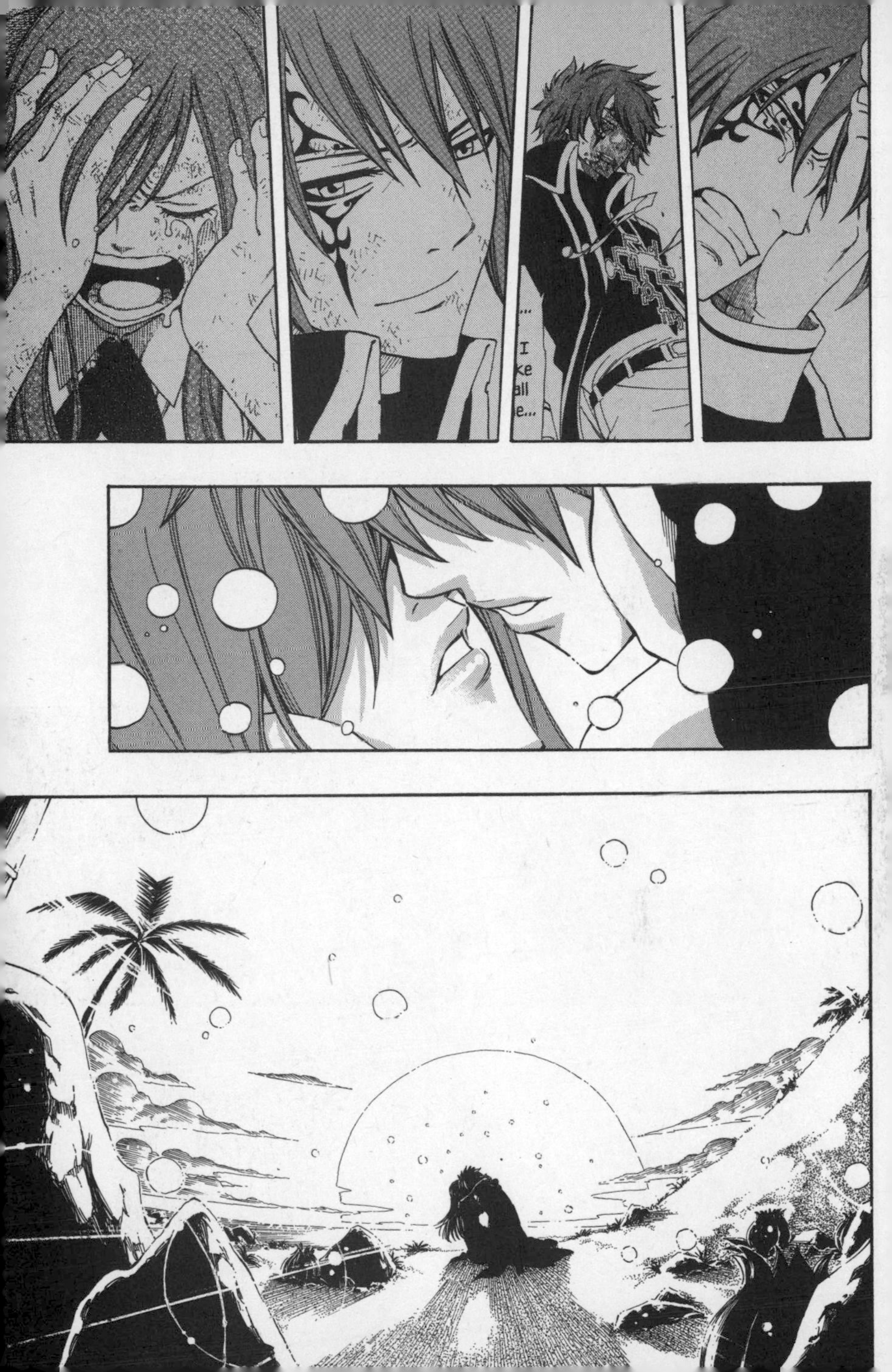
...
I
ke
all
e...

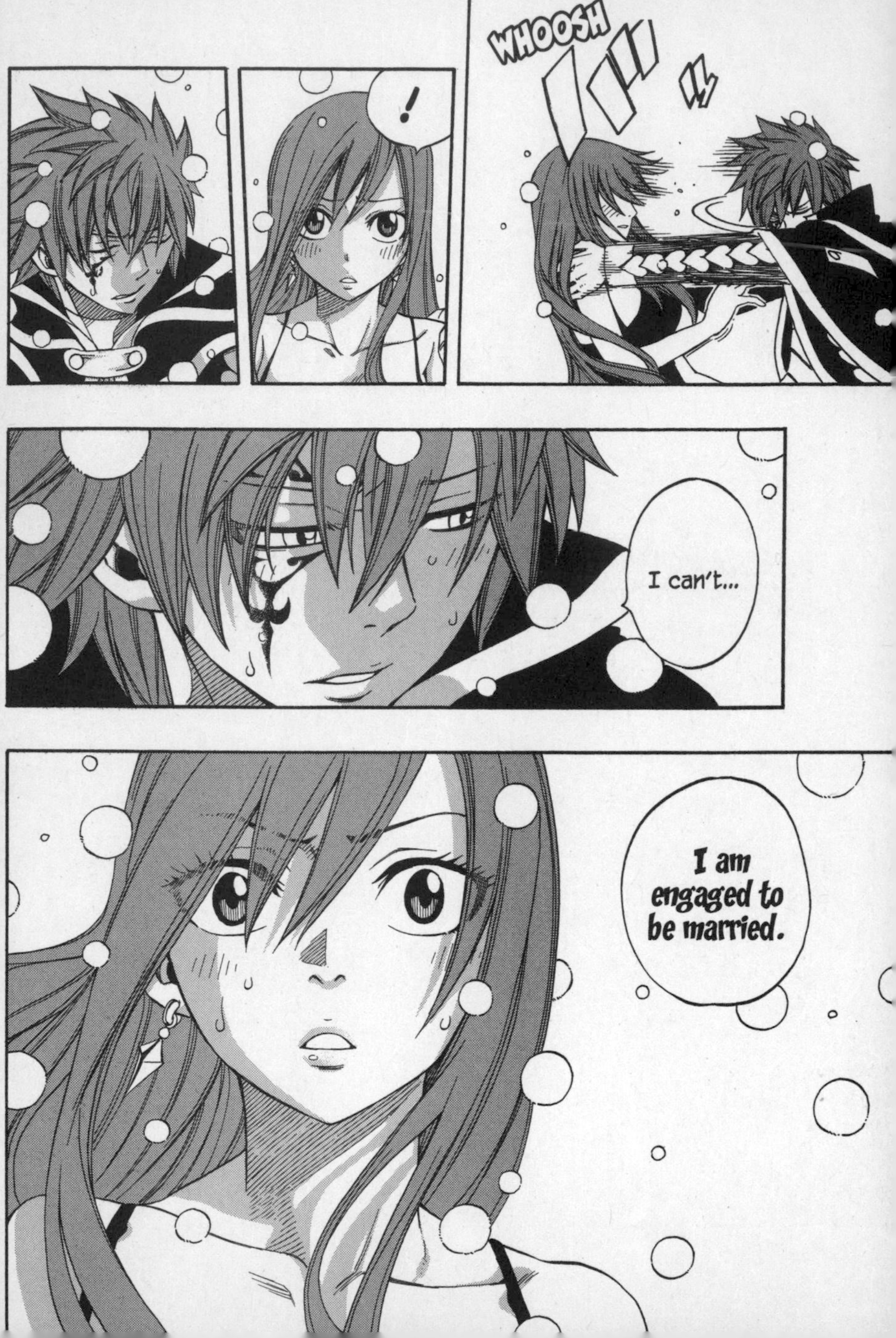
WHOOSH
!!
!
I can't...
I am engaged to be married.

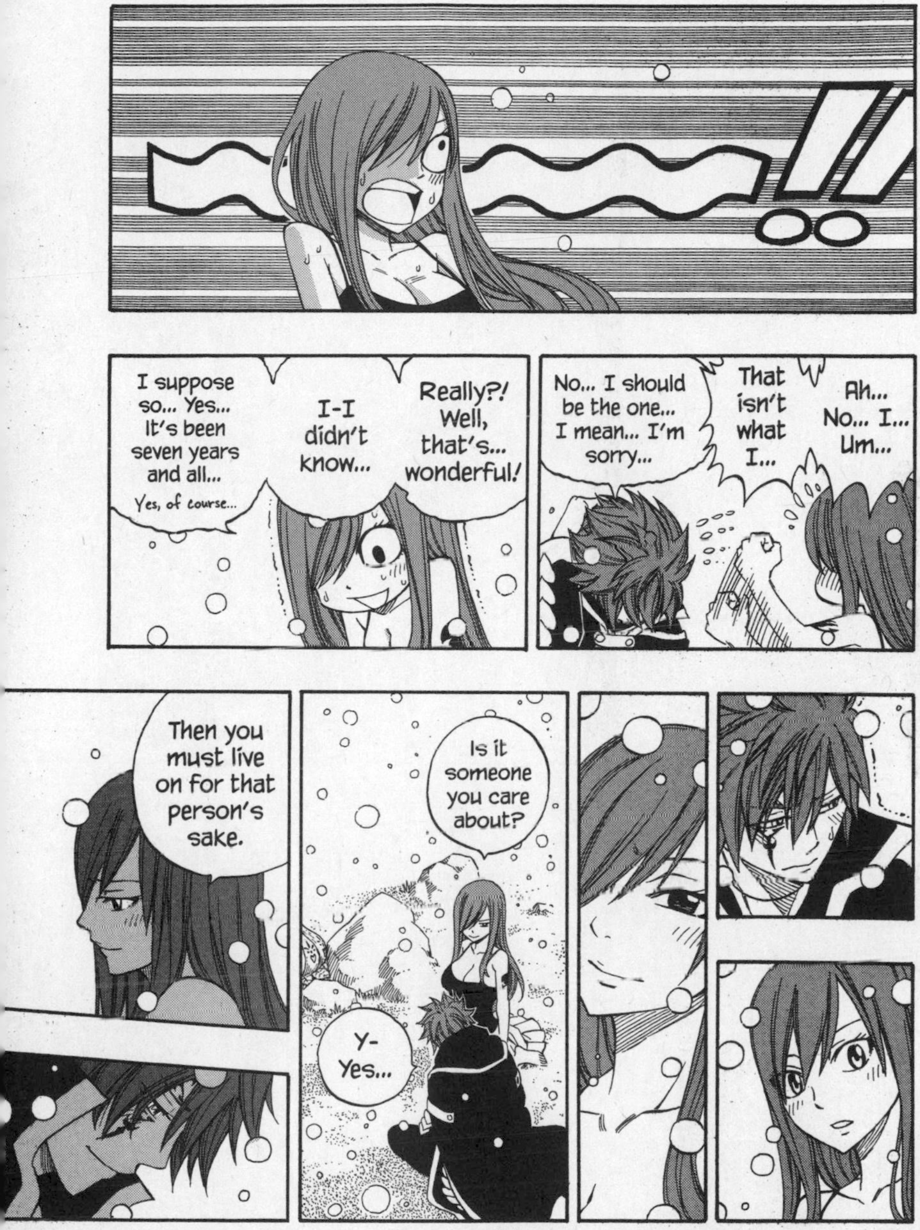
Ah... No... I... Um...
That isn't what I...
No... I should be the one... I mean... I'm sorry...
Really?! Well, that's... wonderful!
I-I didn't know...
I suppose so... Yes... It's been seven years and all...
Yes, of course...
Is it someone you care about?
Y- Yes...
Then you must live on for that person's sake.

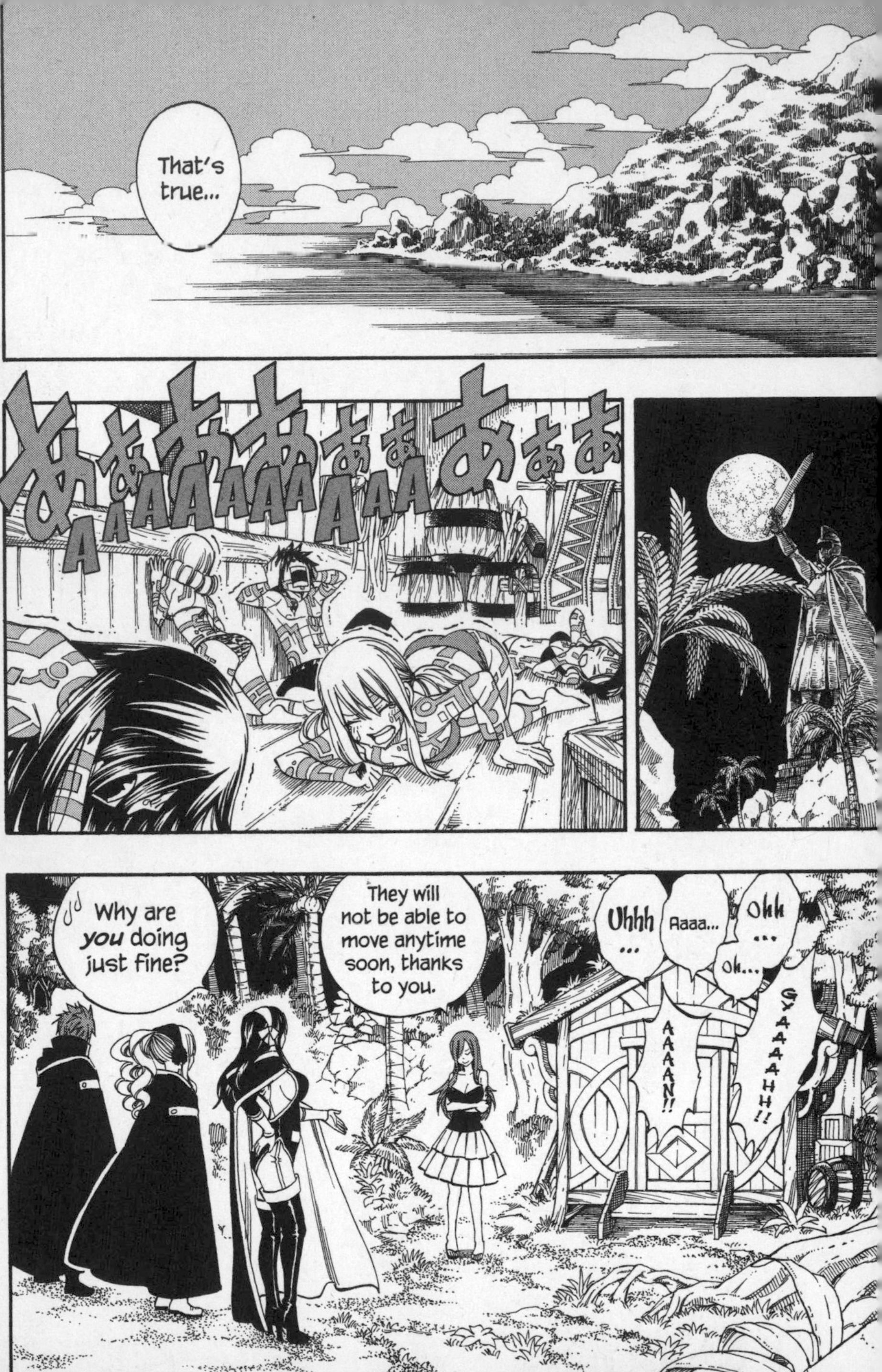
That's true...
ぬぁああぁぁあぁぁ
AAAAAAAAAA
Ohh ... oh...
Aaaa...
Uhhh ...
GYAAAAAHH!!
AAAAAN!!
They will not be able to move anytime soon, thanks to you.
Why are *you* doing just fine?

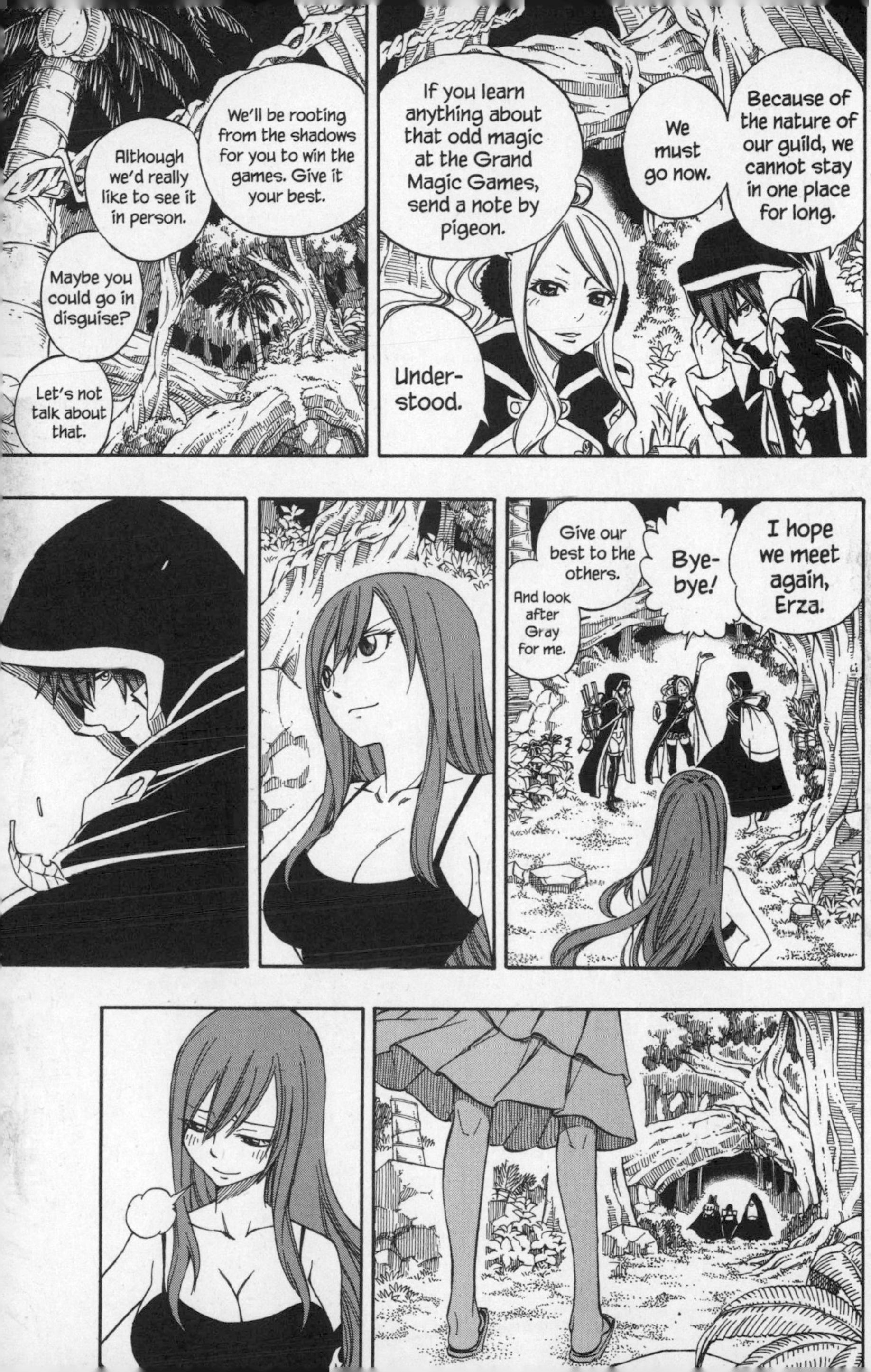
Because of the nature of our guild, we cannot stay in one place for long.
We must go now.
If you learn anything about that odd magic at the Grand Magic Games, send a note by pigeon.
Under-stood.
We'll be rooting from the shadows for you to win the games. Give it your best.
Although we'd really like to see it in person.
Maybe you could go in disguise?
Let's not talk about that.
I hope we meet again, Erza.
Bye-bye!
Give our best to the others.
And look after Gray for me.

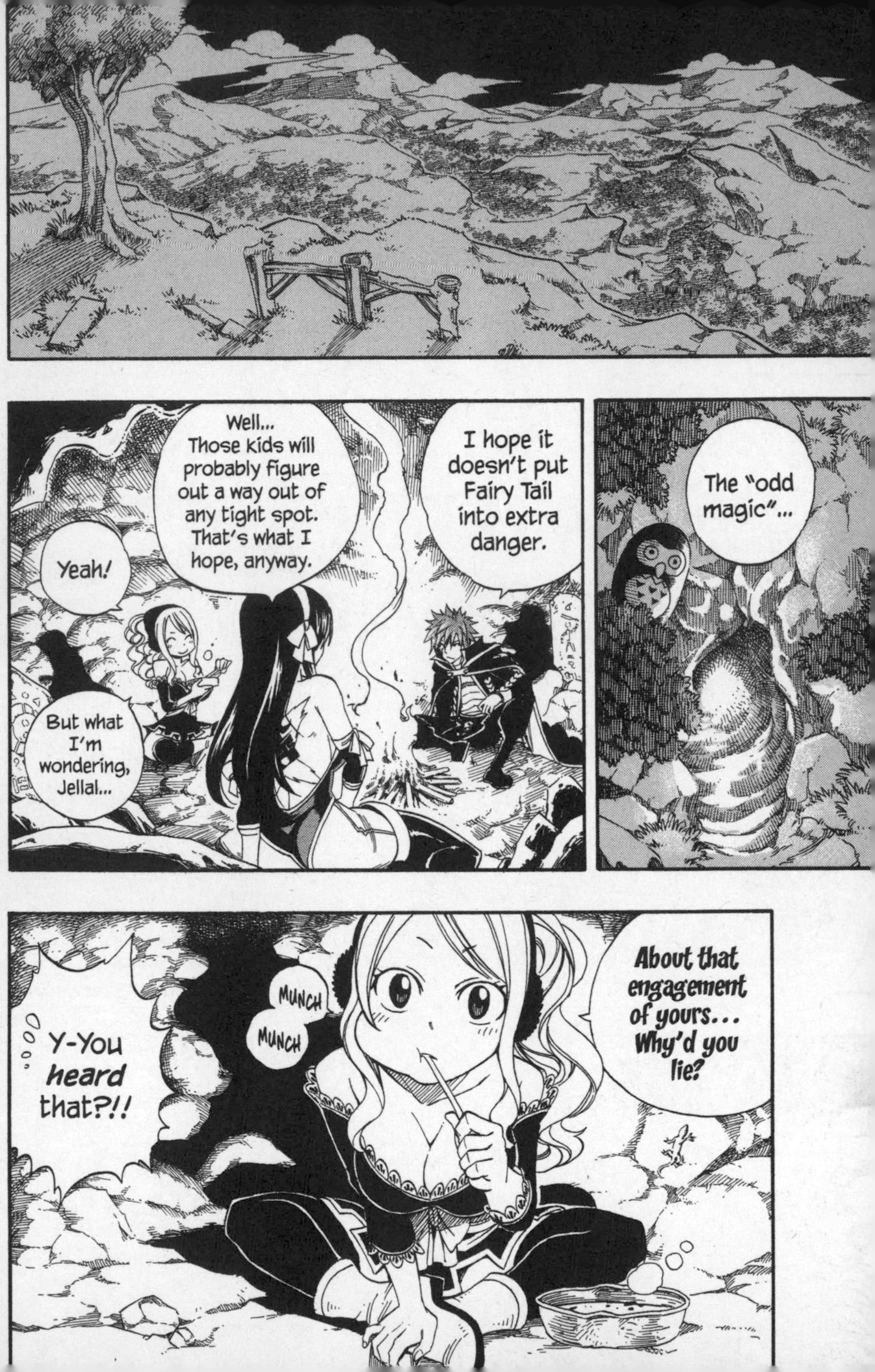
The "odd magic"...
I hope it doesn't put Fairy Tail into extra danger.
Well... Those kids will probably figure out a way out of any tight spot. That's what I hope, anyway.
Yeah!
But what I'm wondering, Jellal...
About that engagement of yours... Why'd you lie?
MUNCH
MUNCH
Y-You *heard* that?!!

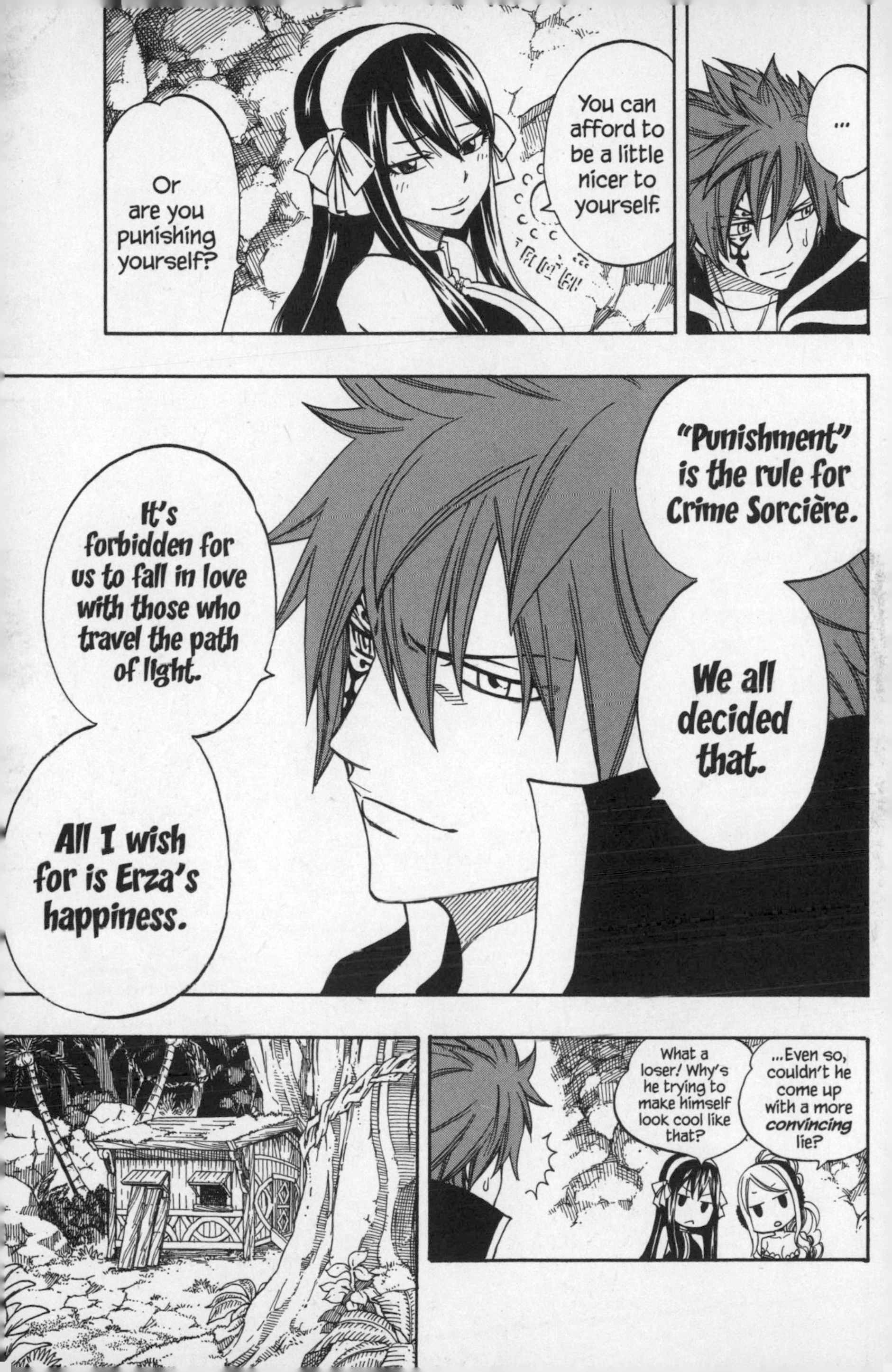
...
You can afford to be a little nicer to yourself.
Or are you punishing yourself?
"Punishment" is the rule for Crime Sorcière.
We all decided that.
It's forbidden for us to fall in love with those who travel the path of light.
All I wish for is Erza's happiness.
...Even so, couldn't he come up with a more *convincing* lie?
What a loser! Why's he trying to make himself look cool like that?

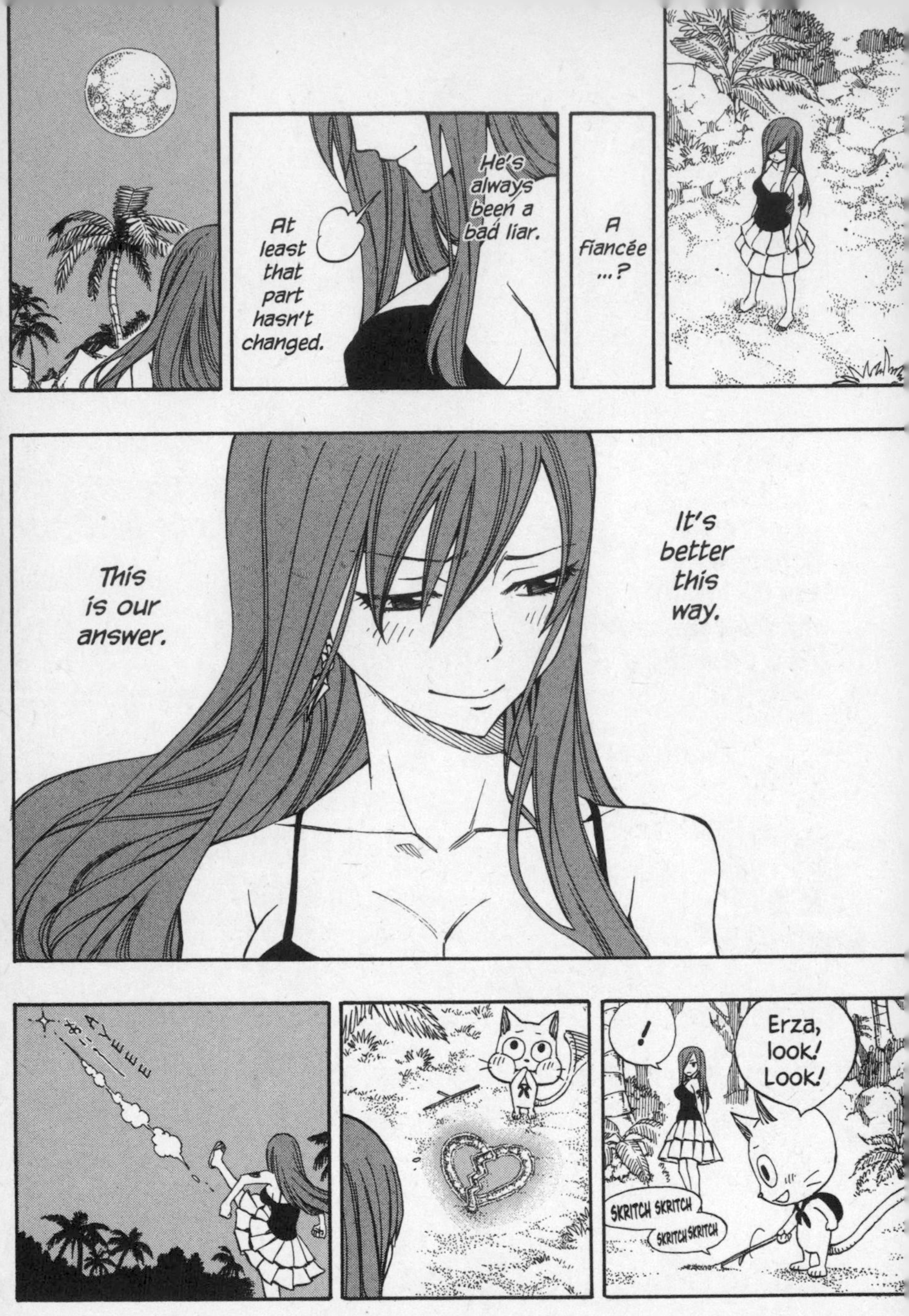
A fiancée ...?
He's always been a bad liar.
At least that part hasn't changed.
It's better this way.
This is our answer.
Erza, look! Look!
!
SKRITCH SKRITCH
SKRITCH SKRITCH
AYEEEE

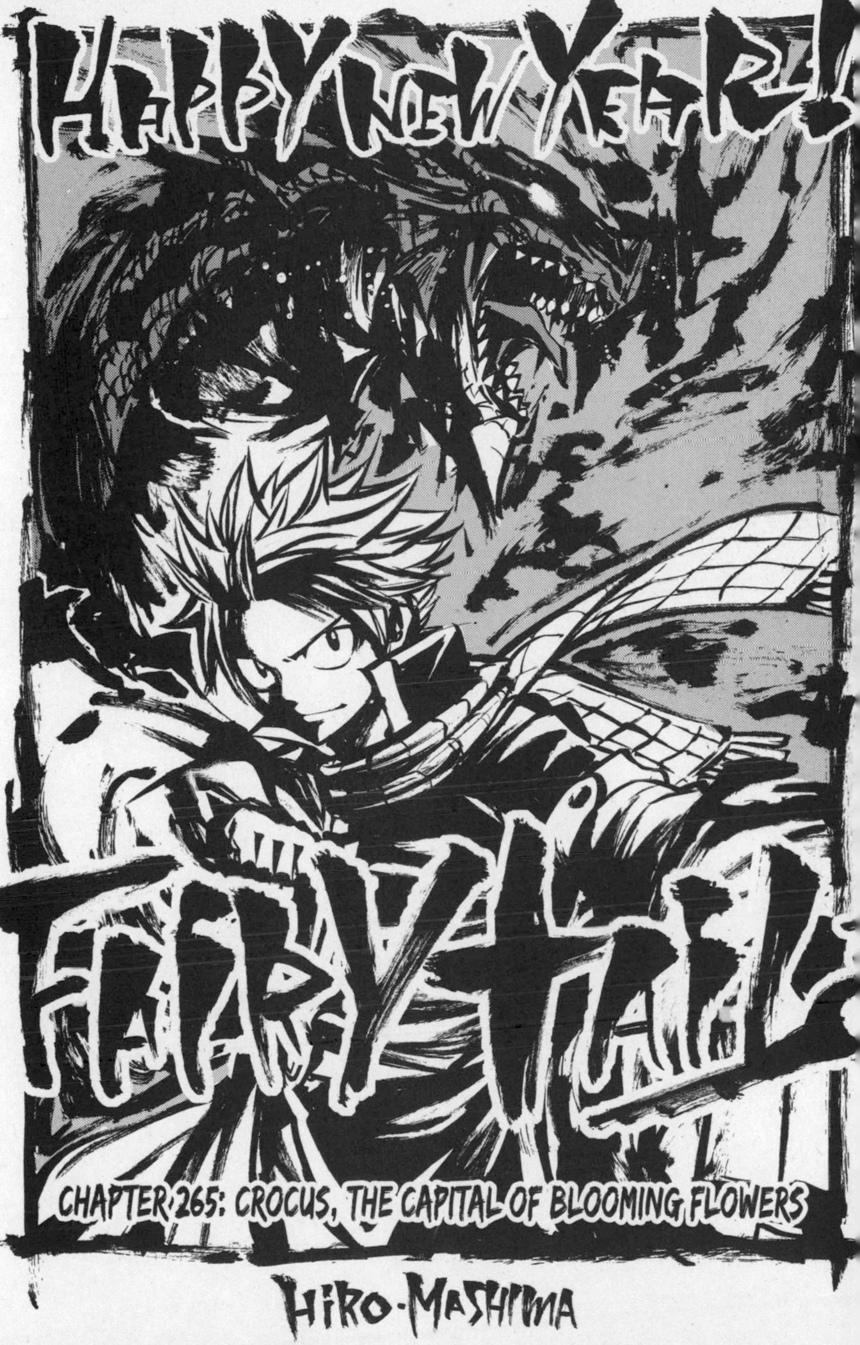
HAPPY NEW YEAR!
FAIRY TAIL
CHAPTER 265: CROCUS, THE CAPITAL OF BLOOMING FLOWERS
HIRO MASHIMA

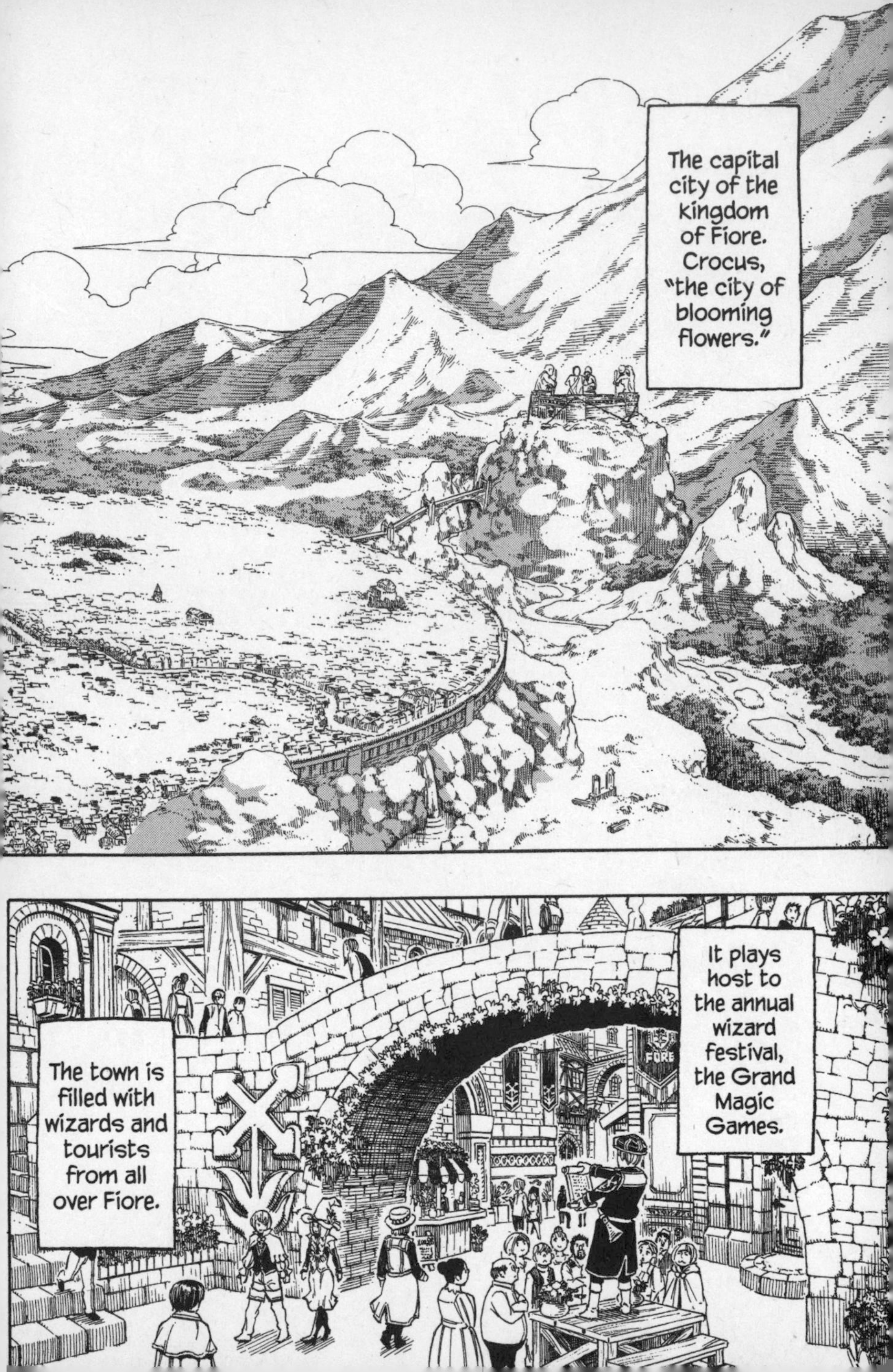
The capital city of the kingdom of Fiore. Crocus, "the city of blooming flowers."
It plays host to the annual wizard festival, the Grand Magic Games.
The town is filled with wizards and tourists from all over Fiore.

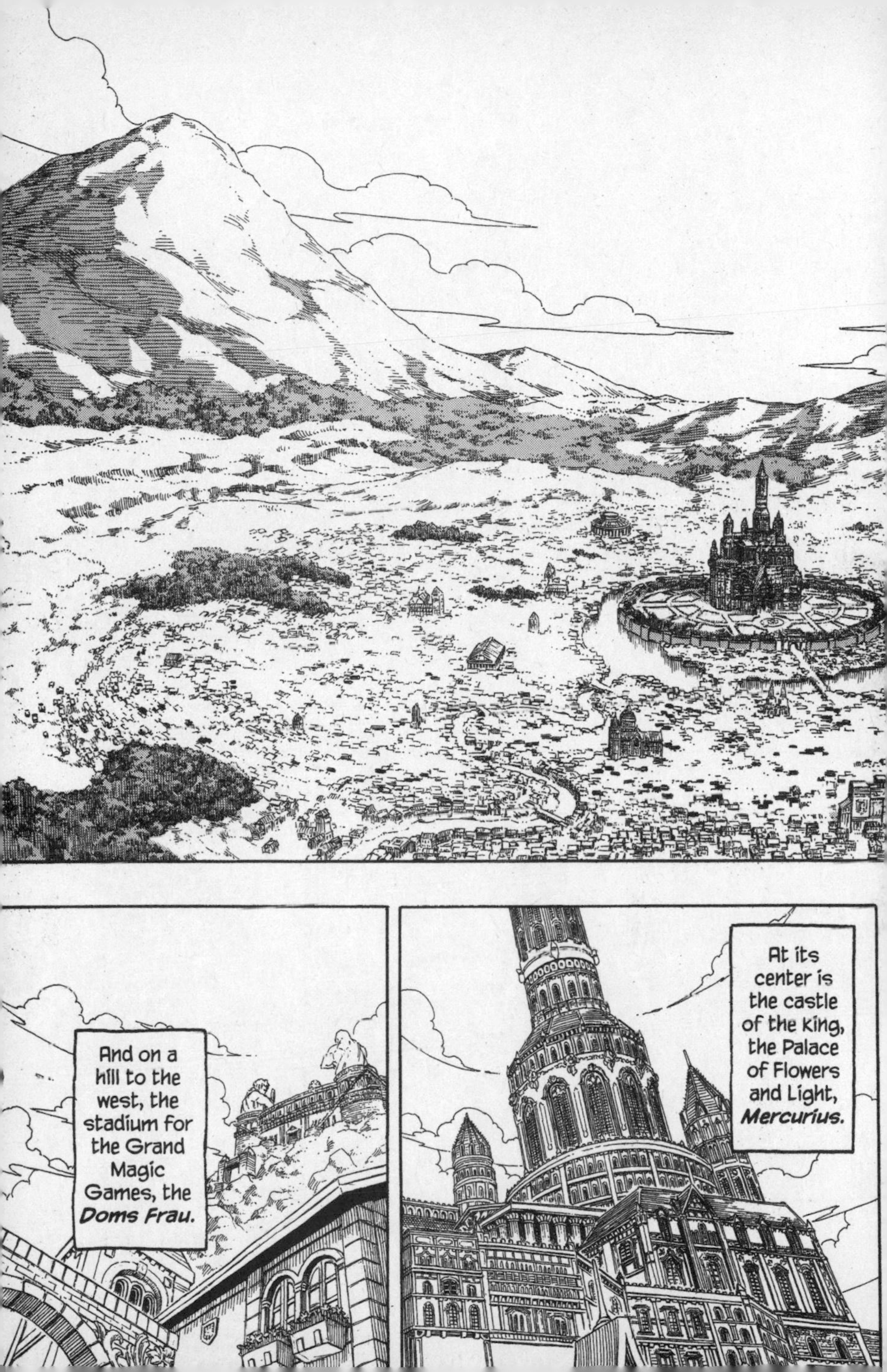
At its center is the castle of the king, the Palace of Flowers and Light, *Mercurius*.
And on a hill to the west, the stadium for the Grand Magic Games, the *Doms Frau*.

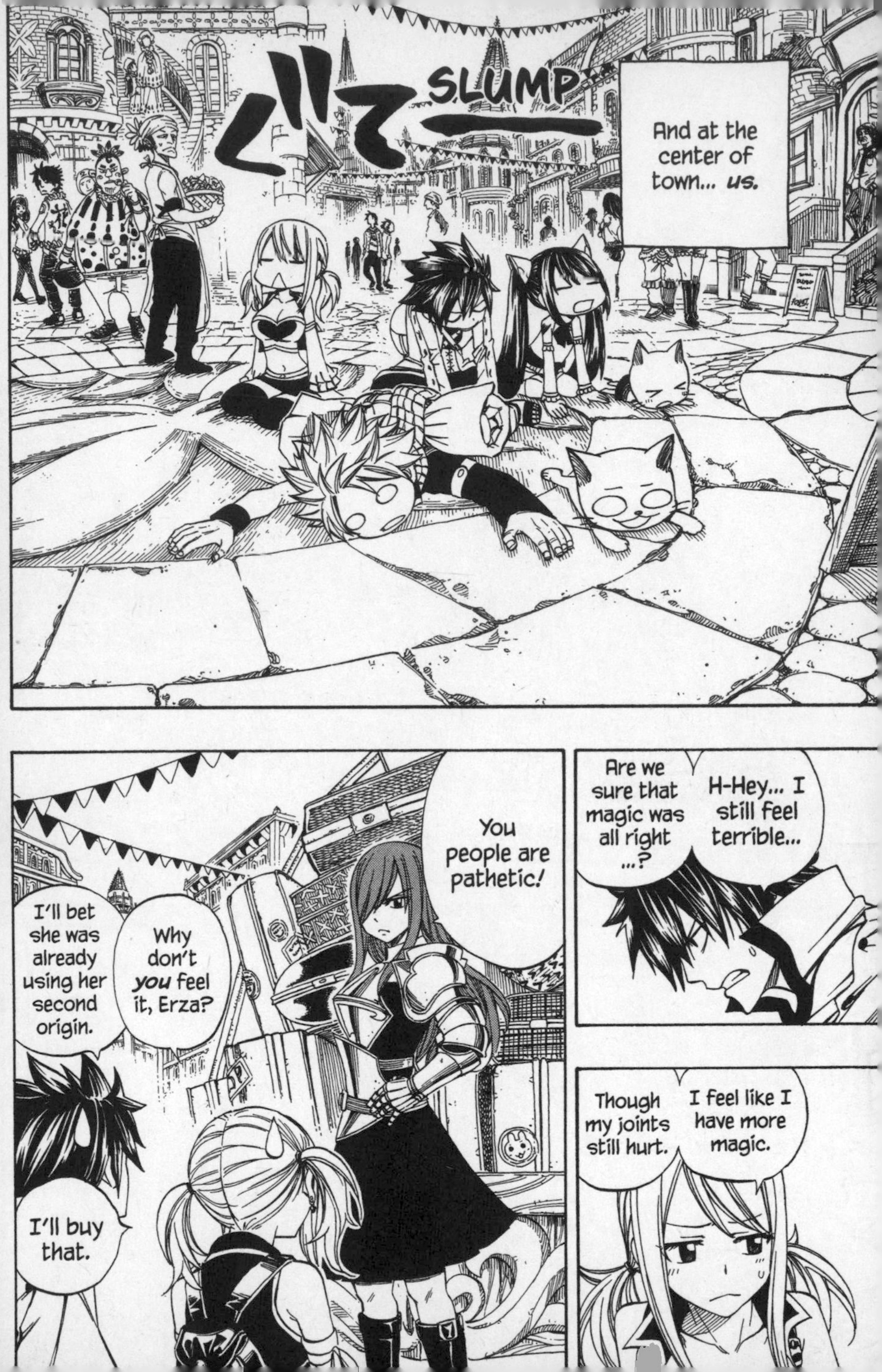

And at the center of town... *us.*
SLUMP
H-Hey... I still feel terrible...
Are we sure that magic was all right ...?
I feel like I have more magic.
Though my joints still hurt.
You people are pathetic!
Why don't *you* feel it, Erza?
I'll bet she was already using her second origin.
I'll buy that.

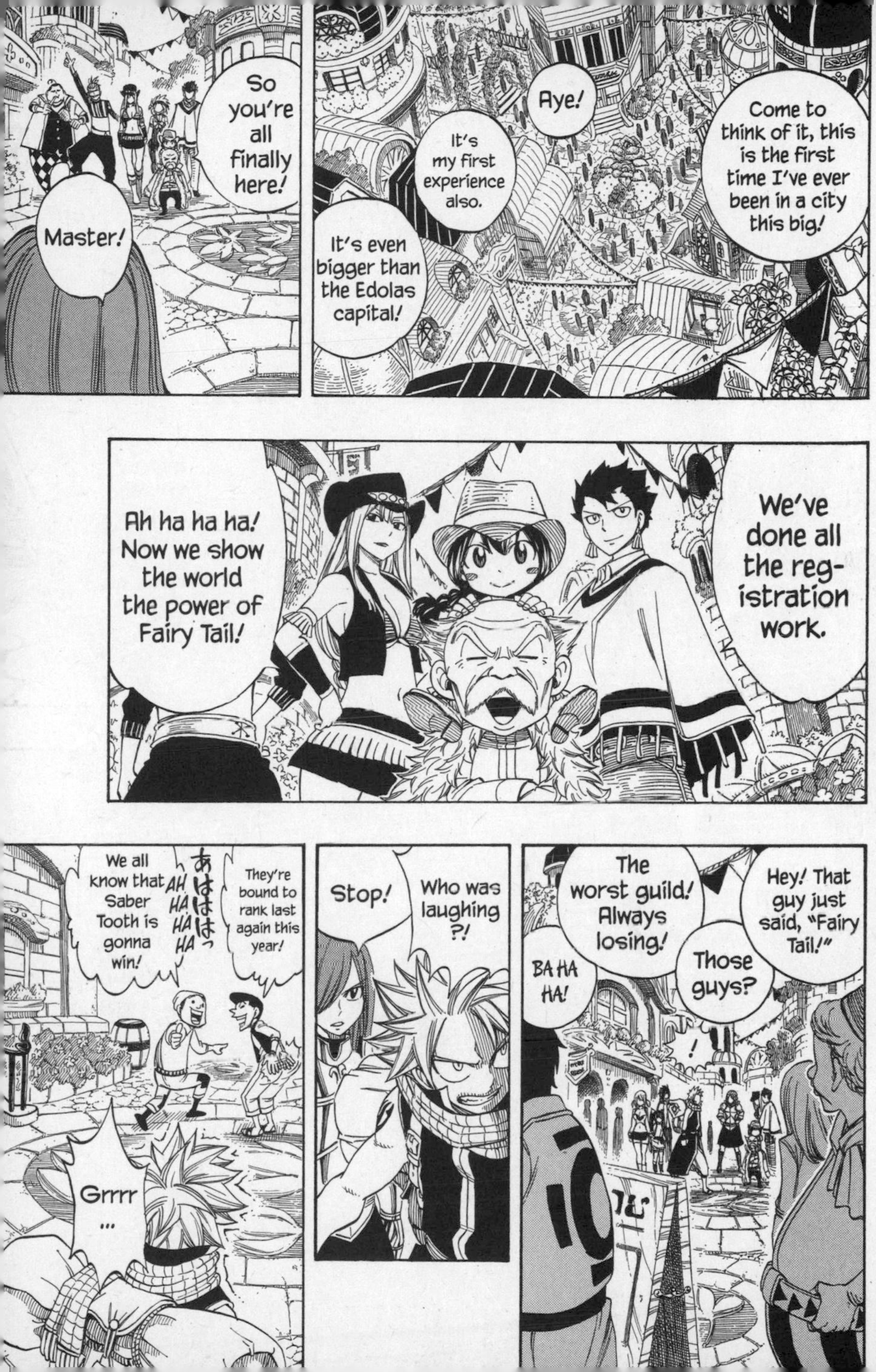

Come to think of it, this is the first time I've ever been in a city this big!
Aye!
It's my first experience also.
It's even bigger than the Edolas capital!
So you're all finally here!
Master!
We've done all the registration work.
Ah ha ha ha! Now we show the world the power of Fairy Tail!
Hey! That guy just said, "Fairy Tail!"
The worst guild! Always losing!
Those guys?
BA HA HA!
!
Who was laughing ?!
Stop!
They're bound to rank last again this year!
AH HA HA HA
あはははっ
We all know that Saber Tooth is gonna win!
Grrrr ...

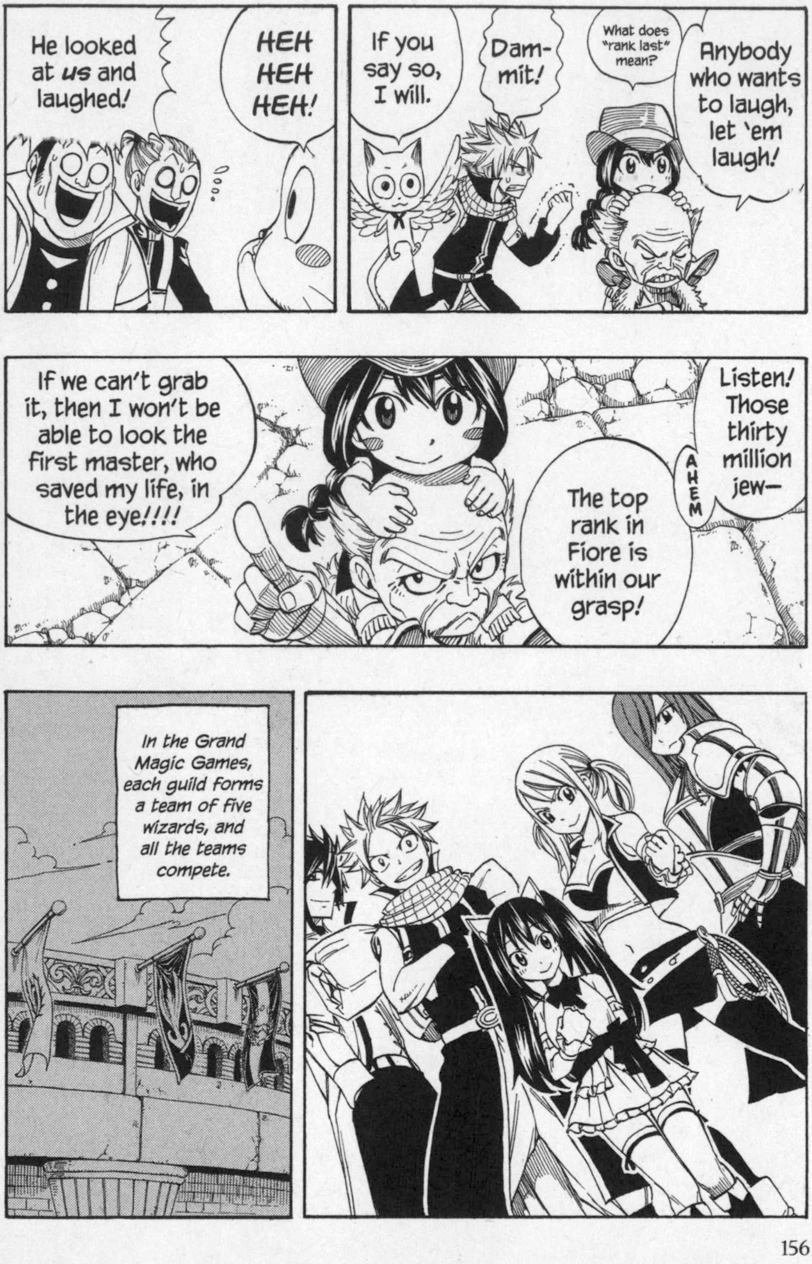
Anybody who wants to laugh, let 'em laugh!
What does "rank last" mean?
Dam- mit!
If you say so, I will.
HEH HEH HEH!
He looked at *us* and laughed!
Listen! Those thirty million jew—
AHEM
The top rank in Fiore is within our grasp!
If we can't grab it, then I won't be able to look the first master, who saved my life, in the eye!!!!
*In the Grand Magic Games, each guild forms a team of five wizards, and all the teams compete.*

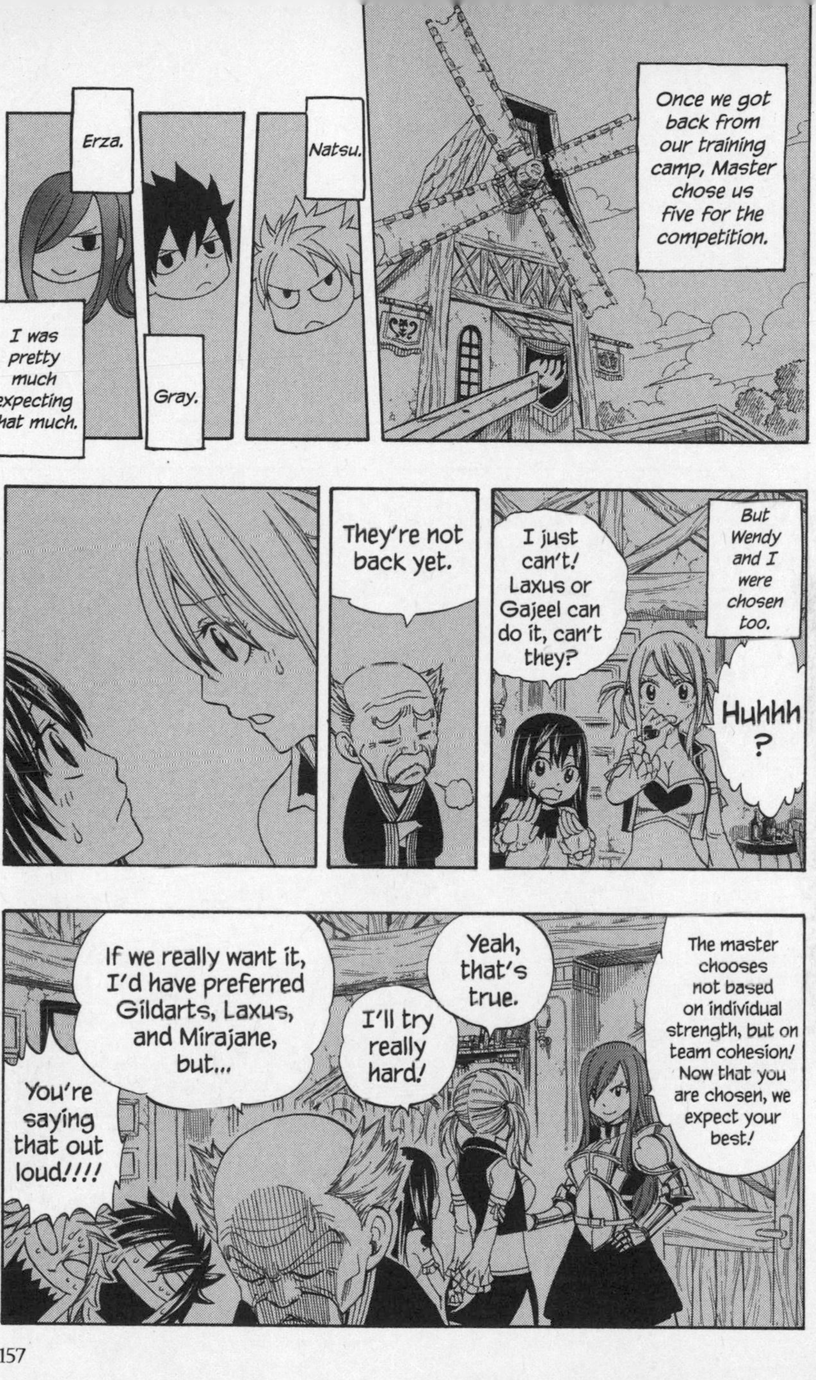
Once we got back from our training camp, Master chose us five for the competition.
Natsu.
Gray.
Erza.
I was pretty much expecting that much.
But Wendy and I were chosen too.
Huhhh?
I just can't! Laxus or Gajeel can do it, can't they?
They're not back yet.
The master chooses not based on individual strength, but on team cohesion! Now that you are chosen, we expect your best!
Yeah, that's true.
I'll try really hard!
If we really want it, I'd have preferred Gildarts, Laxus, and Mirajane, but...
You're saying that out loud!!!!

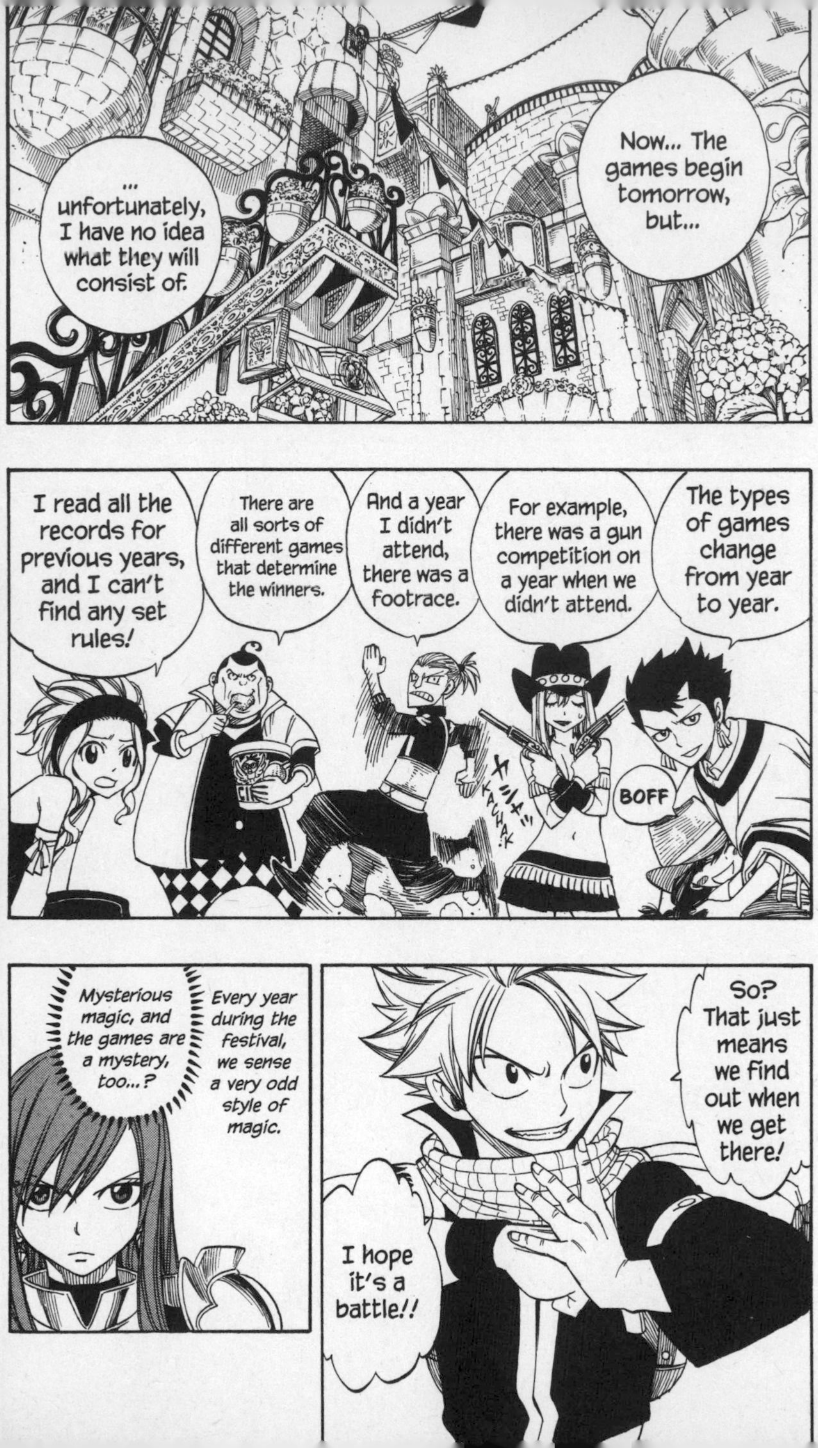
Now... The games begin tomorrow, but...
... unfortunately, I have no idea what they will consist of.
The types of games change from year to year.
For example, there was a gun competition on a year when we didn't attend.
And a year I didn't attend, there was a footrace.
There are all sorts of different games that determine the winners.
I read all the records for previous years, and I can't find any set rules!
BOFF
KACHAK
So? That just means we find out when we get there!
I hope it's a battle!!
Every year during the festival, we sense a very odd style of magic.
Mysterious magic, and the games are a mystery, too...?

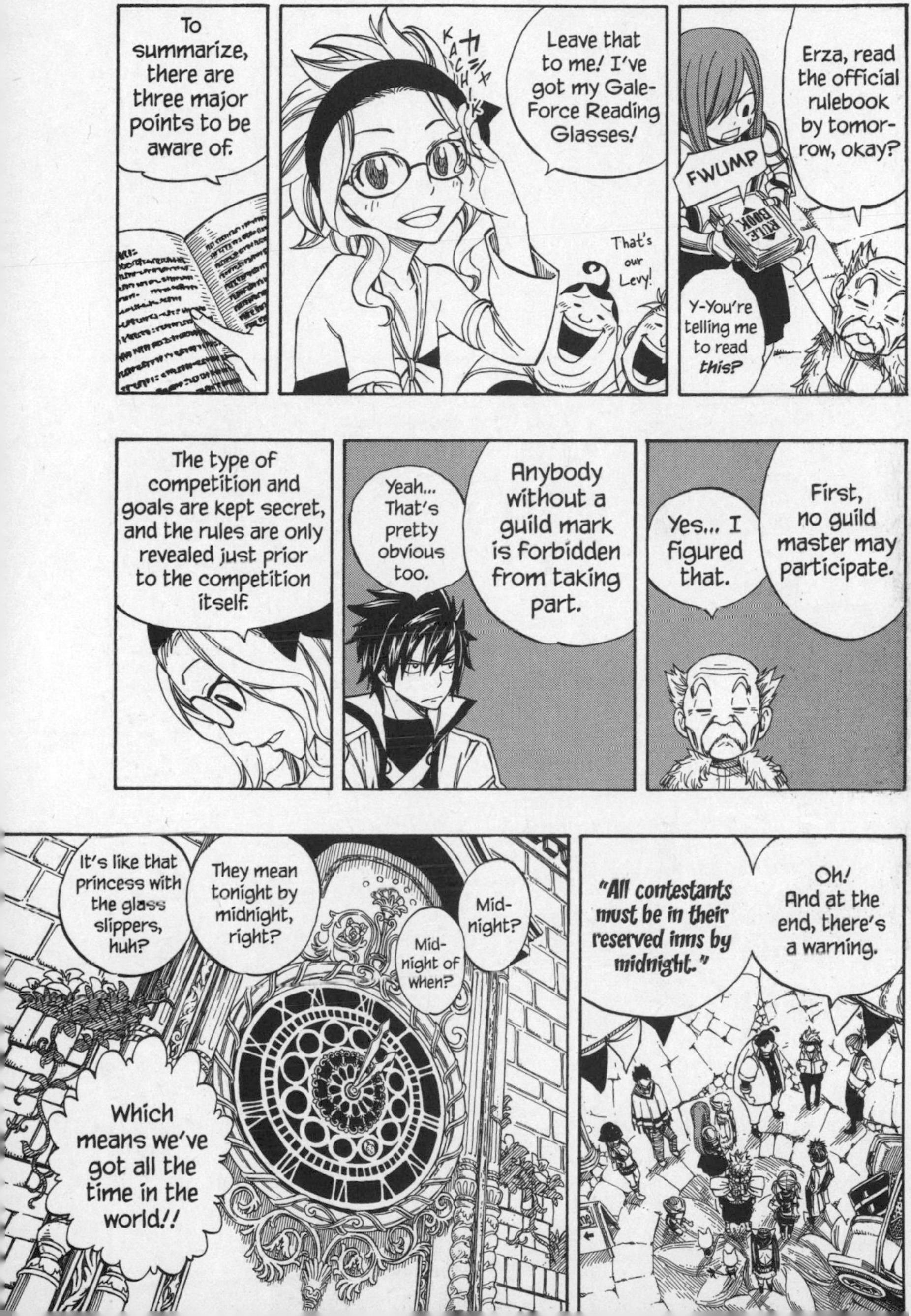
Erza, read the official rulebook by tomorrow, okay?
FWUMP
RULE BOOK
Y-You're telling me to read *this*?
Leave that to me! I've got my Gale-Force Reading Glasses!
KACHIK
That's our Levy!
To summarize, there are three major points to be aware of.
First, no guild master may participate.
Yes... I figured that.
Anybody without a guild mark is forbidden from taking part.
Yeah... That's pretty obvious too.
The type of competition and goals are kept secret, and the rules are only revealed just prior to the competition itself.
Oh! And at the end, there's a warning.
*"All contestants must be in their reserved inns by midnight."*
Mid-night?
Mid-night of when?
They mean tonight by midnight, right?
It's like that princess with the glass slippers, huh?
Which means we've got all the time in the world!!

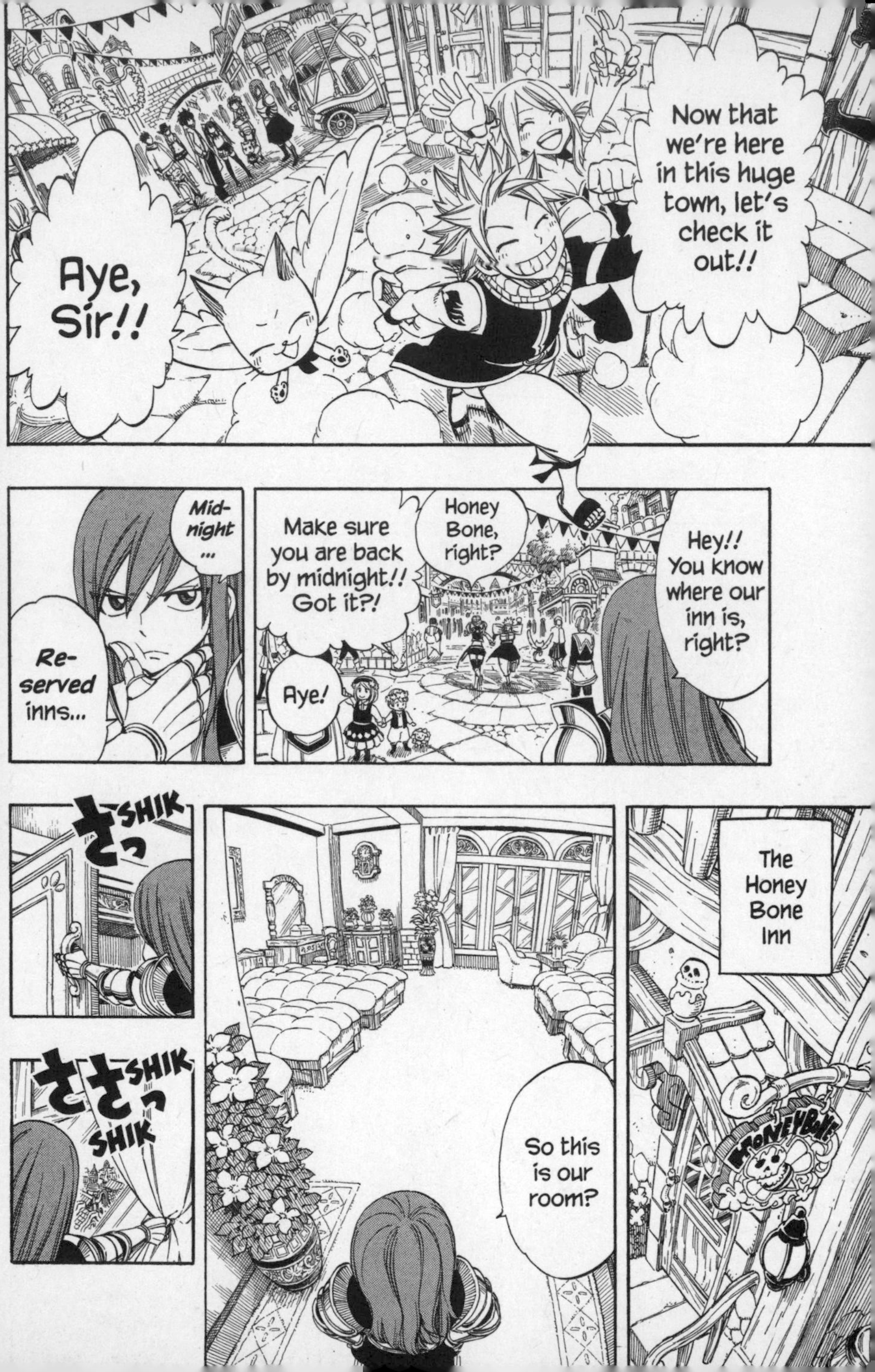
Now that we're here in this huge town, let's check it out!!
Aye, Sir!!
Hey!! You know where our inn is, right?
Honey Bone, right?
Make sure you are back by midnight!! Got it?!
Aye!
Mid-night...
Re-served inns...
The Honey Bone Inn
HONEYBONE
So this is our room?
さっ SHIK
ささっ SHIK SHIK

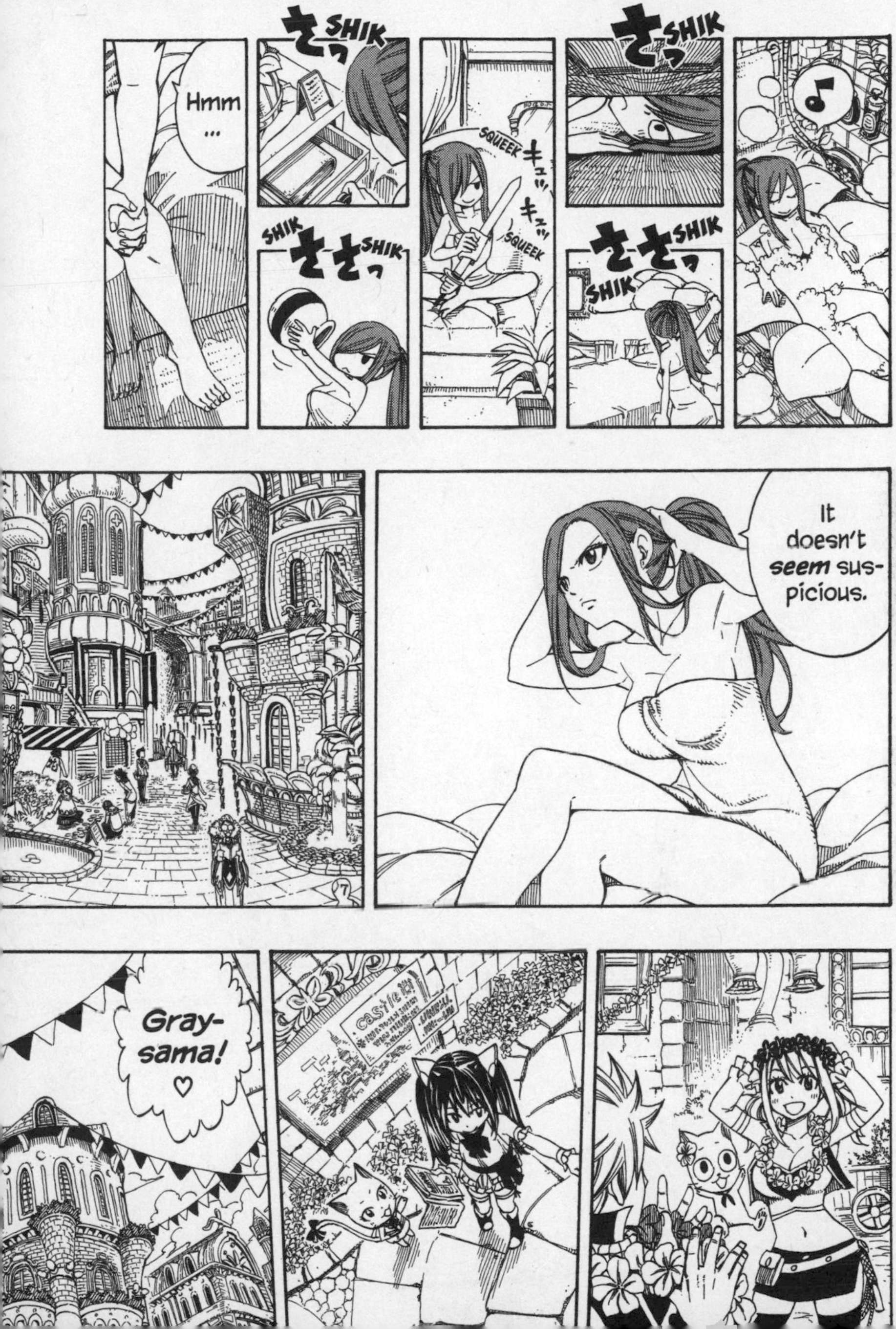

さっ SHIK
SHIK さ さっ SHIK
SQUEEK キュッ
キュッ SQUEEK
さっ SHIK
SHIK ささっ SHIK
Hmm ...
It doesn't *seem* sus-picious.
castle
Gray-sama! ♡

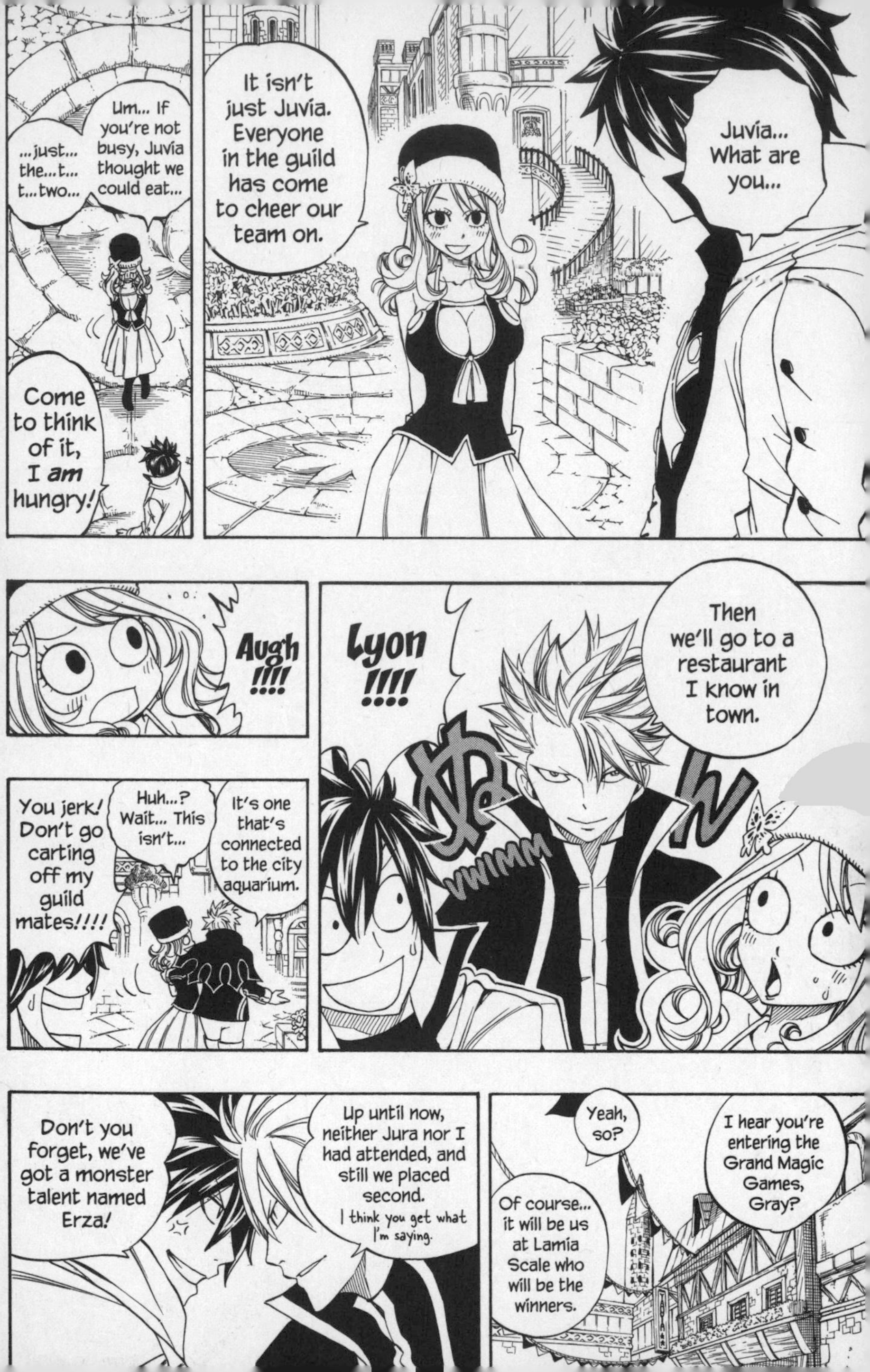

Juvia... What are you...
It isn't just Juvia. Everyone in the guild has come to cheer our team on.
Um... If you're not busy, Juvia thought we could eat...
...just... the...t... t...two...
Come to think of it, I *am* hungry!
Then we'll go to a restaurant I know in town.
Lyon!!!!
VWIMM
Augh!!!!
It's one that's connected to the city aquarium.
Huh...? Wait... This isn't...
You jerk! Don't go carting off my guild mates!!!!
I hear you're entering the Grand Magic Games, Gray?
Yeah, so?
Of course... it will be us at Lamia Scale who will be the winners.
Up until now, neither Jura nor I had attended, and still we placed second.
I think you get what I'm saying.
Don't you forget, we've got a monster talent named Erza!

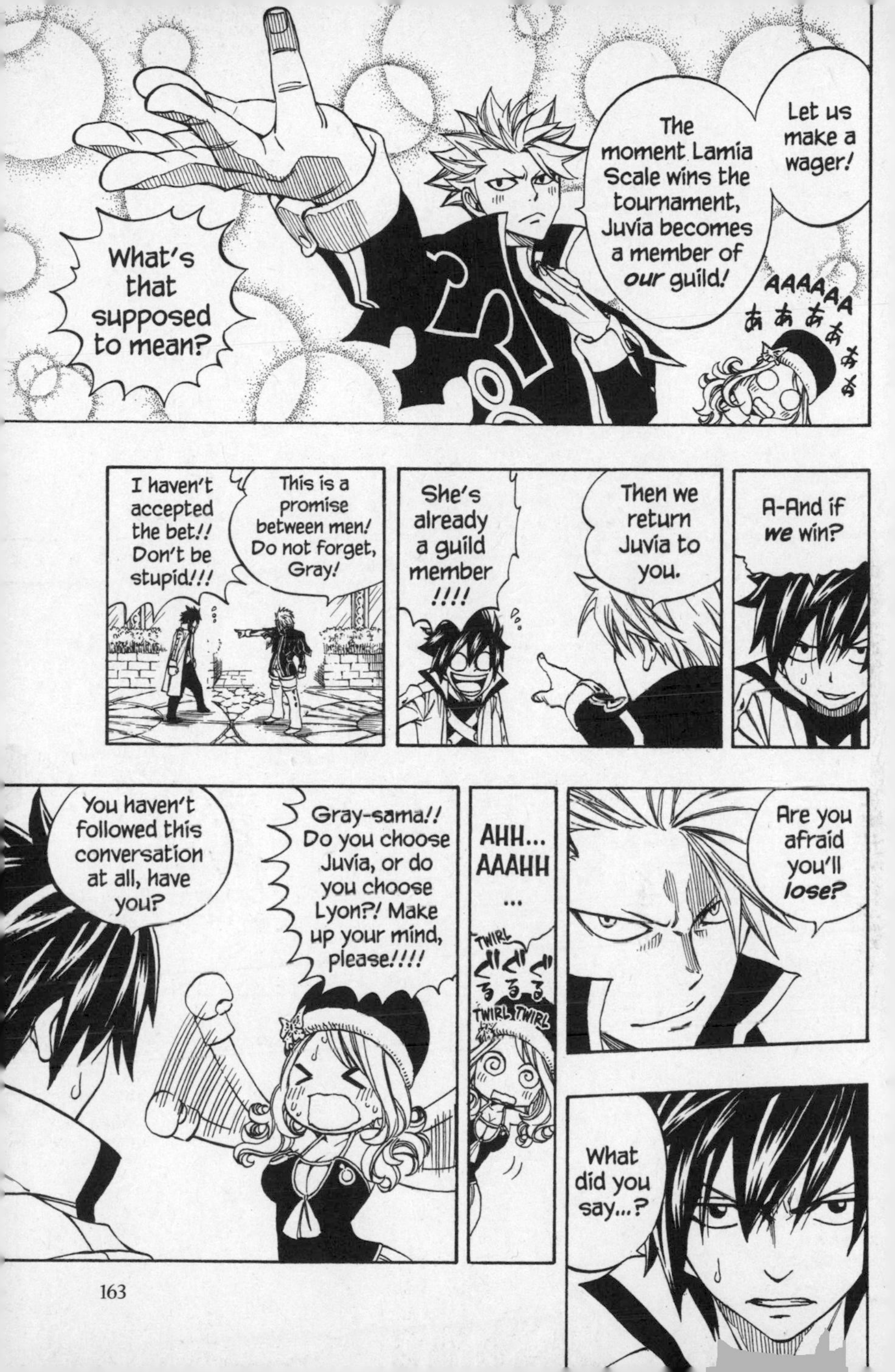

Let us make a wager!
The moment Lamia Scale wins the tournament, Juvia becomes a member of *our* guild!
AAAAAA
What's that supposed to mean?
A-And if *we* win?
Then we return Juvia to you.
She's already a guild member!!!!
This is a promise between men! Do not forget, Gray!
I haven't accepted the bet!! Don't be stupid!!!
Are you afraid you'll *lose?*
What did you say...?
AHH... AAAHH ...
TWIRL
TWIRL TWIRL
Gray-sama!! Do you choose Juvia, or do you choose Lyon?! Make up your mind, please!!!!
You haven't followed this conversation at all, have you?

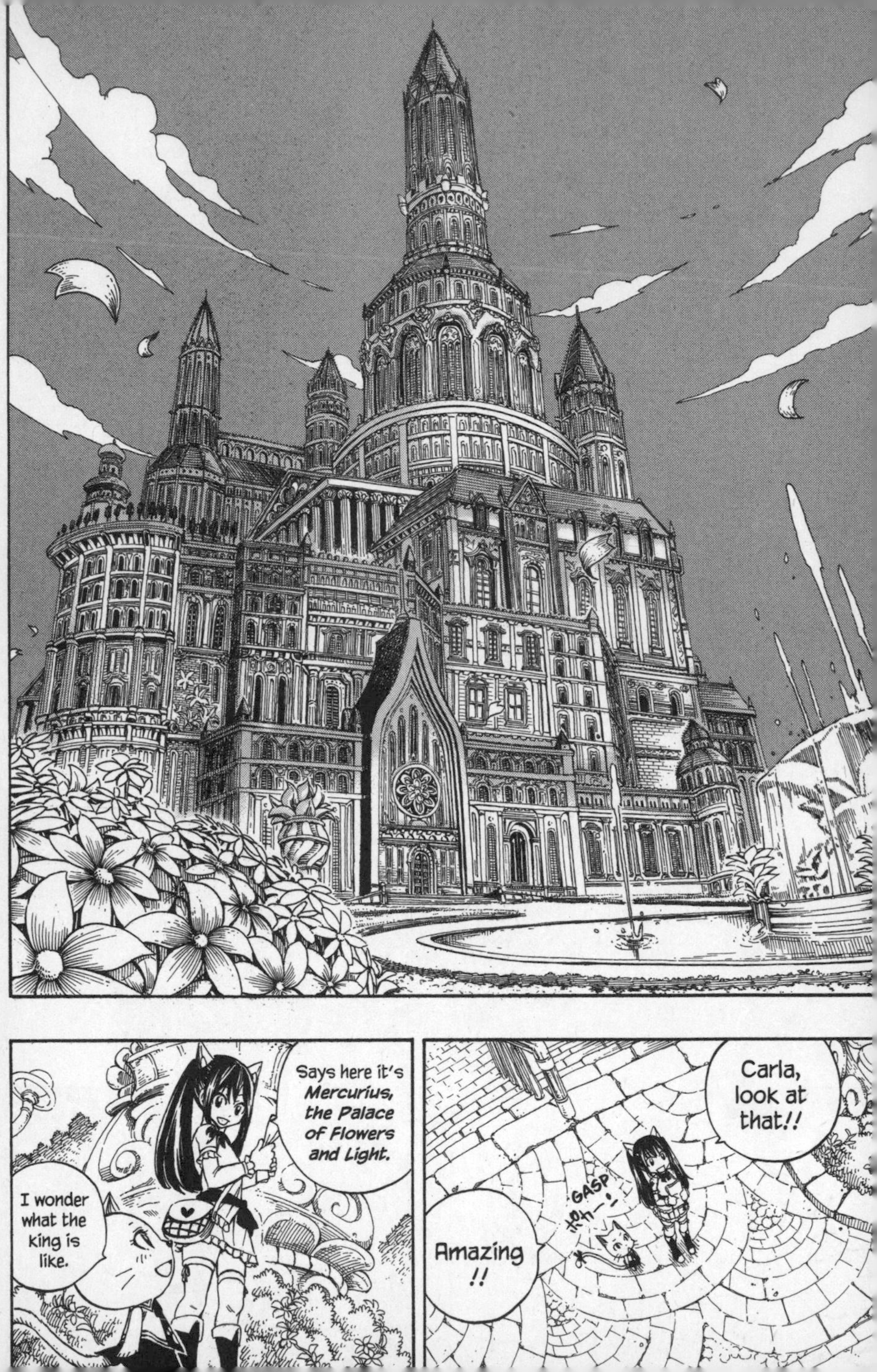
Carla, look at that!!
GASP
Amazing!!
Says here it's *Mercurius, the Palace of Flowers and Light.*
I wonder what the king is like.

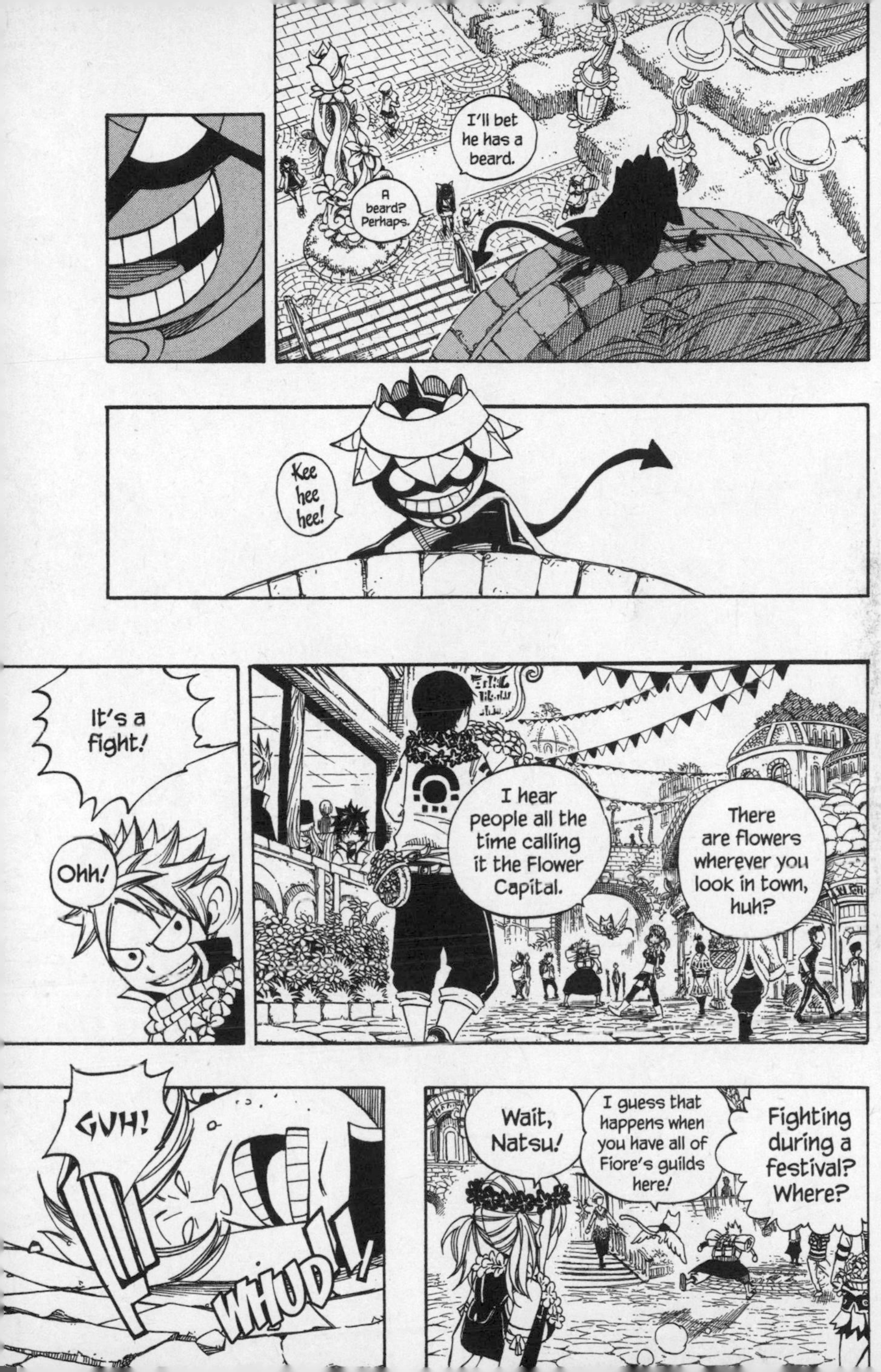
I'll bet he has a beard.
A beard? Perhaps.
Kee hee hee!
There are flowers wherever you look in town, huh?
I hear people all the time calling it the Flower Capital.
It's a fight!
Ohh!
Fighting during a festival? Where?
I guess that happens when you have all of Fiore's guilds here!
Wait, Natsu!
GUH!
WHUD

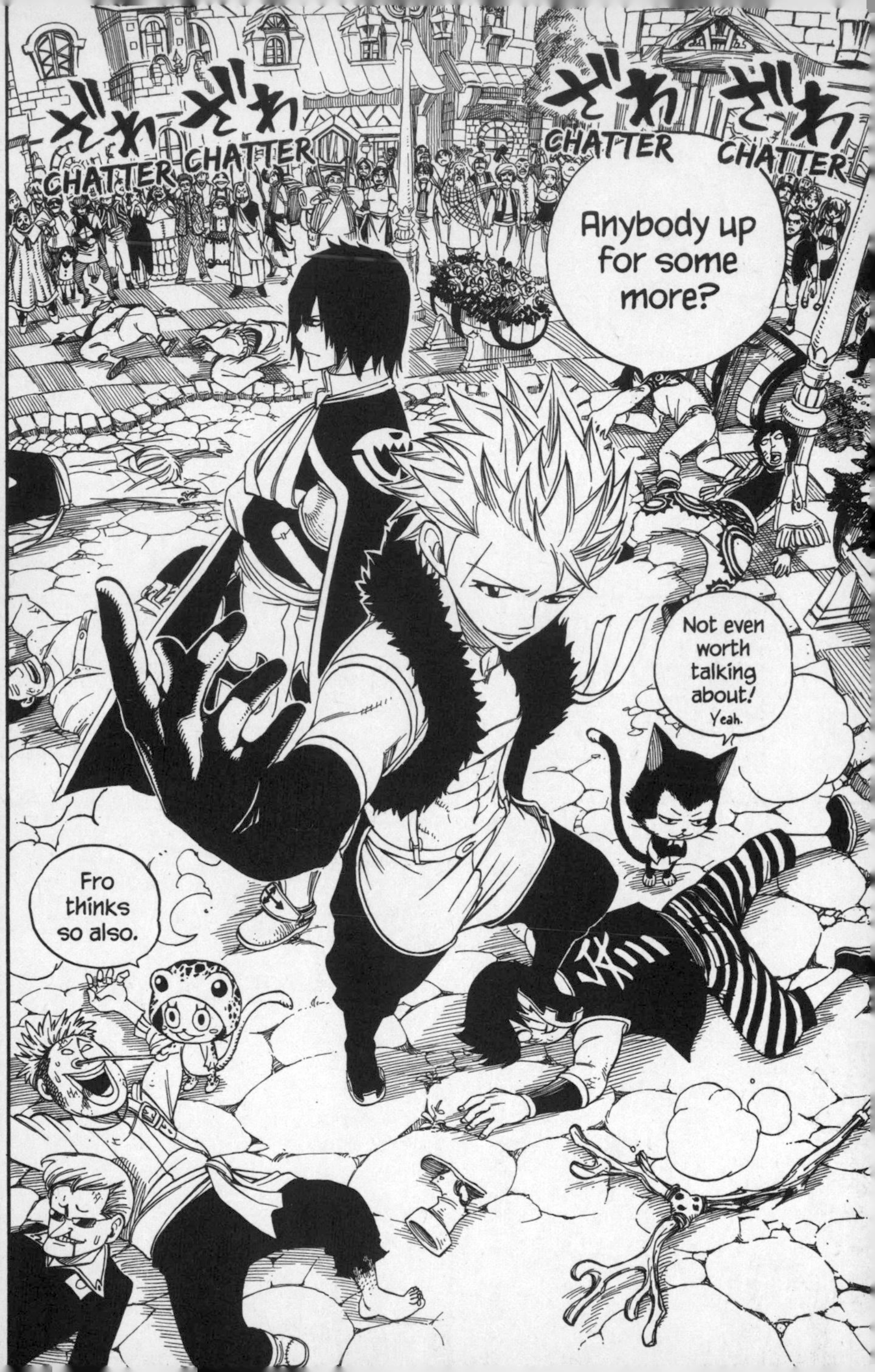
ざわ ざわ
CHATTER CHATTER
Anybody up for some more?
ざわ ざわ
CHATTER CHATTER
Not even worth talking about!
Yeah.
Fro thinks so also.

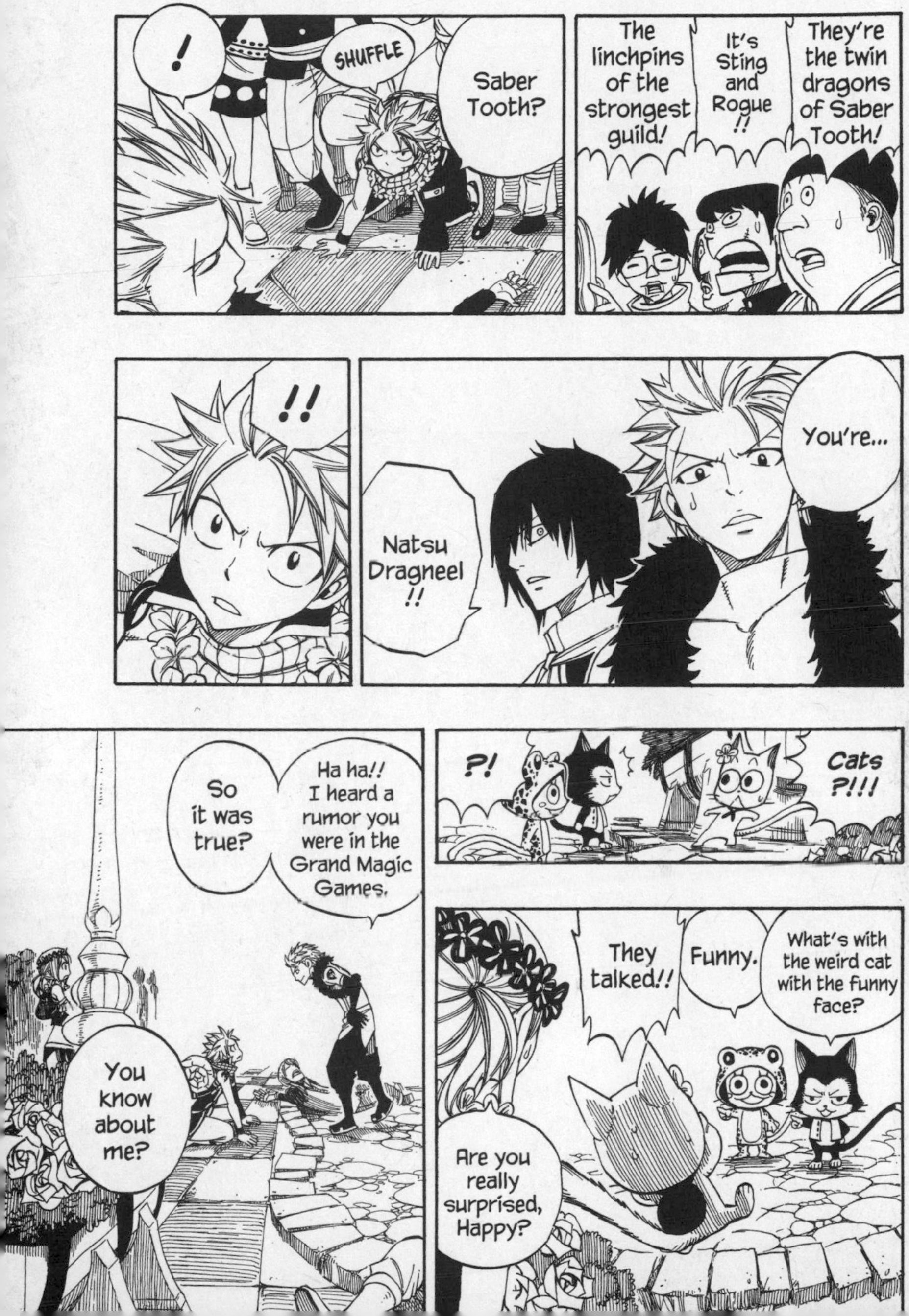
They're the twin dragons of Saber Tooth!
It's Sting and Rogue!!
The linchpins of the strongest guild!
Saber Tooth?
SHUFFLE
!
You're...
Natsu Dragneel!!
!!
Cats?!!!
?!
What's with the weird cat with the funny face?
Funny.
They talked!!
Are you really surprised, Happy?
Ha ha!! I heard a rumor you were in the Grand Magic Games.
So it was true?
You know about me?

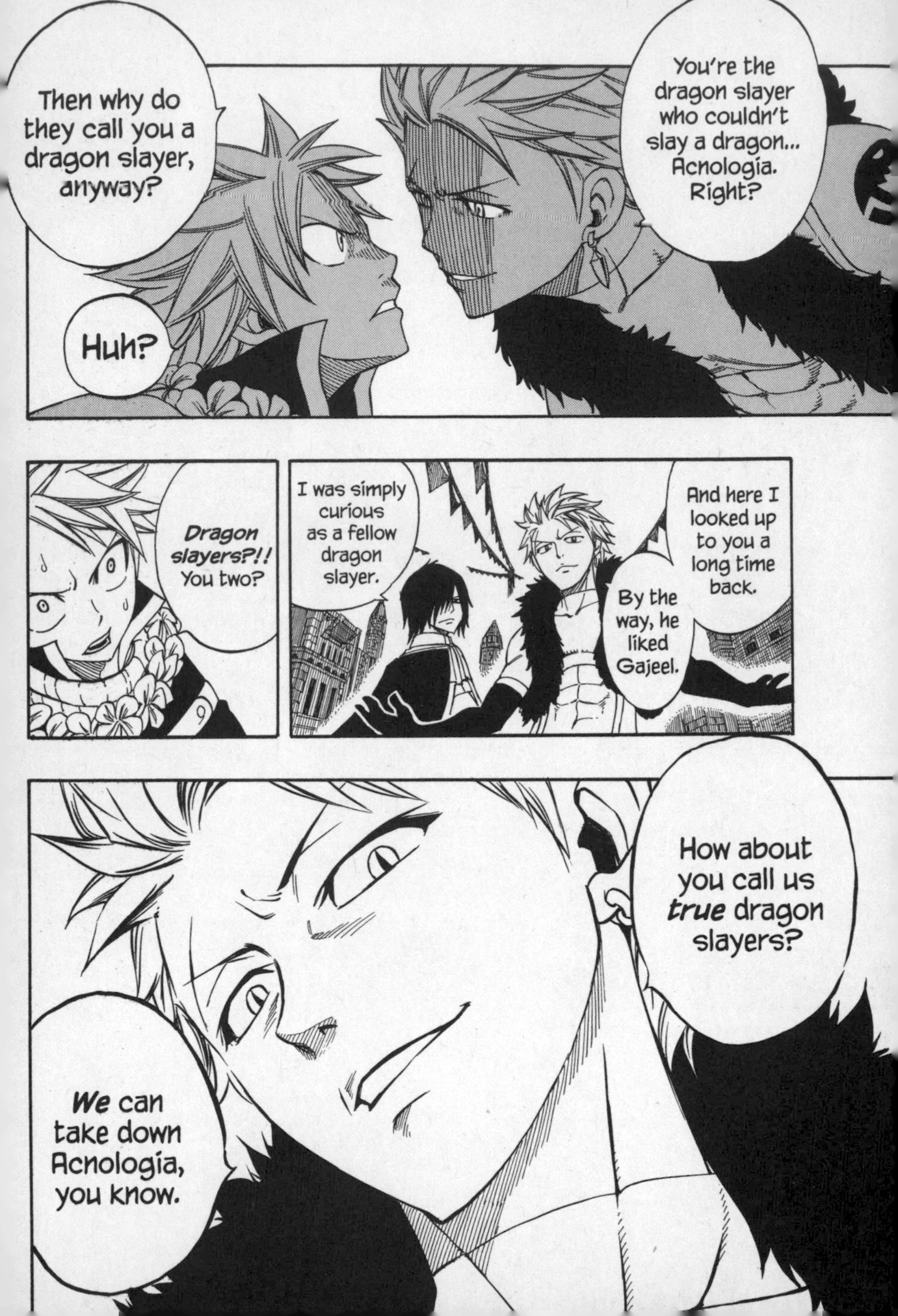
You're the dragon slayer who couldn't slay a dragon... Acnologia. Right?
Then why do they call you a dragon slayer, anyway?
Huh?
And here I looked up to you a long time back.
I was simply curious as a fellow dragon slayer.
By the way, he liked Gajeel.
*Dragon slayers?!!* You two?
How about you call us ***true*** dragon slayers?
***We*** can take down Acnologia, you know.

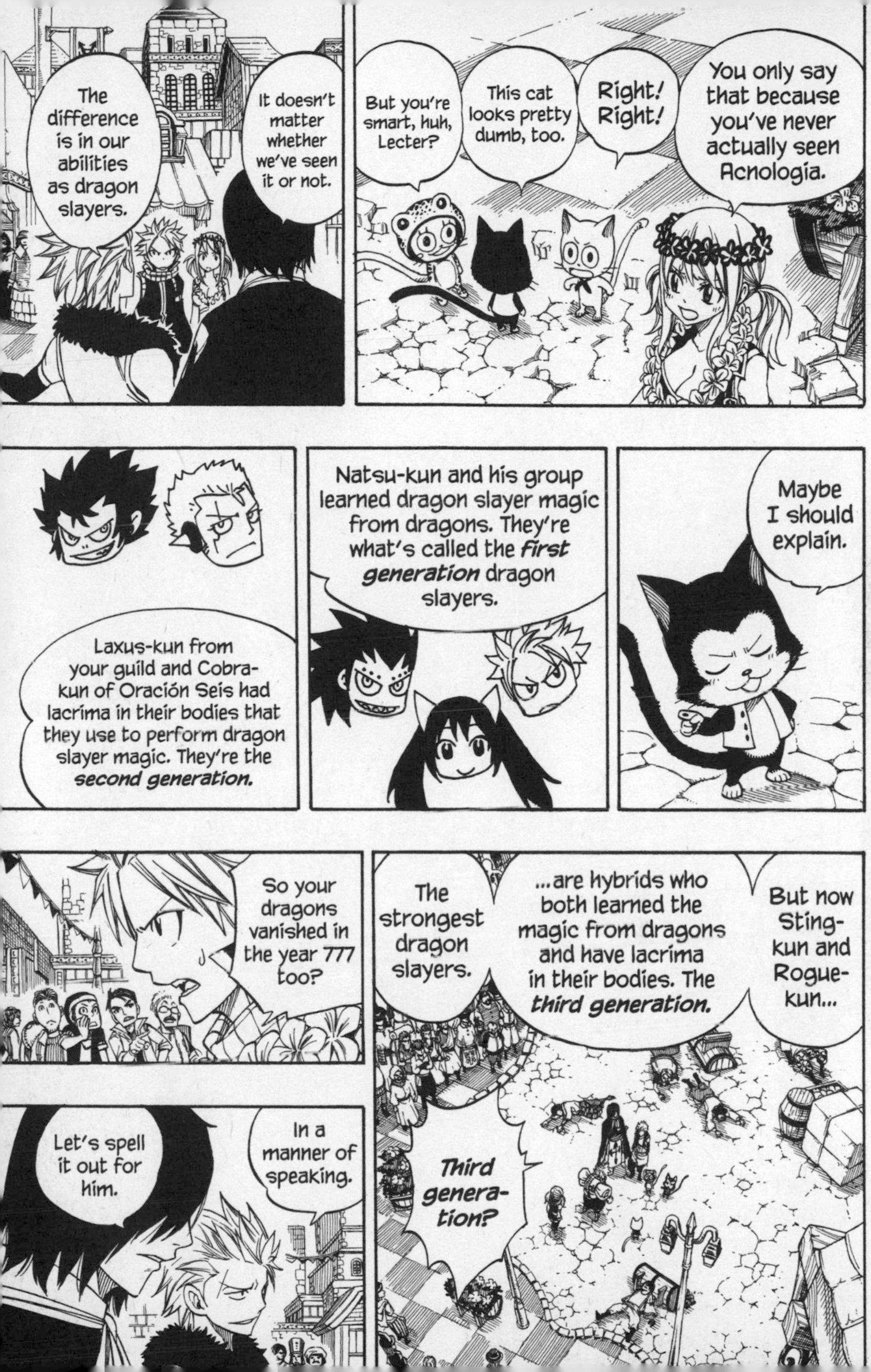
You only say that because you've never actually seen Acnologia.
Right! Right!
This cat looks pretty dumb, too.
But you're smart, huh, Lecter?
It doesn't matter whether we've seen it or not.
The difference is in our abilities as dragon slayers.
Maybe I should explain.
Natsu-kun and his group learned dragon slayer magic from dragons. They're what's called the *first generation* dragon slayers.
Laxus-kun from your guild and Cobra-kun of Oración Seis had lacrima in their bodies that they use to perform dragon slayer magic. They're the *second generation.*
But now Sting-kun and Rogue-kun...
...are hybrids who both learned the magic from dragons and have lacrima in their bodies. The *third generation.*
The strongest dragon slayers.
*Third generation?*
So your dragons vanished in the year 777 too?
In a manner of speaking.
Let's spell it out for him.

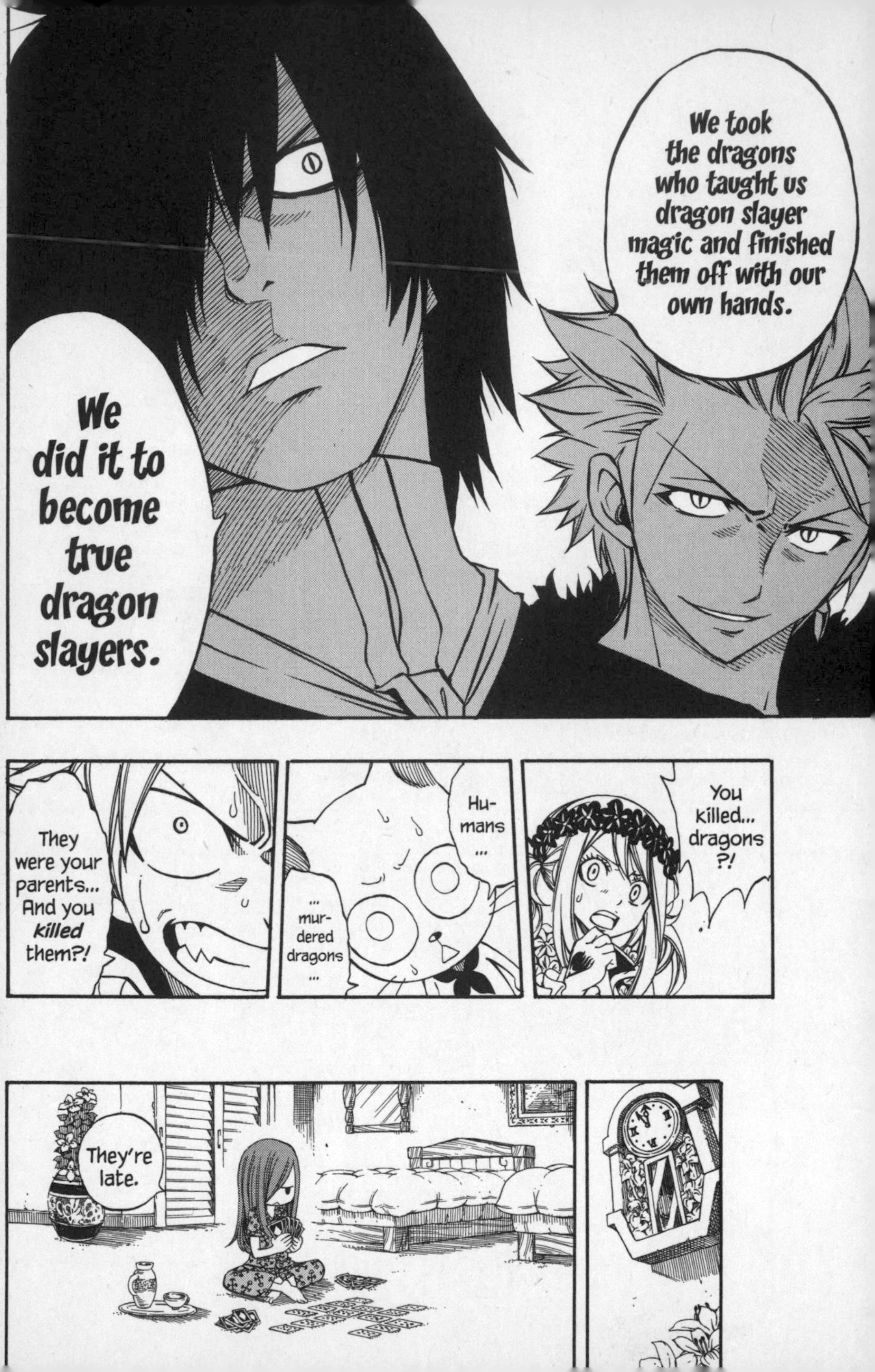
We took the dragons who taught us dragon slayer magic and finished them off with our own hands.
We did it to become true dragon slayers.
You killed... dragons?!
Humans...
...murdered dragons...
They were your parents... And you *killed* them?!
They're late.

# FAIRY TAIL

## Chapter 266: Sky Labyrinth

**FAIRY TAIL**

Name:
**Max Alors**

Age:
**24**

Magic:
**Sandstorm**

Likes:
**Bars**

Dislikes:
**Being alone**

## Remarks

One of his favorite things in the world is talking to people, so while the Sirius Island group was gone, the number of people in the guild decreased, and this pained him. Before, he'd work the guild's gift shop, plan and run events, talk to the public and do master-of-ceremonies work, but as the guild got weaker, his constant talk was reduced a little bit. The people around him started to think he had finally quieted down, but when the Sirius Island group came back, his motor mouth returned.

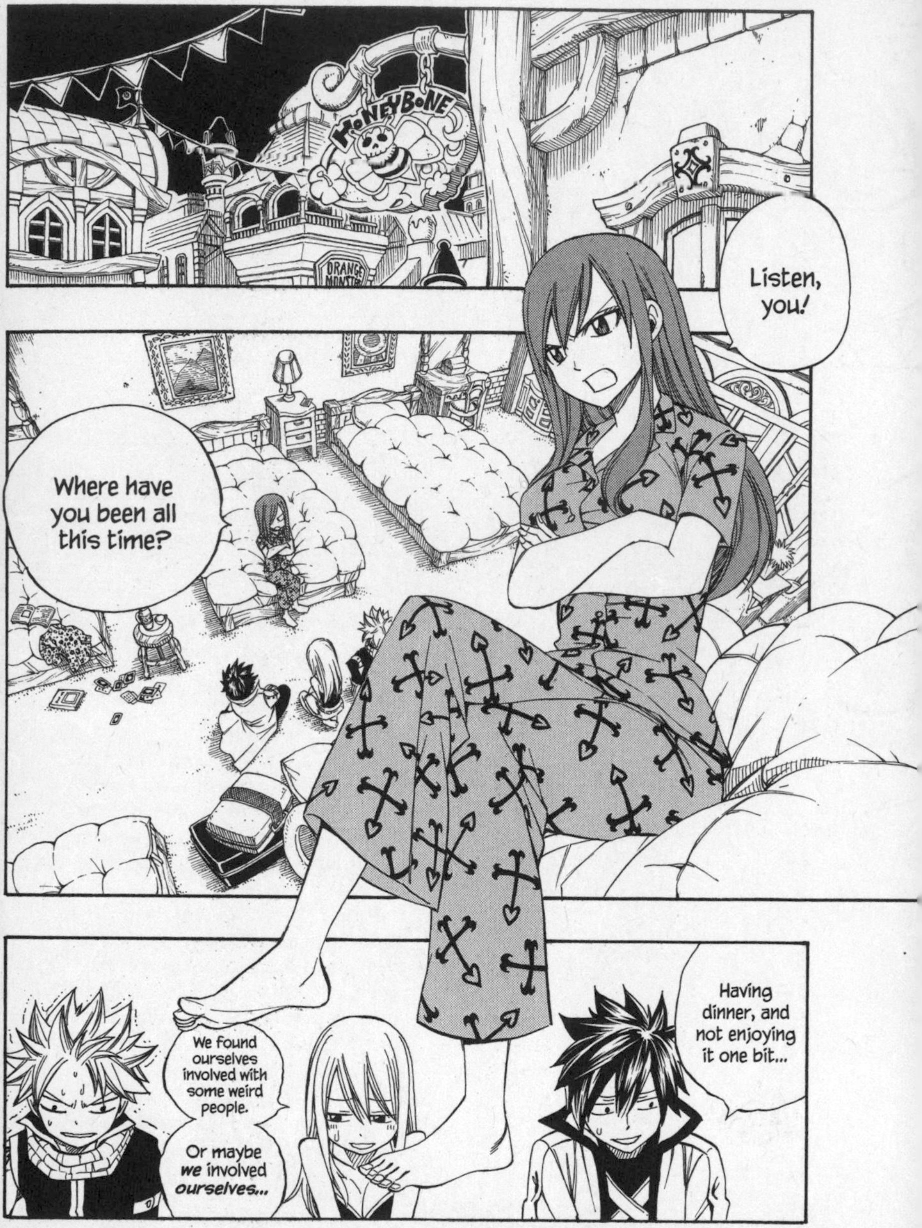
HONEYBONE
Listen, you!
Where have you been all this time?
Having dinner, and not enjoying it one bit...
We found ourselves involved with some weird people.
Or maybe *we* involved *ourselves*...

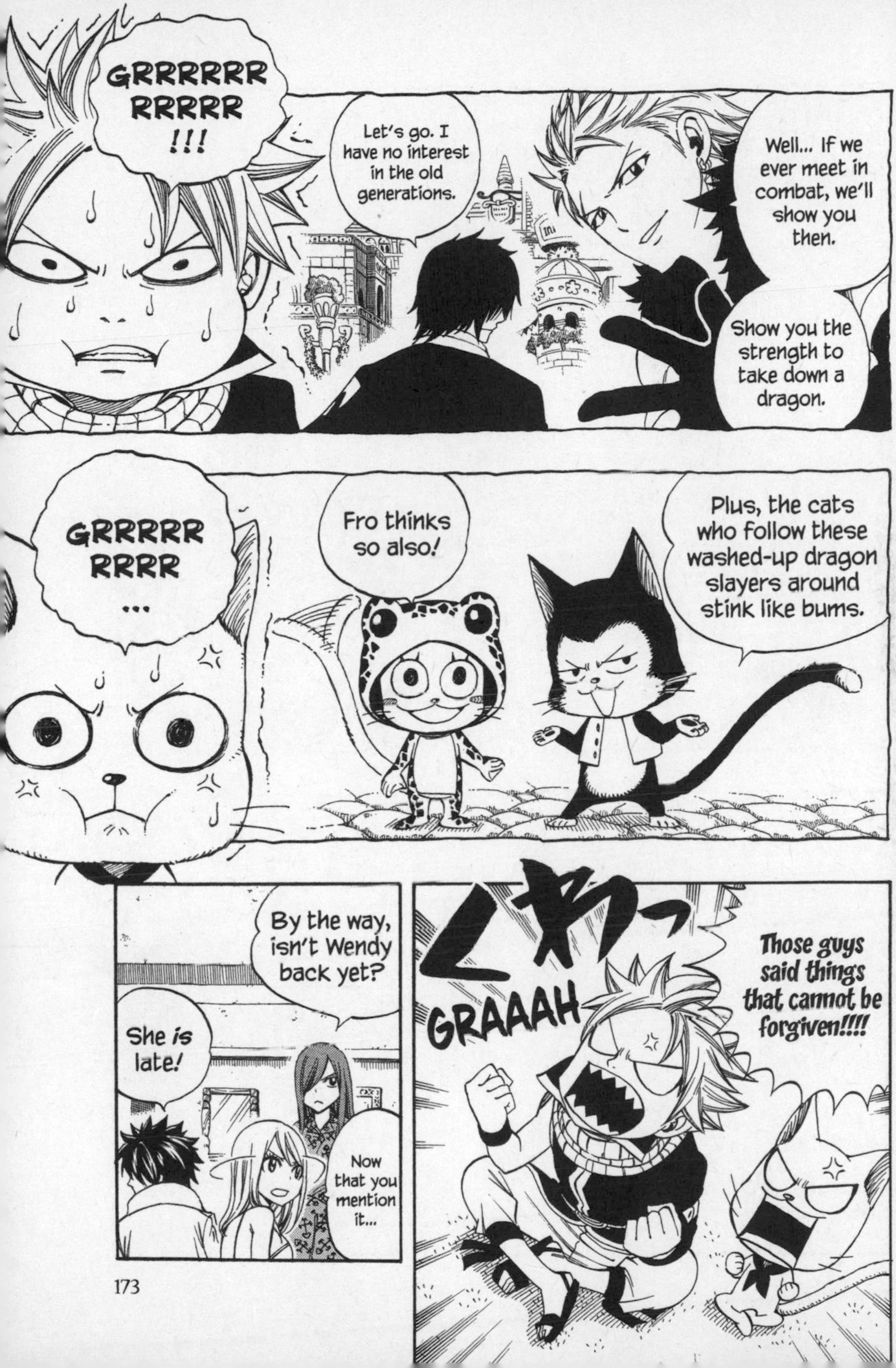
Well... If we ever meet in combat, we'll show you then.
Show you the strength to take down a dragon.
Let's go. I have no interest in the old generations.
GRRRRRRRRRRRR!!!
Plus, the cats who follow these washed-up dragon slayers around stink like bums.
Fro thinks so also!
GRRRRRRRRRR...
Those guys said things that cannot be forgiven!!!!
くわっ
GRAAAH
By the way, isn't Wendy back yet?
She *is* late!
Now that you mention it...

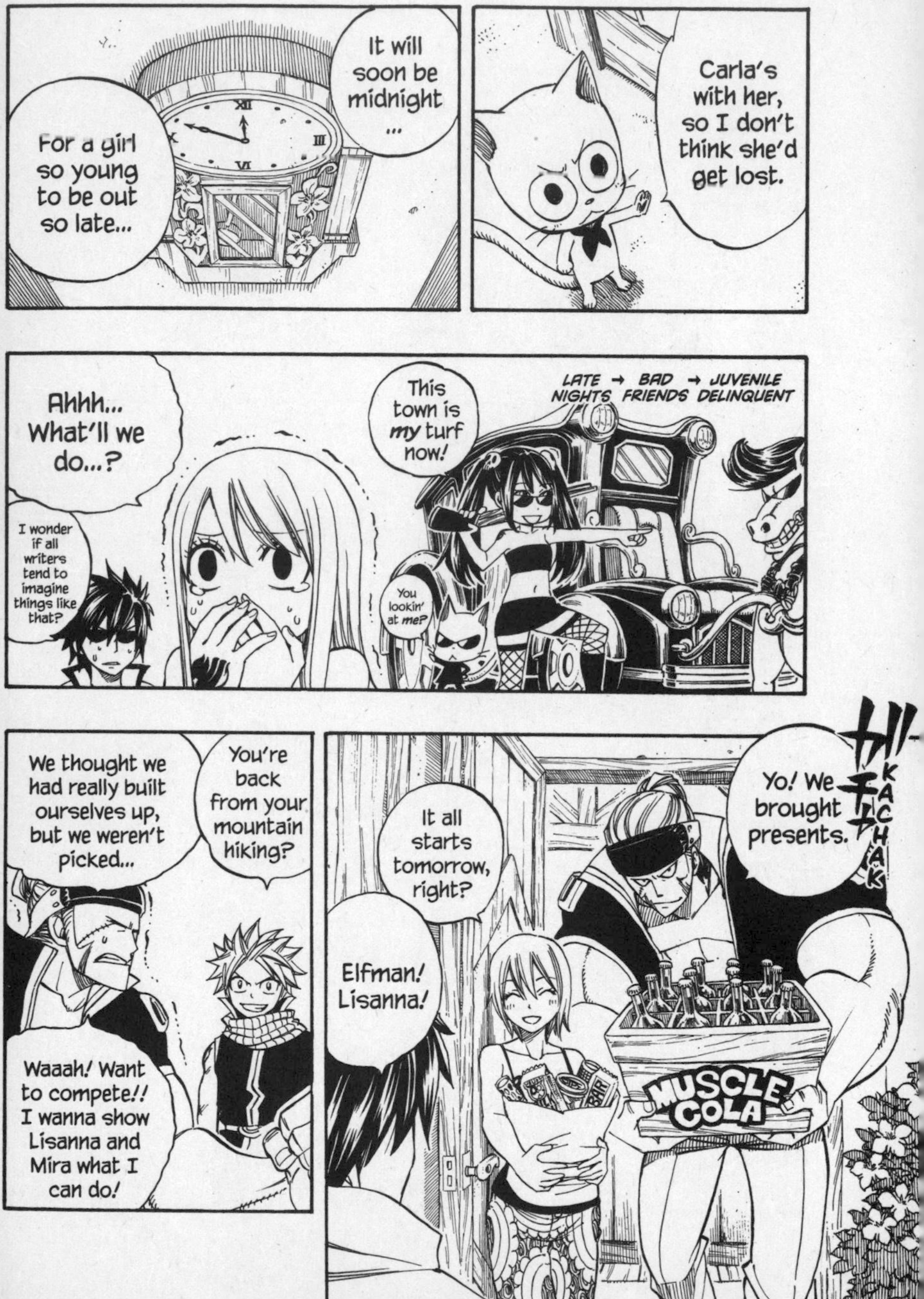
Carla's with her, so I don't think she'd get lost.
It will soon be midnight ...
For a girl so young to be out so late...
LATE NIGHTS → BAD FRIENDS → JUVENILE DELINQUENT
This town is *my* turf now!
Ahhh... What'll we do...?
You lookin' at *me*?
I wonder if all writers tend to imagine things like that?
Yo! We brought presents.
KACHAK
It all starts tomorrow, right?
Elfman! Lisanna!
MUSCLE COLA
You're back from your mountain hiking?
We thought we had really built ourselves up, but we weren't picked...
Waaah! Want to compete!! I wanna show Lisanna and Mira what I can do!

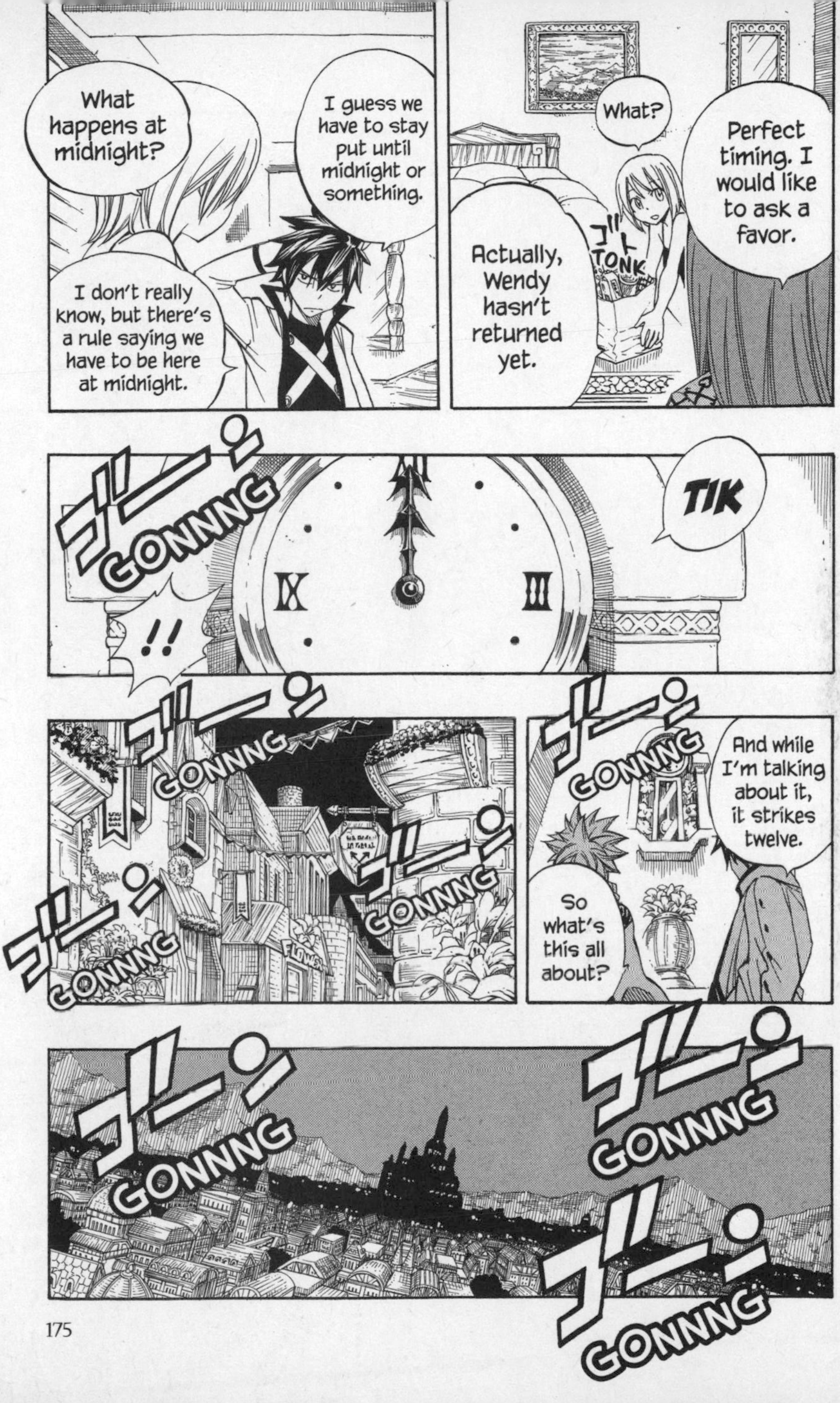
Perfect timing. I would like to ask a favor.
What?
TONK
Actually, Wendy hasn't returned yet.
I guess we have to stay put until midnight or something.
What happens at midnight?
I don't really know, but there's a rule saying we have to be here at midnight.
TIK
GONNNG
!!
GONNNG
And while I'm talking about it, it strikes twelve.
So what's this all about?
GONNNG
GONNNG
GONNNG
GONNNG
GONNNG
GONNNG

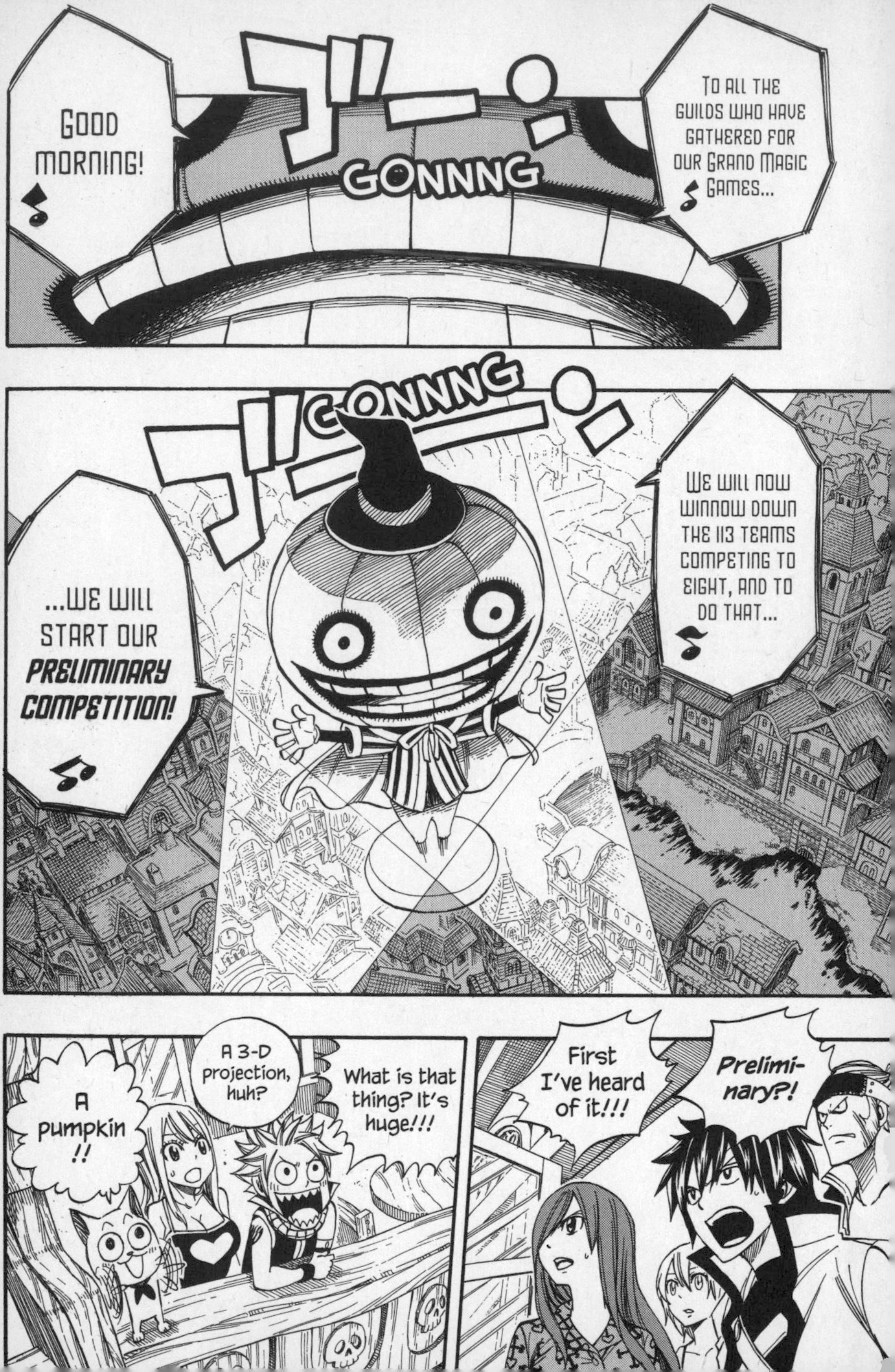
To all the guilds who have gathered for our Grand Magic Games...
GONNNG
Good morning!
We will now winnow down the 113 teams competing to eight, and to do that...
GONNNG
...we will start our *preliminary competition!*
*Prelimi-nary?!*
First I've heard of it!!!
What is that thing? It's huge!!!
A 3-D projection, huh?
A pumpkin!!

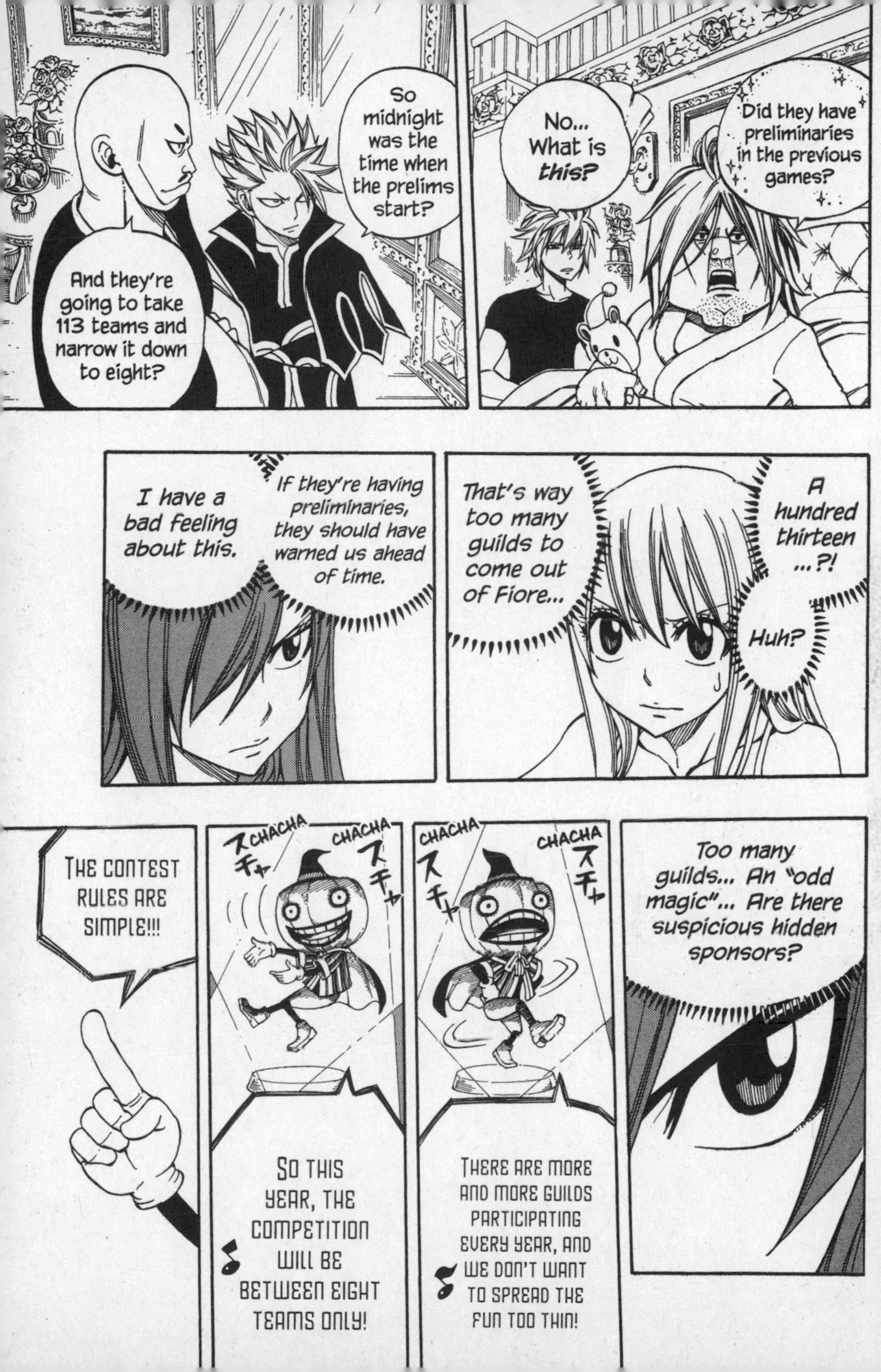

Did they have preliminaries in the previous games?
No... What is *this?*
So midnight was the time when the prelims start?
And they're going to take 113 teams and narrow it down to eight?
*A hundred thirteen ...?!*
*Huh?*
*That's way too many guilds to come out of Fiore...*
*If they're having preliminaries, they should have warned us ahead of time.*
*I have a bad feeling about this.*
*Too many guilds... An "odd magic"... Are there suspicious hidden sponsors?*
CHACHA
CHACHA
THERE ARE MORE AND MORE GUILDS PARTICIPATING EVERY YEAR, AND WE DON'T WANT TO SPREAD THE FUN TOO THIN!
CHACHA
CHACHA
SO THIS YEAR, THE COMPETITION WILL BE BETWEEN EIGHT TEAMS ONLY!
THE CONTEST RULES ARE SIMPLE!!!

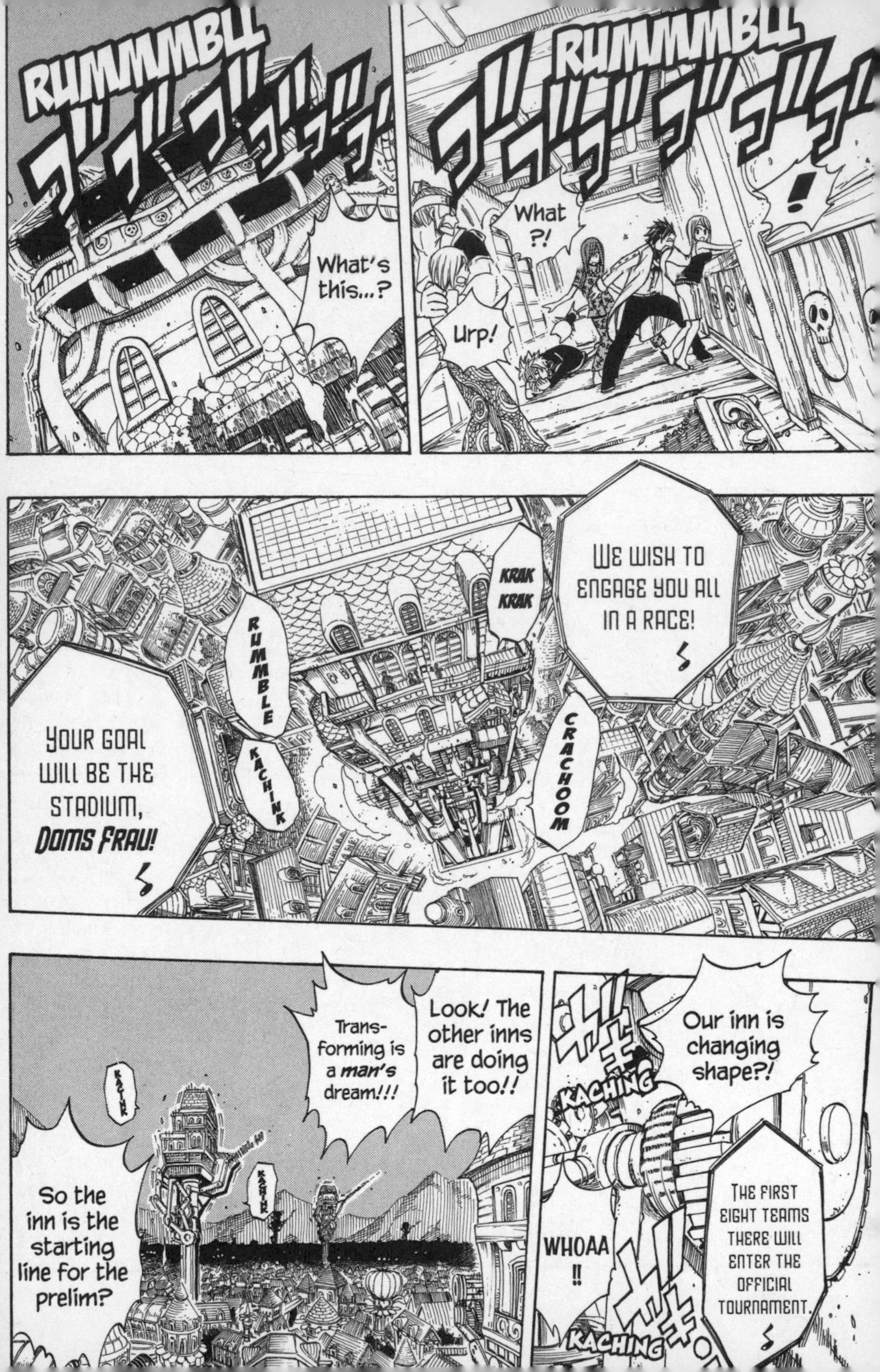
RUMMMBLL
!
What ?!
Urp!
RUMMMBLL
What's this...?
WE WISH TO ENGAGE YOU ALL IN A RACE!
KRAK KRAK
CRACHOOM
RUMBLE
KACHINK
YOUR GOAL WILL BE THE STADIUM, DOMS FRAU!
Our inn is changing shape?!
KACHING
WHOAA !!
THE FIRST EIGHT TEAMS THERE WILL ENTER THE OFFICIAL TOURNAMENT.
KACHING
Look! The other inns are doing it too!!
Trans-forming is a man's dream!!!
KACHINK
KACHINK
So the inn is the starting line for the prelim?

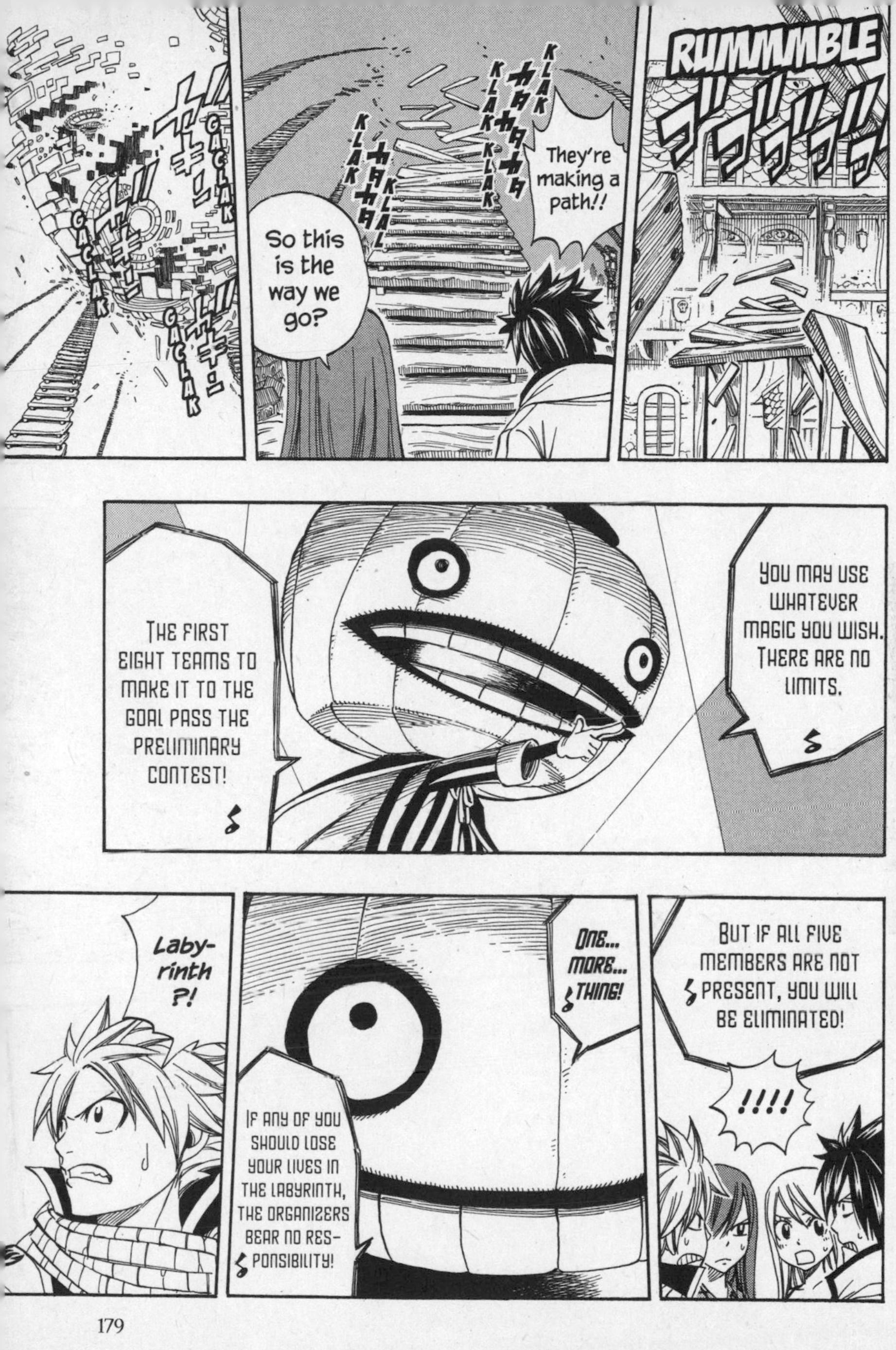

RUMMMBLE
They're making a path!!
So this is the way we go?
KLAK KLAK
KLAK KLAK
KLAK KLAL
GACLAK
GACLAK
GACLAK
You may use whatever magic you wish. There are no limits.
The first eight teams to make it to the goal pass the preliminary contest!
But if all five members are not present, you will be eliminated!
!!!!
One... more... thing!
If any of you should lose your lives in the labyrinth, the organizers bear no responsibility!
Labyrinth?!

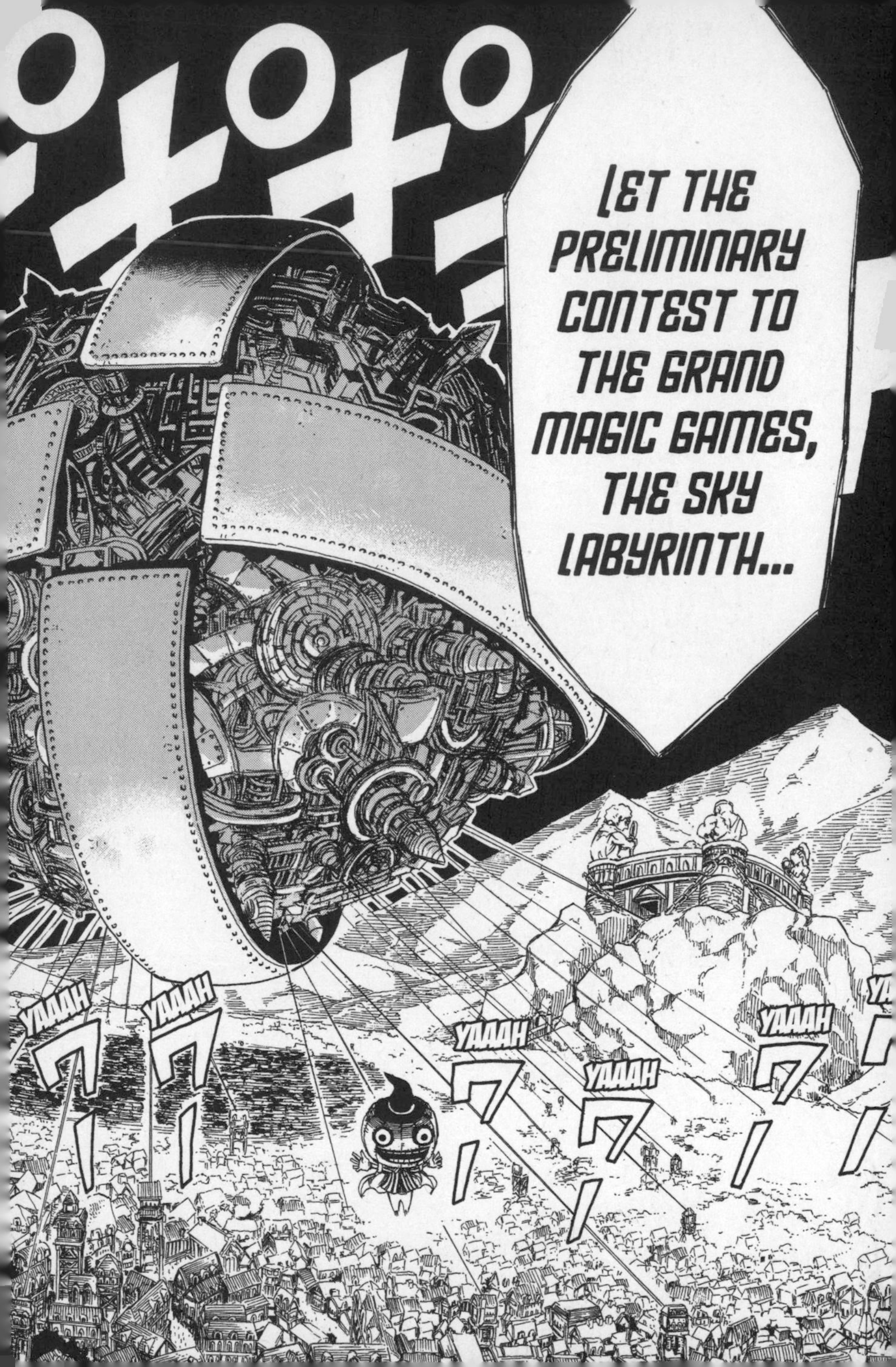
LET THE PRELIMINARY CONTEST TO THE GRAND MAGIC GAMES, THE SKY LABYRINTH...
YAAAH
YAAAH
YAAAH
YAAAH
YAAAH

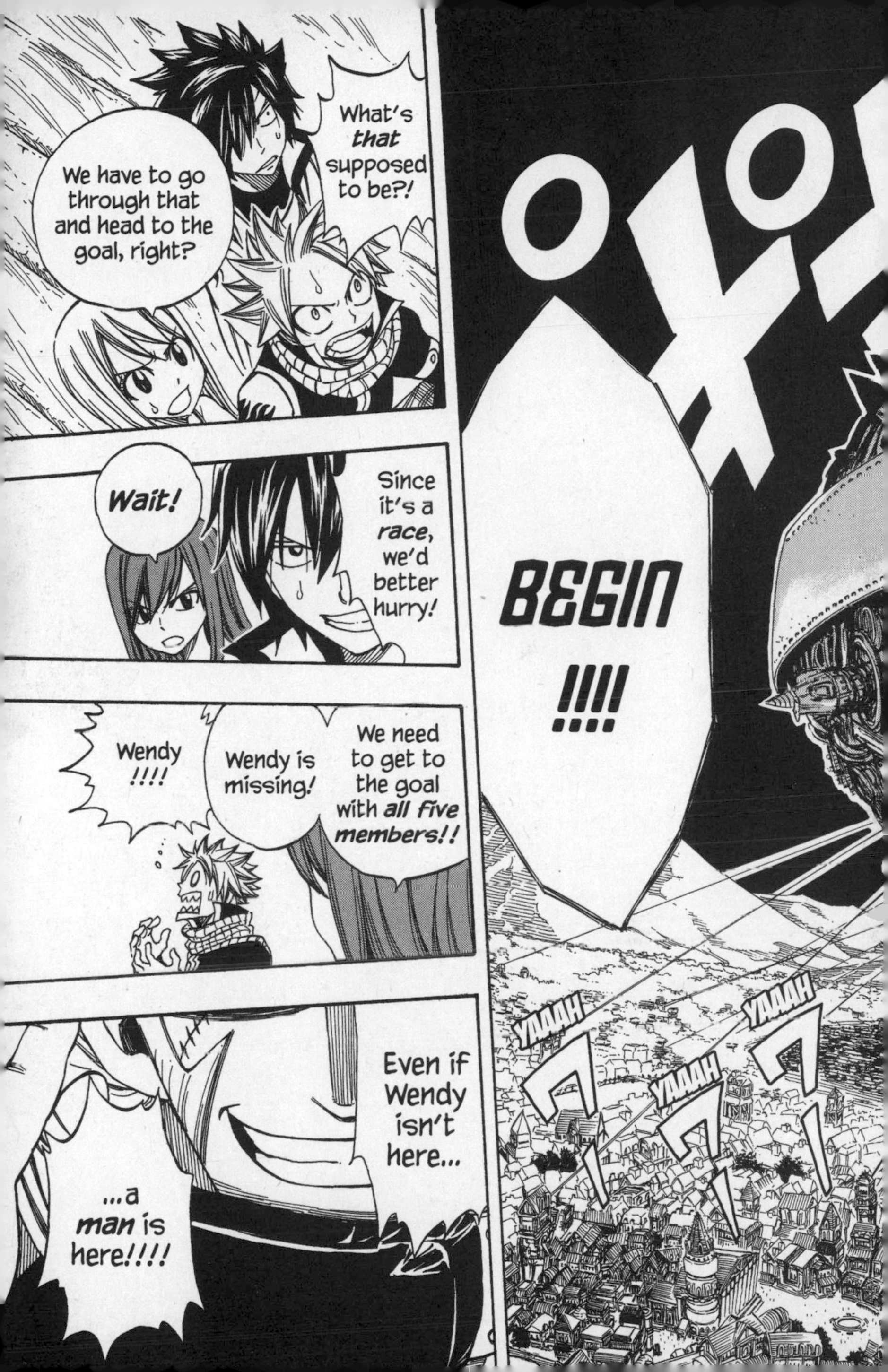
BEGIN !!!!
YAAAH
YAAAH
YAAAH
What's *that* supposed to be?!
We have to go through that and head to the goal, right?
Since it's a *race*, we'd better hurry!
*Wait!*
We need to get to the goal with *all five members!!*
Wendy is missing!
Wendy !!!!
Even if Wendy isn't here...
...a *man* is here!!!!

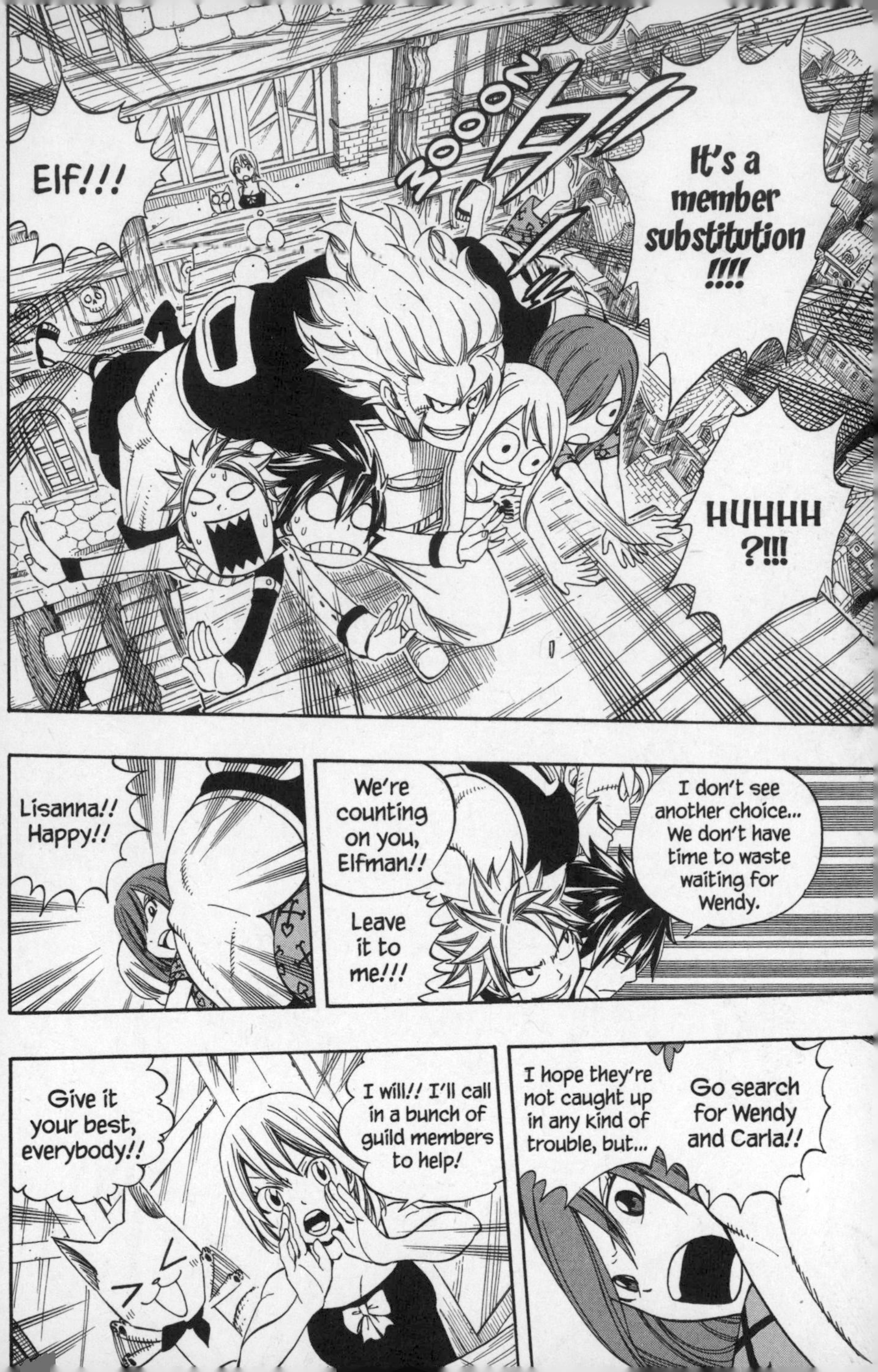
It's a member substitution !!!!
Elf!!!
HUHHH ?!!!
I don't see another choice... We don't have time to waste waiting for Wendy.
We're counting on you, Elfman!!
Leave it to me!!!
Lisanna!! Happy!!
Go search for Wendy and Carla!!
I hope they're not caught up in any kind of trouble, but...
I will!! I'll call in a bunch of guild members to help!
Give it your best, everybody!!

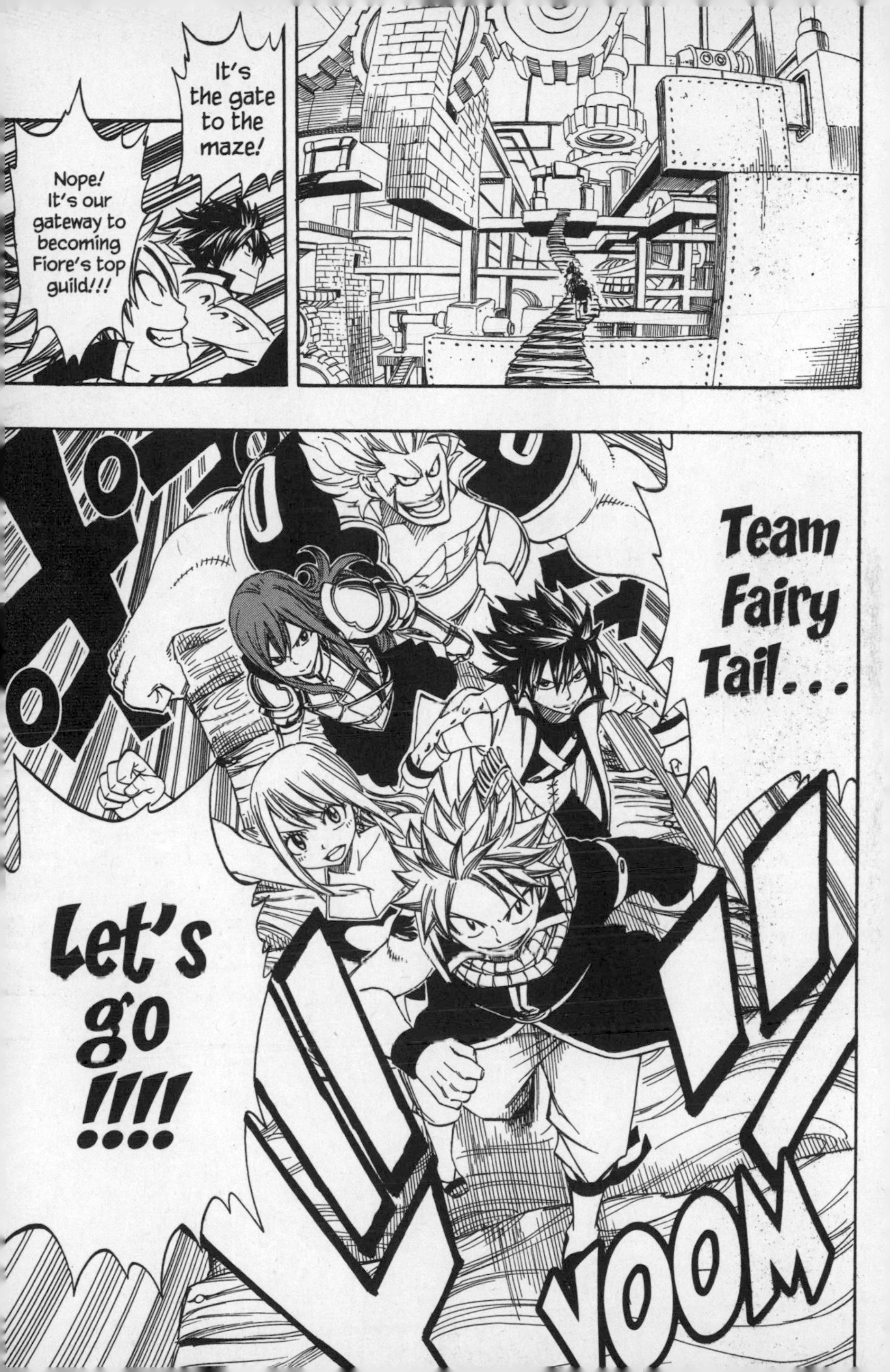
It's the gate to the maze!
Nope! It's our gateway to becoming Fiore's top guild!!!
Team Fairy Tail...
Let's go!!!!
VOOM

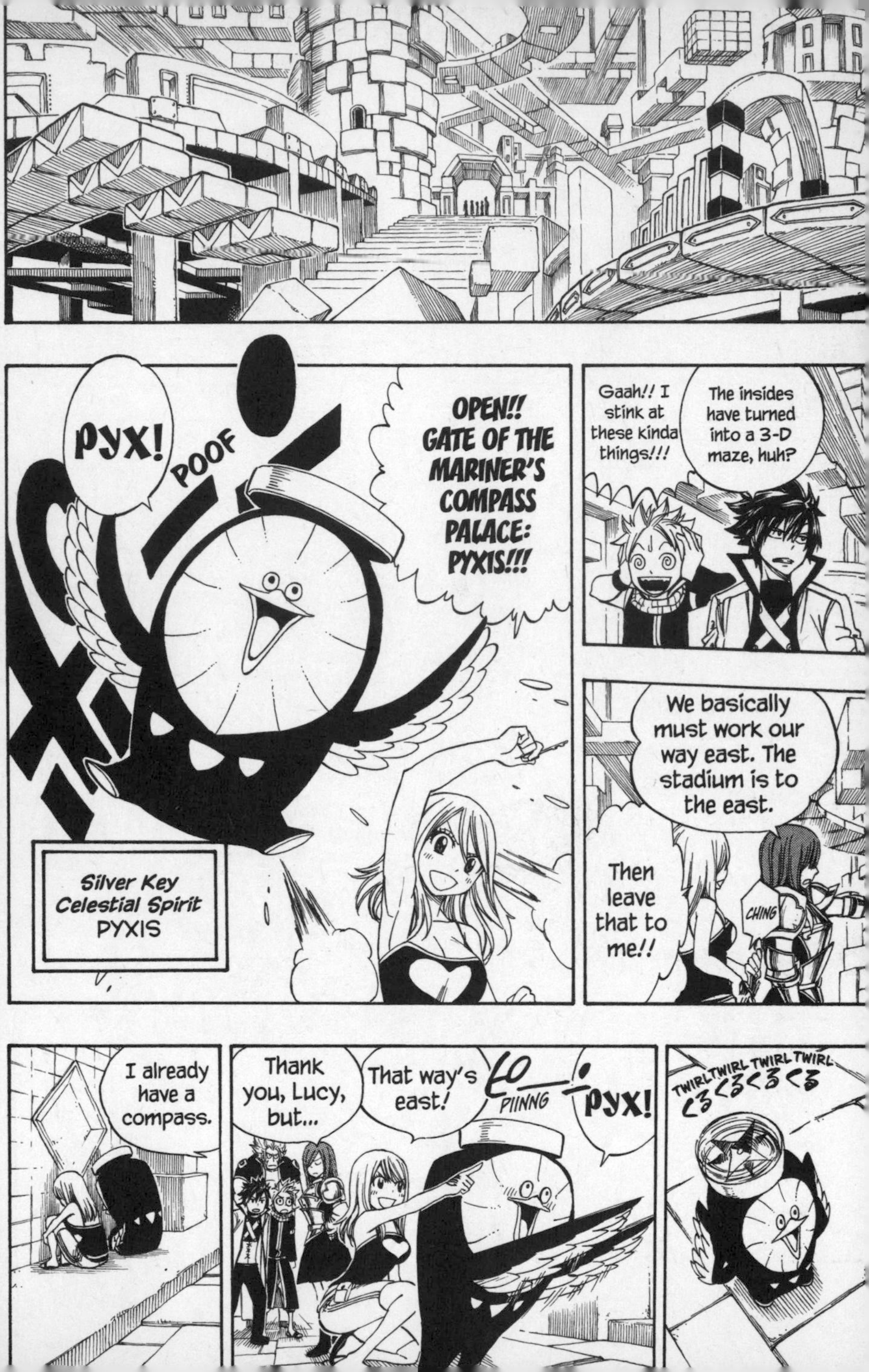
The insides have turned into a 3-D maze, huh?
Gaah!! I stink at these kinda things!!!
We basically must work our way east. The stadium is to the east.
Then leave that to me!!
CHING
OPEN!! GATE OF THE MARINER'S COMPASS PALACE: PYXIS!!!
PYX!
POOF
Silver Key Celestial Spirit PYXIS
TWIRL TWIRL TWIRL TWIRL
くるくるくるくる
PYX!
PIINNG
That way's east!
Thank you, Lucy, but...
I already have a compass.

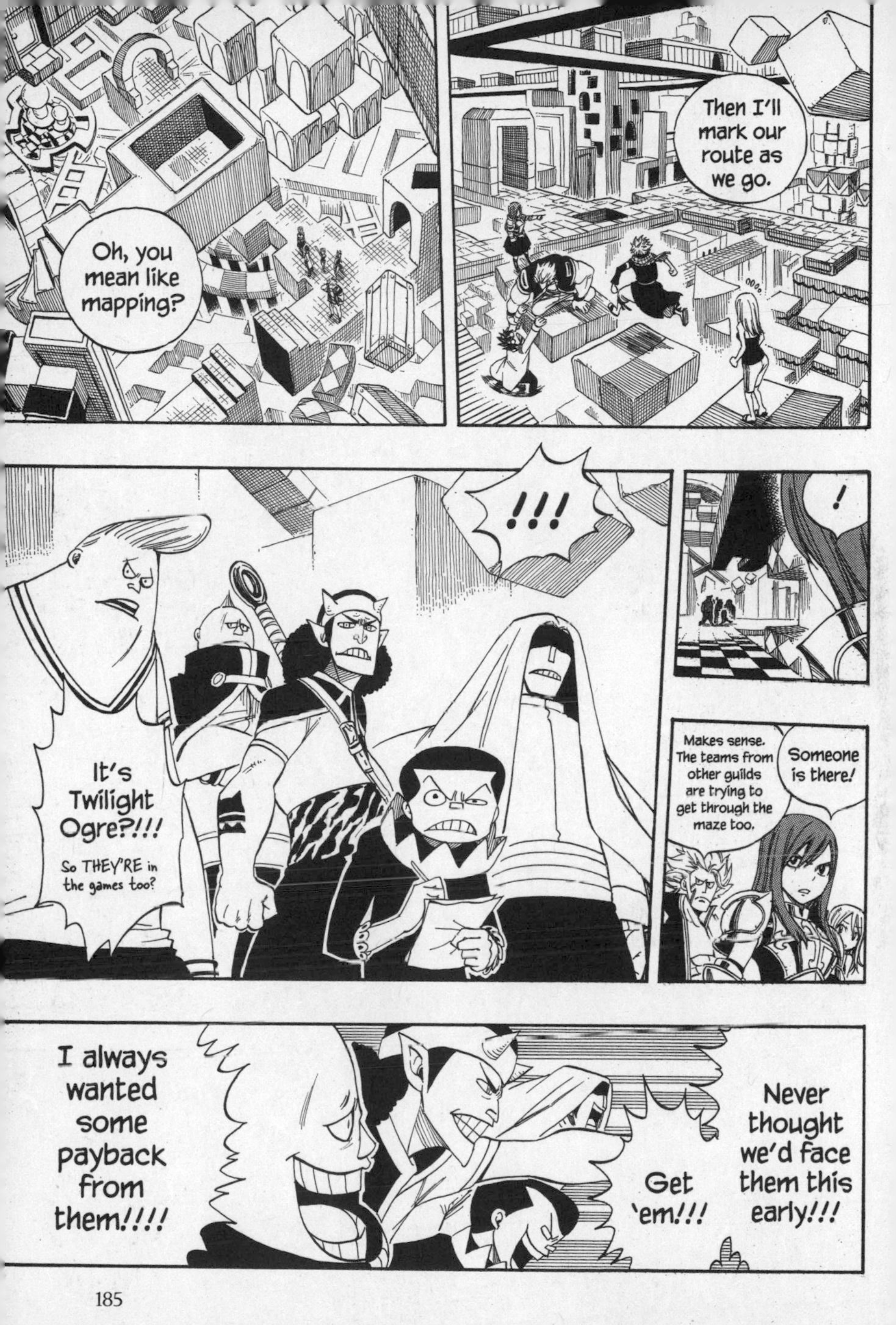
Then I'll mark our route as we go.
Oh, you mean like mapping?
!
Someone is there!
Makes sense. The teams from other guilds are trying to get through the maze too.
!!!
It's Twilight Ogre?!!!
So THEY'RE in the games too?
Never thought we'd face them this early!!!
Get 'em!!!
I always wanted some payback from them!!!!

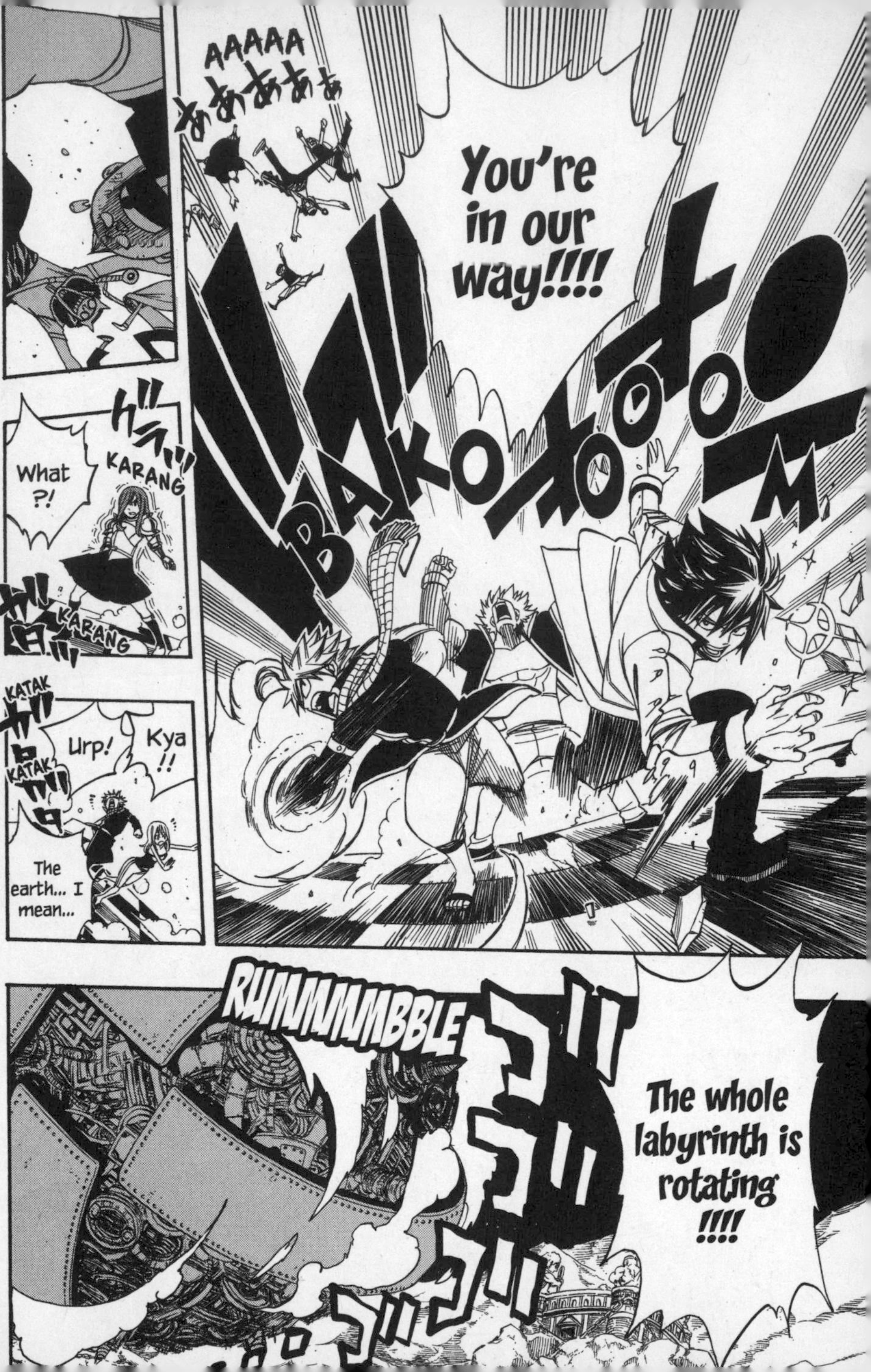
AAAAA
あああああ
You're in our way!!!!
BAKOOOOOM
What ?!
KARANG
KARANG
KATAK
KATAK
Urp!
Kya !!
The earth... I mean...
RUMMMMMBLE
The whole labyrinth is rotating !!!!

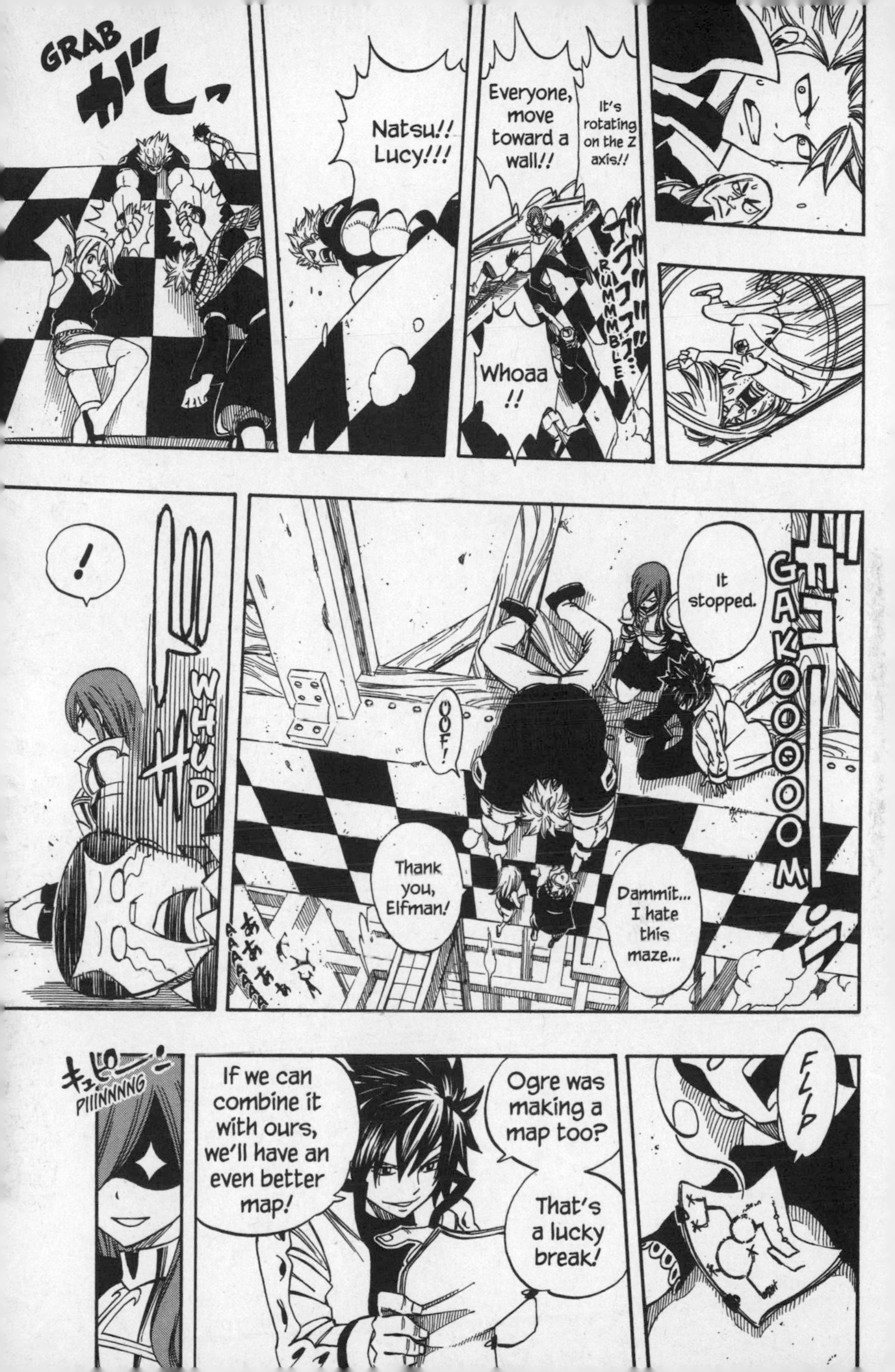
It's rotating on the Z axis!!
Everyone, move toward a wall!!
RUMMMBLE
Whoaa!!
Natsu!! Lucy!!!
GRAB
GAKOOOOOOM
It stopped.
OOF!
Dammit... I hate this maze...
Thank you, Elfman!
!
WHUD
FLIP
Ogre was making a map too?
That's a lucky break!
If we can combine it with ours, we'll have an even better map!
PIIINNNNG

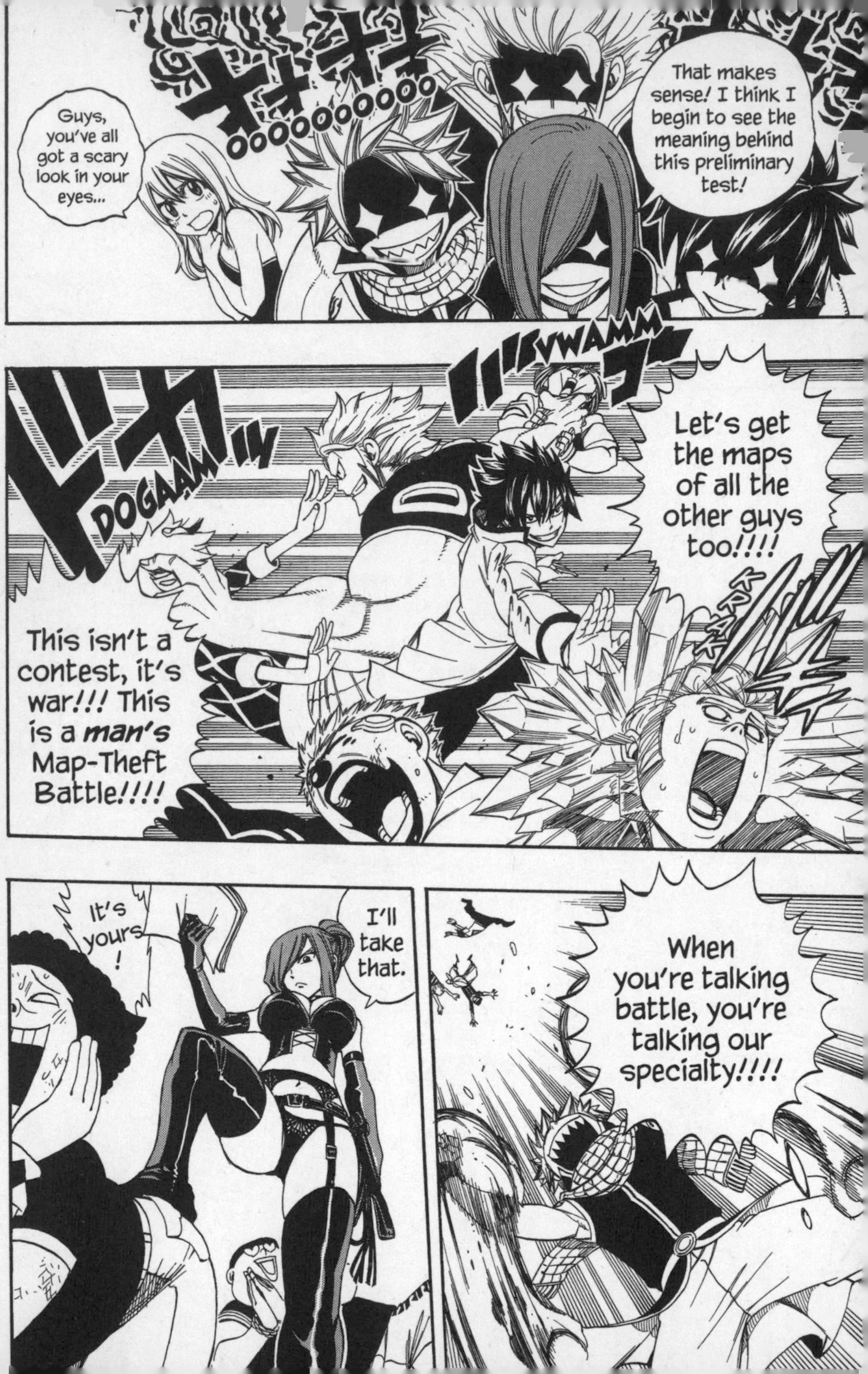
That makes sense! I think I begin to see the meaning behind this preliminary test!
OOOOOOOOOO
Guys, you've all got a scary look in your eyes...
VWAMM
Let's get the maps of all the other guys too!!!!
KRAK
DOGAAAM
This isn't a contest, it's war!!! This is a *man's* Map-Theft Battle!!!!
When you're talking battle, you're talking our specialty!!!!
I'll take that.
It's yours!

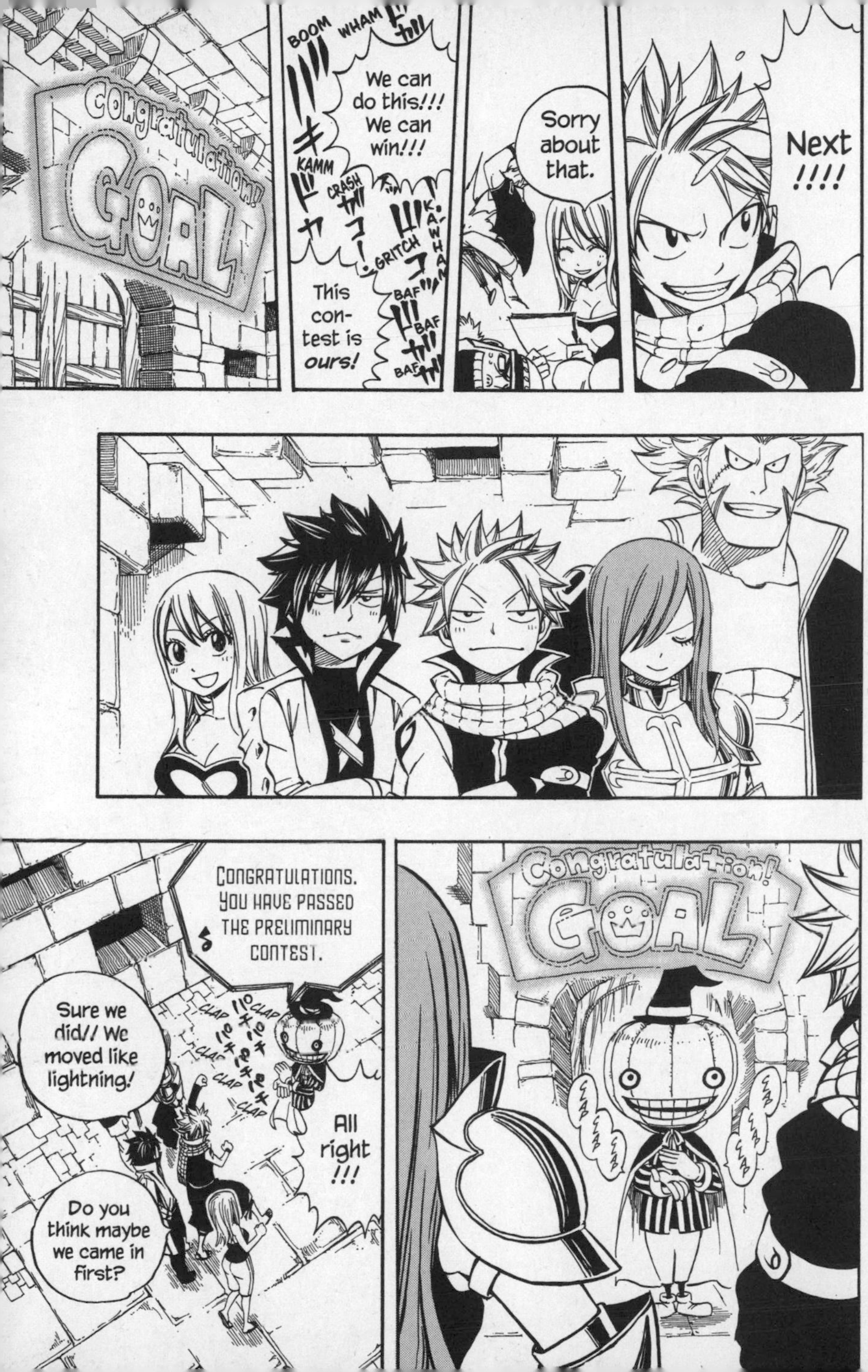
Next!!!!
Sorry about that.
BOOM
WHAM
We can do this!!! We can win!!!
KAMM
CRASH
GRITCH
KAWHAM
BAF
BAF
BAF
This contest is ours!
Congratulation!
GOAL
Congratulation!
GOAL
CLAP
CONGRATULATIONS. YOU HAVE PASSED THE PRELIMINARY CONTEST.
CLAP
CLAP
CLAP
CLAP
CLAP
All right!!!
Sure we did!! We moved like lightning!
Do you think maybe we came in first?

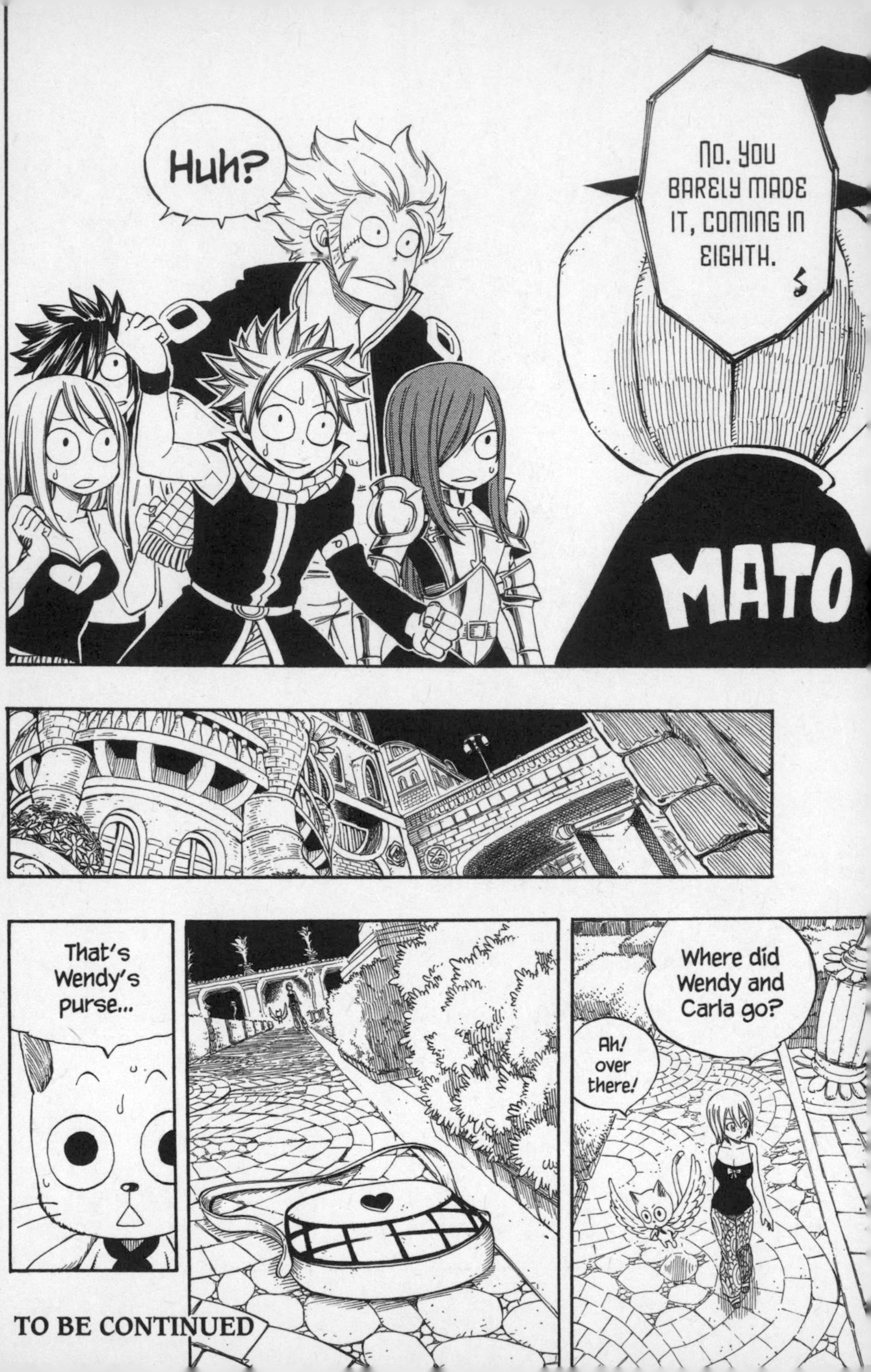
No. You barely made it, coming in eighth.
MATO
Huh?
Where did Wendy and Carla go?
Ah! over there!
That's Wendy's purse...
TO BE CONTINUED

# BONUS PAGES

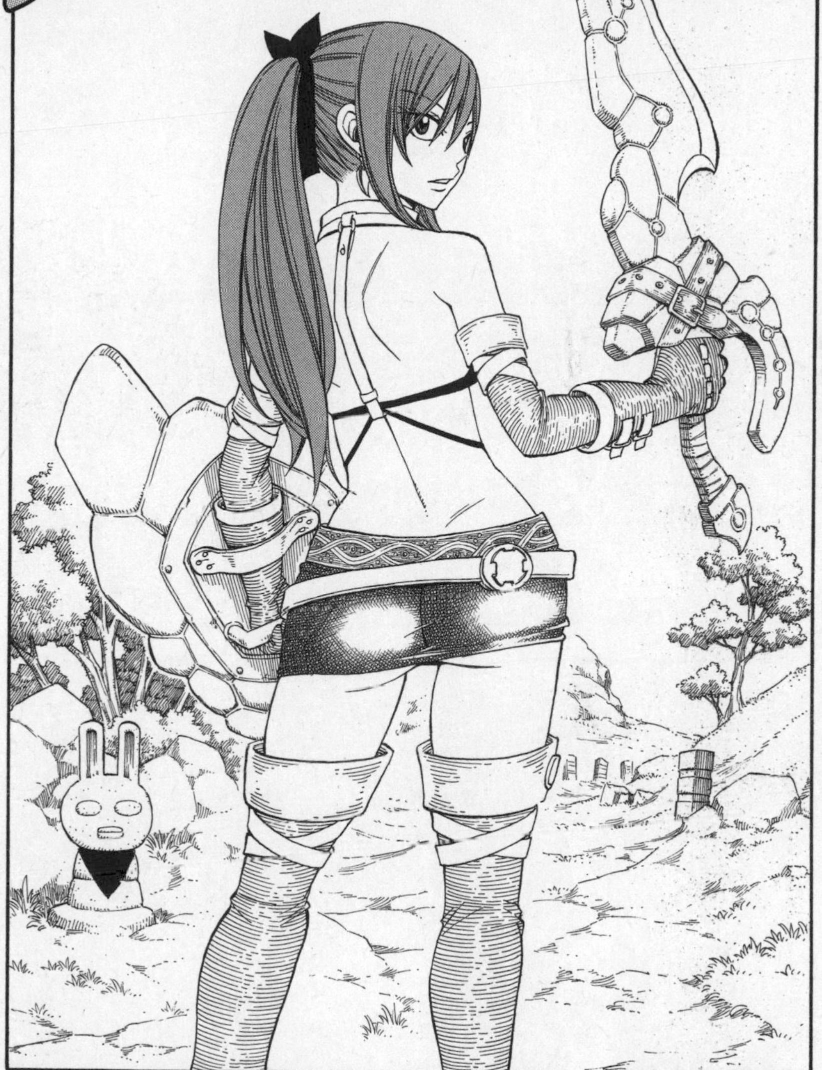

# Spot the Differences

The drawings below look just like page 139! But when you look closer, something's different…

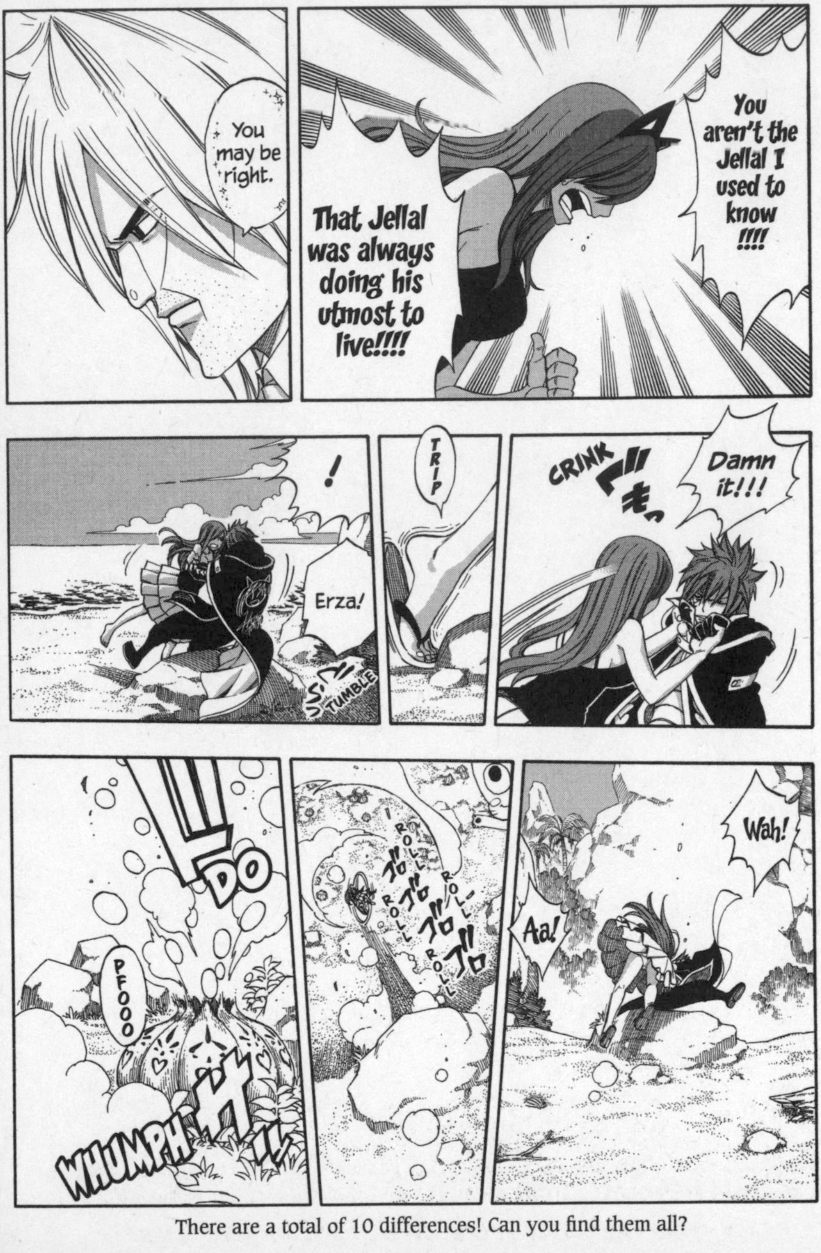
You aren't the Jellal I used to know!!!!
That Jellal was always doing his utmost to live!!!!
You may be right.
CRINK
Damn it!!!
TRIP
!
Erza!
TUMBLE
Wah!
Aa!
ROLL
ROLL
ROLL
ROLL
DO
PFOOO
WHUMPH

There are a total of 10 differences! Can you find them all?

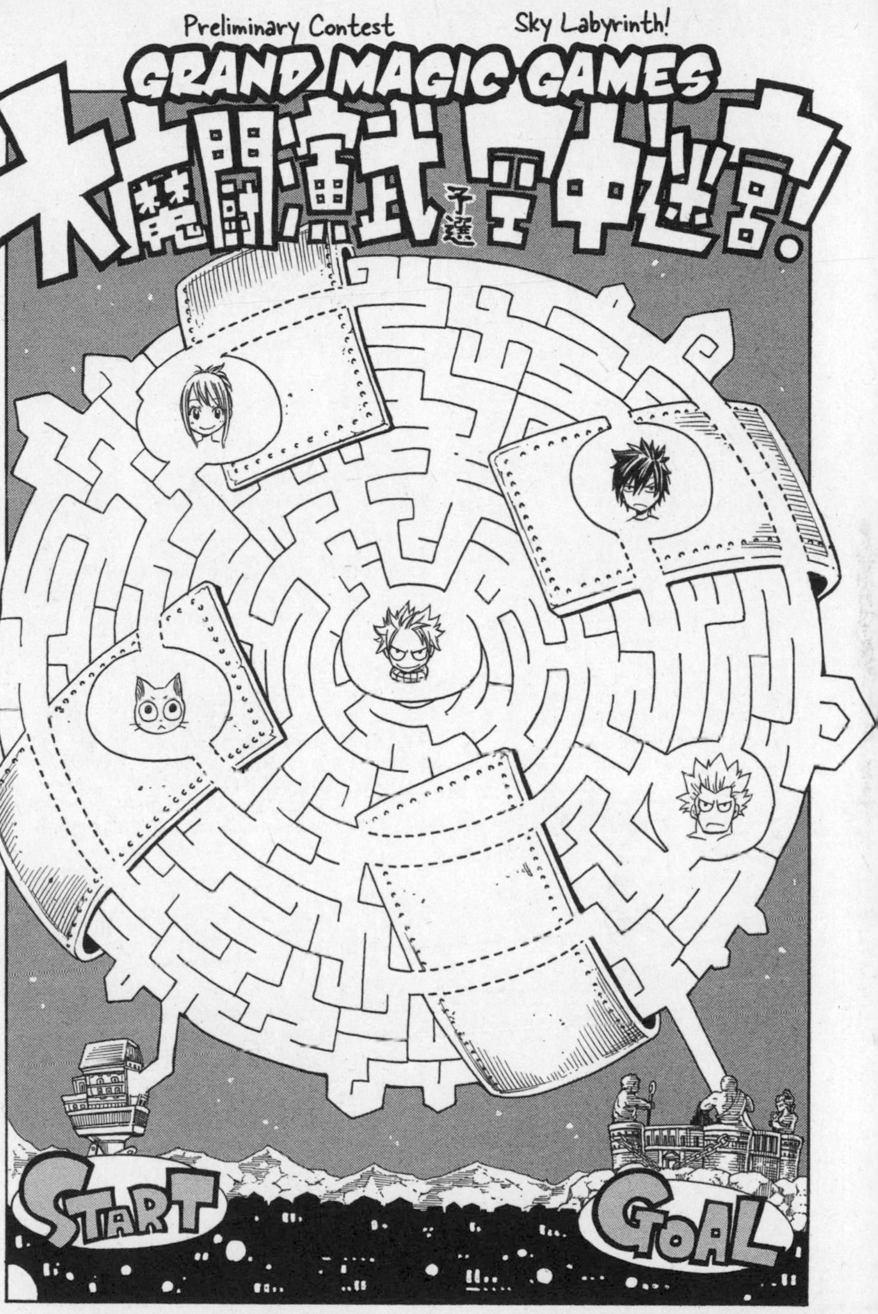
Preliminary Contest
Sky Labyrinth!
GRAND MAGIC GAMES
大魔闘演武 予選 空中迷宮!
START
GOAL

**Can you make it from the Start to the Goal?**

Continued from the left-hand page. ⬇

**Mira:** On to the next question.

***With seven years having passed, what's happened to Master Hades, Rusty, and Kain?***

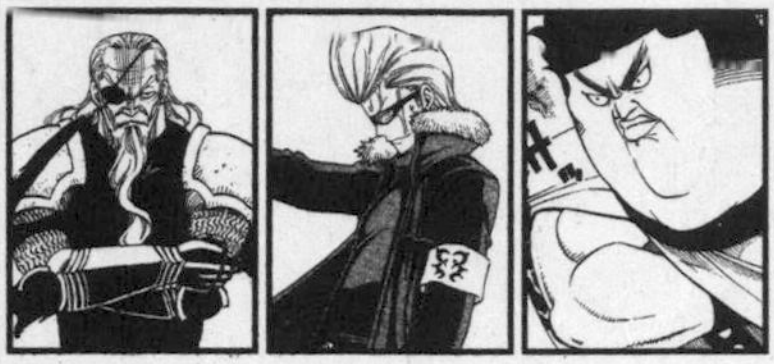

**Lucy:** That's one thing I want to know too!

**Mira:** A similar question, "What happened to Zeref," is coming in a lot too.

**Lucy:** But won't people find out for themselves before too long?

**Mira:** That's true. Let's just say, "expect some fun when we get there!"

**Lucy:** And since it may have some relation to the question above, here's this question.

***Zeref's character and background aren't really clear to me.***

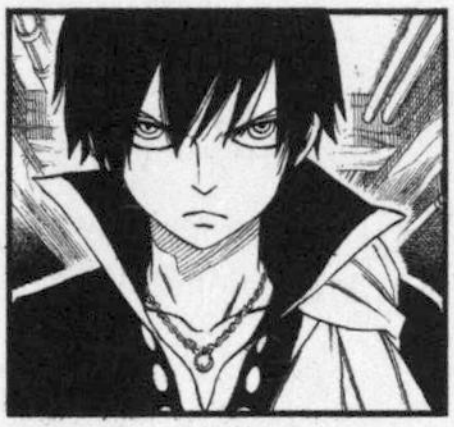

**Mira:** ....................

**Lucy:** ....................

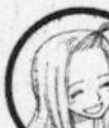
: Come to think of it, he does seem like a complicated character.

**Lucy:** When he was supposed to be asleep, he was actually awake all the time.

**Mira:** When he wants to preserve a life, he unconsciously takes the life instead.

**Mira:** And to keep that from happening, he has to forget the weight of human life.

**Lucy:** A pretty amazing character.

**Mira:** It's still a long time until what is behind his character will be revealed, but apparently we're allowed to give one hint.

**Lucy:** Allowed by who?

**Mira:** Mashima-sensei.

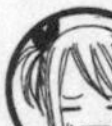
: I hope his editor doesn't get mad at him for it.

**Mira:** He says that he's using a particular trick in regards to Zeref's existence.

**Lucy:** Trick? What's that supposed to mean?

**Mira:** I can't say any more than that. But it seems that Mashima-sensei has taken the unusual step of deciding on things like Zeref's secret past and loads of other small details.

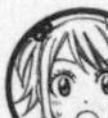
: Eh? Isn't that jumping past proper procedure?

**Mira:** He say's he'll do whatever it takes if it's to surprise the readers! So look forward to some good twists!

**Lucy:** Hmm... Isn't this exactly the same as the answer to the Mavis question?

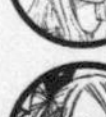
: Well, with Zeref, he's sure that's he's going to draw it someday!

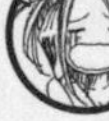
: But I want to know about Mavis too!

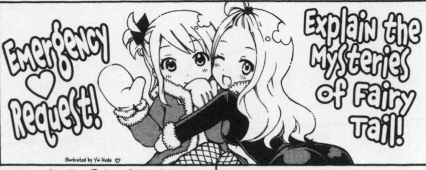

# Emergency ♡ Request! Explain the Mysteries of Fairy Tail!

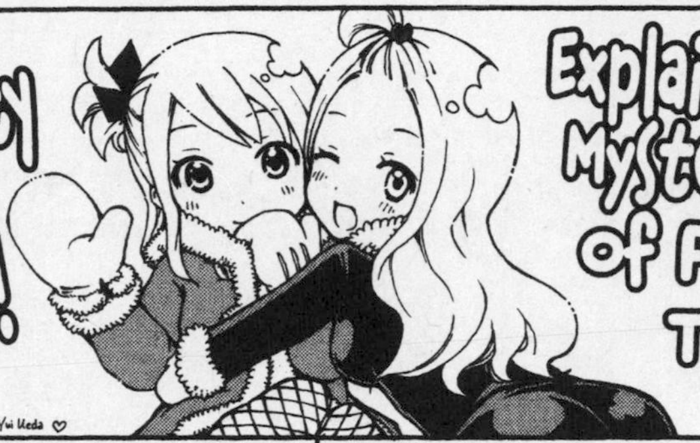

Illustrated by Yui Ueda ♡


***At the Fairy Tail counter...***

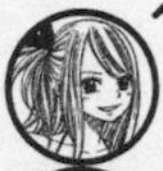
: Wow! ♡ What a cute picture!

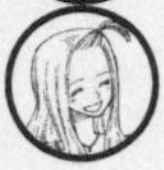
: It isn't one of Mashima-sensei's, you know.

**Lucy:** It looks like it was drawn by one member of his staff, Ueda.

**Mira:** It's kind of nice to have one of these once in a while.

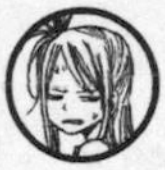
: Although I get the feeling it's just Mashima getting lazy.

**Mira:** Okay, shall we start with the questions?

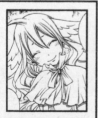

***Why is Master Mavis so young?***

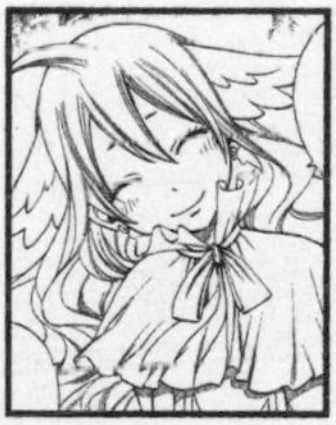

**Lucy:** This question came up a lot!

**Mira:** Sure, there are a lot of questions about her, but ever since the last volume, she's had a lot of pictures sent into Guild d'Art too!♡

**Lucy:** That tells you how popular her character is, huh?

**Mira:** Now, they asked why Master Mavis looks so young, so...

**Lucy:** So...?

**Mira:** We don't know yet.

**Lucy:** Huhhh?!!

**Mira:** So far, nothing in the main story or the side stories have touched upon the subject yet.

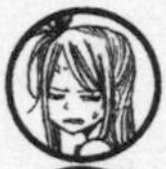
: I get it. He just hasn't thought up an answer yet, huh?

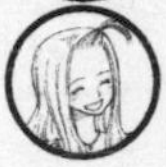
: Actually Mavis's background was part of the very first concepts, and there may (or may not) have been something there to surprise the readers.

**Lucy:** Really? Now you've got me interested!

**Mira:** But!

**Lucy:** There's a "but?"

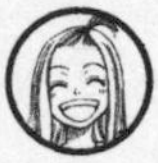
: Even though we've let that slip, the surprise may never enter the story.

**Lucy:** That's no good!! That'll make the readers angry for sure!! If you're going to drop those hints here, then do the story!! You'd better, got it?

Continued on the right-hand page ↗

# TAIL d'ART

The Fairy Tail Guild is looking for illustrations! Please send in your art on a postcard or at postcard size, and do it in black pen, okay? Those chosen to be published will get a signed mini poster! ♪ Make sure you write your real name and address on the back of your illustration!

Saitama Prefecture, Tsubame

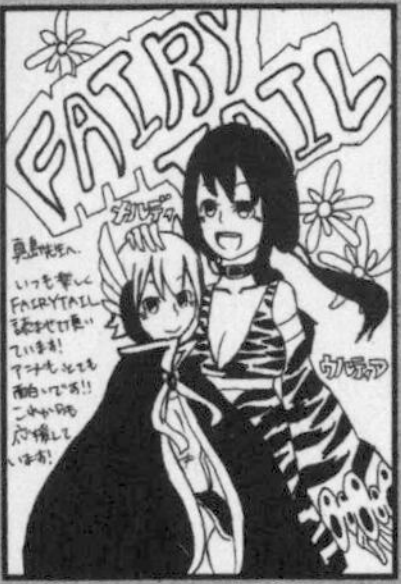
FAIRY TAIL

▲And really quickly, these two show up again. Merudy's grown up a lot!

Hokkaido, Tomihide Tsuda

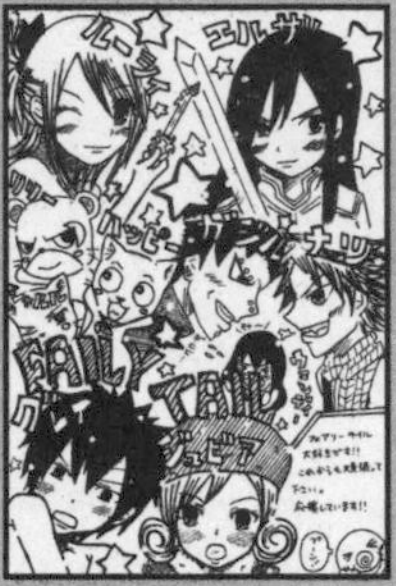

▲Thanks for doing so much drawing!

Aichi Prefecture, Chika Goto

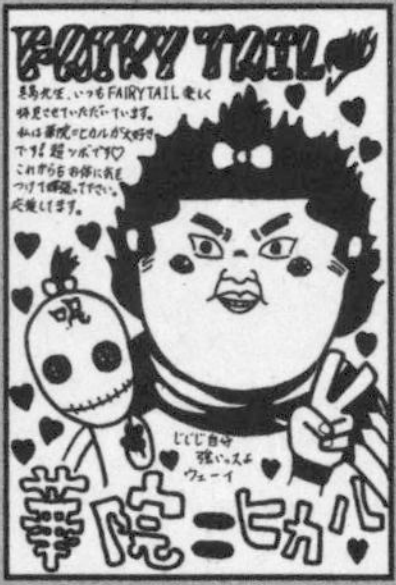

▲Ah! I see you share an attraction to this character with Fairy Tail's director, Ishihira-san.

Saitama Prefecture, do it

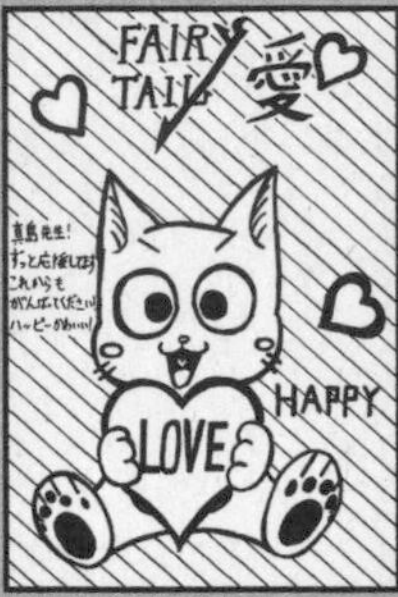
FAIRY TAIL 愛
HAPPY
LOVE

▲From Happy with love.

Hokkaido, Sarasa Kokubun

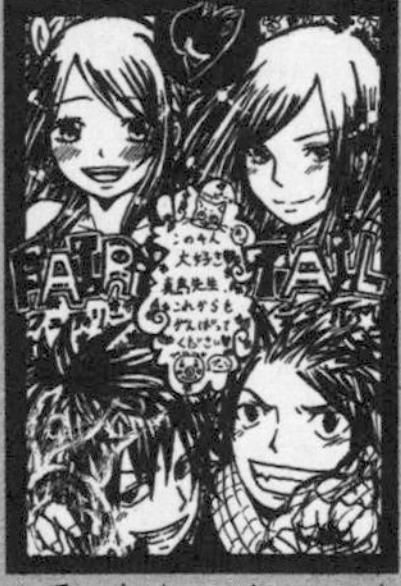

▲They look good surrounded in black! Makes them look cool!

Saitama Prefecture, Miyana

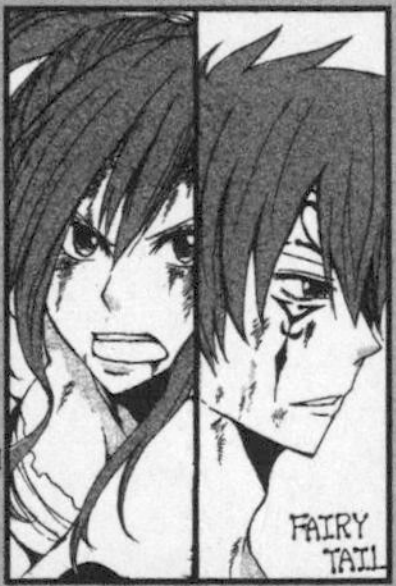
FAIRY TAIL

▲What did you think when these two met again?

Aichi Prefecture, Chun

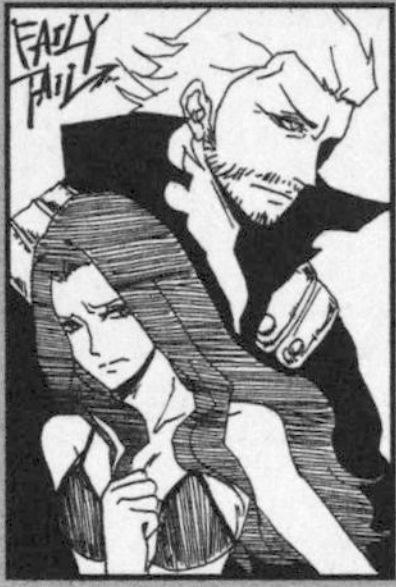
FAILY TAIL

▲Cana is finally able to say what she always wanted to. Great, huh?

Kyoto, Ryō Goto.

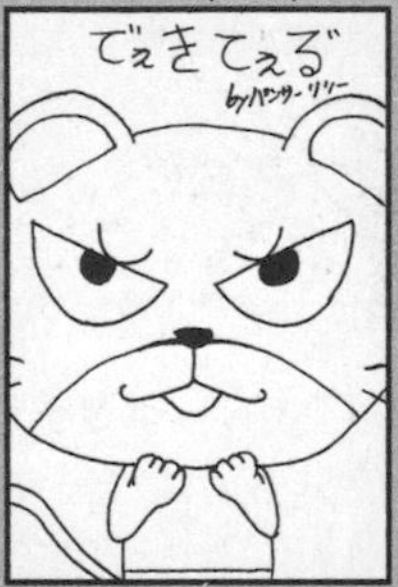
でぇきてぇる
byパンサーリリー

▲Just who is Panther Lily saying, "You're so doing it," to?!

**Send to** Hiro Mashima, Kodansha Comics
451 Park Ave. South, 7th Floor New York, NY 10016

# FAIRY GUILD

Aomori Prefecture, Fûrant

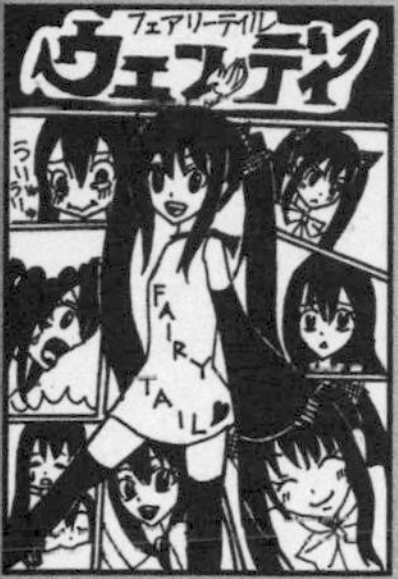

FAIRY TAIL


▲Whoa! Thanks for all the Wendys!

Kanagawa Prefecture, Erika Yamaguchi

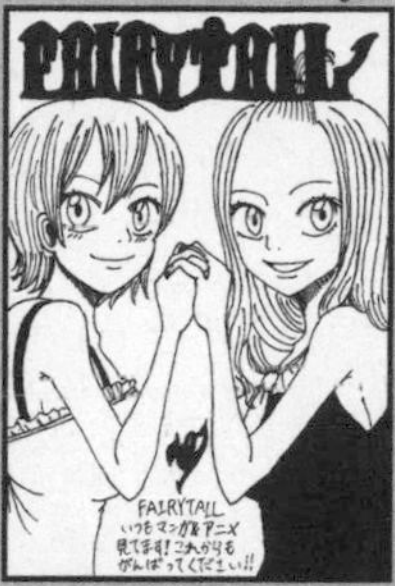

FAIRYTAIL
FAIRYTAIL


▲Sisters who get along really well! Gives off a nice feeling!

Kanagawa Prefecture, Rii-chan

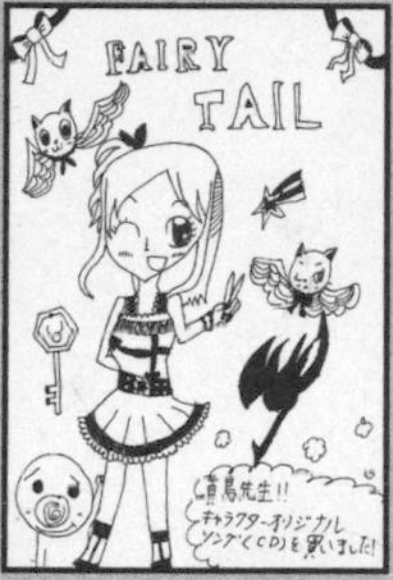

FAIRY TAIL


▲Then what song did you like the best?

Osaka, Kyôka Ruzuki

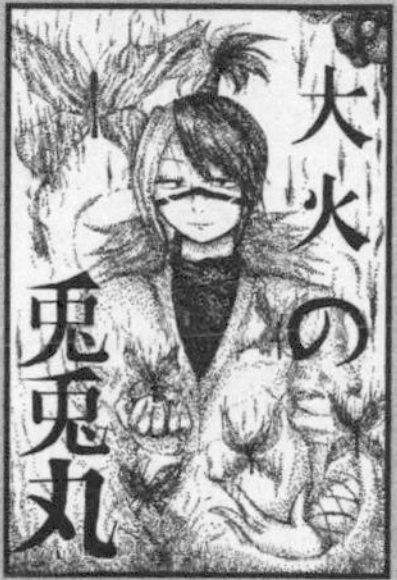

大火の兎兎丸


▲Brings back memories!! But he did show up recently, huh?

REJECTION CORNER

There's so much to harp on, and I really don't know what's going on! ▶

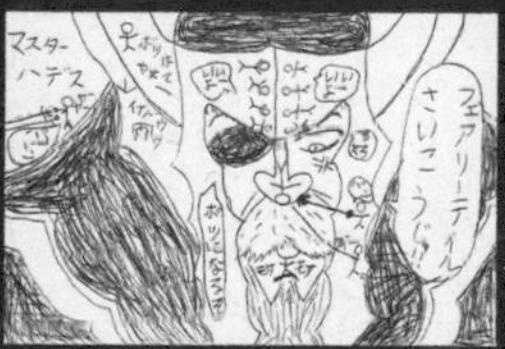

Fukushima Prefecture, Ikuya Saito

It's always those three, huh? ▶

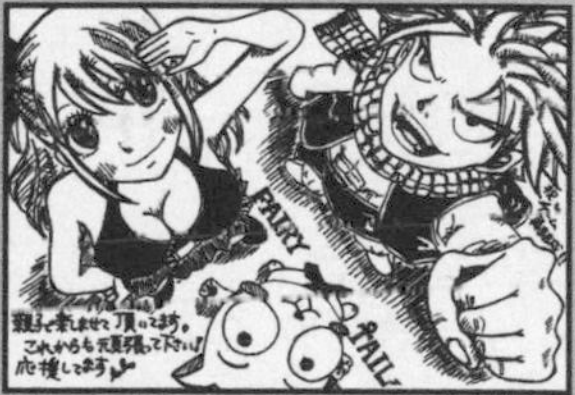

FAIRY TAIL


Kanagawa Prefecture, Teruka

By sending in letters or postcards you give us permission to give your name, address, postal code and any other information you include to the author as is. Please keep that in mind.

Ohh! Now that's cute!! Thanks for cheering me on!! ▶

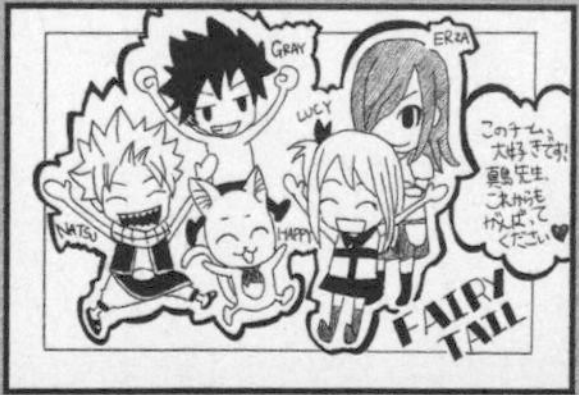

GRAY
ERZA
LUCY
NATSU
HAPPY
FAIRY TAIL


Osaka, Ayaka Inui

# GUILD REPORT NEW FAIRTAIL

1) Bar Area
2) Bar Counter & Kitchen
3) Bathroom & shower
4) Store Room & Records Room
5) Request Board

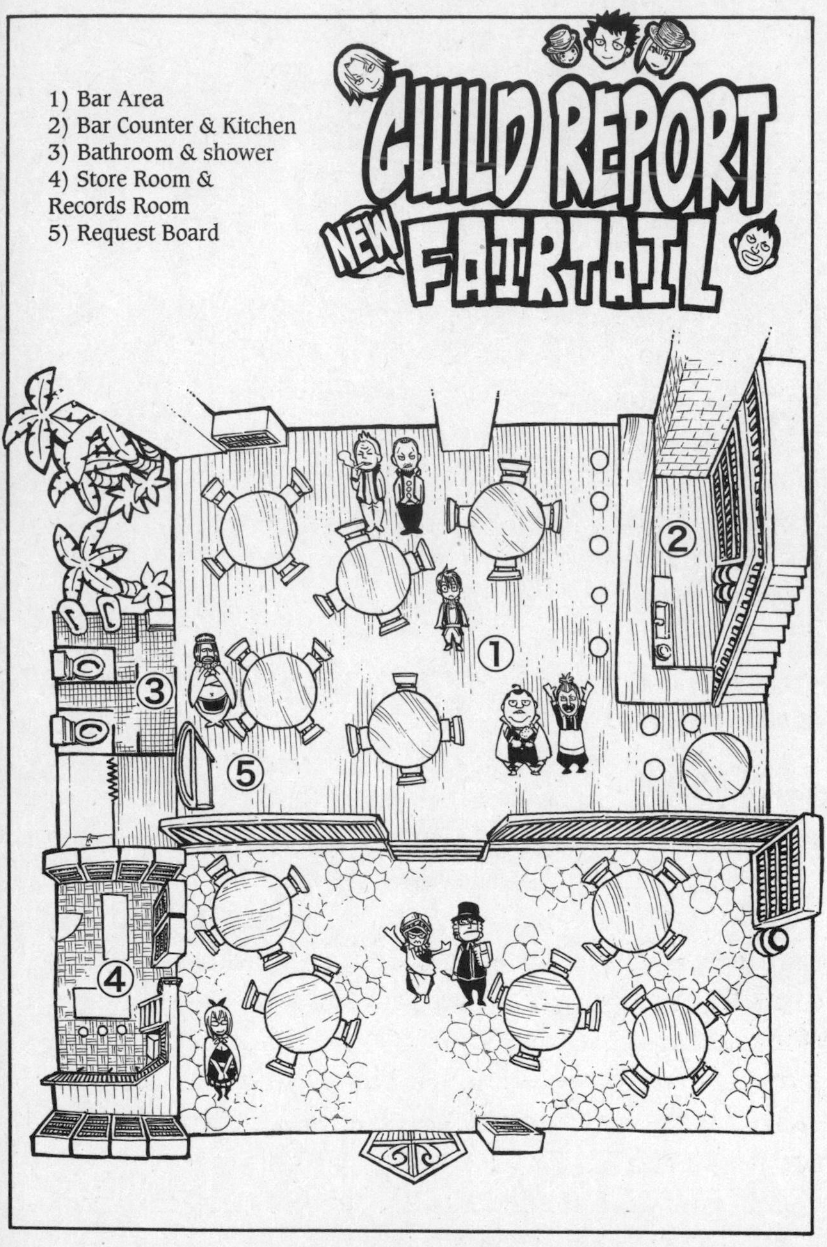

# Afterword
# あとがき

The Grand Magic Games!!!! A festival! A festival! Heave-ho! Heave-ho! And so, although these are the same Natsu & crew who are always putting their lives on the line in their battles, this particular series will focus on them doing battle in order to reclaim the honor of their guild. At first, I thought of the Grand Magic Games as a simple battle tournament, but that's been done so many times, I discarded that idea. (Call me perverse.)

Personally, I just love those hot plot twists, but Fairy Tail, while being a battle manga, is also about the importance of the "bonds within the guild." If this were just battles, that would make it hard to return to that theme. Of course there *will* be battles though. There will be combinations that seem really unusual and competitions that I always wanted to see. I'm planning all sorts of fun things! And more than anything, the character count outdoes anything in Fairy Tail history so far! The contestants and other major characters bring it to over 40 characters!!!! Really, it's a struggle to draw it every week, but it's so fun to draw that "festival" feeling! Up until now, we've had battles against bad people and dark guilds, but I want this story to give you a better view of the Fairy Tail world and all the various types of guilds that are in it.

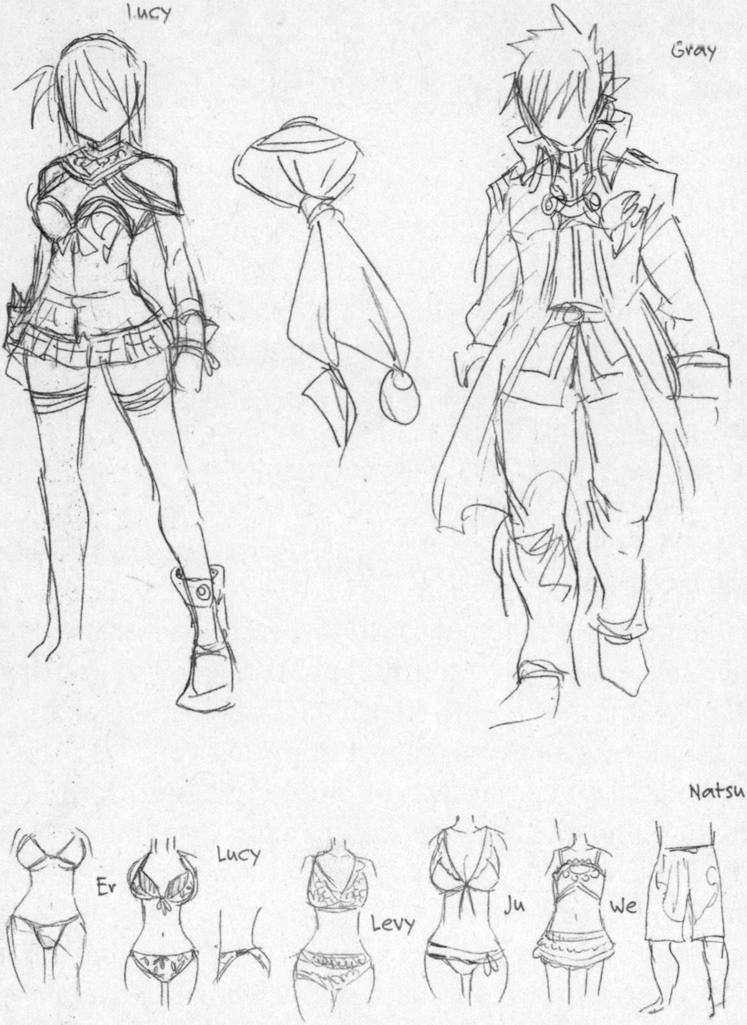
Lucy
Gray
Natsu
Er
Lucy
Levy
Ju
We

# FAIRY TAIL 31

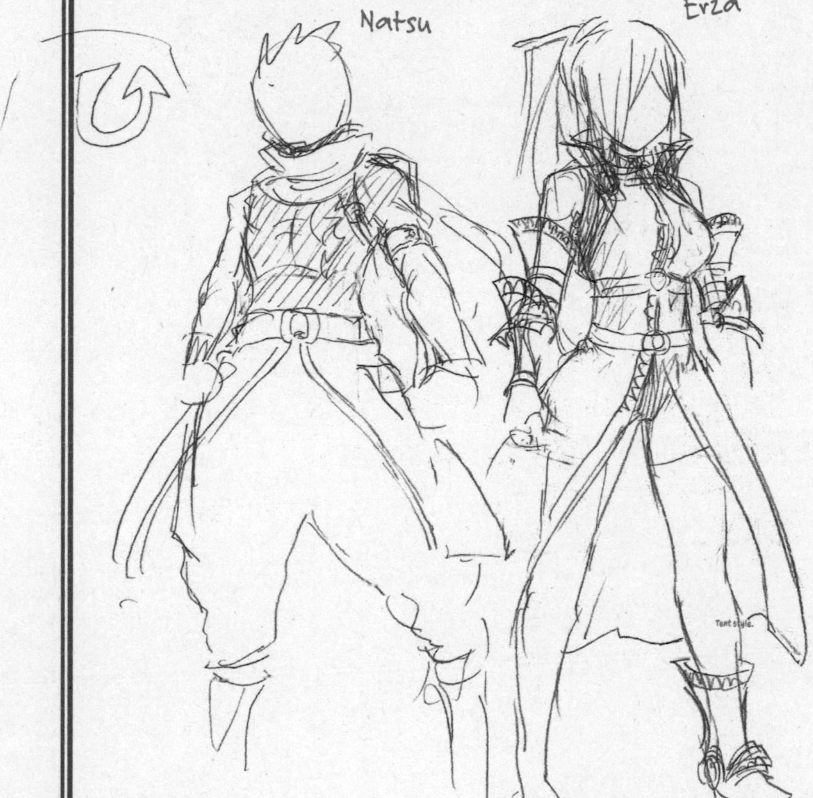

Natsu
Erza
Tent style.


HIRO MASHIMA

**FROM HIRO MASHIMA**

I've got a bad feeling about this.
With the Sirius Island story, I
included an enormous number
of characters, and really whined
about drawing it. With the new
storyline, I've got this really, really
bad premonition. I couldn't be
thinking of having, like, more
than forty characters appearing,
could I? I wonder if I'm going to
survive this...

Original Jacket Design: Hisao Ogawa

# Translation Notes:

Japanese is a tricky language for most Westerners, and translation is often more art than science. For your edification and reading pleasure, here are notes on some of the places where we could have gone in a different direction with our translation of the work, or where a Japanese cultural reference is used.

## Page 26,Frosch

Frosch is the German word for frog. It also happens to be a German brand of household cleaner with a frog logo that was introduced in Japan about a year ago. Coincidence?

## Page 76, Read this word

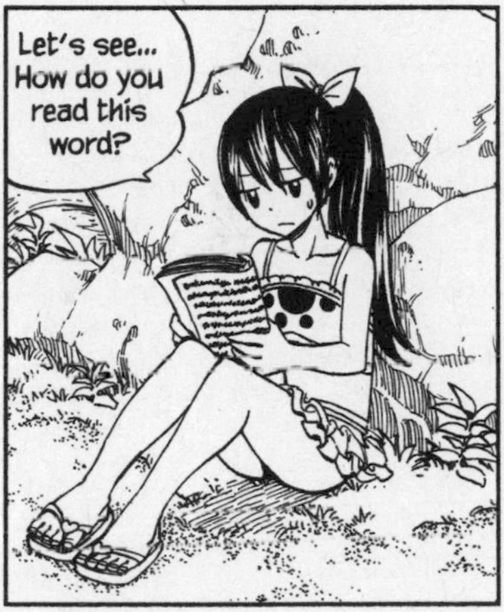

Let's see... How do you read this word?


In the English language, it's common for words with odd spellings to be difficult to pronounce, but in Japanese, there are words made up of kanji where one does not remember (or never knew in the first place) how the word was pronounced. For those who don't know about the Japanese writing system, kanji are ideograms (pictograms look like what they describe whereas ideograms are symbols that may or may not look like what they represent) and as such don't automatically have a sound attached. In some other languages such as Chinese, each ideogram usually has only one pronunciation in any particular dialect, but in Japanese most have at least two and some have many, many more possible pronunciations. So it's not unusual for a fully educated adult to not know how an occasional word is pronounced, and it is very common for children Wendy's age to not know.

## Page 104, Lyra's song

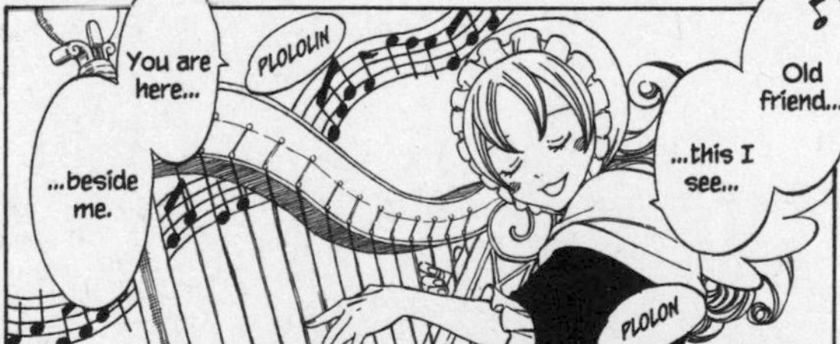

Old friend...
...this I see...
PLOLOUN
You are here...
...beside me.
PLOLON


Although this translator would not blame you if you didn't think the translated English lyrics were very poetic, please rest assured that the translation of the song took no liberties with the meaning in order to add some rhymes to it. The meaning of what Lyra is singing here is almost identical to the meaning of the song in Japanese.

## Page 112, Ohba Babasaama

This character is an old woman, and her name reflects it. Ohba is a word that means "grandmother," and baba is another word that means "grandmother" or "old lady." The saama is probably a nod to the -sama honorific. A little later on the same page, Lyon refers to her as "Obaba," which also means "grandmother" or "old lady."

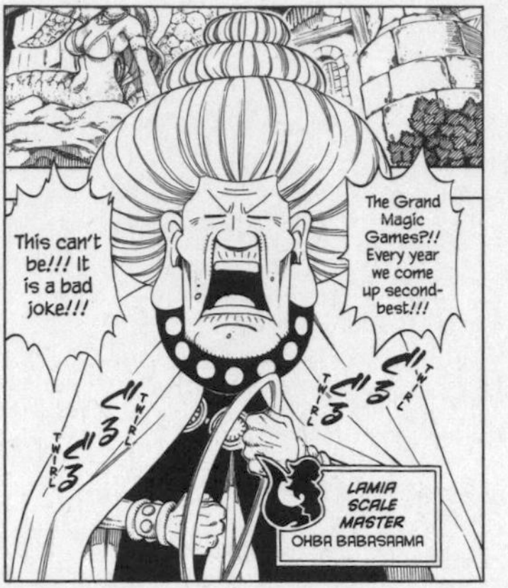
The Grand Magic Games?!! Every year we come up second-best!!!
This can't be!!! It is a bad joke!!!
TWIRL
TWIRL
TWIRL
TWIRL
LAMIA SCALE MASTER
OHBA BABASAAMA

## Page 116, Punishment

The position Virgo is demonstrating in that first panel on page 116 is a torture that was found in ancient Japan. A person is bound by their hands and feet, forced to sit seiza (with their shins tucked underneath their thighs) on a grated wooden board with sharp corners sticking up, and then weights are applied to the tops of their thighs. The corners bite into the person's sensitive shins as the weights press down on them. Generally if the victim was being tortured for information, resistance was met with more weight being applied to their thighs.

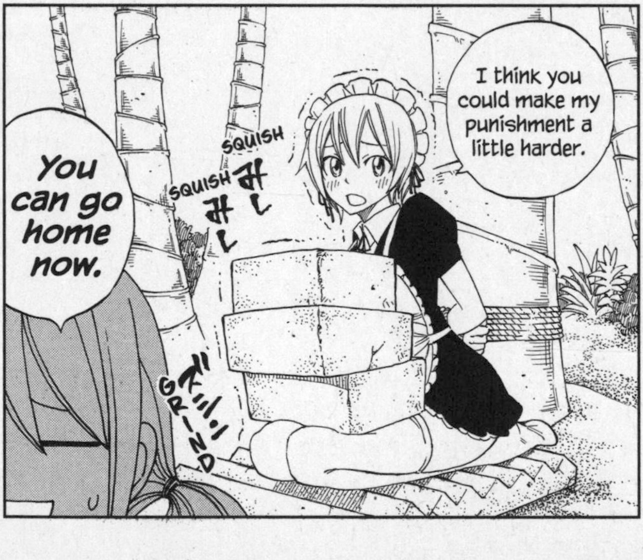
I think you could make my punishment a little harder.
SQUISH
SQUISH
You can go home now.
GRIND

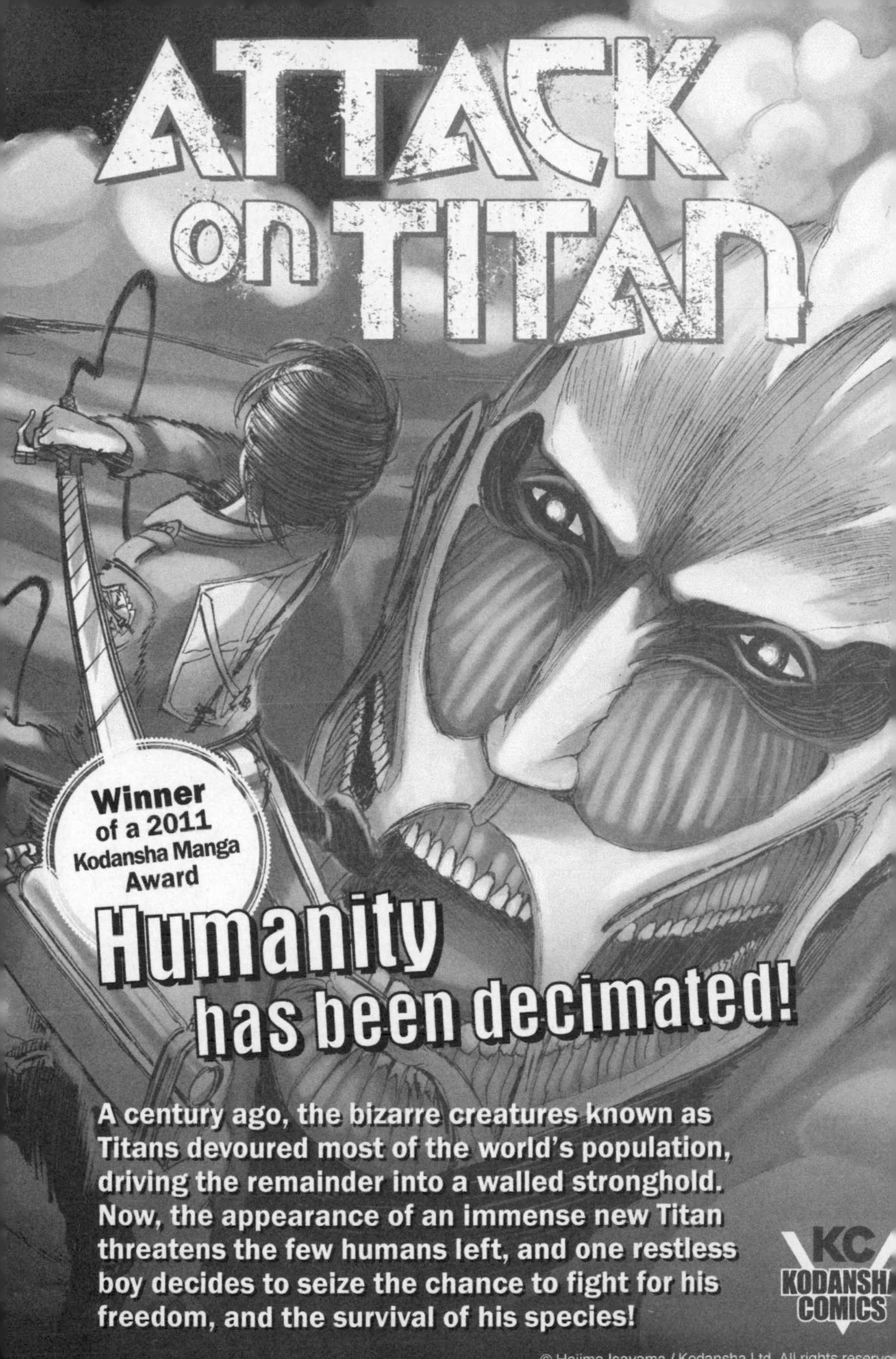
ATTACK on TITAN
Winner of a 2011 Kodansha Manga Award
Humanity has been decimated!
A century ago, the bizarre creatures known as Titans devoured most of the world's population, driving the remainder into a walled stronghold. Now, the appearance of an immense new Titan threatens the few humans left, and one restless boy decides to seize the chance to fight for his freedom, and the survival of his species!
KC KODANSHA COMICS

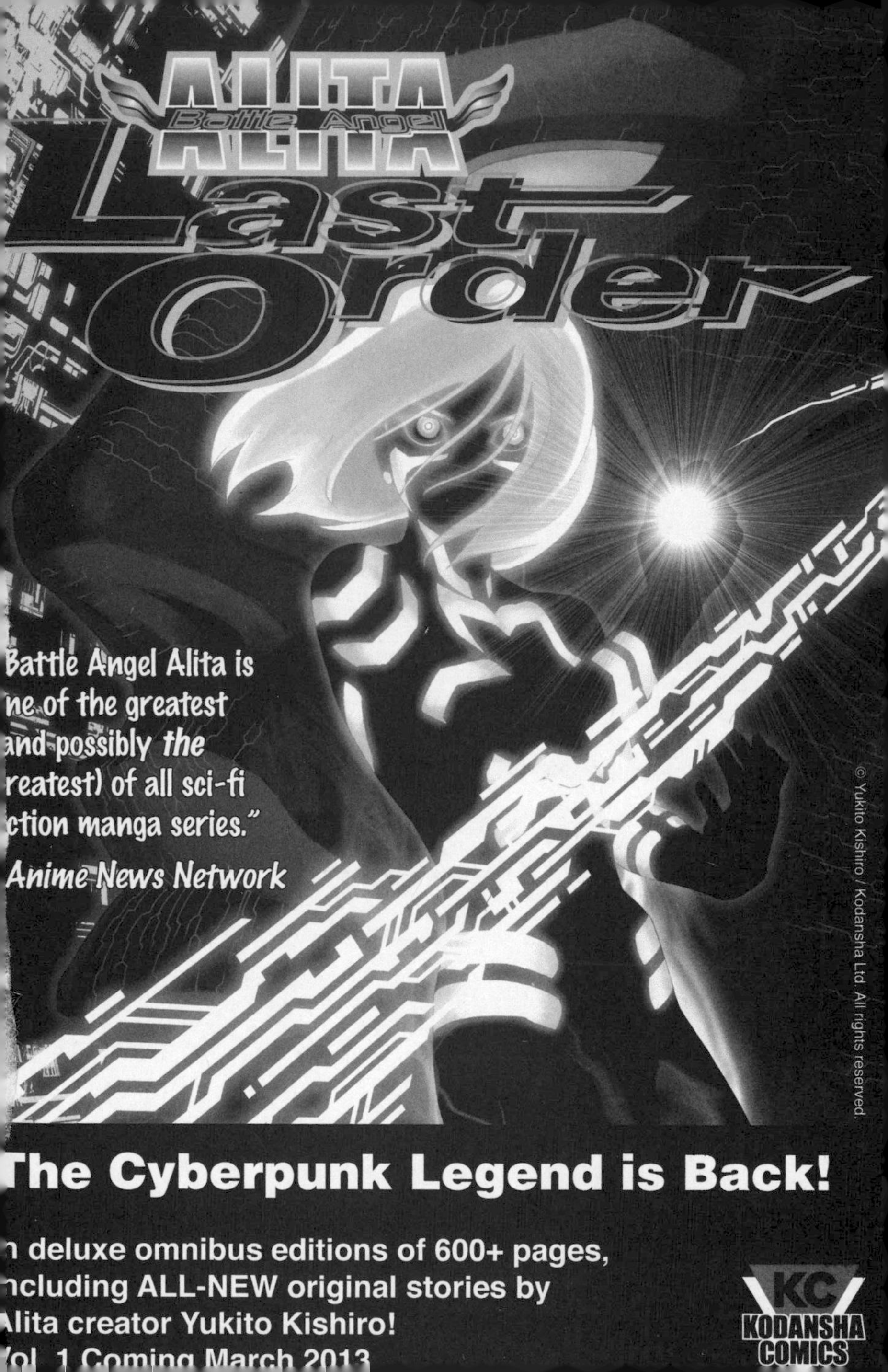
ALITA
Battle Angel
ALITA
Last Order
Battle Angel Alita is
ne of the greatest
and possibly *the*
reatest) of all sci-fi
ction manga series."
Anime News Network

A Kodansha Comics Trade Paperback Original.

Published in the United States by Kodansha Comics, an imprint of Kodansha USA Publishing, LLC, New York.

Publication rights for this English edition arranged through Kodansha Ltd., Tokyo.

First published in Japan in 2012 by Kodansha Ltd., Tokyo
ISBN 978-1-61262-408-2

Printed in the United States of America.

www.kodanshacomics.com

9 8 7 6 5 4 3 2

Translator: William Flanagan
Lettering: AndWorld Design

# TOMARE!

止まれ

[STOP!]

## You're going the wrong way!

## Manga is a completely different type of reading experience.

## To start at the *beginning*, go to the *end*!

That's right! Authentic manga is read the traditional Japanese way—from right to left, exactly the *opposite* of how American books are read. It's easy to follow: Just go to the other end of the book and read each page—and each panel—from right side to left side, starting at the top right. Now you're experiencing manga as it was meant to be!